THE SHEEP FROM THE GOATS

Also by John Simon

THE SHEEP
FROM
THE GOATS

*Selected Literary Essays
of John Simon*

 Weidenfeld & Nicolson
New York

Copyright © 1989 by John Simon

Published by Weidenfeld & Nicolson, New York
A Division of Wheatland Corporation
841 Broadway
New York, New York 10003-4793

Published in Canada by General Publishing Company, Ltd.

Due to limitations of space, permissions appear on
page 454.

Library of Congress Cataloging-in-Publication Data

Simon, John Ivan.
   The sheep from the goats : selected literary essays of John Simon.—1st ed.
      p.   cm.
   ISBN 1-55584-180-5
   1. Literature—History and criticism.   I. Title.
PN45.S433   1989
809—dc19   88-9633
                                                    CIP

Manufactured in the United States of America

This book is printed on acid-free paper.

Designed by Irving Perkins Associates

First Edition

10 9 8 7 6 5 4 3 2 1

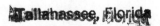

For Patricia Hoag
without whom even the possible would be impossible

ACKNOWLEDGMENTS

I wish to thank my editor, John Herman, for his wisdom and helpfulness, and Barbara Berson and Carol Wilcox for many kind forms of assistance.

CONTENTS

French Literature

German and Austrian Literature

INTRODUCTION

LITERATURE is the arena where some of the oddest games, circuses, gladiatorial combats have been proliferating. Why? Because literature is the melting-pot art for consumers of every kind, from high to low, educated to pseudo-educated, old to young—although the young, to do them prosaic justice, are rapidly becoming exonerated from the taint of reading. There is a great free-for-all in literature, a heaven-storming Babel of tongues, but also a potential for genuine quality because, after all, it does not cost that much to buy a book or even to publish it. There are still highly sophisticated persons who haughtily declare they can do without the movies and that today's debased theater is seldom worth their attention, but few if any people boast of never reading a book, even if some of them make good on that unvoiced boast.

Books offer at prices that are affordable—or, in public libraries, nonexistent—something for every taste, however civilized or swinish, the sublime and the trashy rubbing spines if not shoulders. In the circus of the library and the arena of the bookstore window, shrouded in hieratic exclusiveness or pumped up with sweaty promiscuity, literary reputations rise or fall—or rise *and* fall, fall *and* rise—and, in some cases, just keep rising. Arguably the most widely and prominently reviewed of all the arts, literature provides the stage for dramatic separations of the wheat from the chaff, the men from the boys, the sheep from the goats—all in a muddle that only time can eventually sort out. In the meantime, even time has been known to reverse itself.

The good and the bad, the sheep and the goats, they are the ones the critic is called on to separate for a reading public that has neither the means nor the time, neither the training nor the stamina to make the discriminations it expects the critic to supply. For whatever else is wanted from the critic, this is wanted most: being told "Read this!" or "Don't read this!" and why. And the critic, however pure and speculative and non-opinionated he may rightly wish to be, is, equally rightly, eager to comply. Scourge of goats, champion of sheep, defender of the faith—lovely titles all.

Yet where does this famous trope of the sheep and the goats come from? What does it really mean? Why that particular metaphor? And how does it apply to literature? The answer to the first question is simple enough. It comes from Matthew XXV, concerning the last judgment, where the Son of Man "will separate men into two groups as a shepherd separates the sheep from the goats, and he will place the sheep on his right hand and the goats on his left." The sheep are the "righteous," who go to "eternal life"; the goats, who do not rate a specific epithet, are the ones who did nothing for their fellowmen, and "go away to eternal punishment."

Still, that does not explain why the righteous should be symbolized by sheep, and the unrighteous by goats, rather than the other way round. Clearly, the properties of sheep must have been considered better. They are gentle and obedient, give good wool with which to clothe the naked, to say nothing of lambskin coats. Further, they provide excellent cheese, and their skin was the good, perdurable ancestor of paper—hence a diploma is still affectionately known as a sheepskin. Goats, to be sure, supplied potable milk and fine cheese, though the gourmet consumption of goat cheese as a delicacy is a much more recent practice. Goatskins, too, had sundry uses, but morocco, as a choice leather for bookbinding, is, obviously, of much later date. Above all, however, goats are capricious— from the Latin *caper*, a billygoat—mischievous, randy, foul-smelling, destructively omnivorous, and capable of doing harm with their pointy horns, so unlike the ram's safely rounded ones, convertible into musical instruments. Not for nothing do both satyrs and the devil have goat's feet.

Things change, however. Not only have goat products achieved wider application and higher status of late, but also the very docility of sheep (consider the pejorative "sheeplike" and the unglamorous "sheepish") has fallen into disrepute. You no longer earn high marks for submitting like a lamb to the slaughter; for quite a while the goatee has been a dapper, indeed aristocratic, ornament for the chin. Goatfoot satyrs acquired an image in art scarcely inferior to that of quivering-fleshed nymphs. The capriole is as elegant a caper for a horse as the cabriole is for a ballet dancer; even in crime, a caper is a robbery accomplished with ingenuity and, sometimes, wit. So, to a considerable degree, the goat and its derivatives have been vindicated: sheep, meanwhile, have been appreciably downgraded. Even for sheer beauty, the mountain goat now ranks as high as its rocky habitat.

In short, sheep and goats are no longer what they used to be. To complicate matters further, they are now being crossbred into a new species called the geep, combining the best aspects of each. (Does the shoat, a young hog, unite the worst aspects?) In any case, aggressiveness, the goat's chief hallmark, has become a generally desirable trait in business, sexuality, and various other fields of endeavor. Only in military matters is aggression still in official disfavor, although most people would prefer a goatish army to a sheepish one. If the moral status and metaphorical value of sheep and goats, then, have undergone a sort of Hal-Hotspur turn of the wheel of fortune, can this be without literary ramifications?

Of course not. Accordingly, writers previously neglected and forgotten have shot up in value; others, formerly esteemed and exalted, are being ignored if not downright derided. In

English poetry alone, such eminent sheep as Wordsworth, Tennyson, and Browning (though Robert was not without a repressed goatishness) have been pretty much put out to pasture, while such idiosyncratic goats (at the very least black sheep) as John Skelton, Matthew Pryor, and Thomas Lovell Beddoes have found more and more boosters, and are gradually being elevated to the angora category. It's no longer the sheepish effusions that score for Byron, but his goatish satires and letters. Shelley is being converted from a poet of golden fleeciness to a revolutionary, sexual and political, like Byron, both now viewed as the scapegoats of reactionary forces. Oscar Wilde is being raised to sainthood, not least for his sardonic prose poems. The caprine Dylan Thomas outshines his ovine namesakes Edward and R. S. In America, even a tethered goat such as Wallace Stevens outweighs the progressively more sheepified William Carlos Williams, at best a Judas goat who led his sheepish imitators to the slaughter. Confirmed goats such as Ezra Pound threaten to outshine Poor Tom, the second-best *fabbro,* whose Angoras (cats, not goats) may do better than his lamb-of-godlike three white leopards. Particularly instructive is the rehabilitation of Emily Dickinson from a sheepish nightingale into a feminist nannygoat, and of Robert Frost from a snowy-fleeced bellwether into a troubled and troubling fence-breaker (something goats are known for). And who, nowadays, would gambol with Marianne Moore when he—or, more likely, she—can lock horns with Sylvia Plath?

What goes for Anglo-American poetry goes for the rest of literature, old and new. It would seem to be unsafe to ply the critic's trade, to try to assign stable values to authors and their works. How dare one proclaim the excellence of this or the inadequacy of that if, a few decades later, the values may be reversed: the goat reclassified a sheep, the sheep demoted—or promoted—to a goat. Or we may have on our hands a geep, and not even an ordinary geep: the goatish parts may be the very things that make him an honorary sheep, while the sheepish ones disqualify him from claiming birth under a dancing star in the sign of Capricorn. Thus the critic may give up on being a critic and succumb to Hanslick's syndrome. (Hanslick, of course, was the music critic who, while championing Brahms, excoriated Wagner. But at least he fully recognized Brahms's value, and could claim Nietzsche as a fellow Wagner-deprecator.)

The dedicated critic cannot afford to worry about Hanslick's syndrome; it is better to be time's fool than one's own. If you are scrupulously honest and graphically explicit about what and how you perceive, you serve a critical purpose. At the very least, you represent a well-argued view for the future to take issue with. Some of the best critical formulations have been made against previous ones, and, let's face it, you cannot play squash without a wall. It may be, for instance, that Taine's kind of sociopsychological, historicizing criticism is now obsolete, but it filled a need in its own time, gave later criticism something to kick against, and contributed a conscientious, articulate, and sometimes persuasive voice to the ongoing critical chorus.

It is the critic's task to compare and contrast, sift and explicate, notice the complex and elusive and discuss it clearly and pertinently. Engaged in these activities, the critic cannot but formulate value judgments, but if they are both considered and passionate (not just one or the other), sensitive and consistent, they will have to be stepping-stones in literary history, whether or not they lead in the direction the critic intended. It will emerge from the criticism that, at a given time and for this particular observer, such and such a writer was a sheep or a goat or a geep. That is a critical snapshot. On the basis of snapshots of a certain writer taken at random intervals, the critic fashions the portrait of that writer. To the extent that this portrait (or evaluation) coincides with the judgment of time, the critic has made his mark as being of more than seasonal interest.

But what of the goats and sheep, then, if there is such a thing as the judgment of time? At the risk of seeming contradiction, I will now assert that there does come for certain writers— and, eventually, probably for all of them—a moment when the verdict is in, when the goats remain goats, and the sheep can no longer claim to be goats in sheepskin, and there is no longer any doubt about what either category means. Time, as if it were the voice of the Son of Man, has pronounced a verdict. It is the hope of every serious critic to anticipate that verdict as often and as forcefully as possible. It is the tragedy of every serious critic that he is never long-lived enough to see himself proved right. But his consolation is that he will also be spared being around when his judgments are overturned.

In the pieces that follow—many of them mere book reviews struggling with varying success against the limitations of time and space imposed on most reviewers—I have attempted to impart what makes a work or an author sui generis, and how I rate that particular quiddity. The opinions may be original or not, useful or not, enduring or not. But what they surely are is arrived at idiosyncratically, without reference to prevailing notions, theories, schools of thought. There is no attempt to follow or create a system; if this is a disadvantage, so be it.

My position is definitely old-fashioned and may strike some as painfully simple. It is to look at the work and author steadily (as Arnold put it) and try to see it and him or her whole. And to make the examination and evaluation straightforward, informative, and, I hope, entertaining. Many of these pieces may qualify for what used to be called a book chat. But in an age obsessed with structuralizing, semioticizing, deconstructing, and heaven knows what else, chatting may fill in a lacuna, a need that dared not speak its name. At any rate, these pieces are not intended as substitutes for the works under discussion, as alternatives to or exemptions from reading the writers they deal with. I hope that they alert and instruct, but, I repeat, I hope no less that they entertain. For it is only by fulfilling all three of those functions that they may stir the reader of the review (even if it is negative, but his curiosity is piqued) to be graduated into a reader of the book. Let the book chat, then, function modestly as a Baedeker rather than as a *summa theologica, philosophica,* or other, and it is still serving a perfectly legitimate purpose.

But the book chat presupposes a certain kind of reader who, one hopes, is not extinct, or else our culture is in serious danger. It is the kind of reader who is neither uneducated nor academic, but somewhere in that not inconsiderable in between. Such a reader already knows something about books and writers, and wants to know more about them. But he or she neither knows nor cares about structuralism, semiology, deconstruction. Pavese and Hašek, Kleist and Vallejo may be only names to this reader, but he or she wants some guidance to and about these names, not elaborately obfuscatory routines, performances in which the critic dazzles with his erudition, stuns with his intellectual prestidigitation, calls primary attention to himself. Even if the alternative skirts the obvious and merely revitalizes the known, it can—provided it does so with liveliness and tact, and proves hermeneutic—end up being more useful than the prevailing pyrotechnics.

Or so this geep or shoat among critics thinks. To preserve the authenticity and flavor of these pieces—reviews or critiques, talks or lectures, forewords or afterwords—I have left them pretty much as they were. I have tried to correct obvious errors and, in a few places, make the expression clearer or more felicitous. But I have not attempted to add later and revised judgments based on subsequent information and hindsight; there is no *esprit de l'escalier.* The perceptions and passions of these writings have been preserved, whether they are of moment or merely of the moment.

AMERICAN
LITERATURE

MAILER'S MYSTIC MARRIAGE
Norman Mailer, *Marilyn*

IT is straight out of an Otto Preminger movie. A beautiful and famous woman, Marilyn, has died mysteriously. All that is left of her is a set of photographs by various hands about to be published in book form. The clever editor hires a brilliant young (well, young in everything but years) literary detective, Norman Mailer, to piece together the woman's story and unriddle its dark ending. Norman becomes obsessed with the lovely dead woman, and his proposed preface mushrooms into a 90,000-word mushy and maniacal "novel biography." He awaits the Preminger twist, when the girl in the pictures will prove alive after all and fall into his arms. If not that, at least Mailer believes in karma: "She will soon return to us from retirement," he concludes hopefully. But, lest that be too unmodishly happy an ending, he adds: "It is the devil of her humor and the curse of our land that she will come back speaking Chinese." That time her name will be Anna May Wong.

Most biographies are labors of love; Mailer's *Marilyn* is clearly a labor of lust. Taking on a quick project for easy money, he becomes engrossed in the grossest way. Already at the end of *An American Dream* Rojack got a phone call from his dead girl who told him that Marilyn sends her love; back in the days when Mailer's Connecticut farm was only five miles from the Millers', Norman, as he tells us, hoped in vain that Arthur would invite him over to meet Marilyn. Even further back, in *The Deer Park,* Mailer had created Lulu, modeled, one gathers, on Marilyn. At last, even if only posthumously, the affair can be consummated. "Today [when] one has to look into the highest ranks of the Republican party before finding an American who is not polymorphous perverse," as Mailer, for whom no boudoir holds a secret, observes, what is a little platonic necrophilia? So *Marilyn* gets written, not exactly as a "novel biography," though Mailer, to rival Capote's equally preposterous "nonfiction novel," would have it so, and certainly not as biography or criticism. It can be described more precisely as a new genre called transcendental masturbation or metaphysical wet dreaming.

Who was Marilyn Monroe? To Mailer, she is two books about her (by Fred Guiles and Maurice Zolotow, plus some other publications he could briefly dip into), which he quotes, paraphrases, embroiders upon, and, finally, disputes or disparages. Beyond that, she is the creature of his fantasy, of his yearning for, as well as hostility toward, women. The real Monroe was a noteworthy sexpot and quite inconsiderable actress, though today the very handbooks will tell you otherwise. "The pity was that she had real talent," says *The Filmgoer's Companion*; in *The International Encyclopedia of Film* one reads: "Her considerable talent for comedy and pathos was largely either unrecognized or belittled in her lifetime."

I would say that her flagrant sexiness, as in *Niagara,* was indisputable; that her attempts at comedy, as in *Bus Stop,* were risible; and that her pathos, as in *The Misfits,* was a pathetic fallacy. The legend of her comedic skills seems to have been largely the fabrication of Lee and Paula Strasberg, who saw in her acquisition for the Actors Studio and their personal coaching a boost to their failing fame and fortune. It is they who spread the canard of her as a great stage actress, which, for them, paid off handsomely. For Marilyn Monroe, whom their adulation confused, made megalomaniacal, and turned against the Hollywood where she belonged, the result was merely that she was speeded along on the pill-paved road to perdition.

But Mailer, despite the ocular evidence of twenty-four of her thirty films, which he seems to have sat through in rapid succession, thinks Monroe a great actress and great woman. She is "a proud, inviolate artist" who "inhabits every frame of the film" she is in; she "possessed the talent to play Cordelia," and became "so superb an actress" that "her taste by the end of her career was close to superb." We are told that "one might literally have to invent the idea of a soul in order to approach her." If a goddess didn't exist, we'd have to invent her.

Why limit oneself to criticism when one can create hagiography? So Mailer writes: "This woman, then, is better seen as Madame Bovary and Nana all in one, both in one, each with her separate unconscious. [But] one unconscious could almost serve for Nana and Bovary both. It is when Nana and Joan of Arc exist in the same flesh, or Boris Karloff and Bing Crosby, that the abysses of insanity are under the fog at every turn. And there is Monroe with the pictures of Eleonora Duse and Abraham Lincoln on her wall, double Monroe, one hard and calculating computer of a cold and ambitious cunt . . . and that other tender animal, an angel, a doe at large in blonde and lovely human form. Anyone else, man or woman, who contained such opposite personalities within his body would be ferociously mad. It is her transcendence of the opposites into a movie star that is her triumph. . . ."

Already in the very first paragraph of the book we read: "Across five continents the men who knew the most about love would covet her, and the classical pimples of the adolescent working his first gas pump would also pump for her, since Marilyn was deliverance, a very Stradivarius of sex, so gorgeous, forgiving, humorous, compliant and tender that even the most mediocre musician could relax his lack of art in the dissolving magic of her violin." Alas, great hagiography—even of this secular and profane sort—seldom makes for good writing.

What is truly shocking about *Marilyn* is not so much that

Mailer is writing a biography of someone he didn't know and
doesn't bother to research properly; nor is it the absurd overestimation of that person's talents and scope; nor yet the metaphysical balderdash about karma and double souls and Chinese
reincarnation; nor even the arrogance and foolishness with
which he figures out by spurious near-anagrams of their
names that Marilyn and Mailer were destined for each other
(or really the same person, I'm not quite sure which). The
capital offense of this book is the rant, the bombast, the fus-
tian, the sheer ludicrous and ugly overwriting of it. If the
content is worthy of Preminger's *Laura,* the style is rather like
Popeye the Sailor's arm after the ingestion of spinach: Mailer
flexing his verbal muscles to the point where his prose is not a
good read but a grisly roller-coaster ride along a biceps gone
berserk.

Vulgar errors abound. Most typical is the mixed metaphor,
as when Marilyn is "a sweet peach bursting before one's eyes"
while looking "like she'd stepped fully clothed out of a choco-
late box for Valentine's Day"—a chocolate-covered peach, presumably, to whom, in the next sentence, "sex was, yes, ice
cream." Such an indigestible diet of metaphors leads inevitably
to the scrambling of digestive and other organs; so Darryl
Zanuck, a hundred pages later, finds Marilyn's surpassing his
low estimate of her "ulcerous to the eye of his stomach," and
Marilyn's vacuous countenance becomes "in part the face
DiMaggio has been leaving in her womb." I haven't the space
here for examples of mere errors of grammar and syntax,
misuse of words, illiterate inversions, and the like; at least let
me instance the carelessness that exudes from such repetitions
as "receive a good reception" and "Dougherty's version is by
way of Guiles: 'Are you happy?' he decides to ask by way of a
greeting."

The tastelessness is less in the prurience than in the ineptitude. We read, for example, that "a male photographer [wants]
to photograph his woman nude, ideally her vagina, open and
nude"—as if a vagina were not *ipso facto* open and nude. We

read that "more than one Hollywood star would yet brag of early morning blow jobs fresh as milk while having his studio lunch in the commissary"—where it is rather hard to determine what is blown and what is eaten, and just where breakfast stops and lunch begins. Again: "Darryl Zanuck liked to put his own meat into a star's meat, so that the product was truly stamped Twentieth Century–Fox. In his eyes [Marilyn] had to be Schenck's meat and Hyde's potatoes. No glory to his own sausage." We begin to wonder what oral-infantile fixation obliges Mailer to keep mixing up sex and eating, the erotic and the esculent.

If Marilyn is looking at some mushrooms, to Mailer she is probably "comparing them to differences she has now discovered in the penis of the husband and the lover." Note also the bad grammar. When he lusts for his heroine most, in *Gentlemen Prefer Blondes* ("never . . . will she appear so fucky again"), Mailer expatiates: "Never again will she seem so close to a detumescent body ready to roll right over the edge of the world and drop your body down a chute of pillows and honey." Food once more, but that must be some sticky, clogged-up chute!

Yet Mailer needs neither sex nor food to be nauseating; he can do it with mere hyperbole. If Marilyn exasperates her fellow actors on the set, this becomes in Mailer: "She is an extermination camp to millions of cells in each of the brains of her co-workers as she gasses their patience"—six million dead Jews in search of an author who can convert them into a metaphor for Monroe's neurosis.

Or consider this Sargasso Sea of verbiage through which we must fight toward the simple notion that young Marilyn, although a narcissist, need not have been a virgin: "While an actor's face can be the human equivalent of Potemkin's village, and glamour no more than a measure of the distance from the glow of the flesh to sentiments of sewer gas in the womb, not every woman who is transcendently sexual on the screen must therefore be transcendently frigid in bed. It is simpler to assume that sexual attraction is finally based on something in sex itself, or that for some years, at any rate, there is the power to find some sexual return in a phallus or vagina as well as in a mirror or lens." Eureka!

Of course, Mailer can write simply, too. But then there is always the Charybdis of the adman's or press agent's sweet banalities lying in wait for him. So we read of Marilyn that "to kiss her is to drift in a canoe" or that "she is Lady Girl of the working class, and our own Rubens of the 4x5 Speed Graphic." Marilyn's longing for power to compensate for an orphan's dreary childhood becomes catchily "Yeats's beast slinking to the marketplace," although that particular beast slouched toward Bethlehem. Again, in *The Misfits,* Marilyn "is not so much a woman as a mood, a cloud of drifting senses in the form of Marilyn Monroe—no, never has she been more luminous." You can read stuff no worse than that in any studio's publicity handouts.

From verbal aggrandizement we go, quite naturally, to ideological magnification. Thus Mailer's Marilyn is at various times compared or contrasted to Napoléon, Nixon, John F. Kennedy, the Kennedy clan as a whole, George Wallace, and Saint Joan, and even, most curiously, likened in her ways of cleaning her first conjugal apartment to Joseph Conrad learning English.

To buttress such gilt (yes, gilt) by association, Mailer will outstrip any casuistic Biblical exegete. Asked if she had anything on for her calendar poses, Monroe (or her press agent) replied, "The radio." Mailer explicates this as not necessarily trying to be funny, but rather an awareness that one is much less nude "with the protection of sound." If Monroe on the set keeps flubbing the simple line "It's me, Sugar" by twisting it into "It's Sugar, Me," Mailer glosses this as "searching into nuances of identity . . . working out a problem in psychic knots worthy of R. D. Laing." And if the actress doesn't wash to the point of stinking, this is an existential act: "Marilyn, like many another artist, may not wish to wash if in the scent of the previous day some clue to experience can linger."

For such a master Jesuit, it is simple legerdemain to speculate that Monroe's suicide may have been a cleverly disguised
murder, either by the FBI-CIA or by the Mafia—an Either/Or
at which Kierkegaard himself would have boggled—and that
this death set off the series of cataclysmic political assassina-
tions that were soon to start rending the country. Moreover, it
is probably Marilyn, "the First Lady of American ghosts,"
who gives "a witch's turn to the wheel in Chappaquiddick."
This is no longer mere bad writing or bad thinking; it is
perfect madness.

Despite a few flashes of common sense, some insights, and
an occasional bit of lucid exposition, *Marilyn* is a very poorly
written, very demented book, by someone whom our deluded
critics persist in treating as a major, perhaps our best, writer.
And it won't do to say that Mailer has only lately gone around
the bend: there is less than a Chappaquiddick wheel's deviation
between these onanistic lucubrations on the late sex star, the
nude and deceased, and that supposedly brilliant first novel on
the naked and the dead.

[1973]

CLINGING TO A. BURR

Gore Vidal, *Burr: A Novel*

IN an essay called "Literary Gangsters" Gore Vidal wrote about me, among other good things, "There is nothing he cannot find to hate. Yet in his way, Mr. Simon is pure; a compulsive rogue criminal, more sadistic Gilles de Rais than neighborhood thug. Robert Brustein—is not pure; he has ambitions about his station. Mr. Simon knows that he is only an Illyrian gangster and is blessedly free of side; he simply wants to torture and kill in order to be as good an American as Mr. Charles Manson, say, or Lyndon Johnson." Well, Aaron Burr was, by most accounts, a rogue, and it is presumably on the principle of it-takes-one-to-know-one that I was picked to review this book about him.

But yesterday's rogues become today's heroes. Writing early in 1970, Vidal's paradigms of depravity were Manson and Johnson. Since then, we have had sympathetic accounts of the Manson family, and a President who makes LBJ look far too good to be bracketed with the likes of me. As for Aaron Burr, from this distance, and considering that he never reviewed one of Vidal's plays, he can look positively marvelous. So he becomes the proud, witty, sagacious, fundamentally honorable hero of this historico-picaresque novel, all the things that the real-life Burr may not have been. Or, again, may. Vidal's Burr is enterprising and shrewd: the one forces him into understandable conflict with those whose cupidity or stupidity opposes his enlightened self-interest; the other, as Vidal sees it, makes a sardonic skepticism about human nature unavoidable. So Burr emerges as a gentleman adventurer, a bit of a plotter but loyal to the best causes, and certainly no traitor. Well, why not?

What has always puzzled me, though, is why a respectable writer, such as Vidal sees himself as being, would want to write a historical novel. When you think of it, which would you rather have written: *Bleak House* or *A Tale of Two Cities, Middlemarch* or *Romola, Madame Bovary* or *Salammbô,* or even *Lie Down in Darkness* or *The Confessions of Nat Turner*? There are virtually no distinguished historical novels about the distant past, and why should there be? Let us not be so crude as to say that a novelist must write about what he has experienced, what he knows; but let us not be so rash as to suppose that the intuition and imagination of a writer, which must be exercised even when dealing with firsthand knowledge, cannot be over-extended, overtaxed. A historical novel is liable to be burdened with excessive scholarship or diluted by too much guesswork; it may sound farfetched, anachronistic; or it may simply, and often rightly, seem to be an evasion of the troublesome, too painfully involving present.

In his afterword, Vidal defends his choice of the historical novel over straight history as allowing him to be meticulous yet free—free, above all, to "attribute motives," which is to say, interpret history. But surely that is what all good historians, at least since Thucydides, have done—interpret history—the more scrupulous ones making it clearer where fact ends and conjecture begins. I think that the clue to Vidal's problem is in the very title of his book, *Burr: A Novel.* The reason for including the genre in the title may, of course, be to explain to those who shun heavy reading that this is, after all, only a novel; but it may also be, conversely, Vidal's attempt to convince the world and himself that this *is* a piece of fiction. Our novelists are finding it harder and harder to write novels, hence the desperate stratagems of a Capote with his "nonfiction novel," of a Mailer with his "novel biography," and of Vidal now with his tautological title.

That is not to suggest that *Burr: A Novel* does not qualify as historical fiction. In fact, it rather ambitiously subsumes both established modes of the historic novel. One is to take a famous and fascinating figure, and concentrate on him or her, often writing in the first person; thus, for example, Robert Graves's *I, Claudius.* The second, somewhat less risky, approach keeps the great figures of the period in the background (*War and Peace*), or out of sight (*Vanity Fair*), and concentrates on fictitious characters. *Burr* takes place partly between 1833 and 1836, when a young lawyer-writer, Charlie Schuyler, records the reminiscences that his employer, old Aaron Burr, dictates to him, and partly in the time covered by these memoirs— from the Revolution to Burr's trial for treason. We see the young and mature Burr through his own eyes, and the old Burr through Charlie's, with Charlie's independent adventures mixed in. The memoir sequences are history fictionalized, whereas the framework is fiction historicized. Vidal, whose stepfather is a descendant of Burr, spent two decades researching the book, and is covering territory with which he is comfortably, almost cavalierly, familiar.

The dual method has its felicities. It permits Vidal to see Colonel Burr as he saw himself and as others saw and evaluated him, allowing for instant ambiguity. It permits, moreover, a somewhat arbitrary, personalized overview of history, and a certain foreshortening by an old man impatient with the niceties and more tiresome details of memoir writing; in other words, the mere scattering of nuggets before an avid amanuensis. Finally, the bifocal view enables us to draw conclusions about the differences between the theorizing of the Founding Fathers, and the practical realities as they became set under Jackson, Van Buren, and their heirs—ourselves. (This, by the way, is no simplistic contrast between a glorious dream and a smudged actuality, but more about that anon.)

The binary approach has its drawbacks, too. The early period of this republic is much more spectacular than the 1830s, and Colonel and Vice President Burr are much more captivating than poor old Aaron Burr, to say nothing of poor young Charlie Schuyler. As a result, we end up racing through the "present-day" passages with only moderate interest, impatient to get to the flashbacks, when Burr and this country really got cracking. Besides, put history, or what passes for it, alongside second-rate fiction, and what passes for fiction will always be the loser.

Not that *Burr* is a bad novel; actually, by contemporary standards, it is quite a good one. Vidal, after all, is something very few American novelists have been: a wit. Humorists we have had aplenty, but novelists who could actually write sparkling repartee have been rarer among us than saints, and rather more sorely missed. If you look at today's crop of novelists, except for Vidal, only Wilfrid Sheed can be considered a reputable wit, and even he is English-born. If for nothing else but their rarity, therefore, wits are precious hereabouts.

I cannot argue that *Burr* is a prime example of the novel of wit; still, it does contain much that is witty, and for this I am grateful. For instance, when Hamilton compares himself to Domitian, Burr catches the misidentification of the emperor turned cabbage-grower, corrects him—"Diocletian"—and wryly reflects: "I fear that Hamilton had only glanced at Gibbon while I had made the mistake of reading the master's every word." Or, close to death himself and learning of Dolley Madison's widowing, Burr comments: "Dolley will do well, with or without money. I am told that Daniel Webster is in love with her and since he takes every bribe offered to him, he will have enough money to keep her in style." Again, Burr will remark: "Bentham was certainly drawn to democracy, having experienced so little of it."

There is a lot of this stuff—some better, some worse—strewn throughout the 428 tall octavo pages of this novel; but the ultimate wit lies in the satirical, debunking, irreverent notions of the work as a whole. Our Revolutionary myths are demythified, our heroes put into—indeed spanked with—slippers. Washington emerges as a vainglorious and incompetent general, a pompous and self-aggrandizing would-be monarch, with skill only for political intrigue; Hamilton as a canting, megalomaniacal, dissembling, but often perceptive royalist *manqué;* Adams and Monroe as mediocre bores; and Jefferson, the archvillain of the piece, as a brilliant strategist and opportunist of genius, and also a liar, coward, selfish schemer, inconsistent wordmonger, paltry tinkerer, and consummate hypocrite. The good guys are Madison, Gallatin, and, above all, Jackson, but they are fairly inconspicuous by comparison. Vidal makes out a plausible and eminently readable case for his reinterpretations; yet even if one accepts them, as I tend to do, one feels that there must have been more and better sides to these men than a valet's view of history full of backstairs gossip has room for, true as it may be within its limits. Though Vidal is no linear descendant of Burr, he may well be one of the twelfth-century troubadour Peire Vidal, of whom the ancient chronicle relates that he "talked the greatest nonsense about . . . slandering others."

In his afterword, Vidal claims that some of his own assessments differ from Burr's, and here we get to the area of the book's basic weakness: a want of strong, memorable, living characters. Charlie and his girl, Helen, various journalists, writers, politicians, wives, are all intelligently conceived and observed, but they lack that racy, idiosyncratic, autonomous selfhood that severs the umbilical cord between a character and the mind that gave birth to him. Even Burr is much more real when commenting about rivals, politics, life in general, than when he is simply being himself in the quotidian details of his personality. In fact, Burr, Charlie, and a number of lesser characters speak the same language—the author's—down to such shared tics as elliptical sentences chary of pronouns. Consequently, it becomes almost impossible to accept a character's view as being anything but Vidal's own.

Altogether, Vidal's manner is that of the gifted, incisive amateur, who explains people more accurately than he can evoke them. And granted that his vignettes of early America, with pigs foraging along New York's Broad Way and guests shooting partridges out of the windows of Washington's best hotel, are fetching and no doubt authentic, when he has to create a scene in greater detail, it is all too apt to read like this: "In silence, we watched the steamboat from Albany make its way down the centre [Vidal goes in for British spelling] channel of the river. On the decks women in bright summer finery twirl parasols; over the water their voices echo the gulls that follow in the ship's wake, waiting for food." Note that in this description there is not one vital, original image or word.

What draws Vidal to Burr is, clearly, the man's—or eidolon's—aristocratic fastidiousness, gentlemanly connoisseurship, and antidemocratic irony. Vidal goes so far as to bring on the already dead Edward Livingston in order to allow him to pronounce anachronistically Burr's epitaph: "He would have made a better President than Mr. Jefferson because he was in every way the nobler man."

Illyrian gangster that I am, I still happen to share Mr. Vidal's dandified mistrust of the plebs and its politicos, and so must confess that, perhaps for the wrong reasons, I rather enjoyed this book and recommend it threequarterheartedly to America at large. With uncanny intuition, or sheer luck, it arrives on the scene in the wake of Vietnam, Agnew, Watergate, and Nixon, and so neatly matches the mood of the nation as to make it an immediate best-seller despite its undemocratic, unpopular views. If it can make its readers more politically sophisticated, without plunging them into cynicism or driving them, defensively, into a backlash of total disbelief, we must all be beholden to its author.

[1973]

DE TENUISSIMIS CLAMAVI

Joan Didion, *The White Album*

WOULDN'T you like to be Joan Didion? A lovely young woman whose every novel is hailed as superlative by the critics and whose every collection of essays is saluted as so much better than her fiction? Oh, to be married to an understanding fellow writer: to have an adopted daughter whom you love so much that you measure time and history by her ages (the new house you moved into when she was five, the terrible flood when she was twelve); to be of good Western pioneer stock, yet equally at home in chic, sophisticated New York and eccentric, manic California; to be able to pack yourself off, when you need solitude for the writing of a book, to the luxurious Royal Hawaiian Hotel in Honolulu or to the child-hood house in Sacramento, where your loving parents will still make you feel protectedly secluded in your adolescent surroundings.

In New York, even your daughter would be talking to Carl Bernstein; in Los Angeles, Janis Joplin and David Hockney would drop in at your house, and Roman Polanski would spill red wine on your white dress. When you were not interviewing or profiling Nancy Reagan or Eldridge Cleaver, you and your husband would be writing screenplays for Otto Preminger or Barbra Streisand (what matter if they never got made—the fun, as one of Miss Didion's essays informs us, is all in the wheeling and dealing), and the *Los Angeles Times* would name you one of its "Women of the Year." But, oh, the price you would have to pay for it! Sensitivity such as Miss Didion bulges and bristles with takes its toll, and she wastes no time in informing us of it in her new collection of essays, *The White Album*.

She has, first, to pay for it with a disorder that might be some form of multiple sclerosis, which alerts her to "what it [is] like to open the door to the stranger and find that the stranger [does] indeed have a knife." A thorough psychiatric examination reveals attacks of vertigo and nausea, but also that "in quality and level of sophistication [the] patient's responses are characteristic of . . . high average or superior intelligence." Worst of all, perhaps, are the migraines that condemn Miss Didion, from three to five times a month, to whole days in bed, in pain and lost to the world. The only consolation is that, just as the vertigo and nausea do "not now seem to [her] an inappropriate response to the summer of 1968," so the "migraine personality . . . tends to be ambitious, inward, intolerant of error . . . perfectionist." Yes, horrible as attacks of vertigo and nausea, not to mention weekly migraines, may be, their ache is mitigated when seen as an earnest of concern with a world gone haywire and the kind of perfectionism that has the victim "spending most of a week [presumably the parts unencroached on by headaches and nausea] writing and rewriting and not writing a single paragraph."

But that is not all that sensitivity costs you. It also costs you peace of mind and inflicts strange compulsions. Having met and followed around two Zuma Beach lifeguards on their daily rounds, Miss Didion is haunted by them: "Although I have not gone back, there is no day when I do not think of Leonard McKinley and Dick Haddock and what they are doing, what situations they face. . . ." And water itself absorbs her even more than its guardians: "I will be talking to someone in Los Angeles, say, or in New York, and suddenly the [Hoover] dam will materialize. . . . I will be driving down Sunset Boulevard, or about to enter a freeway, and abruptly those power transmission towers will appear before me. . . ." She is fascinated by whence and how her drinking water reaches her; it is a reverence for water taking "the form of this constant meditation upon where the water is . . . [on] the movement of water through aqueducts. . . ." She even wanted to *be* the water one day, and she wants it still. And when she is not yearning for the aqueous state, she longs for a moist atmosphere: "All my life I had been trying to spend time in one greenhouse or another, and all my life the person in one greenhouse or another has been trying to hustle me out."

And then there are the fears and disturbing obsessions. First the permanent kind, such as the one that began when a stranger entered her house and claimed to be from Chicken Delight, only to be routed by the appearance of her husband. The intrepid author takes down the license number of the intruder's panel truck. "During those years I was always writing down the license numbers of panel trucks . . . circling the block . . . parked across the street . . . idling at the intersection."

Some fears are only semipermanent. During certain years, when she visits her mother-in-law, she must avoid at all cost looking at six lines of a goody-goody framed poem on the wall; during her many stays in Hawaii, she has "never driven into Schofield [Barracks, which she seems to visit frequently]" without hearing the six lines of the blues that end *From Here to Eternity*. Heading for the California State Water Project Operations Control Center, she thinks almost constantly of six lines by Karl Shapiro; driving one day from Sacramento to San Francisco, she must turn the radio all the way up "to erase six words from her mind," Ezra Pound's *Petals on a wet black bough,* for they "signal [that year] the onset of anxiety and fright."

On a flight to Hawaii, she cannot stop thinking of six overheard words spoken by a male passenger to a woman: "You are driving me to murder." (Six is a distinctly unlucky number for Miss Didion.) Sometimes, though, the haunting is more vague: "Quite often I reflect on the big house in Hollywood, on 'Midnight Confessions,' and on [the murder of] Ramon Novarro and on the fact that Roman Polanski and I are godparents to the same child. . . . ." Wistfully she concludes that writing has not yet helped her find the answers; but when, I wonder, has she time to write, what with those constant obligations to think of Leonard McKinley and Dick Haddock, Hoover Dam and quotations from Karl Shapiro and James Jones, those compulsions to write down license numbers of panel trucks, to follow the course of California water in her mind, to get hustled out of greenhouses, and meditate on Ramon Novarro and her shared godparenthood with Roman Polanski?

The life of a sensitivity freak is not an easy one, I tell you. Throughout *The White Album* Miss Didion must walk through a forest of doomsday symbols so alarming that she cannot see a single tree. And all the time she is driven to confess her fatal virtues, her devastating, apocalyptic awareness. Thus the bottle of Château Léoville-Poyferré she is treated to in a fashionable Bogotá restaurant is, at "$20 American," merely "indifferent"; thus she cannot tell you the real reason Governor Reagan's unfinished mansion makes her shudder "without getting into touchy . . . and finally inadmissible questions of taste, and ultimately of class"; thus she feels dreadful guilt on one of her sojourns at her Honolulu luxury hotel: "To sit by the Royal pool and read *The New York Review of Books* is to feel oneself an asp, disguised in a voile beach robe, in the very bosom of the place." After reading such outpourings of hypersensitivity in quotidian conflict, one feels positively relieved to be an insensitive clod.

Joan Didion can write well enough, observe and overhear oddities sharply, and display sumptuously a Cassandran intellect. But I don't want to read about Honolulu, for instance, through the voile veil of her constant desire (as she puts it) to have me know precisely who she is and where she is and what is on her mind. Can't she let her sensitivity be an automatic by-product, as in her better essays it sometimes is? There is a world out there beyond what the world means to Joan Didion.

[1979]

FROM SENSIBILITY
TOWARD SENSE

Susan Sontag, *Under the Sign of Saturn*

ACCORDING to an adage that often performs also as an analogy, if we watched ourselves walking, we could not walk at all. In the process of speculating about just how we propel ourselves forward by putting one foot in front of the other, we would end up paralyzed or falling on our faces. Whether or not this is the truth about ambulation, it unfortunately is not true of criticism: entire schools of contemporary criticism watch themselves—anxiously, self-importantly, gloatingly—perform in essays that, far from freezing, flow unremittingly on. If anyone becomes numb, it is the reader, unlucky fellow, who finds himself in the position of an innocent traveler pressed into archaeological spadework without being given the necessary equipment or training. Structuralist and semiological criticism, and their various offshoots, have not only buried the texts they belabor under impermeable rubble, they are also hellbent on burying us.

Susan Sontag is not uninfluenced by the prevailing French or French-derived criticism, witness the tribute to Roland Barthes in her new collection, *Under the Sign of Saturn*. Although she is basically a comprehensible, generally even lucid, critic, she has a tendency to sprinkle complication into her writing, as for instance in the opening section of her essay on Antonin Artaud, the longest and most interesting in the book. One is reminded of the story about Mallarmé dawdling at a café table over a funerary poem for Verlaine and explaining his holding up the obsequies with: "I am just adding a little obscurity." Aside from the short mortuary tribute to Barthes, a similar one to Paul Goodman—the latter really a lament over his snubbing her, as well as a portrait of herself as an isolated artist in a Paris garret—and the piece on Artaud that served as the introduction to his *Selected Writings,* Sontag's book includes essays on Walter Benjamin (himself no mean shedder of obscurity), on Elias Canetti, on Hans-Jürgen Syberberg's seven-hour film about Hitler, and on "Fascinating Fascism," which deals with both Leni Riefenstahl and a coffee-table book of photographs called *SS Regalia.*

What is the sign of Saturn, and why are these writers and filmmakers under it? Miss Sontag quotes Walter Benjamin, the complicated German philosopher-critic who alone can compete with the French master obfuscators in current popularity among the literary elite: "I came into the world under the sign of Saturn—the star of the slowest revolution, the planet of detours and delays. . . ." The umbrella of Saturn does not really cover every one of the other artists discussed, but they are all, in one sense or another, extreme cases—*cas limites,* as the French would say: artists who are at the limits of the possible or the permissible. Sontag refers to them admiringly as "the great, daring mapmakers of consciousness *in extremis.*"

Actually, some do not enjoy her full favor; she is against Leni Riefenstahl, Hitler's favorite filmmaker, at least ideologically. It is characteristic of Miss Sontag's new critical stance that moral considerations matter. Thus she shows us Riefenstahl's career as a triptych: the early mountaineering films where Leni was both star and director, and physical effort triumphed; the Nazi period's panegyrics to bodily beauty, strength, and achievement—*Triumph of the Will* and *Olympia*; and the more recent book of photographs about a handsome but vanishing

African tribe, *The Last of the Nuba*. In her *Sturm und Drang* phase, Miss Sontag would have hailed Riefenstahl's aesthetic achievements and disregarded the political and moral aspects; now, at last, she gives us a carefully researched and documented moral-political case against Riefenstahl and her alleged reformation, though Sontag rightly concedes a certain philosophy to the Nazis and admires the unquestionable cinematic values of the Nazi filmmaker's two great documentaries.

Here Sontag reintroduces the concept of "camp," which she championed without ever fully admitting it, essentially to renounce it, albeit not without some reservations and regrets. She speaks of "formalist appreciations" backed up by "the sensibility of camp, which is unfettered by the scruples of high seriousness: and the modern sensibility relies on continuing trade-offs between the formalist approach and camp taste." This is an irresponsible statement: neither in her celebrated "Notes on 'Camp'" (1964) nor in "Fascinating Fascism" (1974) does Sontag show how "high seriousness" or "the formalist approach" trades off with camp taste; indeed, not even the meaning of "modern sensibility" is made entirely clear.

But, then, Sontag has a trying habit of issuing wonderfully challenging statements throughout this collection (and elsewhere) without elaborating and elucidating them. She will tell us, "I admire Norman Mailer as a writer, but I don't really believe in his voice," a voice that she finds "too baroque, somehow fabricated." Since her statement occurs in the tribute to Paul Goodman, whose voice, apparently, "is the real thing," we must, perhaps, settle for this foreshortened explanation of what is wrong with Mailer; yet, whatever the context, we must be told how someone with an inauthentic voice can still be admired as a writer.

Similarly, we learn next that although Goodman "was not often graceful as a writer, his writing and his mind were touched with grace." This means one of three things. Either grace as a writer can coexist with gracelessness in the writing, or being touched with grace is in some mysterious way different from having it, or Miss Sontag tosses off hasty, high-sounding paradoxes without thinking through what, if anything, they mean.

The last hypothesis gains credibility when considered in conjunction with other assertions in the book. We are told that the major works of Baudelaire and Lautréamont "are equally dependent . . . upon the idea of the author as a tormented self raping its own unique subjectivity." Quite aside from the clumsiness of that image, the extremely disciplined verse and controlled audacity of *Les Fleurs du mal* are in no way comparable to the torrential flow of poetic prose and surreal vision of *Les Chants de Maldoror*; as for the artist's driving himself to the limit and beyond, this applies equally to a good many nineteenth- and twentieth-century poets. But what really confuses the issue is Miss Sontag's wording: what is this "idea of the author"? Is it in the author's or in the reading public's mind? Is it a legitimate concept or a self-deluding notion? Or is it merely verbiage?

Again, when Sontag casually asserts that "Walt Disney's *Fantasia,* Busby Berkeley's *The Gang's All Here,* and Kubrick's *2001* . . . strikingly exemplify certain formal structures and themes of fascist art," we cannot accept her parenthetic aside without any further discussion; at the very least we want to know *which* structures and themes. And if it is true, it requires an examination of what that says about contemporary American society. In fact, if Sontag could prove her glibly dropped point, an essay on *it* would be much more interesting than the demonstration of Riefenstahl's virtually self-evident fascism.

But to return to camp. Sontag tries to exonerate it, first, on the basis of "continuing trade-offs" between it and high seriousness—which conjures up the image of a close collaboration between Matthew Arnold and Ronald Firbank; soon, contradictorily, she attempts a defense on the grounds of something quite ephemeral: fashion. "Art that seemed eminently worth defending ten years ago [i.e., in '64 as against '74], as a minority or adversary taste, no longer seems defensible today, because the ethical and cultural issues it raises have become serious, even dangerous, in a way they were not then." This is, to put it mildly, bizarre.

To begin with, can something that ceases to be defensible as art in a mere decade still be considered art at all? Whatever outlives its artistic usefulness in ten short years is precisely a fleeting fashion and the exemplar of nonart. Second, is critical evaluation meant to be a kind of politics of contrariness? That would automatically foster the enshrinement of what the majority resents or ignores—the very procedure that, for a while, raised camp to the level of art.

The giveaway follows apace: "The hard truth is that what may be acceptable in elite culture may not be acceptable in mass culture, that tastes which pose only innocuous ethical issues as the property of a minority become corrupting when they become more established. Taste is context, and the context has changed." Yet how did camp become a majority taste? It achieved its eminence precisely because the brilliant, young, glámorous Susan Sontag published "Notes on 'Camp' "—to be sure, in *Partisan Review,* not exactly the stomping grounds of hoi polloi, but where are the temples of the unco-optable nowadays? Soon enough the media latched on to that essay and its topic, and especially to its eloquent, charming, highly salable author. Nothing succeeds better than highbrow endorsement of lowbrow tastes: who would not, at no extra cost, prefer to be a *justified* sinner? Miss Sontag's "hard truth" strikes me as very soft indeed.

Next, by what right, human or divine, is what is good for the elite taboo for the masses? This kind of intellectual *droit du seigneur* may well be the epitome of fascist criticism. If, as responsible critics, we preconize, say, Proust, Mallarmé, Joyce, and Beckett, it is not because we want to keep them to ourselves; it is, on the contrary, in the hope, often forlorn, that we may bring more people to the pleasure and insight to be gathered from them. If, on the other hand, our taste is deleterious and culpable—or foolish and irresponsible—we have no business promulgating it either in *Partisan Review* or in *Time* maga-zine. Taste is precisely *not* context, but that which transcends context; everything else is addiction, fashionable or unfashion-able, and, even if pleasing for the moment, headed for the wastebasket. But, of course, this is presuming that taste refers to aesthetics and not to erotics, and that we do not, as Miss Sontag did in another famous 1964 essay, "Against Interpreta-tion," celebrate and demand a mere "erotics of art."

Miss Sontag no longer militantly espouses this outlook, but she continues to hover in its vicinity. Scattered throughout *Under the Sign of Saturn* are such bits of questionable praise as that for Artaud's "aesthetics of thought . . . theology of culture . . . phenomenology of suffering." Now, I can see how one might worship culture, though I am not sure how this applies to Artaud; I can likewise see how a phenomenology of suffer-ing might make for a riveting case history for psychiatrists and even some lay readers. But "aesthetics of thought"—surely this is just the "erotics of art" turned inside out and being sneaked, in sheep's clothing, through the back door.

And touting Artaud, that "hero of self-exacerbation," as "the greatest prose poet in the French language since the Rim-baud of *Illuminations* and *A Season in Hell*" rashly ignores the Mallarmé of *Divagations* and does scant justice to Valéry, Claudel, Gide, and Jules Renard, among others. Of course, if your criterion is self-exacerbation—"the greatest *quantity* of suffering in the history of literature"—your candidate may be the greatest prose poet *before* Rimbaud as well, although even then one might wonder about what kinds of scales, or calipers, are needed for the quantitative assessment of suffering. Or does one judge simply by the loudness of the screams?

Yet how silly of me to raise such questions in these post–R. D. Laing and post–Michel Foucault days. Obviously, Miss Sontag is influenced by both these "minority or adversary" thinkers, as witness her condemnation of Jacques Rivière's moving attempts to bring Artaud back to relative sanity (a lost cause, if ever there was one, but nevertheless moving), followed by her Foucaultian definition of sanity as what makes sense to a particular culture, a particular society; whereas "what is called insane denotes that which in the determination of a particular society must not be thought." Aside from the fact that this statement overlooks the not insignificant distinction in most societies between thought and action, it implies that to a shallow society profundity will appear insane, i.e., madness is context, and the context changes. Yet even if there is something arbitrary about most prevailing definitions of madness, there is nothing specious about regarding acts of violence against others as dangerous, illicit, or mad.

But do not consider the foregoing strictures a complete rejection of Miss Sontag's book. Whenever she takes the trouble to be a historian, as in her pointing out the ahistoricity of Riefenstahl's view of the Nuba, or a theological historian, as when she traces Artaud's indebtedness to Gnosticism, she performs with noteworthy acumen and ability. So, too, when she analyzes the quiddity of a work and its background, as with Syberberg's *Hitler, a Film from Germany,* a seven-hour endurance test she had the stamina (or eccentricity) to see five or six times, to discuss at length with its author, and (apparently) to read up on in great detail. Although my own regard for this film is qualified, I have nothing but respect for a critic who goes to such lengths to understand and interpret (yes, interpret; no "against interpretation" here!) a difficult work.

Regrettably, in the case of this film, too, Miss Sontag indulges in what strikes me as exaggeration. Just as she asserted that "the course of all recent serious theater in Western Europe and the Americas can be said to divide into two periods—before Artaud and after Artaud" (which, assuming that it is meant as more than a chronological division, sounds like a whopping overstatement), she now tells us that *Hitler* is "probably the most ambitious Symbolist work of this century," a masterpiece having "in the era of cinema's unprecedented mediocrity . . . something of the character of a posthumous event." It is "like an unwanted baby in the era of zero population growth." The trouble with *Hitler,* as I see it, is precisely that it is the equivalent of too many babies in any era, an act of overpopulation on screen—and of decimation in the auditorium.

That, however, is one of the hallmarks of Miss Sontag's criticism: a boundless enthusiasm for certain favorites that ignores or minimizes their shortcomings. In Elias Canetti she loves "his staunchless capacity for admiration and enthusiasm, and his civilized contempt for complaining." This may be splendid in a novelist and essayist; in a critic, complaining is often necessary where it hurts most, and enthusiasm frequently in need of a little staunching. Thank goodness, Miss Sontag no longer comes out in enthusiastic defense of such stuff as Jack Smith's *Flaming Creatures,* yet not even Canetti, whose work I hardly know, should (in my opinion) be praised unqualifiedly for his tribute to "a brown bundle emitting a single sound (e-e-e-e-e-e) which is brought every day to a square in Marrakesh." Canetti's "I was proud of the bundle because it was alive" strikes me not as a moving tribute, but as endorsement of a horrible misery for the sake of displaying one's enlightened affirmation of life.

Susan Sontag can write well: "One is always in arrears to oneself" is exquisite and compelling; "Surrealism's great gift . . . was to make melancholy cheerful," though debatable, is equally stimulating and exquisite. There is much to be said, too, for this maxim: "One cannot use the life to interpret the work. But one can use the work to interpret the life." Other boldly hurled apothegms boomerang. I find it hard to accept, in a context of her high praise for Walter Benjamin, that "his major essays seem to end just in time, before they self-destruct."

Rash and unhelpful, again, is the assertion that, though one can be inspired, scorched, and changed by Artaud, "there is no way of applying him." Can any poet-seer be applied? Sontag's argument is not helped by careless use of words: how can Artaud be "profoundly indigestible"? On some deeper level than that of the stomach? And I should be happier if Miss Sontag stopped hinting, especially about the dead, and instead of referring to Barthes as "consciously interested in the perverse" and as "a man of his sexual tastes," allowed her observations to come out of the closet.

She might also, profitably, stop reaching for grand but nebulous criteria. To praise, as she does, identification "with something beyond achievement" is very much like arguing "against interpretation." A critic as capable of subtle and illuminating interpretations as Susan Sontag should come down all the way from the cloudy heights of metacriticism.

[1980]

PENTIMENTAL JOURNEY

Lillian Hellman, *Pentimento: A Book of Portraits*

I AM glad that Lillian Hellman entitled her new book of memoirs *Pentimento* and so taught me a fine new word. In a prefatory note, she explains: "Old paint on canvas, as it ages, sometimes becomes transparent." One can then

> see the original lines: a tree will show through a woman's dress, a child makes way for a dog, a large boat is no longer on an open sea. That is called pentimento because the painter "repented," changed his mind. Perhaps it would be as well to say that the old conception, replaced by a later choice, is a way of seeing and then seeing again. That is all I mean about the people in this book. The paint has aged now and I wanted to see what was there for me once, what is there for me now.

That is nicely phrased and sounds promising. For pentimento usually means a painter's changing his mind about the specific way in which a particular thing is to be shown— whether a leg is to be bent or straight. It is not so much a child making way for a dog, or a tree for a woman's dress, as getting the foreshortening of an outstretched arm down correctly, or catching the exact curve of a brow. So, I assumed, a collection of verbal portraits would show how the sitter looked to Miss

Hellman then and now: the past impressions would show through the present's overpaint in such a way that they would comment on, correct, reassess each other, allowing for certain paradigms of change and permanence to emerge in the process. This, however, is rarely what Miss Hellman gives us; rather, she lets the tree peep through the woman's dress until we see the tree for what she now takes it to mean, not as a fascinating set of cross-references between what was and is, or what was and is no more.

But, all right, let the book be no more than a pentimental journey into the past; if well done, that is quite good enough. And indeed it soon becomes apparent that Miss Hellman is using the portraits—or pentimenti—of this book to continue and fill out her autobiography, which, under the title *An Unfinished Woman,* appeared in 1969. That book ended with three *portraits-souvenir* (to use Cocteau's term) that were themselves pentimenti *avant la lettre,* so to speak; more important, the last sentences read, "All I mean is that I left too much of me unfinished because I wasted too much time. However." The terminal "however" was no mere stylistic cuteness, although it is that, too; very likely it was meant as an allusion to Ibsen's dying word, *tvertimot,* meaning "on the contrary." He was giving the lie to his nurse's optimistic statement about his condition: Miss Hellman, a neo-Ibsenite, gives the lie to the notion that her time has been largely wasted. What a difference between these *tvertimot*s: one a bleak facing up to the grimmest of finalities, the other a hopeful acceptance of one's life as not having been such a botch after all. Which might explain why Ibsen's plays are dramas and Miss Hellman's mostly melodramas with vaguely happy endings. But let us come back to *Pentimento.*

The book is made up of seven essays of varying length, five of them dedicated, at least ostensibly, to obscure but noteworthy individuals. "Bethe" concerns a rather primitive but handsome cousin of Miss Hellman's imported by rich New Orleans immigrants, the Bowmans (Lillian's mother was *née* Bowman), to become wife and sedative to a young ne'er-do-well of a Bowman. The marriage fails and Bethe becomes the mistress of a local mafioso, and a social outcast. Fourteen-year-old Lillian, precocious and highly impressionable (as what author, at least in his own reminiscenses, wasn't?), learns from Bethe how much more meaningful than marriage an unsanctioned union can be. The mafioso is killed; Bethe gets involved with lesser men, and is suddenly carried off by a severe attack of pneumonia.

The trouble with an essay like this is that, viewed from the outside, Bethe is not a particularly interesting character, and the child Lillian could not possibly have penetrated to her core. The purpose of the memoir, however, has not much to do with Bethe, anyway; it is mostly meant to explain why Miss Hellman's longest and closest relationship was with Dashiell Hammett, whom she never actually married. The key passage reads: "Then I don't believe I ever thought of her again through a pleasant marriage that was not to last, until the first afternoon I slept with Dashiell Hammett. As I moved toward the bed I said, 'I'd like to tell you about my cousin, a woman called Bethe.' Hammett said, 'You can tell me if you have to, but I can't say I would have chosen this time.' " According to one's taste, one may consider this candid or unappetizing. The business of dismissing the marriage with the single epithet "pleasant" I find insensitive and unappealing. A marriage, even a brief one, cannot be honestly summed up with a solitary modifier more appropriate to a pony ride or ice cream cone. And if that marriage was indeed pleasant, why was it so brief? From our forthright, outspoken author, we have the right to expect something more.

The next essay, "Willy," begins as a portrait of overrefined but shallow Aunt Lily, whom Willy married for her money and soon came to detest. He had been an adventurer in Central America for years; now, through Lily, he became an important part of a corporation like United Fruit, and, as a buccaneer and slave boss (even if only by proxy), rich and powerful. The adolescent Lillian and this middle-aged man became attracted to each other during a brief car trip to the bayou country; years later, after a fight with Dash, Miss Hellman is back in New Orleans, rediscovers Willy, and almost goes off with him on a romantic expedition to Central America. But, afraid of losing Dash, she changes her mind, and learns later that Willy, in dire financial straits, drove up to the bayou country and died there in a car accident.

I am not quite sure about the purpose of this memoir. Willy is not intrinsically compelling—his satanic deeds are executed by others, and at home he is merely an acrimonious, routinely unfaithful husband. The trip to the bayous shared by this older man and the awakening girl never takes on the poetic intensity and mythic reverberations that might lift it out of the commonplace, and the "plot" lacks dramatic, or even melodramatic, interest. Lily and Willy and their son Honey are a peculiar enough threesome, but that is not what is explored here.

Here, too, a basic lack in this memoir-writing becomes apparent. Miss Hellman does not possess the gift of seeing the odd, funny, telling detail that would make humdrum events achieve their uniqueness, their trivial but touching dignity. Consider Max Beerbohm, in "No. 2. The Pines," on his way to see Swinburne. Now, a visit to Swinburne may be momentous, but its preliminaries are quite mundane: apprehension and nervousness. Yet Beerbohm makes them memorable:

> I had expected a greater distance to the sanctuary—a walk in which to compose my mind and prepare myself for initiation. I laid my hand irresolutely against the gate of the bleak trim frontgarden, I withdrew my hand, I went away. Out here were all the aspects of common modern life. In there was Swinburne. A butcher-boy went by, whistling. He was not going to see Swinburne. He could afford to whistle.

It is that butcher-boy that makes this a great moment in memoir-writing; but in *Pentimento* there are few if any such butcher-boys.

Consider now Miss Hellman's way of telling an episode in which Uncle Willy takes her, a successful young playwright, for a drive:

> Toward midday we went through the town of Hammond and Willy said, "In a few minutes." The long driveway, lined with moss oak, ended at a galleried plantation house. "We're home," he said. It was a beautiful, half empty house of oval rooms and delicate colors. Beyond the great lawns were strawberry fields and, in the distance, ten or twelve horses moved slowly in a field. I said, "I like my farm in Pleasantville. But there's nothing like the look of Southern land, or there's no way for me to get over thinking so. It's home for me still."
> "I'll give you this place," he said. "I'd like you to have it."
> Late in the afternoon, after a long walk in the strawberry acres, I said my aunts would be hurt if I didn't have dinner with them. We had an argument about that, and then we started back to New Orleans.

Now this is good, straightforward journalistic writing. But it is not absorbing, not a penetrating human document. Clearly the essence of what went on between Willy and the young Lily is, willingly or not, left unrecorded. This strikes me as a human or, at the very least, an artistic failure. Nothing really comes alive here: not the people, not the house, not even that unique "Southern land." The butcher boy is missing

One finally gets the uncomfortable feeling that this hazy portrait of Uncle Willy serves chiefly to show us Miss Hellman as a pioneer liberated woman, perhaps even a *femme fatale*: if, after all, she had not ditched Willy at the last moment to hotfoot it back to Hammett, Willy might not have died in that drunken car crash. Of course, one purpose that all but one of these essays serve is, sooner or later, to introduce Hammett as a character, to bring the events and characters into some sort of test-tube relationship with him from which he emerges with a uniqueness even more manifest than the Southern land's. So here is the crucial long-distance phone call, the turning point in the "Willy" story:

> I phoned the Beverly Hills house from the restaurant. I said to
> Hammett, "I'm in New Orleans. I'm not coming back to
> Hollywood for a while and I didn't want you to worry."
> "How are you?" he said.
> "O.K. And you?"
> "I'm O.K. I miss you."
> "I miss you, too. Is there a lady in my bedroom?"
> He laughed. "I don't think so, but they come and go. Except
> you. You just go."
> "I had good reason," I said.
> "Yes," he said, "you did."

This is the stichomythic, tough, ironic dialogue Hellman and
Hammett usually exchange in the book, and it is plainly meant
to be mythic as well as stichomythic: they see themselves as
Hemingway characters living out a fabulous Hemingway
affair. But besides being sophomoric, these conversations re-
created with total recall are also a bit suspect: surely Miss
Hellman couldn't have written down all these charged monosyllables in her diary, or remembered them, understatement
by pregnant understatement. She becomes even more suspect,
however, when she is putting casually profound statements
into her own adolescent mouth. Thus when a policeman questions her about why she tried to see Bethe the day after her
mafioso lover was killed, child Lillian replies: "I don't know. I
read about Mr. Arneggio last night. Love, I think, but I'm not
sure." From no young schoolgirl do I buy this "Love, I think,
but I'm not sure," especially if it is set down by that same girl
at the age of sixty-six or sixty-seven.

Yet this memoir-writing presents even graver problems.
Though Miss Hellman is evidently a memory artist, she never
gives us the look, the essential characteristics, the feel of a
person in one of those rapid sketches that cleave to a reader's
remembrance. There is not one character in *Pentimento* whom,
however much I may get to know him or her in other ways, I
can clearly visualize, despite the painterly title and promise of
this memoir. For example, when the grown-up Lillian sees

Willy again, we get what may be the longest physical description in the volume: "He was much older: the large body hung
now with loose flesh, the hair was tumbled, the heavy face
lined and colored sick." That "colored sick" is not bad; but
compare this to a recollection by G. K. Chesterton of a schoolboy whom he calls Simmons: "It was a hesitating face, which
seemed to blink doubtfully in the daylight. He had even the
look of one who has received a buffet that he cannot return. In
all occupations he was the average boy; just sufficiently good
at sports, just sufficiently bad at work to be universally satisfactory. But he was prominent in nothing, for prominence was
to him a thing like bodily pain." From Miss Hellman's
accounts I can reconstruct certain persons, and when Willy's
son is described as "thin-boned, yellowish," I even have a dim,
ectoplasmic view of him. But Simmons I can see inside and
out.

The next essay, "Julia," is the most striking in the book. Julia
was a beautiful, very rich Christian girl, Lillian's favorite
schoolmate, who later went to Vienna to study medicine,
grew fascinated by Freud, and, eventually, became his patient.
She had an affair with an American fellow medical student,
from which a daughter was born. But the chap married
another girl, a shallow ex-classmate of Julia's and Lillian's. An
idealist, Julia was soon embroiled in Marxist political activities; when budding Nazis attached the workingmen's quarter
in which she lived, Julia was badly injured and laid up, tempo-
rarily unable to speak, in a Vienna hospital. Here Lillian visited her and sat by her bedside, clasping her hand in harrowing
silence. Later, in 1937, Lillian receives word from Julia: would
she consider the risky business of smuggling $50,000 into
Germany for the freeing of some political prisoners? Only if
she wanted to, of course. Fearfully, Lillian complies and, after
some Hitchcockian experiences, sees Julia again in Berlin. One
of her legs has been amputated as a result of that Vienna
incident, but Julia is hopeful—about coming to America
again, about her little daughter named after Lillian, about

foiling the Nazis. Later, Miss Hellman, who is never again to
see her friend alive, learns that Julia was horribly killed by the
Nazis, but that her body has been smuggled out into a London
funeral parlor. There Miss Hellman picks up the mutilated
body and takes it back to America for cremation. Julia's family
will have nothing to do with Miss Hellman, their scapegrace
daughter's corpse, or Julia's daughter if she could be located.
They want Julia's money all to themselves, and nothing else.

It is a grim, exciting, and moving story, well told. But upon
reflection, some things seem wrong with it. Miss Hellman,
though she was receiving letters and presents from her, doesn't
know much about Julia in Europe; as in a Greek tragedy, all the
heroic, bloody, spectacular events take place offstage. But here
there are no messengers even to report those awesome happen-
ings. As a result, the centerpiece of the essay is Miss Hellman's
smuggling of money into Germany, and this throws the whole
thing out of whack: however great and tragic Julia may have
been, the acts of bravery and devotion that we actually read
about are Miss Hellman's.

And something else—a problem that runs through the
whole book. It is all very well that the writing is mostly spare,
clipped, understated. (Not always, by the way. We also get bits
of bathos as when her childhood notebooks are described by
their author as "filled with question marks: the large, funny,
sad questions of the very young.") But the essential technique
and tenor of most of this writing is melodrama, as it was with
Miss Hellman's playwriting. Consider, for instance, the dropping of ominous hints: "My letter was returned, unopened and
resealed, and it was to be another year before I knew why."
(Why, incidentally, does an unopened letter have to be
resealed?) Or, again: "He said he was forty-two, and I didn't
know that night why he coughed so much after he said it, nor
why he stared at me so hard when we reached my door."
These are cliffhangers, the devices of melodrama: we are
meant to be on tenterhooks until, many pages later, our thirst
for the answer is quenched. So, too, we are told at the beginning of "Julia" that all the names have been changed because

some of the people are still living or because Miss Hellman is "not sure that even now the Germans like their premature anti-Nazis." Since she gives only first names, anyhow, this seems captious, to say the least; but the real reason, surely, is neither tact, which Julia's relatives don't deserve, nor the Germans, who tend nowadays to grovel before premature anti-Nazis, but the creation of an atmosphere of mystery and melodrama. Still, "Julia" contains some of the book's best aperçus, e.g.: "Neither of us knew much more than the bare terms of each other's [sic] life, nothing of the daily stuff that is the real truth, the importance." Or a passage about not trusting people's memories of childhood, which, without being earthshaking, is perfectly cogent.

The next essay is called "Theatre," and in it the author reluctantly tells a little about her experiences on Broadway and in Hollywood, while professing not to know why people would be curious about such things. She relates quite deftly, nevertheless, anecdotes about the great and near-great of stage and screen, but when it comes to assessing her own plays and their productions, the comments are chary if not niggardly. This could be modesty, but I somehow find it hard to believe in the modesty of a person who drops, ever so offhandedly, a remark like "I . . . didn't care as much about money as the people around me," a statement I know from unpleasant personal experience to be untrue. But about that—to use one of Miss Hellman's own devices—more later. I am likewise suspicious of a playwright who deplores the general incompetence of drama critics, only to make an exception of Walter Kerr. Checking one of Kerr's books, I find that Miss Hellman has "a clear head, a level eye, and a fierce respect for the unchanging color of the precisely used word." With so clear a head and so level an eye, one would naturally see Mr. Kerr in his true, unchanging colors.

In this section of the book Miss Hellman moves rapidly and adroitly from one subject to another, and her ability to leap from comments on her *Watch on the Rhine* to her friendship with Henry Sigerist and thence to her even better friendship

with Edmund Wilson is impressive in its acrobatically associa-
tive way. She is even witty here, once or twice ("savories—that
upperclass English habit of drowning the bad with the
worse"), but humor, by and large, is not her strong suit, what
there is of it coming mostly from the acts of, or quotations
from, others.

The next essay, about Arthur W. A. Cowan, a highly eccentric millionaire lawyer, playboy, philanthropist, culture lover
and vulgarian, makes for diverting reading. But here, again,
although this difficult, likable and also exasperating person, a
pathetic dilettante of gigantic proportions, is captured well
enough, deeper insights into him are not forthcoming. Indeed,
the most memorable passage in the essay has nothing to do
with Cowan, but epitomizes Miss Hellman's feelings about
the McCarthy era, during which she behaved with rare and
exemplary courage, at great personal cost. Still, even if Miss
Hellman does not go into this, it is hard to escape an impression of smugness when she tells about Hammett's being the
only one around to recognize that a gun Cowan brandished
threateningly was, in fact, a toy, and that it was deposited, in
their summer house, "on top of the collected works of Yeats."
Since this detail has nothing to do with anything, I must
assume that the reader is meant to be impressed by the culture
of people who line their summer house with the collected
works of Yeats. My uneasiness is compounded by the fact that
there was not then, as there is not now, an edition of the
"collected works" of Yeats, only of the collected poems and
collected plays—which makes me wonder just how much
attention Miss Hellman ever devoted to that prestigious tome.

Next comes a very short story-essay, "Turtle," about a snapping turtle on the Pleasantville farm, a creature that clung to
life so tenaciously that, even after Dash had shot it twice
through the head and then, with an ax, severed its neck down
to one last piece of skin, it managed to crawl away from its
executioners and disappear into the garden before finally giving up the ghost. Whereupon Lillian is moved to speculate

about the meaning of life, for which Dash taunts her with his Hemingwayesque ironies, and she insists on not eating this amphibian Rasputin but burying it instead. Final irony: some four-footed predator digs up and devours the turtle, leaving only a few bones over which Dash erects a mocking cenotaph. In his rapturous review of *Pentimento* for *Book World,* Richard Poirier calls this piece "a moral tale," though what the moral is he makes no clearer than does the piece itself. It may be that women are, after all, more sensitive than even the most brilliant of men, or that one should eat every turtle one bags.

The short final essay is called "Pentimento," and its point, I regret to say, eludes me. In it, we see Miss Hellman, now teaching literature at Harvard, making insomniac pilgrimages in the dead of snowy nights to the nursing home where she would have installed Hammett had he survived that long; and we see also Helen, her faithful black maid, enlisting the help of a passing undergraduate, Jimsie, to get her mistress back into bed. A friendship develops first between maid and student, then between student and mistress; subsequently, Jimsie undertakes to get Helen's corpse back to her native South Carolina. We also learn about Jimsie, who gives up dazzling work in chemistry at Harvard to do no less dazzling work in astrophysics at Oxford, which he also gives up to go back home to rural Oregon and become rich by carving wooden rosettes for a woman decorator. He now lives with a girl called Carrie, who cooks and scrubs, and of whom he declares that she's O.K. Miss Hellman does not find O.K. enough for her, but Jimsie considers it sufficient. Then, as Miss Hellman is treating the rich visiting woodcarver to a restaurant meal he finds he cannot, after all, pay for, they reminisce about Helen, who gave him the coat he is still wearing. It emerges that the ex-chemist-astrophysicist, who merely tolerates Carrie, loved Helen. " 'Too bad you never told her so. Too late now.' 'I told it to her,' he said, 'the night I looked up your word, pentimento.' " And so the essay and book end.

Even Richard Poirier, who talks about the book's "immense

literary worth" and "moral value" and about its creating "in us perceptions about human character that have all but disappeared from contemporary writing," fails to interpret this sketch for us, except for muttering darkly about "a kind of emotional range-finding." Mark Schorer, however, in the *Times Book Review,* explains it as "a gentle eulogy to Hammett but more especially to Helen," in which case why all this stuff about Jimsie's curious career and the final apotheosis of Miss Hellman's word, pentimento? But perhaps I just cannot see the tree from all that woman's skirt painted over it.

"I remember best what things look like and forget what it has been like to be with them," Miss Hellman writes and is, I believe, profoundly mistaken. For it is not nearly so much the characters in this book—not even the two maiden aunts and several Negro servants who are treated with genuine affection—who come to visible, tangible life, but, rather, her own moral, intellectual, and, above all, emotional responses to them. The book is, ultimately, a more or less clandestine autobiography, and it is the contours of Miss Hellman's persona that the pentimento reveals underneath the portraits of others. This, too, would be fine if something significant about the author were to become clear; but even such a proposition as "All my life I believed in the changes I could, and sometimes did, make in a nature I so often didn't like, but now it seems to me that time made alterations and mutations rather than true reforms," which is as philosophic as the author gets, is not demonstrated by the course of the book. Except for the facts that she is loyal, courageous, outspoken, hot-blooded, a heavy drinker, and "not good with actors and directors," we do not find out much about Miss Hellman either. There is another definition of pentimento, I discovered from P. and L. Murray's *A Dictionary of Art and Artists*: "several attempts to fix a contour with precision in a drawing." Perhaps this best fits the case of this blurry self-portrait.

But the book provided me with my own pentimento. When working on her adaptation of Anouilh's *The Lark,* Miss Hellman commissioned a colleague of mine at MIT to do a sample translation of representative speeches by the main characters; though she had a trot to work from, it did not provide Miss Hellman with the nuances of the voices of the various dramatis personae. She would pay a hundred dollars for some forty or fifty pages of polished translation. Even by 1955 standards, this was less than munificent. My friend offered me half if I would assist him. Dazzled not so much by the paltry sum as by the chance to meet someone who could initiate me into the arcana of the theater, I agreed. This work, about which Miss Hellman said she was in no great hurry, was only three-quarters finished when she called it off impatiently, offering to pay us half. My friend was too disgusted to demur, but I called up Miss Hellman to stand up for our rights, politely but firmly. She became unpleasant on the phone, denouncing our tardiness and the paucity of work—she had, of course, understood single-spaced pages, insisting that that was how actors' sides were always typed. When I pointed out that this was in no case to be the actors' text and was clearly a piece of literary typing, always double-spaced, she became hysterical and announced that if we wanted to sue her, she had the best lawyers in New York, etc., etc. We had, of course, never even thought of a suit in connection with so footling a sum, but the matter got ugly because my thesis director, a friend of Hellman's, threatened to have me thrown out of Harvard graduate school. The matter was finally settled by Miss Hellman's paying us the full amount and our signing a statement that we would have no further claims against her on her forthcoming version of *The Lark*. My thesis director also compelled me to write a letter of apology, which he demanded to see before I sent it off. It contained a quotation from Chaucer, and passed muster.

The storm subsided, and the whole affair wouldn't be worth mentioning but for one thing. To this day, Miss Hellman thinks I am vengefully persecuting her, and I was told that she believes that my friend Charles Thomas Samuels's unfavorable

Times review of her collected plays was written to my specifi-
cations, if not, indeed, dictated by me. But the fact is that I,
like Charles Samuels, never thought much of Miss Hellman's
plays. Well before the *Lark* incident, during a Harvard Law
School Forum, Miss Hellman wondered out loud why the play
of hers she liked best, *The Autumn Garden,* had failed; she could
find no explanation. In the question period, I rose to ask her
whether that Chekhovian pastiche did not simply seem passé
in an era when Brecht, Sartre, and Camus were producing
their most innovative stage works. Miss Hellman threw up her
arms and said she couldn't answer that question, whereupon
the moderator, Marc Connelly, an insignificant playwright
with a once inflated reputation, jumped to her defense: there
was no such thing as something new in drama, he contemptuously informed me, only recasting of the old. I tried to answer,
but wasn't allowed to.

All this came back to me as I read in *Pentimento* about "the
mixture of commitment and noncommitment" Miss Hellman
finds inside herself, stemming "from bohemia as it bumped
into Calvin." I recalled how, during the aforementioned tele-
phone conversation, I had said to Miss Hellman that she was
being unduly Calvinistic about something or other. "But I'm
not a Calvinist," she remonstrated querulously and rather lit-
eral-mindedly, "I'm a Jew!" "I know, I know," I replied, trying
hard not to sound either uninformed or anti-Semitic. And
here, a couple of decades later, it is: Calvin, from Miss Hellman's own pen. However.

[1973–1974]

CATALOGUING
AS LITERATURE
Elizabeth Hardwick, *Sleepless Nights*

"SLEEPLESS Nights, A Novel by Elizabeth Hardwick," says the jacket. Yet the book has little or nothing to do with sleepless nights, is certainly not a novel, and was not really written by Elizabeth Hardwick.

Let me start with the last proposition. The work is in truth a collaboration between Rainer Maria Rilke, who wrote *The Notebooks of Malte Laurids Brigge,* of which *Sleepless Nights* is an almost shameless imitation, and Elizabeth Lowell, the prestigious former wife of Robert Lowell and longtime associate editor of the prestigious *New York Review of Books,* who just happens to use Hardwick as her *nom de plume*. I doubt whether Miss Hardwick could have imagined her book without the Rilkean model, and I am quite sure that it would not have been published had it been signed Smith or Jones. Second, her collection of more or less random jottings, in segments varying in length from a couple of lines to a couple of pages, is even less novelistic than *Malte,* where a kind of plot line evolves from an emotional progression. Finally, though Hardwick's work may be the product of many sleepless nights, it has almost no bearing on acute insomnia or any other theme or topic that would give it cohesion, to say nothing of unity.

There is, to be sure, a narrator of sorts—Elizabeth—and we are treated to splinters of her consciousness, recollection, philosophizing in whirling snippets of prose suffering from delusions of poetry. This Elizabeth is—despite partial denials by Miss Hardwick in interviews—the author, but the author in search of fictional characters because, I presume, she considers fiction safer than autobiography: if you allow an ostensible piece of fiction to lapse into autobiography, that tends to be called candor, even though it is merely a failure of the imagination; but if you allow autobiography to trail off into fiction, it cannot be construed as anything but lies.

What, then, does this Elizabeth share with us? Something about her family, especially about her mother (as does Malte in *Malte Laurids Brigge*); some memories of famous or obscure friends and acquaintances (as does Malte); some chance encounters, particularly with lowly, touching people and wrenching failures (as does Malte); and a good many literary allusions and reflections (as does Malte). But, unlike Rilke, Miss Hardwick tells us very little about the protagonist's current life as a toiler in literature, and there are merely obscure references to lovers and very scant ones to a husband. The book disintegrates even more because it misses the cunning, hidden structure of *Malte,* where the veiled autobiography of the hero gathers unto itself exemplary lives, historical anecdotes, meditations on art to convey the strategies of an existence crumbling under the brunt of poverty, illness, and excessive sensitivity unbolstered by creative potency (one model for Malte was the prematurely deceased Norwegian "decadent" poet-novelist Sigbjørn Obstfelder). The anonymous personages and the one named celebrity, Billie Holiday, in Hardwick do not add up to a significant design, any more than Elizabeth and her aperçus compose themselves into an identifiable view of life or artistic vision.

When Malte, for example, meditates on Henrik Ibsen, we get not only a splendid evocation of an artist's success and failure, but also a portrait of genius as it verges on madness and confirms Malte's own frustrations and neuroses. Here, in contrast, is a typical one-page segment from *Sleepless Nights*:

> Pasternak's line: *To live a life is not to cross a field.* It is not to climb a mountain either. Leconte de Lisle spoke enviously of Victor Hugo as having the "stupidity of the Himalayas." The murderous German girl with the alpenstock, her hiking boots, calls to the old architect, higher, higher! He falls to his death and this is Ibsen's disgust with the giddiness up there, or the assumption of up there. For himself, he adjusted his rimless spectacles and the corners of his mouth turned down when fervent young girls thought he was dumber than he was. Ibsen was not a happy man. Work all day, more than a little schnapps in the evening, and back home at the hotel, the resort, the pension there was his strong wife who after she had little Sigurd Ibsen said: That's it, that's enough.

It should be noted that this segment does not hook on to the one preceding it, and has the most arbitrary and tenuous connection to what follows. "Pasternak's line," by the way, is a Russian proverb incorporated verbatim into one of Yuri Zhivago's poems. Hardwick's next observation is a non sequitur; she might as well have said life is not spelunking or tobogganing, except that that would not have led into the equally irrelevant but impressive quotation from Leconte de Lisle. The Himalayas, though, suggest height—even if the statement is really about stupidity—bringing us to Master Builder Solness falling off his hubristic steeple. But Hilda Wangel, the heroine of *The Master Builder,* is Norwegian; if Hardwick means her probable real-life prototype, Emilie Bardach, she was not German either—she was Viennese (a very different thing), and not at all murderous. Moreover, what kills Solness has nothing to do with Ibsen's "disgust with the giddiness up there, or the assumption of up there"—whether "assumption" in the alternative explanation means "taking possession" or "notion"; but, then, Hardwick's writing is often murderously opaque.

Furthermore, it is simply not true, as the passage implies, that old Ibsen took his young groupies in stride; and the statement that he "was not a happy man" is a vulgar truism about any advanced artist, especially a tormented genius like Ibsen, and tritely expressed. As for the conclusion, Susanna Ibsen's "That's it, that's enough," its inclusion here seems to derive from the *"Ich mag nicht mehr"* of Rilke's Ingeborg in *Malte,* but the line is much more moving coming from a deathbed than, as here, from a childbed. So we are left to wonder what—aside from a few platitudes, irrelevant eso-terica, and misinterpretations of a great play and playwright—this entire independent segment has to offer.

Similarly, just before this passage, we get a somewhat longer, equally unilluminating episode about Elizabeth's hav-ing to share a Canadian train ride with a group of raucous men, presumably salesmen returning from a convention. She evokes them with some sharpness, but without the sympathy, wit, or insight that would justify their presence in the book. Large parts of the description are crude bits of list-making: "I have paid attention to clothes, shoes, rings, watches, accents, teeth, points of deportment, turns of speech." On the preced-ing page, we got two other forays into the art of cataloguing: "With the weak something is always happening: improvisa-tion, surprise, suspense, injustice, manipulation, hypo-chondria, secret drinking, jealousy, lying, crying, hiding in the garden, driving off in the middle of the night." Notice that, as in the list above, after a number of one-word items comes a pair of more elaborate ones. The pattern is promptly repeated: "Tickets, migrations, worries, property, debts, changes of name and changes back once more; these came about from reading many books." I doubt whether they came *from* reading many books, but they surely come together *for* the making of this dubious tome.

To return to the Canadian salesmen, their evocation is sud-denly interrupted by the following segment: "Borges asks the question: 'Are not the fervent Shakespeareans who give themselves over to a line of Shakespeare, are they not, literally, Shakespeare?' " There is no earthly way to divine the connection between this insert and the segments about the Canadian loudmouths that surround it; the temptation is to view it either as some sort of gratuitous free association or as an attempt to impress with erudition, arcaneness, the ability to see connections so far beyond the reader's vision as the hearing of a dog stretches beyond the human ear.

Consider now a couple of sentences about an ex-lover meeting Elizabeth near (or at) the hometown library. "Everything washed in a harsh, hard light"—surely "washed in light" is a platitude, and "harsh, hard" facile word-mongering comparable to the jingle "the blank glare of square bungalows" a page earlier. "His curiosity flamed over a word, an adjective over the seductiveness of the fact that I was taking down a volume of Thomas Mann from the library shelves. Eros has a thousand friends." What, besides desperate straining after lyrical sensitivity and gnomic utterance, does this mean? The very syntax is confused and obfuscatory: is that "adjective" in apposition to the "word" over which the man's curiosity flamed? Or did the flaming curiosity become a kind of adjective hung, like a fiery festoon, over Elizabeth? How, by the way, does an adjective flame? And what, exactly, was seductive: that Elizabeth went in for such heavy reading as Thomas Mann, or her graceful movement in lifting the book off the shelf? If the former, the shelves are supererogatory; if the latter, Thomas Mann is just window dressing. And doesn't Eros have a thousand sources or accomplices, rather than "friends"?

Or take this: "The music seemed to cut into his flesh, leaving a sort of scar of longing never satisfied, almost a wound of feeling." Surely, "a scar of longing never satisfied" and "a wound of feeling" are too close in meaning for both to be needed; if, somehow, they are not redundant, Hardwick fails to show how the latter expands on the former. She is talking here about a homosexual friend's passion for jazz, and about his difficulties in resolving what popular music meant to him:

"What was it? . . . the sea itself, or youth alone?" (Ellipsis the author's.) That, I am afraid, is schoolgirl drivel at its most pitifully grandiose.

Nobody comes fully alive in this book—not Billie Holiday, for instance; not Alex, an ex-lover who reappears in Elizabeth's life. Try this segment:

> It is almost seven. Should Alex walk in the door as a type, a genre? Perhaps that effort is a mistake. What is wanted is history, the man in the raincoat, wearing the loops of his ideas, the buttons of his period. Some men define themselves by women although they appear to believe quite the opposite; to believe that it is *she,* rather than themselves, who is being filed away, tagged, named at last like a quivering cell under a microscope.

Even the grammar is a mess here: if "women" is the antecedent, "she" has to read "they"; but "themselves," to be correct, would also have to read "they," making the sentence impenetrable. The imagery is still more chaotic. What is that historic raincoat whose loops are made of ideas, and buttons out of the period? How do we get from filing cabinets and tags to a microscope? And cells under a microscope do not quiver ordinarily; it is Miss Hardwick's sensibility and prose that do so—extraordinarily. In any case, what does all this tell us about Alex, Elizabeth, or their relationship?

I can cite some better passages, too, like this one about living in a cheap Manhattan hotel:

> No star was to be seen in the heavens, but the sky was always bright with the flicker of distant lights. No tree was to be seen, but as if by miracle little heaps of twigs and blown leaves gathered in the gutters. To live in the obscuring jungle in the midst of things: close to—what? Within walking distance of all those places one never walked to.

These lines have visual acuity, good rhythm, and unattitudinizing truthfulness to recommend them, yet such felicities are relatively rare; soon the panoply of pretension engulfs them.

Thus Miss Hardwick will toss in a prose translation of the second stanza of Hölderlin's "Hälfte des Lebens" without any more explanation or identification than the casual remark "He [an amorous doctor] called upon the help of European poetry." But the translation is so unpoetic that, except to the initiate, it suggests neither poetry nor help. Or consider how Hardwick lets one of her characters, Louisa, peter out:

> She will not do too much nor [correctly: or] too little and this is what is wanted. She will have an apartment, a lover, will take a few drugs, will listen to the phonograph, buy clothes, and something will happen. Perhaps it will be good—or at least what she likes.

Such an anticlimatic string of clichés cannot etch Louisa into our minds.

Repeatedly, as well, Miss Hardwick makes us doubt the veracity of her statements; her writing lacks the authority that either the truly lived or the authentically envisioned confers. In her native Lexington, Kentucky, she recalls, for instance, "two sensual hotels where the wastebaskets contained memorandums of assignations and the hyperbolic, misshapen prose of illicit love letters." Has she truly been there, even in her imagination? I doubt that the Lexington horse traders write any memorandums of assignations or many illicit love letters in however misshapen prose; if they do, these documents must get tossed into quite different wastebaskets—in the kitchens of stagnant housewives, say—unless, as is more likely, they are preserved hidden among the pages of old schoolbooks. A person neither carries such integumenta to an assignation, nor has time to write them there; the wastebaskets fill up with much more mundane articles. Incidentally, after *The Sensual Woman, The Sensual Man,* and *The Sensual Couple,* can a responsible writer still commit the words "sensual hotels" to serious print?

Even in her aphorisms Miss Hardwick fails to achieve the ring of truth. "Envy is not the vice of the frozen intellectual. How can it seize the mind when boredom arrives before it, always ahead of time, ready?" I could match Miss Hardwick's lifetime royalties on all her books—past, present, and future— if someone would offer me a nickel for every envious intellectual I could scare up, in and out of the academy. Nevertheless, side by side with this kind of nonsense, Hardwick is perfectly capable of good, homely observations laced with ladylike bitchiness when she does not set her stylistic, philosophical, and poetic sights too high. She can write of a party: "No person of talent had brought along a new, beautiful young girl, who being new and not knowing all the names would seem rude and superior, thus sending arrows of pain into the flesh of the older people who were known for something." Not bad at all—particularly those "older people who were known for something," with that "something" truly sealing their doom.

But such pointillistic virtues—like hitting a small nail neatly on the head with a tiny but precise hammer—are canceled out, again and again, by the aforementioned preciosities, pretensions, and platitudes. It's no good being able to write felicitously "his long yellow teeth emerged like fog lights out of the taciturn lips" if you lapse forthwith into "and then a lifetime with its mound of men climbing on and off." Surely it is not the mound that does the climbing; yet assuming the trope worked, it would still be coarse.

And always there are the devices out of *Malte Laurids Brigge* (in fact, there is a reference, albeit an insignificant one, to the book itself): there are passages purporting to be letters to unidentified friends; there are lists of names of obscure people dimly resonating in the memory—in this case various servant women; there are introductory sentences where the scene is set with the verb deliberately omitted: "At our high school dances in the winter, small, cheap local events." This corresponds in *Malte* to such things as "Die Existenz des Entsetzlichen in jedem Bestandteil der Luft" ("The existence of the horrible in every particle of the air").

   In an interview, Miss Hardwick, citing some of her reading, spoke of "*The Notebooks of Malte Brigge* [sic]—miraculous, perfect work." In his review of *Sleepless Nights,* John Leonard also latched on to this utterance, and to the parallels it suggests. He concluded by declaring *Sleepless Nights* "like Rilke's *Notebook* . . . miraculous and almost perfect." At least he had the decency to slip in that "almost." Otherwise, his review, like all the others I have read, is a rave. Now, *that* is perfectly miraculous, with no "almost" about it.

[1979]

LIFE OF AN ANTIHERO

Donald Spoto, *The Kindness of Strangers:*
The Life of Tennessee Williams
Dotson Rader, *Tennessee: Cry of the Heart*

WE have simultaneously two new biographies of Tennessee Williams—equally albeit differently unsatisfactory. Yet
because their few virtues are likewise antithetical and thus
complementary, to read both of them may provide some sense
of Tennessee Williams the man, though not the author.

Donald Spoto's book, bearing the threadbare title *The Kind-*
ness of Strangers, is sedulous, pretentious, pedestrian, erratically
researched, pontifical, and hopelessly shallow. Dotson Rader's
tritely and histrionically titled *Tennessee: Cry of the Heart* has the
advantage of being based on firsthand knowledge of Williams
during the later years and has a dash of bravura; but it is more
sloppily written, disorganized, unresearched, self-serving,
and awash with scandalous tales about Williams and everybody else famous or near-famous whose name Rader can drop
and reputation darken. You cannot always trust Spoto, who is
clearly too dull-witted for the task at hand; you generally
mistrust Rader, who is out to be sensational, to settle personal
scores and, concomitantly, aggrandize himself. So you have
your choice between the perceptions of a diligent but obtuse
truffle hound who seldom gets at the truffles, and a worm's-

eye view, neither uncrafty nor unfunny, but no less limited in
vision and fairly slimy to boot.

There are three main troubles with Spoto. First, he has no
qualifications whatever as a critic or literary historian, despite
many hollowly grandiose gestures in that direction. (Even his
books on Hitchcock, his specialty, are paltry stuff. See my
review of his *The Dark Side of Genius: The Life of Alfred Hitchcock,* in *The New Leader,* May 16, 1983.) Second, he writes in an
exceedingly flat, unsyntactical style that comes to grief
whether it sinks to lower-than-sea-level platitudes or circuitously ascends into the cloudily opaque. Third, he harps on
his moral disapproval of Williams's sexual indulgences (one
mention would be quite enough), yet at other times he
attempts to justify the playwright's worst excesses with such
an empty term as "Dionysian or Bacchic impulse," to which
he resorts some dozen times; but he is incapable of an incisive
and convincing psychological interpretation of his subject.

As for Rader, he takes Williams's supremacy for granted
("the greatest playwright of the age" *tout court*), never bother-
ing to cast so much as a passing glance at the work. He is
content to wallow in anecdotes, scabrous or otherwise, while
he tries to make out a case for himself as (a) a major political
activist during the Vietnam War who almost succeeded in
radicalizing the apolitical Williams; (b) the closest and truest
friend of the playwright, his confidant and platonic lover; and
(c) a fellow author of sufficient talent and acumen to be able to
present an accurate and penetrating portrait of his illustrious
boon companion. Rader's writing is ungrammatical, messy,
and would-be literary ("He panted heavily, like an old dog in
the sun or a child molester spotting a sandbox in the park"),
and no one at Doubleday has corrected his misspellings of
well-known proper names. At least Rader is not humorless,
has genuine affection for Williams, and does stumble on the
occasional suggestive phrase or tell some believably devastating stories, as about the contemptible Yevgeny Yevtushenko.

You can get the outline of Williams's life from *The Kindness of*

Strangers: the birth in the Bible Belt in Columbus, Mississippi,
in 1911; the unhappily married, largely destructive parents,
and the kindly and supportive maternal grandparents; the family's frequent uprootings before reaching St. Louis, and the
incessant changes of domicile there; the excessive closeness to
Rose, the older sister, who became weirder and weirder and
was finally lobotomized at her mother Edwina's behest; the
difficulties of young Thomas Lanier Williams (Tennessee's
baptismal name) at school and in college; the self-distancing of
Tom from his younger brother, Dakin; Tom's trip to Europe
with the aforesaid grandfather, the Reverend Walter Edwin
Dakin, who would later lose his money, apparently as the
result of a homosexual escapade (though on this, as on many
such things, Rader is more explicit).

Also: the sacrifices of Grandmother Rose to support Tom
when he dropped out of the famous University of Missouri
journalism school; the ten miserable months of working in the
shoe factory where Cornelius, the father, was profitably
employed before his drinking and wenching started to take
their toll; the intensive toil over poems, stories, and, eventually, plays, which gradually began to be published or produced
in magazines and small theaters; and then the beginnings of
making it as Tom—now Tennessee—moves to New York and
enters his alliance with the agent Audrey Wood. She was to be
everything from friend to mother, from secretary to business
manager, to this man helpless in practical matters. Nonetheless, years afterward when his creative powers were failing and
delusions gaining, he turned on her with paranoiac ferocity
and signal ingratitude.

Tennessee made a couple of feeble stabs at heterosexual
relations; it was not until his late twenties as a struggling
writer in New Orleans, that he had his first homosexual experience and discovered his sexual destiny. From then on, it was
an endless chain of pickups and affairs, a very few more
serious, but always there was that psychic priapism that ruled
out monogamy. Only two relationships of some duration seem

to have mattered. One was with a young dancer, Kip, whom Williams loved during a Provincetown summer: a sweet draft dodger from Canada, he subsequently married, and died at age twenty-six of a brain tumor. Tennessee, if we are to believe Rader, carried Kip's pictures in his wallet "some twenty years," until they "disappeared mysteriously." Said Tennessee at seventy: "Kip lives on in my leftover heart."

The other major love was Frank Merlo, Williams's companion for many years. He was a decent, loving Sicilian-American, whose benign influence on the playwright could not, however, convert him to monogamy. Their relations deteriorated, and when Frank was dying in New York Hospital of cancer, Tennessee could barely bring himself to visit. One day, as Frank seemed to be dozing off, and Tennessee was starting to tiptoe out, Merlo said, "No, I'm used to you," and died. According to Rader, these were "five words that [Williams] could not forget, and when, even twenty years later, he would recall them, tears would come to his eyes." The attentive reader will note the schematic recurrence of "twenty years" in these sad love stories; whether this casts doubt on either Williams's or Rader's veracity, or whether it is simple, blameless coincidence, he will have to decide for himself.

After Tennessee's huge successes on stage and (to a lesser extent) screen, after the impressive celebrity and wealth, his life went into depressing decline. Although Spoto finds merit in several of the later critically and financially unsuccessful works, he, even more than Rader, portrays the middle-aged and older Williams as a man suffering from hypochondria, paranoia, erotomania, dromomania, fateful fascination with all sorts of perversion, drug addiction (vast excesses of medicines, stimulants, depressants, and one mention of cocaine), and schizophrenia. Spoto's picture, with its repeated outbursts against the male whores and parasites hanging around the playwright, is grim indeed; Rader's, with its many gossipy anecdotes, is at any rate one of relieved gloom.

Gore Vidal, in his critique of these two books in *The New*

York Review of Books, presents a third, characteristically revisionist, picture. Vidal has mild contempt for Spoto and such
loathing for Rader that he will not let his pen trace the latter's
name. In any case, he perceives both authors as pandering to
"brains already overloaded with tales of celebrity-suffering,
the ultimate consolation—and justification—to those who
didn't make it or, worse, didn't even try." He further insists
that "since those who write about [Williams] are usually more
confused about human sexuality than he was, which is saying
a lot, some instruction is now in order."

So we get an essentially cheerful Williams who "never
doubted that what he liked [i.e., homosexuality and promis-
cuity] was entirely natural." Only because sexual taboos,
being the most truly ecumenical, are the most effective "arbitrary prohibitions" of a ruling class that rules largely through
prohibitions, says Vidal, did Williams believe to the end of his
life that he was on the "bad team," proclaimed "evil, sick,
vicious." All this merely meant, we are assured, that "he
suffered from a sense of otherness, not unuseful for a writer."
At the end of the essay-review Tennessee and Gore are on a
restaurant terrace in Key West in the early fifties, and the
playwright—martini in hand, bare feet on the terrace rail-
ing—smilingly declares, "I like my life."

No doubt there is truth to this picture too, particularly for
the younger Williams in his artistic and vital prime, the years
of Vidal's closest fraternization with him. Still, things cannot
be that simple for someone who feels he is simultaneously
"entirely natural" and "evil, sick, vicious." Vidal concedes
hypochondria alone from the above-cited nosology, but something like manic depressiveness emerges from his description
and, *a fortiori,* from those of Spoto and Rader. Even assuming
that much of this may have been drug-induced, what induced
the drugs? Every account indicates periods of raucous eupho-
ria, followed by others of crushing depression, and if perhaps
"not unuseful" to the writer, they were surely not unharrow-
ing to the man and those around him who became the butts of

his rages. In later life he changed agents almost as fast as friends, and friends nearly as often as shirts, for I am told that he was neat about his person despite the slovenliness and filth in which he often lived.

Something was clearly deleterious about the parental home: Edwina, especially as she grew older, seems to have been quite demented; Cornelius became increasingly shiftless and less visible. Rose, Tennessee's adored sister, had to be institutionalized for life; Dakin kept running for high political office without any qualification or prospects; Tennessee had attacks of hysteria very early on, and, in 1969, was briefly committed by his brother. But the assessments of Williams's traits vary, as much from one page to the next of the same biography as from one biographer to the other. Spoto, after attributing great wit to Williams, cites few if any devastating witticisms. Rader merely makes out a case for humor—sometimes jolly, often bitchy, and most frequently confined to ribald stories about other people. (Ned Rorem, who knew Tennessee well, asked me recently: "Didn't you find him a bore?")

There are similarly divergent reports of Williams's willingness to spend money. He certainly helped friends and needy artists, yet Spoto cites him, when already very rich, unwilling to pay fifty dollars for the coveted Van Gogh *Letters*. Rader tells of his never buying paper and using instead the back of mail from others. In matters of courage, he appears to have been self-contradictory—composing, for example, a brave letter protesting the denial of a passport to Arthur Miller, then losing the nerve to post it. He was, unquestionably, a consistently tireless writer, and even if one concedes that writing was therapeutic for him, one has to admire his doggedness in the teeth of despair. He could be realistic about the quality of his work or totally deluded—though probably less so than Spoto, who calls far too many of the plays masterpieces, and the movies brilliant.

My own recollections of Williams are meager. As a graduate student at Harvard, I attended one of his Cambridge appearances. It was a question-and-answer session—he couldn't and didn't give lectures. Someone asked what he thought of existentialism, Sartre being the rage in that fall of 1947, when *Streetcar* was trying out in Boston. Williams allowed as how he did not know anything about it but maybe somebody in the audience could offer a brief description. Eager grad student that I was, I volunteered. "If that's what it is," Williams cackled, "I've been an existentialist since the age of ten." Afterward we talked, and I told him how the *Harvard Advocate* had turned down my review of *Streetcar* because no play could deserve such an unqualified rave. (Few plays do, but *Streetcar* may well be one of them.) He invited me to lunch at the Ritz, where he was staying, and I was thrilled.

I was less so when, on the appointed day, he answered the doorbell in his robe, under which his pajamas seemed more unbuttoned than necessary. Spoto relates an incident, as told by Stephen Silverman, of Williams years later receiving an entire press delegation "half-naked and very coquettish." In my naïveté, it took me a while to figure out that I had not been invited either for my expertise in existentialism or for my critical astuteness. Thereupon I proceeded to talk almost exclusively about women. Tennessee got my message and behaved irreproachably; he may even have buttoned up his pajama jacket.

Two things struck me about him. First, the dullness, in fact cliché-riddenness, of his conversation. It was Armistice Day. Through the windows, we could see soldiers waiting atop their tanks and armored cars to join the parade. Icy winds blew across Boston Common. "Those poor boys," Williams remarked, "must be cold as a witch's teat." I froze too: such a platitude from our most poetic dramatist! Then, speaking rapturously about Garbo, he gushed: "When she came into the room, she seemed to be walking on air." I won't say that was when I lost my illusions, great writers subdivision, yet it was distressing.

The other thing I couldn't help noticing was an unhealthy

curiosity, a rampant voyeurism. He explained that we could not linger over lunch because soon someone was coming to take him on a tour of the state insane asylum. "Whenever I come to a new city, I like to visit the local mental institution," he informed me, expatiating a bit on this theme. He brushed aside my questions about Jessica Tandy and Kim Hunter, saying the only interesting female in the cast was a middle-aged black woman in a bit part, and suggested that I have a blond fellow student he had seen me with call him. That was Bill Becker, now of Janus Films, and wildly heterosexual. So neither Williams nor I got much out of that lunch.

Our subsequent meetings, about one per decade, were mere hellos or handshakes. Once, in a Manhattan restaurant, he sat at the next table and, without recognizing me, asked what time it was. It was very late. Still later, when I criticized his grammar in a language column I was doing for *Esquire*, he wrote a letter to the editor, as pitiful as it was irrelevant, saying that Mr. Simon should know that, nowadays, he, Williams, wasn't writing symphonies any more, only chamber music. This must have been his standard answer to critics deploring the falling off of his work (a sad truth I hadn't mentioned in that column), for Rader quotes him as saying, "I used to write symphonies. Now I write chamber music, smaller plays." As if that ill-fitting metaphor covered the gap between, say, *The Glass Menagerie* and *Clothes for a Summer Hotel.* The fault, of course, was almost always the critics'. Parroting his mentor, Rader writes: "[The critics] certainly defeated Tennessee. One of the few times I saw him cry was when he read a review about his work by John Simon."

Rader, on the other hand, confirms Williams's reliance on clichés in his conversation. Within the same gripe about Irene Selznick, who didn't invite him to one of her dinner parties, Tennessee says both "All she loves is the almighty dollar" and "All I ever was was just a meal ticket for her." The proclivity for madhouse visitations I find in neither book (it may be my sole contribution to Williams lore), but Spoto reports that the playwright, during his friendly visit with Castro, "attended public political executions in Havana"; in Spain, he chided his friend Marian Vaccaro for getting sick at bullfights, which he loved.

A manifest memoir like Rader's does not require a critical stance; a biography like Spoto's, with professed critical standards and assessments, does. In its place, we get: "What was new in Tennessee Williams was his rhapsodic insistence that form serve his utterance rather than dominating and cramping it." Note the faulty parallelism along with the platitudinous insight and the historical absurdity. "New"? Had not Chekhov, Ibsen, Strindberg, O'Neill—Williams's models— done the same thing? Or consider: "*Iguana* was becoming a journal of Williams's soul passed through the prism of his poetic-dramatic art." Greater mastery of truism is unimaginable. Or this: "*Summer and Smoke* is one of Tennessee Williams's masterworks for the stage, a play of the eternal conflict between flesh and spirit—although these are often schematically represented." A schematic masterwork—that is certainly something new. And further: " 'The tables have turned with a vengeance,' Alma observes, in Tennessee Williams's most poignant assertion that balanced unions between right mates are very rare indeed." And just how does a seven-word utterance consisting of not one but two clichés become "most poignant?" Pathetic, perhaps.

Pathetic as well—beyond the bad thinking, the ungrammatical writing, the appallingly scrambled images ("Williams was surrounded by a pack of glamour-hungry jackals who used sex like a flyswatter"), the clichés paraded as deep insights, the total irresponsibilities (the "plays" of Kurt Weill!)—is Spoto's need to impress us with his threepenny erudition. Describing a clutch of hysterical or bitchy women around Tennessee, Spoto writes: "Euripides himself, in *The Trojan Women,* or Shakespeare in the opening of *Macbeth,* or Goethe describing a *Walpurgisnacht,* could not have assembled a team more ready for what Jane Bowles called an exercise in feminine wiles." When he tries to correct Williams's wretched German in his title *Kirche, Kutschen und Kinder,* he comes up with the equally incorrect *Küchen* for *Küche.* But what can we expect from a biographer who has Dakin "recalling" something that took place long before he was born?

Dotson Rader, although less literate than Spoto, does write with some gusto at times verging on flair. Unfortunately this does not make up for his slapdashness, inaccuracies, self-promotion, mawkishness, and, above all, disingenuousness. Rader casually informs us, "I was living at the Dakota then." A prestigious address, but no mention of Ruth Ford, the considerably older actress and star of the Margo Jones production of *You Touched Me,* who for several years kept the openly homosexual (and self-confessed onetime male hustler) Rader in a style he was scarcely accustomed to in *her* Dakota apartment. (Somebody once asked me what kind of relationship this unlikely pair could have. "A Ford and a Datsun?" I said. "Auto-eroticism.")

On Williams the writer neither Spoto nor Rader can come up with anything approaching the following simple, compelling insight from Vidal: "Just as Williams never really added to his basic repertory company of actors: Cornelius and Edwina, Reverend Dakin and [grandmother] Rose, himself and [sister] Rose, he never picked up much information about the world during his half-century as an adult. He also never tried, consciously at least, to make sense of the society into which he was born." He remained throughout his life the man who, having at age ten discovered existentialism, did not need to read Sartre or anyone else. Yet by turning his world into a sealed-off, stifling, exacerbating hothouse, he was able to convey with steamy intensity his moving but limited vision. No wonder that after two or three powerful plays Tennessee Williams was irreversibly depleted.

[1985]

BROTHERS UNDER THE SKIN

Eugene O'Neill and Tennessee Williams

TENNESSEE Williams's friend Gore Vidal called the playwright "the Bird," and a rare bird, *rara avis,* he was. But like that other Avis, he seems to have been condemned, hard and harder as he may have tried, to being always rated second after Eugene O'Neill. "Our best playwright after O'Neill" is the way many, myself included, have tended to put it. For some reason, leading playwrights throughout history have often come, or been made to come, in tandem: Racine and Corneille, Lope de Vega and Calderón, Gozzi and Goldoni, Goethe and Schiller, Goldsmith and Sheridan, Shaw and Wilde, Chekhov and Gorky, and, depending on whether you're looking at the Elizabethan or the Jacobean Shakespeare, Shakespeare and Marlowe or Shakespeare and Ben Jonson.

I don't know why there was so frequently a pair of divine twins, Castor and Pollux, among playwrights, and why, as in the starry couple of Dioscuri, only one was truly immortal. Perhaps the reason is that there has to be, as in the Miss America contest, a close runner-up who can take over in case nude photographs of the winner come to light. Or it may be that we need either a real or an imaginary second-best so that we can deliver critical pronouncements on how and why A is better than B—or even, if we are particularly clever, on why B is actually as good as or (the height of revisionist bliss) superior to A.

Be this as it may, O'Neill and Williams are the two master dramatists of America, a phenomenon of which no one was more keenly, painfully aware than Williams himself. Here is a passage from Dotson Rader's highly unreliable memoir, *Tennessee: Cry of the Heart*:

> I noticed a program on the floor from some Eugene O'Neill Festival a year or two before. I showed it to [Tennessee]. He took it from me, smiled, and still holding it went back to sleep.
>
> Five or six years before, when I had first stayed with him in Key West, he had found a long letter from Eugene O'Neill in a filing cabinet in his studio. Still in the original envelope, it was stained with wine and cigarette burns. But Tennessee read it to me, first explaining that he had received it after the opening of *The Glass Menagerie* in New York. O'Neill began his letter, the only one he ever wrote to Tennessee, with generous praise for *Menagerie* and its author. However, soon the body of the letter was darkened by O'Neill's warnings to the young playwright about the treachery of Broadway producers, the disloyalty of the audience, the egotism and callousness of reviewers, in short, the many difficulties of being a playwright in the United States, a country that seemed to have a compulsion to elevate its artists to great heights only to bring them roughly to ground. He warned him about the destructiveness that lay in wait ahead, booze and vicious women, wives who devoured the soul and spit it out (he didn't have to worry about Tennessee on that score), and he wrote at length about the terrible loneliness he felt, an isolation that Tennessee, too, would come to know, however great his gifts.
>
> It was very moving and a very sad letter, and I don't know what became of it. Years later, when Beverly Grunwald came to Key West to interview Tennessee for *Women's Wear Daily* . . . I asked him to read the O'Neill letter to her. He couldn't find it.
>
> What I learned from the letter, and from Tennessee's ruminations on the literary genius and personal wreckage of Eugene O'Neill, was that he considered the author of *Long Day's Journey*

into Night to be his only competitor in the pantheon of American playwrights. He thought O'Neill was, after himself, the
nation's greatest playwright, and he was right in that belief. Yet
he was jealous of O'Neill all his life, indeed obsessed. While he
never disparaged him, he firmly believed that there existed an
ongoing conspiracy, directed by Leslie [this should be Arthur]
Gelb and his wife, both employees of the *New York Times,* to
destroy his reputation in order to ensure O'Neill's place as the
first-ranking of America's dramatists. Whenever he received a
bad review from the *Times,* something that occurred with heartbreaking regularity once Clive Barnes had left to become drama
critic for the *New York Post,* Tennessee blamed the hated Gelbs.

"Baby, they have done it again!" The unkinder the notice, the
more steamed he became at the Gelbs. "You know, they think
they own a monopoly on Eugene O'Neill because they wrote
the definitive biography of his life, the *authorized* biography.
They have made a cottage industry out of him, and they are out
to protect their financial stake, and that means destroying me!
They are the Keepers of the Flame, and they fight to destroy
anyone's reputation whose work might reduce the intensity of
that light."

For days after a bad review he muttered on ominously about
the evil Gelbs using the power of the *Times* to ruin him. He may
have been right.

Curiously, his admiration for the work of Eugene O'Neill
never diminished, nor did his respect for the suffering of his sad
life ever cease.

By 1980, when I last visited him in Key West, Tennessee's
self-respect had grown so weak, his feelings of failure so
unshakable, his desperation so acute that he sought even to
impress me. . . .

This is how he did it. He went into his studio and got the
playbill from the O'Neill Festival I had found three years
before. On its cover was a large, handsome sepia photograph of
the playwright taken shortly before his death. Tennessee excit-
edly showed it to me. On it was written, with a ballpoint pen,
"To Tennessee, with love, Eugene O'Neill."

He asked me to take it to the art store and have it beautifully
framed.

A few days later, when I brought the framed picture home,

Tennessee made quite a ceremony of housing it prominently on display on the small wicker table by the sofa . . . in the living room. To make room for it he removed the framed photograph of Hart Crane, shoving it in a drawer.

Watching him, I felt I might cry, so unhappy was I made by his desperate act, this need for approval from the dead. I knew Tennessee had signed the picture himself, I knew his handwriting as well as my own. I knew the Festival, for which the playbill was printed, had taken place long after O'Neill had died. It saddened me to think that he thought he could fool anyone with it, and sadder still that he felt he had to try.

When I was last in his home in Key West, in July 1982, the O'Neill picture, with its framed inscription, was in the break-front behind the dining table.

This passage prompted the following response from Gore Vidal in his review of Rader's and Donald Spoto's Williams biographies in the *New York Review of Books:*

Toward the end, [Williams] had personified the ringleaders [of the anti-Williams cabal]. They were a Mr. and Mrs. Gelb who worked for the *New York Times*. Because they had written a book about Eugene O'Neill, the Bird was convinced that the Gelbs were using the *Times* in order to destroy him so that they could sell more copies of their book about O'Neill who would then be America's *numero uno* dramatist. Among Crier's [i.e., Rader's] numerous errors and inventions is the Eugene O'Neill letter. . . . The letter was written not after *Menagerie* but *Streetcar,* and Tennessee never read it to Crier or to anyone else because neither Tennessee nor I, in Rome in 1948, could make head or tail of it. O'Neill was suffering from Parkinson's disease; the handwriting was illegible. The Bird and I had a running gag over the years that would begin, "As Eugene O'Neill wrote you . . ." Except for O'Neill, the Bird's sharp eye saw no dangerous competition.

The trouble is that I cannot entirely trust Vidal's testimony either. Moreover, I do not think that Dotson Rader, on the evidence of my slight acquaintance with him and his writing, has the imagination to invent that story of Williams's reading him the O'Neill letter. How, in any case, would he have hit upon the correct notion of the existence of such a letter and its importance to Williams? (His misdating it, by the way, is perfectly consistent with Rader's general sloppiness.) Now, since Williams and Vidal were, apparently, both given to making up fictitious outpourings from O'Neill to Tennessee, isn't it plausible—indeed likely—that Williams produced the illegible letter and treated the gullible Rader to a bogus reading of it, rather like that false inscription on the photograph, whose existence not even Vidal challenges in his review? Certainly the supposed content of the letter fits both what O'Neill might have written and what Williams would have wanted him to say. And Williams clearly had the inventiveness and wit to improvise such a reading.

What emerges, then, is a love-hate, an admiration-rivalry Williams must have felt for O'Neill. Donald Spoto quotes Howard Barnes's review of *Streetcar* in the *New York Herald Tribune,* which contains the statement "Williams is certainly the O'Neill of the present period." There is also a letter printed in *Represented by Audrey Wood,* in which that invaluable agent and friend is trying to raise the spirits of a Williams in a state of depression after the failure of *The Milk Train Doesn't Stop Here Anymore,* and writes, in January 1964: "You are an acknowledged artist whose accomplishments in the theatre are not matched by any other American dramatist, with the possible exception of O'Neill—and with all his greatness, he lacked your magic with theatre dialogue."

In the revised edition of their *O'Neill,* the hated and evil Gelbs include the following: "Late in 1946 O'Neill answered a letter from Tennessee Williams, who had written him in praise of *The Iceman.* He said Williams's note had been particularly welcome because it came at a time when he was 'down in the dumps.' ('O'Neill,' Williams said, years later, in recalling the alleged exchange of fan mail, 'gave birth to the American theatre and died for it.')" The difficulty is that—as Louis

Sheaffer, the most reliable and authoritative O'Neill biographer, has shown—the Gelbs, whether evil or not, are pretty unreliable, and this exchange of letters is not mentioned in Sheaffer's definitive O'Neill biography. Significantly, the Gelbs give no source for their information.

What all this is meant to suggest is simply that there existed a Williams-O'Neill nexus, if not in any documented epistolary exchange, then, at any rate—and with equal consequence—in Williams's mind, as there is one in any serious consideration of American drama. I think we can trust Albert Bermel, who, in the July/August 1984 issue of *American Theatre,* quotes José Quintero, whom we can also trust: "Tennessee Williams said the impact of O'Neill on him was enormous. He could write like Williams because he had a predecessor who wrote like O'Neill." This remark points us in the direction of perceiving important similarities between the two playwrights rather than, as has been customary, significant differences—though these, too, of course, exist.

Even on the most superficial level, parallels between the playwrights can be traced. Both had difficult early family situations: forbidding, ungenerous fathers and adored but impossible mothers toward whom they felt as much guilt as they felt animus toward the fathers. O'Neill had a beloved brother who became an alcoholic; Williams, a sister who was to become confined to mental institutions. In other words, both experienced what Thomas Mann has called disorder and early sorrow, which, however oppressive to the person, may prove incitements to the artist. O'Neill had serious problems with his health just as Williams *thought* he had; if Tennessee's were mostly imaginary, they felt no less real for that. Both men had strong sexual drives, and the troubles O'Neill had with women, Williams had with men.

Far more important, though, than such biographical similarities are the parallels between the two men as artists. Both of them were prolific writers, even if Williams wrote fiction and poetry as well, whereas O'Neill stuck to plays. Yet for all their large outputs each man is remembered mostly for two plays that tower above the rest of his productions: *The Iceman Cometh* and *Long Day's Journey into Night* for O'Neill, *The Glass Menagerie* and *A Streetcar Named Desire* for Williams. Here, however, there is a difference: Williams's best work was written early, followed by a gradual but steady decline; O'Neill's in his last years, when he kept getting better, the two masterpieces flanked by a brace of other meritorious plays, *A Moon for the Misbegotten* and *A Touch of the Poet*. Dying at the relatively early age of sixty-five, O'Neill might have gone on to other successes; for Williams, dead at seventy, with a string of critical and audience failures stretching behind him, no such claim can be made.

Yet however much this may incline us in favor of O'Neill, what finally counts is the oeuvre, and *Summer and Smoke* and *Cat on a Hot Tin Roof* can hold their own against *Moon* and *Poet*. So isn't it time to start examining how similar in intention and effect the best plays of O'Neill and Williams are instead of playing their authors off against each other? That there was a direct influence we know from the fact, among others, that Williams saw O'Neill's *Diff'rent* at the Provincetown Playhouse in the summer of 1940; and we cannot doubt what many, including the evil Gelbs, pointed out—that Emma Crosby in O'Neill's play was the forerunner of Blanche DuBois and Alma Winemiller.

What I want to consider in greater detail is the kinship between the two pairs of masterworks, a kinship not based on any traceable influence but on a meeting of minds. The first marked resemblance between our two playwrights is that neither of them gave a hoot about politics. It is true that American literature, dramatic or otherwise, is much less concerned with politics than is any of its European counterparts, yet it is also true that there have been a good many exceptions. From O'Neill's and Williams's drama, however, you would barely have gleaned that there were such things as two world wars and a rather uneasy time between them. Certainly, World War I creeps into *Strange Interlude,* but it is rather less real than the Boer War in *The Iceman Cometh,* where, however, there is some discussion of the radical left. In Williams, there are Nazis at the periphery of *The Night of the Iguana* and a vague sense of a police state in *Camino Real,* but none of this gives either playwright a remote claim to being political.

It is, conversely, common knowledge that O'Neill was concerned with social conditions, whereas Williams was not, and this is supposed to give the older playwright an edge over the more recent one. True, O'Neill's lesser plays are intensely social, yet how true is this of the masterpieces? *Journey* is first and last family drama, and even those derelicts in Harry Hope's saloon are treated not as victims of society but as people haunted by private demons that can be exorcised only by alcohol and self-delusion. Similarly, *Menagerie* is a family comedy-drama, and *Streetcar* a play in which social conditions are noted—the dying of the Old South, the rise of a crasser but sturdier new one—yet the principal concerns are personal rather than societal.

Still, *Iceman* and *Streetcar* are related to each other as crypto-social plays: both are characterized by their love for the outcast. In *Iceman,* this is obvious enough, though it should be stressed that love is extended not only to the various boozers, but also to the whores and their pimps. In *Streetcar,* the author's sympathy for Blanche is weakest, indeed nil, when her lack of understanding and compassion drives her young homosexual husband to suicide. Conversely, the greatest amount of authorial feeling for Blanche is expanded when she becomes most pariah-like: during her years of desperate sexual indulgence in Laurel as Belle Reve was crumbling, and at the end, as Blanche's own sanity shatters into madness.

Blanche, moreover, incurs a not dissimilar demerit through her treatment of Stanley. Being a cultured, upper-class representative of the Old South, she patronizes the lower-class Kowalski, treating him not only as an inferior, but even as a primitive beast. There is a sexual element in this, to which I shall return, but there is also sheer condescension. Coming from an undistinguished middle-class family, Tennessee Williams suffered from the contumely of genteel, snobbish Southerners in his childhood and youth: no doubt some retributive animus informs his attitude toward Blanche. I recall my amazement when, as a graduate student at Harvard, I briefly made his acquaintance at the time of *Streetcar*'s Boston tryout, and found him much more sympathetic to Stanley than to Blanche.

I now have no doubt that, however much Tennessee identified himself with Blanche, however much he *was* Blanche in certain ways—rather like the Flaubert who uttered his famous "Madame Bovary, c'est moi"—he also felt a measure of self-hatred that he took out on Blanche, putting her through the wringer in more ways than one. Furthermore, he must have felt a strong sympathy tinged with sexual attraction for the kind of brash, acquisitive, unhypocritical, dominant young man Stanley represents, and Blanche's provocative taunts, echoing her cruel incomprehension of her young husband, must be reckoned as, at least in part, triggering her undoing. So we cannot dismiss *Streetcar* as having no latent social content, even if it may have remained hidden from its very author. But isn't it the nature of great works of art to have a life of their own, beneath and beyond even their makers' awareness? I might go a step further and assert that any work of art that is no more than exactly what its author, consciously and deliberately, put into it may be craftsmanlike and effective, may even be of importance, but will not, cannot be great.

To return to our parallelism, however, consider the supreme theme of illusions, so essential to all four of the plays we are discussing. It is, of course, central to *Iceman,* where every character lives in his illusions or, with greater accuracy, delusions about himself and the world, including Hickey, the one fellow who claims to have rid himself of crippling pipe dreams and proposes to do as much for the rest of the dramatis personae. O'Neill clearly inherited the theme from the Ibsen of

The Wild Duck, but it is also a theme that, in one form or another, has been with us since the year one, or, more accurately, since some 430-odd years earlier, when Sophocles wrote his *Oedipus Rex,* another play about a wiseacre who wants to put an end to illusions or delusions, and succeeds only in putting an end to his happiness, however specious.

Illusions, though less obviously, are equally important in *Long Day's Journey into Night.* James Tyrone cannot get over his early dire poverty, and lives, despite his prosperity, convinced that he must pinch pennies the way others might pitch them. It has become an obsession with him that cost his wife's health and caused her morphine addiction, threatens the health and very survival of his younger son, Edmund, and earns him the fierce resentment of both Edmund and his elder brother, Jamie. Jamie, likewise shortchanged by his father, is well on his way to becoming a wastrel, but he, too, has illusions about his life to come. As for Mary, the wife and mother and drug fiend, her illusions are at least sweet and benevolent—a happy family living in affection and harmony—but are all the more pitiful for that. Only the autobiographical Edmund, thanks to his dedication to art and the clarity of perception his vocation exacts, is able to cut through this web of lies, but at what cost to himself the life of Eugene O'Neill sadly attests to.

It follows that O'Neill was of two minds about illusion. He perceived it as distinctly necessary to making life tolerable in *Iceman;* in *Journey,* on the other hand, he castigates it as the poisoner of the will to achieve, strangler of generous impulses—an opiate that, unlike the one in *Iceman,* does not console the desperate but paralyzes the potentially gifted. Perhaps those who have nothing to lose need illusions, whereas those who have something more to rely on cannot afford them; perhaps what O'Neill is saying is that the pipe dream is a slower, gentler form of suicide than facing reality with inadequate equipment.

Illusion is a principal theme in Williams, too, but his attitude toward it is even more complicated. In *Menagerie,* Amanda

lives amid all manner of delusions about the past and the
future, while trying to be practical about the present as she
moves heaven and earth to make a success of Laura. But prac-
ticality about the otherworldly Laura, unfit for life, is misplaced, delusory. Amanda's maneuverings are about as helpful
as her making Laura wish for happiness on the new moon. Yet
Williams clearly sympathizes with Amanda's absurdity even as
he does with Tom's common sense and Laura's resignation,
and much more than with Jim's prosaism. Nevertheless,
Amanda is also ridiculous and a menace—a monster of misplaced energy.

If we look now at *Streetcar,* the problem gets knottier.
Blanche, like Amanda, is a creature mired in illusion, but also a
practical schemer who sets about entrapping Mitch. Concerning the past, she has illusions for others, for show; for herself,
she sees its horror clearly. About the future, she does have
illusions: she thinks she can be happy with Mitch, something
highly unlikely given their enormous differences. She even
tries to coax Stella, a commonplace young woman, out of an
ambience that suits her for the sake of some delusory better life
away from Stanley, and reality finally catches up with her and,
apparently, crushes her. The madhouse she is taken to may be a
place in which she can forever indulge her delusions—her
version of Harry Hope's saloon; or it may be calamitous,
depending on whether it is informed by the mercilessness of
the matron or by the humanity of the doctor.

Is facing the facts, tearing the veil of illusion, any better?
When Stanley verbally, and Mitch physically, rend the par-
ticolored lanterns from the light bulbs (surely an allusion to
the colored lights Stanley and Stella see when they make love),
is anyone better served by the revelations? That paper lantern
takes us back to the song Blanche was singing in the hot tub,
"It's only a paper moon / . . . But it wouldn't be make-believe /
If you believed in me!" Belief can make Blanche young and
innocent and loved again—or can it? Herein lies the tragedy of
Streetcar: no one is quite right, no one is quite wrong. Illusions

are simultaneously a deception, and thus bad, and a balm, and thus good. The ambivalence about illusion that O'Neill expressed consecutively from one play to another, Williams packs into one and the same play. It is not even a case of shifting, as in *Iceman,* away from illusions, as Hickey's arguments prevail; then back again to them, as Hickey's reasoning proves to have been of no help even to himself. No, it is the deepest kind of ambivalence or ambiguity that inheres in every step of the play, at every stop of the streetcar on its way to desire and death.

If, then, O'Neill and Williams are not entirely unrelated in matters of social consciousness—if, moreover, they are akin in their perceptions of the role of illusion in life—they become positively brothers under the skin on the subject of love-hate, in which all four plays are saturated. In both of the family plays, *Journey* and *Menagerie,* the atmosphere is fraught with anger at one's next-of-kin that sometimes is cloaked in loving concern, but presently strips for naked warfare. Only that isn't the end of it, either; under the phony love and real bitterness is yet another layer of genuine love: festering, impotent, neither to be shaken off nor to be sustained with impunity. In *Long Day's Journey* people are constantly apologizing for their outbursts; I have always wanted to count the number of apologies, but my mathematics isn't good enough.

What in O'Neill is done, as it were, sequentially—insult, apology, insult, remorse—gets fused in Williams. It is evident that Amanda is driving both her children away, but whereas Tom can eventually escape outward into the world, sister Laura can escape only into her unreal inner world. In the play, that is a world of fragile glass bric-a-brac, and equally frail, flickering candlelight; in real life, for sister Rose, it was insanity. But if we read the play carefully, we see that Tom and Laura's attitude toward their domineering mother is one of bristling meekness, of subservience frantically seeking a way out. At the same time, we perceive that Amanda-Edwina is also disguising her profound disappointment with her ineffectual children who are foiling her social aspirations just as distressingly as her husband foiled them. Her excess of smothering effusiveness must be a mask for resentment. So I think it is very cavalier to dismiss plays such as *Menagerie* and *Journey* as merely "personal" or autobiographical or solipsistic; in their intensely honest criticism (which includes self-criticism), they rise to being social documents as well.

The love-hate motif, however, looms just as large in the two more overtly social plays. In *Iceman,* there are, offstage, the relationships between Parritt and his mother, the mother and Larry, and Hickey and his wife, Evelyn; onstage, we have the relationships between the bartenders, Rocky and Chuck, and their girls, as well as the one between the Boer and the Briton. Not to be ignored either is the curious triangle involving Harry Hope, his dead wife, and her brother, Ed Mosher; or the frustrated surrogate-father and son relations between Larry and Parritt. Everywhere one looks there is smoldering love-hate, now drowned in booze, now coming hissingly alive again. And so it is in *Streetcar,* between Stanley and Blanche, Blanche and Stella, at times Stella and Stanley, and eventually Blanche and Mitch, not to mention the comic upstairs version of Steve and Eunice.

In trying to sketch in a few significant similarities or equivalences between the works of Williams and O'Neill, it was not my intention either to reverse the usual order at the finish line or to confirm it. I do, however, wish to begin here what others, better qualified, should continue: turning the two dramatists not into opposites, each serving to point up the lacks of the other, but into forces complementing, corroborating, reinvigorating each other. If pressed, I would still have to assert that because O'Neill had the greater range and variety, and perhaps a nobler zeal to discover the new through experimentation, he deserves to win in a photo finish. Yet *Camino Real, Slapstick Tragedy,* and *The Two-Character Play* are, in their way, experimental too, and though unsuccessful, just how successful is, say, *The Great God Brown*? Drama, in any case, is not horse racing; if anything it is more like cat-skinning, for which there exists more than one way.

But there is only one way to end this discussion: by calling attention to the major advantage Williams had over O'Neill, the one Audrey Wood reminded Tennessee of in the letter quoted earlier, and known to every thoughtful critic. I mean, of course, language. For the one thing O'Neill never quite managed was that sublimated poetry that makes a play-wright's prose sing out at the right moments; it is the thing such supposedly major playwrights as Arthur Miller and Lillian Hellman could never shout their way into hailing distance of, a thing that Thornton Wilder, Lanford Wilson, and a few others share with Williams to varying degrees.

What exactly is this theatrical prose poetry? I can't tell you what it is *exactly* any more than I can define poetry *tout court*. It can, however, be analyzed—in terms of rhythm, cadence, sonority, imagery, etc.—either in sustained passages or in brief spurts such as the one I shall examine here. At the end of Scene VI of *Streetcar*, Mitch and Blanche have found each other; he has timidly kissed her and declared himself. "Her breath," says the stage direction, "is drawn and released in long, grateful sobs," and then she exclaims: "Sometimes—there's God—so quickly!" Why do these five or six words in seven syllables work so potently?

First, there is the extreme concision: not "heaven" or "there is," but "God" and "there's"—one syllable apiece. Second, the scansion, stressed by the dashes representing sobs or pauses but also emphasizing the three metrical feet: a trochee, an iamb, an amphibrach. The English language, and with it English poetry, is predominantly iambic; but not even in verse, let alone in prose, could one string together unalloyed iambs and expect anything but doggerel. So Williams—who, let us not forget, was also a poet and author of at least one extraordinary poem, "Life Story"—uses a line of iambic trimeter, but varies it cannily. At the beginning, he introduces a traditional deviation, the reversal of an iamb into a trochee; at the end, by another traditional variation, an extra syllable is added to create a feminine ending, a dying fall. A lesser writer might have concluded with a perfect iamb, "Sometimes there's God so fast," and merely confirmed his mediocrity. The way that accented-unaccented "quickly" gently dissolves into silence exactly reproduces Blanche's emotional state.

Third, sonority. The line affects us so deeply also because of the way the two dark-voweled syllables, "God" and "so," are followed by two high-pitched, airy ones: "quickly." After the slow, long, opaque sounds of those two o's—the second more closed and prolonged than the first—the brisk brightness of "quickly" takes off, flies heavenward. Finally, the imagery. A lesser playwright might have written, instead of "quickly," "soon." But that would have conveyed only shortness of time. "Quickly," however, suggests also an agent, someone doing something with speed, and so God becomes personalized. Furthermore, "heaven" or "paradise," though longer words, are less inclusive: "God" is absolute in its very monosyllabicity, and all-encompassing. It is also fresher than "heaven" or "paradise" or "bliss," all tired unto death; and God is not only bigger, he is also more intimate: the one who looks after us, as Blanche needs to be looked after.

Since O'Neill's letter to Williams, if it ever certifiably existed, has certainly disappeared, we shall never know for sure how O'Neill regarded his younger colleague. But letter or no letter, O'Neill was a great help to Williams. Just as the blocked Ibsen, when all else failed, looked up at the portrait of Strindberg conspicuously hung above his desk, and proceeded—out of envy, ambition, or spite—to write like a demon, so Williams must have had O'Neill's picture before him to prod him on. Whether an actual picture, as Dotson Rader claims, or a mental image, hardly matters. Icon or eidolon, it urged him on, and Williams responded by pouring out some of the most sumptuous and moving images ever bestowed on the stage.

[1986–1987]

ASSAYING HARDER

Maureen Howard, ed., *The Penguin Book of Contemporary American Essays*

PITY the poor anthologist, for whatever he or she does will be wrong. All literate persons carry their own compendium of favorite poems, stories, perhaps even essays, around in their heads: to confirm this selection is to be redundant; to deviate from it, dangerously mistaken. Just try telling the mother of a numerous brood which of her children she should prefer to the rest! On the subject of what is the best in an art form, people can get almost as violent. Yet when you are anthologizing stories or poems, you can at least invoke a Great Tradition to lean on or shy away from.

The problem becomes far thornier when your subject is the essay, particularly the contemporary essay: there is nothing much to go on. Hence the editor of a tome like *The Penguin Book of Contemporary American Essays* is on virgin ground, and confronted by a critic or reader with a redoubled "Show me!" attitude who is all the crankier in the absence of a Great Tradition for a touchstone. So I must, at any rate, commend Maureen Howard for her courage.

Technically, though, the book is a disaster. The essays are not dated in the text; one has to rummage among the copyright pages to dredge up, with difficulty, the time and place of original publication. The minuscule bio-bibliographies of the

authors fail to offer birth and death dates. "There is no preferred way to read this collection," says Howard in her introduction, and truer words were never spoken. If there is an
organizing principle behind the running order, it is far from
perspicuous. The introduction itself, moreover, says nothing
about the history of the essay, indulges in little or no speculation about its present or future, and does not even provide
useful definitions by the editor or others. Instead, it is confined
largely to thumbnail summaries and a rehearsal of the virtues
that made Howard choose each piece. In the November 18,
1984, issue of the *New York Times Book Review,* Philip Lopate
published an article entitled "The Essay Lives—in Disguise,"
whose very title tells more about the state of the form than this
introduction.

Worse, she is academically sloppy. By way of etymology, for
example, we are told merely, "Essay—from the French *essai,* a
trial or to try," as if the same French word were both noun and
verb. At the very least, Howard could have indicated the
relation to "assay," with the resultant suggestion of weighing
and testing.

Still more shocking is her slatternly reasoning. It appears
that the essay thrives because of our continuous exposure to
TV: "In seeing so much, hearing so much, it seems inevitable
that the essay, that thoughtful form with its way of stopping us
with an urgent, particular voice, considering, playing out an
idea, would come back in force." To whom do those initial
dangling participles refer: to "us" or to the essay? Is the
"urgent, particular voice" an extension of or reaction to all that
bombardment by images? Does the "would come back" imply
the future or describe the present?

Two paragraphs later, Howard tries again: "If I must declare
a thesis at all, it is that during a time when the social sciences
have dealt us a surfeit of information on our society and
ourselves with no solutions, during a time when we have
overdosed on visual images accompanied by meager under-
nourished texts—the news magazines, the nightly roundup—

many of our best American writers have been drawn to the imaginative possibilities of short nonfiction."

Aside from the fact that the idea, fuzzy as it is, comes from the piece by Michael J. Arlen opening the collection, this, like the preceding statement, is starvation fare. To the extent that I can make sense of it, it means that because the social sciences provide information with no solution, and the news media offer images without adequate words, the best American writers rush in to fill the vacuum: provide solutions for the problems and texts for the pictures in the form of essays. This hardly qualifies as thinking, let alone scholarship, criticism, history of ideas, or, indeed, essayistic writing, something I think we are entitled to expect from the editor.

A final example. Apropos of one of the essays, she remarks: "Once again that image of looking, really looking and taking in what we see. There's not an essay in this lot that doesn't make a claim for it." Nor is there an essay that does not claim to use words, sentences, and paragraphs. So the hallmark of a true essay is that it really looks out into the world. And what does fiction do? Or poetry? But enough. Clearly, the most important aspect of the anthology is the essays it contains, and even a pudding-headed gastronome may offer us proof in her puddings.

There are refreshing features. For one, the collection is catholic, eclectic. It is not restricted to personal reflections, biographical and autobiographical pieces, views on literature and the arts—textbook stuff, if you prefer, which it actually goes too far out of its way to avoid. Howard, more precisely, tries to eschew the obvious in three ways. She does not include some of the old standbys, say, E. B. White and Edmund Wilson, yet age cannot be the criterion here, since she does admit Dwight Macdonald and Eudora Welty. Second, she tends to choose the unexpected by expected writers. Who could have foreseen that the worthy John Updike would be represented by "Eclipse," a two-page anecdote-cum-confession concerning his atavistic fears of a solar eclipse, a piece that ends in attitudinizing overstatement? Or that Lewis Thomas would appear with a three-page piece, "Computers," a flimsy and poseurish production, full of easy affirmation?

Third, she includes surprising writers: the columnist Russell Baker, and the journalists Lillian Ross, A. J. Liebling, Garry Wills. Among critics of the arts (assuming that television is an art), we get only Michael J. Arlen. His unremarkable effort discovers that TV adaptations vulgarize literature, and that our images have not caught up with our words. Then there is M. F. K. Fisher on her favorite foods, a nice enough personal essay for a food writer, but not quite good enough for a writer. There is an impressively dull piece on a spectacular subject: Charles Rembar on whether Nixon should be impeached, and whether the impeachment should be televised—written, alas, with all the liveliness of a legal brief. You can't deny range to Howard's florilegium, whatever you think of the scent.

Personally, I find some of the selections malodorous; none more so than A. J. Liebling's "Ahab and Nemesis" and William Gass's "The Artist and Society." The Liebling is a clever—too clever—celebration of boxing. I happen to think that boxing is a bestial blood sport and should not be celebrated, let alone have its celebrations anthologized. More to the point, however, is the trivial cuteness of the writing: standard procedure in slick sports analysis, it should hardly be rewarded with the honorific "essay." Liebling's central subject is the Rocky Marciano–Archie Moore 1955 heavyweight title bout, and he comments on a self-pitying letter he got from the contender: "A fellow who has as much style as Moore tends to overestimate the intellect—he develops the kind of Faustian mind that will throw itself against the problem of perpetual motion. . . . Archie's note made it clear to me that he was honing his harpoon for the White Whale." Faust and Melville to plumb Archie's psyche? That is arch intellectualizing of brutishness, excusable as an isolated lapse, but not when it is the staple of the entire essay.

Take this further sample. Liebling is describing what he calls

Marciano's "pattern of ratiocination": "A kind, quiet, imperturbable fellow, [Marciano] would plan to go after Moore and make him fight continuously until he tired enough to become an accessible target. After that he would expect concussion to accentuate exhaustion and exhaustion to facilitate concussion, until Moore came away from his consciousness, like everybody else Rocky had ever fought." The irony serves merely to allow Liebling to appear to deny his bloodlust while indulging it. The best place to anthologize a cutesy essay that exalts concussive pummeling is the wastepaper basket.

William Gass, one of the most overrated writers in America, is represented by an essay that purports to explain the relationship stated in its title, "The Artist and Society." He begins and ends with an image of a caged bear that seems to owe something to Rilke's "Panther"; for the rest, Gass is indebted only to his own blend of preciosity and pretentiousness, with an occasional bow to the then trendy and since exploded psychiatrist R. D. Laing. We get such things as "Nonpersons unperson persons" and "Reality . . . is rare—rarer, let me say—than an undefeated football season." This can perhaps be justified as the popular college prof soliciting high marks from his students, a stance that may account for some dubious sexual allusions, too. Yet what can excuse the following:

> Israel makes war, and there are no symposia published by prizefighters, no pronouncements from hairdressers, not a ding from the bellhops, from the dentists not even a drill's buzz, from the cabbies nary a horn beep, and from the bankers only the muffled clink of money. . . . But critics, poets, novelists, professors, journalists—those used to shooting off their mouths—they shoot (no danger, it's only their mouth's wash they've wallowed their words in) . . . but neither wisdom nor good will nor magnanimity are [sic] the qualities which will win you your way to the rostrum . . . just plentiful friends in pushy places and a little verbal skill.

Note the unhelpful prolixity, the image-mongering of the first sentence with that precious archaism "nary"; observe the playing to the anti-intellectual (or student) galleries in that mouth-shooting play on words; savor the inept hypallage "pushy places." If you say "brazen lie"—where it is the liar, not the lie, that is brazen—ascribing the weight, hardness, arrogance of brass to the lie itself makes it more real, repellent. But what does "pushy places" (for pushy people in high places) do to make the concept more visual and tangible? Nothing; it's just showing off.

Throughout Gass uses baroque imagery, and tries constantly to shock. So the artist "knows the fish is offset from its shadow; knows the peck of the crow does not disturb the beauty of its beak or the dent it makes in the carrion." The obfuscatory trope-tossing might be mitigated by the essay's having something new to say; regrettably, it comes down to not much more than Matthew Arnold's seeing life steady and seeing it whole, albeit bloated, bedizened, belabored.

Gass concludes with a chic ambiguity: "After all, we are—artists and society—both swaying bears *and* rigid bars. Again, it may be that the *bars* are moving, and the bears, in terror-stricken—are standing behind them . . . no, in front of them—among them—quite, quite still." The image twists in every direction until it wiggles its way out of meaning. And has punctuation ever churned more frenziedly, except when Evelyn Waugh parodied the postcards of English schoolgirls traveling on the Continent? It's shooting off mouth's wash, to which Gass is eminently entitled, embodying as he does almost the whole range of conditions for oral marksmanship: though he is not a poet, he is a critic, novelist, professor, and journalist.

Several other essays here are only slightly less offensive. Norman Mailer's "The Ninth Presidential Paper—Totalitarianism" is the usual jumble of megalomania, phantasmagoria, marketable paranoia, and unprovable assertions—for example, "travel is reminiscent of the trauma of birth, is also suggestive of some possible migrations after death." Further, "The best short poem of the twentieth century, I would think, is Yeats' *The Second Coming*"—this in 1963, when the century still had thirty-seven years left to surpass itself poetically. In any case, only one who would rather *not* think can declare any poem, fine as it may be, the century's best. Present, too, is the endless rambling about cancer—literal, metaphorical, metaphysical—Mailer's favorite polemical device. Slightly mitigating the folly of such writing is the odd sneaky insight, the pawky deviation into sense, on this ramble through the funhouse of Mailer's mind.

The pieces by the journalistic writers named earlier are good enough for ephemeral publication, not for a chrestomathy. Others are effective specimens of scientific writing, e.g., Stephen Jay Gould's paleontological detective work on the Irish elk; or witty send-ups, e.g., Donald Barthelme's report on *The Ed Sullivan Show,* where the slightly skewed angle of vision renders everything condignly absurd—but aren't there worthier targets for satire? Howard Moss's affectionate memoir of Jean Stafford is pleasant, slight stuff that fails to penetrate very deep and takes the subject's greatness too readily for granted.

After this winnowing, at last, we are left with material that earns its place in the volume. Leslie Fiedler's "Afterthoughts on the Rosenbergs" strikes me as first-rate socio-politico-historical commentary. It is a shiningly reasonable sorting out of vexed, rankling questions, the whole thing couched in arresting yet fastidiously unfussy language, making us feel equally sorry for what became of those poor dupes and for what became of Leslie Fiedler, who once could think and write as lucidly, as beautifully as this.

Equally meaty is Dwight Macdonald's "Tolstoy, Orwell and Socialism," offering fine discriminations in a field that has become a dumping ground for preconceptions and oversimplifications. James Baldwin may somewhat overstate his case in "Fifth Avenue, Uptown: A Letter from Harlem," yet up to just before the end he manages to channel undeserved hurt and justified anger into measured, dignifiedly scathing condemnation. In "The Geography of the Imagination," Guy Davenport shows how exhilarating erudition, close analysis, and the history of ideas can be as he leaps in seven-league boots from the past to myth to topography—from Poe's writings to Grant Wood's most famous painting and Spengler's philosophy—and fashions it all into one grand, disheveled piece of scholarship on the rampage, diminished solely by not acknowledging some of its sources.

Ralph Ellison reminisces eloquently and evocatively about the birth of bop in "The Golden Age, Time Past," almost making me, through its sheer stylistic élan and imaginative brio, take bop as seriously as he does. Edward Hoagland's "Hailing the Elusory Mountain Lion," in which a great deal of researched nature lore is joined to lived outdoor experience through graceful, unostentatious writing, moves ahead with the surefooted grace of the cougar. No less alert and incisive, though with an added ontological-metaphysical dimension, is Robert Finch's meditation on a huge, hugely dead finback whale, beached on a stretch of Cape Cod sand, where it becomes an intense but ephemeral tourist attraction. Eudora Welty's "A Sweet Devouring" is immediate, pure recollection of how in her youth she discovered literature, and is itself a small, unsentimentally tender addition to it.

In "On Keeping a Notebook," Joan Didion is not yet so mannered as she was to become, not yet such a depressing mixture of frazzled sensitivity (or is it sensibility?) and steely self-aggrandizement. Granted, the seeds are there, but this is an instance of almost justified narcissism: this *is* the way *that* kind of person becomes a writer, and there is enough shrewd observation to offset the purblind self-importance. Consider: "Only the very young and the very old may recount their dreams at breakfast, dwell upon self, interrupt with memories of beach picnics and favorite Liberty lawn dresses and the rainbow trout in a creek near Colorado Springs. The rest of us are expected, rightly, to affect absorption in other people's favorite dresses, other people's trout." How skillfully that "rightly" plays off that "affect"; here is a tension of not quite overcome doubt, not wholly swallowed etiquette.

There is even better writing in Elizabeth Hardwick's "Boston: The Lost Ideal." The essay is a quietly devastating portrait of cultural twilight and urban decay, of the decline of a quasi-aristocracy into terminal quaintness beyond class and virtually beyond classification, save that Hardwick dissects them sovereignly—and wittily, too—with the scalpel of her loathing. Katherine Anne Porter's "St. Augustine and the Bullfight" is circuitous, self-serving, and quite disingenuous; but its power of evocation is very strong, and its knack for making minutely calculated strategies out of seemingly offhand syntax creates an aura of intimacy with the reader that offsets the ultimate lack of a clear point.

Paul Fussell's "My War," one of the most honest, graphic, controlled, and profoundly unsettling conjurations of the experience and consequences of being in a war that I have ever read, may be the best piece in the book. Astoundingly, it somehow manages to be objective in the midst of autobiography, to render a not unfeelingful detachment more potent than the most percussive breast-beating. So *The Penguin Book of Contemporary American Essays* is, after all, not a total loss.

But what about the state of the essay, beleaguered in the here and now, and facing a shrinking prospect? An essay, as I see it, is the untrammeled self-expression of a writer gifted with originality, endowed with a felicity of style, and blessed with enough space from an editor or publisher. Because these three are not easily come by in conjunction, the essay, that piece of thinking out loud, nowadays often exhibits too little thinking and too shrill a loudness. The contemporary essayist is cramped, however, not only by niggardly publications ("No more than a thousand words, please!") and overpragmatic publishing houses ("Who the hell reads essays nowadays?"), but also by a loss of the literary culture—or, indeed, any kind of culture—on reciprocal accommodation with which he depends. Nor can we ignore the depredations of fiction writers, and occasionally poets, who are really crypto-essay-ists. If one writer will give you both fiction and the essay, gobs of the latter rattling around in the belly of the former, why not buy the two for the price of one?

Nonetheless, read Flannery O'Connor's "The King of the Birds" (1961), reprinted in the collection *Mystery and Manners,* and tell me the essay is dead. Should you want more recent evidence, delve into Jacques Barzun, Wilfrid Sheed, Cynthia Ozick, Eleanor Clark, James Dickey, Ned Rorem, Susan Sontag, Gore Vidal, Erich Heller—to name several others neglected by Maureen Howard—and you will not have to fear for the essay's life. Not yet.

[1984]

PLYING A PERIPLUS

John Updike, *Hugging the Shore*

JOHN UPDIKE has, on the evidence of his allusions, digressions, entire frame of reference, read not only the mighty library of diverse books reviewed in *Hugging the Shore,* his third collection of critical pieces, but also just about everything of value there is to read. Compared to him, I have read almost nothing: only half the books he discusses here have I even dipped into or read about, few consumed cover to cover, and only the merest handful actually reviewed. But perhaps what Lady Bracknell says about a man who desires to get married—that he should know either everything or nothing—extends also to the mating of books and their reviewers, and so, at least by my ignorance, I may qualify.

What kind of a critic is this renowned novelist? One, apparently, who takes to reviewing as a gentleman farmer, who really lives by something else, grows his alfalfa and lettuce. This third critical collection begins, "Writing criticism is to writing fiction and poetry as hugging the shore is to sailing in the open sea. At sea, we have that beautiful blankness all around, a cold bright wind, and the occasional thrill of a gleaming dolphin-back or the synchronized leap of silverfish; hugging the shore, one can always come even closer to the land with another nine-point quotation." An image derived from that most ancient mode of sailing, the periplus, which did not

dare stick its prow into the great billows of risk and exhilaration, but, plodding close to land, got the job done. Is this,
then, condescension to criticism from a fiction and verse
writer? I doubt it, otherwise why a book of some 900 pages
(containing, to be sure, a few personal, noncritical essays and
introductions to or interviews about one's own writings as
well)? Or is it modesty vis-à-vis other writers? I doubt it,
otherwise, again, why a book of such length from which
nothing that Updike reviewed in the last eight years at *The
New Yorker* seems to have been omitted?

Could the faintly patronizing passage be a form of conscious
or unconscious honesty—a description of the sort of criticism
Updike writes, which is, above all other things, safe? Here I
must return to my landlubber trope: the gentleman farmer
takes pride in his crops, but he can afford to grow what amuses
him; hence my choice of alfalfa and lettuce was wrong: it
should have been something more distinguished—Belgian
endives or Spanish saffron. As the chief book critic for a
magazine that adverts only to select items, Updike need
review only his personal choices or works of presumptive
merit respectfully submitted to him by the book-review editor. Though some of these prove to be clinkers, they are tony
clinkers susceptible of elegant, ironical deflation rather than
requiring bloody and maculating dismemberment. So the
reviews can, for the most part, afford to be genteel. Thus if
Saul Bellow strings out an enormous list of nouns unseparated
by commas, to Updike it simply "seems a rather too determined exercise in relaxation." In Anne Tyler, whom he generally overpraises, Updike notes, only ever so glancingly, "one
possible weakness: a tendency to leave the reader just where
she found him." More pointedly, but still observing the
Queensberry rules, he writes about Kingsley Amis and his
Jake's Thing, "Though he himself is a poet good enough to
be generously represented in *The New Oxford Book of Light
Verse* (which Mr. Amis edited), it is a rare sentence of his
prose that surrenders to the demons of language, that abdi-
cates a seat of fussy social judgment, that is there for its own

sake, out of simple awe, gratitude, or dismay in the face of creation."

Yet is there anything wrong with being a genteel critic—with hugging the shore so as not to rock the boat overmuch? Not enormously. In fact, even during a periplus one can experience the odd gust of cold bright wind, the occasional whale or shark (never mind dolphins and silverfish) that strays close to land, and a beautiful blankness on three sides with a not unpleasing prospect of shore on the fourth, which is still a panorama worth considering. Indeed, criticism can be written just as imaginatively and imagistically as any other kind of prose, the very thing *Hugging the Shore* so winningly demonstrates. The effectiveness of Updike's muted critical tone is similar to the one our author defends in the French African fiction of Sembène Ousmane as having "that light, level accent . . . which voices its perceptions, however withering, with a certain pleasant dispassion, with a thinking man's articulations."

Perhaps the one real trouble with a periplus is that it takes longer than sailing straight across the sea. The principal problem with this tome is that there is too much of it. Updike is one of the rare and valuable critics who review a book as a piece of bookmaking as well, and nothing from paper not white enough to "a dust jacket that looks like butcher's paper," from the Schocken Kafka where "the print seems small and the price big" to the University of Chicago's *Carnival* by Isak Dinesen, which, among other good things, "sits holdably in the hand," escapes his aquiline notice. Yet despite his pious wish in the foreword to his previous such collection, *Picked-Up Pieces* ("Let us hope, for the sakes of artistic purity and paper conservation, that ten years from now the pieces to be picked up will make a smaller heap"), the current heap, amassed in only eight years, is by eight-elevenths bigger than the preceding one, twice as heavy, and unlikely to sit holdably in your hands unless they also pump iron. The situation could have been easily remedied by omitting the above-mentioned non-critical pieces and judiciously pruning the critical ones.

Still, there is so much of genuine worth scattered through-out that the stocking of our brains may well compensate for the strain on our muscles. *Hugging the Shore* reviews not only fiction by a host of writers from all continents except Antarc-tica, but also poetry, sociology, theology, criticism, history, art history, and even books by Doris Day and Louise Brooks, for both of which glamorous ladies our galant critic tempers his strictures even more than usual. About the only thing Updike doesn't deal with here is the close competition—Mailer, Sty-ron, et al.; but Vonnegut is here, overpraised as a less conse-quential rival would be by a gentlemanly fellow novelist for "the generosity of his imagination and the honesty of his pain" and "a fine disdain for the merely personal"—if only that were all that was being finely disdained! Updike is similarly over-considerate of his *New Yorker* colleague Muriel Spark, in whose *The Takeover* "we have been ushered into the cave of an enchantress, and have there been dazzled, distracted, and peremptorily, as is befitting, dismissed." Nothing about being turned into swine.

An impressive aspect of Updike's criticism, however, is the generosity of spirit with which he tries—and often manages—to like and make likable writers quite unlike himself. Here he is on Céline: "A first-person narrator is a survivor, or he wouldn't be there on the page. This minor technical fact mutes the sense of death that Céline ostensibly evokes. . . ." On Henry Green: "A vision so clear can be withering; it takes great natural health to sustain a life without illusions." On Jean Rhys: "As a writer, she startles us with what it doesn't occur to her to overlook." On Borges (a bit ambiguously, to be sure): "Few major writers granted long life have proved so loyal to their initial obsessions and demonstrated so little fear of repeating themselves." And this, which goes beyond literary appreciation: "In the prize ring of life few of us would have lasted ten rounds with Colette."

He is equally good and honest at seeing the weaknesses of writers who so resemble him that he might easily have remained blind to their blind spots. Thus John O'Hara's art lacked "love of language . . . language as a semi-opaque medium whose colors and connotations can be worked into a supernatural, supermimetic bliss." About late Bellow: "Literature can do with any amount of egoism; but the merest pinch of narcissism spoils the flavor." About Flann O'Brien, whose former work Updike loved: "Each chapter makes a fresh grab at the greased pig of a plot. . . ." Concerning Bruno Bettelheim, whose interpretations of fairy tales he likes as much as he does fairy tales themselves: "While in the spell of this most benignly paternal scholar of our hearts, we forget that his own enchanting presumption of life as a potentially successful adventure may be itself something of a fairy tale." And this shrewd comment on Italo Calvino's later work, despite high regard for the earlier: "Calvino contemplates the death not of the notorious old moribund Novel, but of the Story, of the hopeful impulse that makes beginnings and seeks outcomes and imagines adventures in the middle."

Yet the modern reader, bombarded with and often subdued by critical theories, may not be satisfied with such examples of good taste and twenty-twenty insight. What are the theoretical underpinnings of this criticism, he asks; what school does it belong to or might it serve to found? I am happy to report that it is purely gustatory criticism, and that Updike has much—and, for him, positively wicked—fun with the structuralists and semiologists. So in his review of *The Origin of Table Manners,* wherein he turns the tables on Claude Lévi-Strauss when he refers to it as "combining the 'raw' opacity of savage myths with the 'cooked' obscurity of close structural analysis. . . . The exact methodology [of the latter] is not easy to grasp, though Lévi-Strauss pauses every hundred pages or so to sing its praises." The entire review is exemplary, as when Updike notes that in reading Lévi-Strauss "one is witnessing a performance fundamentally artistic, less a pragmatic servicing of reality than the execution of a fiendishly difficult, self-imposed intelligence test."

It is rather disappointing, therefore, that though Updike begins by equally effectively putting in its place the earlier work of Roland Barthes, he later capitulates to the trend. Thus "*S/Z* is a nearly unreadable book about reading. . . . The reader emerges as from that machine of Kafka's which engraved commandments upon the transgressor's skin, lexically enriched but lacerated; I cannot remember another book ostensibly in the English language which gave me such pains to peruse." This is right on the nose, as are Updike's comments on another Barthes arcanum, *The Pleasure of the Text.* All that was in 1975, however; by 1976, Updike is more indulgent with *Sade/Fourier/Loyola,* and by 1980 he has become a deep imbiber from the Barthesian well. *New Critical Essays* is pronounced to be "serious and delightful in content," and this posthumous volume elevates Barthes irreplaceably above his disciples. As a supposed example of Barthes's acuity, Updike adduces the following observation about La Rochefoucauld's maxims with their symmetry and antithesis: "This game is in the service of a very old technique, that of meaning; so that writing well is playing with words, because playing with words is *inevitably* [italics mine] coming closer to that intention of opposition which governs the birth of a signification." Anyone who can find a signification of consequence born from the above playing with words can at best draw some incriminating conclusion about Barthes, but no helpful one about La Rochefoucauld. For Barthes, meaning was so very old a technique that it could no longer be recalled.

Why this sudden indulgence? Do semiologists, as Indians were once alleged to, become good only when they are dead? Is *New Critical Essays* better than previous Barthesiana? No; the pieces in it are old, and contain such seminally asinine statements as "this game is at the service of a very old technique, that of meaning. . . ." In fact, the piece on the famous *moraliste* dates from 1961. The answer lies in Updike's temperament or temperance, if not indeed in his curious, elusive, sometimes self-contradictory Christianity, which the author himself describes in this volume as "a helpful peripheral presence." Peripheral it may well be, but whether such Christian forbearance is actually helpful to a critic is an open question. I am not against understatement such as this mildest of detergent ironies to which you can entrust the most delicate fabric of words (in this case, Andrei Bely's *Petersburg*): "Such a determined, doctrinal insubstantiality is, if not a defect, a virtue that takes some getting used to." Here at least we know where we stand; but when a wretched fiction of Robert Pinget's, *The Libera Me Domine,* is exonerated because "human events . . . have a permanently unsettled shape once past the instant in which they occur," the ground underfoot becomes too shifty for the erection of stable criteria.

In his last Barthes review, Updike states his position: "An ingenious sympathy . . . uncovers more treasures than an impatient judgingness." Fine, except that a sympathy so ingenious as to leave all others far behind is apt to discover treasures so rarefied that they don't exist. Love of literature is certainly a tool without which a critic gets nowhere, but the love must not be divorced from a *patient* judgingness. A "wayward tenderness" such as Updike charmingly praises in the novelist R. K. Narayan is not the proper equipment for a critic, any more than is an overdose of Christian *caritas* that takes on a missionary zeal. I suppose that Wallace Stevens would pass muster with Updike even if this "unambiguously atheistical" poet had not "retained a religious disposition," albeit one discernible only to a sympathy so miraculously ingenious that it can turn pagan wine into holy water. But what about an utter horror and nonentity such as William S. Burroughs, for whom Updike likewise conjures up Christian excuses? "*Port of Saints* is claptrap, but since it is murderous claptrap we feel we owe it some respect." Already the other cheek is overextended, but there is worse: "Burroughs would be unbearable if he believed in death; but since he no more believes in finality than the id or the animator of Tom and Jerry cartoons, a St. Elmo's fire of perverse tenderness can be seen to play about his lurid tab-

leaux. . . . " And, most amazing of all, "in a sense, such bohemians [carry] forward under a new banner the old Christian
war of the soul against the body." We haven't seen such
enforced mass conversions to Christianity since the Spaniards
conquered South America.

If Updike has a critical program, however, it is a simple and
sensible one. He wants, as a reader, to be "poked awake by a
flash of beauty or crackle of truth"; he believes that some of the
greatest writers produce "an autobiography transformed by
the needs of art and a mysterious obligation to give the world
back its glory." Of John McGahern, the Irish author, he
remarks that he "writes well, and for the usual reasons: he
observes well, hears faithfully, and feels keenly." Does this
mean that Updike favors straight realistic fiction? Not to the
exclusion of different modes, as witness his admiration for
Pinget, Bruno Schulz (whom he allows to be like Borges "a
cosmogonist without a theology"), much though not all of
Beckett (not "the chop-logic of *Watt* and all the hopeless dron-
ing of *The Unnamable*"), Vonnegut, early and middle Calvino,
most of Nabokov, García Márquez, and many more.

It is, however, true that when the antirealist mode combines
with a certain cosmic bleakness and metaphysical pessimism,
Updike may tune out. I think he includes himself more than
banteringly in the following "we": "Novel readers are ruth-
lessly sentimental. We want characters to marry, out of our
own needs to be done with them, to have them off our consciences." But is this the promised end of fiction? To take only
one obvious example, does it apply to Proust, whom Updike
rightly reveres? How eloquently he defends *A la Recherche*
against Harold Pinter's preposterous screen adaptation: "Pinter's characters are on the attack with every phrase, 'at' each
other, alert for advantage; Proust's dialogue is often an intersection of monologues, conveying with comic amplitude our
deafness to one another amid the vanity of our pretensions and
the lonely immensity of musing space we each of us harbor."
Now, that is multivalent, imaginative, aureate but not over-

burdened criticism of the best sort, criticism that can and must be read as *writing* first. Still, I for one find it regrettable that Updike the novelist and verse writer to some extent influences Updike the critic, so that writers such as Cheever, Bellow, Anne Tyler, Muriel Spark—sometimes even the utterly specious D. M. Thomas—benefit unduly; whereas others such as Milan Kundera, Günter Grass, Flannery O'Connor (whom he passingly equates with Carson McCullers!) are judged too severely, and still others converted to Christianity (the "Godly half" of Jean Rhys's writing) or simply defanged (W. H. Auden, "this sanest and most generous of modern poets").

Yet even if Kundera's splendid *Book of Laughter and Forgetting* is faulted for not bringing to its "heavy-heartedness that touch of traditional religious resignation which converts depression to . . . cosmic humor," at least Updike recognizes the tragic grandeur of Kundera's experiences, "a profound and jagged fall [that] makes the life histories of most American writers as stolid as the progress of a tomato plant. . . ." Similarly, it is inspiriting to see Updike's taste and honesty grapple successfully with the acerb pessimism that, for Updike, isolates behind the barbed wire of sarcasm so much of V. S. Naipaul. Yet if a safely middle-of-the-road but often poetic realism is to be preconized, can we seriously demur if the argument is as sumptuous and stimulating as this:

> Every moment is, in a sense, a dealt hand. The combinations that the human mind invents are relatively facile and unmagical compared to reality's tumbling richness. Behind the artist's transformative sorcery lurks, like a sheepish apprentice, an irrational willingness to view the accidents of the actual as purposeful and the given as sacred. . . . Fiction has no reason to be embarrassed about telling the same story again and again, since we all, with infinite variations, live the same story.

And Updike is not really procrustean; I have nothing but wonderment for an intellectual curiosity and aesthetic catholicity that can not only find much to praise in but also actually read through the works of writers as diverse as Stanislaw Lem and Ursula K. LeGuin on the one hand and Paul Tillich and Karl Barth on the other.

Elegant and inveterately civilized as Updike's writing is, it is not, however, free from surprising lapses, some of which also implicate *The New Yorker*'s nearly superhuman copy-editing. Thus the word "smithy" is used as if synonymous with blacksmith, "regretful" as if meaning regrettable, "triune division" for what can be only tripartite division, and the inept neologism "polylingual" for either multilingual or polyglot. We get also a misplaced subjunctive in "I asked him if he were sure of this," and occasional unfortunate wordplay as in "less promptu get-togethers" and "this saucy spaghetti of ideas . . . seems in consumption as clear as consommé, and goes down like ice cream." There is a trio of whopping errors in German, an excessive eagerness to use "upon" where "on" would read and sound better, a seeming unawareness of the difference between idiot and cretin, and the by now extraordinary misspelling of Jean Genet as "Genêt." A sentence or two may not quite parse; more distressingly, there are instances of ludicrously mixed metaphors: "poems . . . that come out of the creator like toothpaste from a tube, generating their music of self-reflexive allusion as they flow along," and "I want to write books that are hard and curvy, like keys, and that unlock the traffic jam in everybody's head." But these lapses are all but forgiven when one confronts the sustained excellence with which Updike tackles such unlikely books for belletrists as Isaiah Berlin's *Vico and Herder* and Peter Gay's *Art and Act,* a work of art history.

The inevitable question we must finally ask is how does Updike's reviewing compare with that of Edmund Wilson— not so much because Wilson's alpenstock ("mantle" seems cumbersome for so intrepid and agile an explorer) at *The New Yorker* was handed down to Updike, as because every serious author of short journalistic criticism in America must be measured against that august touchstone. There has been no one yet to match Wilson's tireless venturesomeness, intellectual ubiquity, stylistic pungency and pugnacity, and that breath-taking jostling of idiosyncrasy and common sense that kept the reader, whether approvingly or disapprovingly, always agog. Yet Updike, in his more relaxed and only slightly less decath-lonic fashion, does not trail far behind. Whether one holds his more celebrated fiction in low or high esteem, one cannot deny that his criticism enhances his stature as that rarest of American birds, the man of letters.

[1983]

THE LAST OF THE VINE

Randall Jarrell, *Kipling, Auden & Co.*

WITH the publication of *Kipling, Auden & Co.,* the fourth and final collection of Randall Jarrell's essays and reviews, it behooves us all to join in grateful rejoicing: America has one more major critic of literature, the arts, culture, and, therefore, life. Alas, Jarrell wanted to be a major poet, but was only a fine minor one; being a critic, even a great one, meant relatively little to him. Perhaps that is partly why—in 1965, aged fifty-one like his beloved Rilke—he died of letting a car run him over.

Yet Jarrell should have known better, and in a way did, since he wrote: "A good critic—we cannot help seeing when we look back at any other age—is a much rarer thing than a good poet or a good novelist." For "a critic is half writer, half reader: just as the vices of men and horses meet in centaurs, the weaknesses of readers and writers meet in critics." So, "unless you are one critic in a hundred thousand, the future will quote you only as an example of the normal error of the past. . . . Critics are discarded like calendars. . . ." Jarrell was that one critic in a hundred thousand who remains a perennial, undiscardable calendar.

With his initial collection of criticism, *Poetry and the Age* (1953), Jarrell established himself as a remarkably viceless centaur: both a careful reader whose perception never flagged, and a writer whose lucidity and elegance no amount of prodigality could deplete. And somewhere between the perceiver and the purveyor was the sifter, the assayer with enough love not to be blind to faults others overlooked, enough purity not to be jaded about virtues others discounted. Here were capital reassessments of Frost, Whitman, Stevens, and Williams, among others, as well as reflections on poetic "obscurity," on the nature and value of criticism, and on the "situation of the poet." Not only did these essays state their subtle points with exceptional clarity, they also managed to be almost continuously epigrammatic. We read them, as Jarrell said about Malraux's art criticism, "Breath[ing] irregularly and jerk[ing] our heads from side to side, like spectators at a tennis match."

Again in his second collection, *A Sad Heart at the Supermarket* (1962), in the first posthumous one, *The Third Book of Criticism* (1969), and now in *Kipling, Auden & Co.,* we find that "a passage of ordinary exposition" is not ordinary at all, but an extraordinary exposé or a panoramic insight, with shocks of recognition or revelation coming at us from one edge of the page to the other, leaving us indeed in the head-jerking exhilaration of spectators at tennis, one of Jarrell's two or three favorite sports.

Insights and judgments expressed with supreme limpidity and wit—such a gift cannot pass unnoted and unresented by those who do not possess it. Add to this the vengefulness of poetasters who were the victims of Jarrell's skewering ironies, and it is small wonder that his reputation still lags behind that of a Lionel Trilling, whose loftiness hovered far above the vulgar necessity of straightforward negative reviewing; or of an Edmund Wilson, whose occasional attacks disappeared into the aura of the grand old man of letters with the happy knack of making his very crotchets rays in his halo.

Consider what Jarrell could do in the earliest of these pieces, a review of ten books of fiction written when he was twenty-one. About Erskine Caldwell, he remarks: "A writer may be just as sentimental in laying undue emphasis on sexual crimes as on dying mothers: *sentimental,* like *scientific,* is an adjective that relates to method, and not to matter." Pretty astute for such a young critic, especially if you realize that twenty-one in a critic corresponds to roughly fifteen in a poet or composer. Or take this, about Gale Wilhelm: "Her characters, like Hemingway's, are noble. I can recall some characters in literature who I thought were virtuous in the highest sense—Prince Myshkin, for instance—but none of them was ever *noble.*" Already Jarrell had read so much, and so well, that there is nothing arrogant about his sounding as if he had read all books; his distinction between virtuous and noble characters could come, in fact, only from reading widely and wisely.

A few years later, in a review of poems by Reuel Denny, we find: "Mr. Denny is wonderfully academic—here at last is what everyone has been dreading, a poet to take Robert Hillyer's place (going on the safe assumption that Mr. Hillyer is dead) . . ." and this at a time when, as Jarrell must have known perfectly well, Hillyer was as alive as ever he was. About Joyce Kilmer he said: "I do not want to give the impression that his poems are unusually absurd—unusually anything; if they had not existed, it would have been necessary only to copy them." Notice how the mild irony of "unusually absurd" yields to the sarcasm of "unusually anything," and how this in turn leads into the quiet annihilation wrought by that slight substitution: *copy,* where the allusion to Voltaire led us to expect *invent.*

The wit advances by leaps of the imagination and bounds of stylistic suppleness. Here is Jarrell at twenty-six about Pound in 1940: "I had thought of Ezra Pound as the one thing constant in this fleeting world. Continents sank under the sea, empires fell: Vienna fell, Canton fell, Warsaw fell: the unmoved sage sat on at Rapallo, like Idiosyncrasy on a monument [again that fine effect by changing one word]—the warm Italian breeze bore out over a universe of cretins his condemnations and invective, his *wd*'s and *cd*'s and *shd*'s, his American slang unparalleled outside the pages of an English novel." The irony spreads—like one well-pitched blot of ink devouring an entire sheet of blotting paper—from the man to the work, from the preposterous notions of the *Cantos* to their stylistic caducity. And Jarrell continues, brilliantly and justly destructive, but without disallowing that Pound "is obviously one of the most talented poets of our time," until he answers his own question: What has happened?

> Mr. Pound has never submitted to a fact (or anything else, for that matter) in his life. He has taken all culture for his province, and is naturally a little provincial about it . . . he has shouted so long into the intense inane that his yells, by a natural protective metamorphosis, have taken on something of the character of their surroundings. Early in his life Mr. Pound met with strong, continued, and unintelligent opposition. If people keep opposing you when you are right, you think them fools; and after a time, right or wrong, you think them fools simply because they oppose you. . . . Mr. Pound's universe became more and more a solipsistic one; the form, logic, and amenities of his criticism some time ago assumed the proportions of a public calamity. . . . Writing good poetry is only occasionally difficult: usually it is impossible. But writing what seems to you good poetry is always easy. . . .

I have merely skimmed some of the cream off this dazzlingly thought-out and expressed evaluation; under the cream there is, actually, more cream. Let's go on, however, to the equally definitive—and succinct—assessment of Conrad Aiken's verse: "He could write fairly pleasing and interesting poetry about any subject whatsoever; deprive him of his favorite words and he would be simply unable to write poetry at all."

The danger of writing about Jarrell (as many have noted) is the temptation to do nothing but quote him; thus I would love to reproduce *in extenso* the notice of Marya Zaturenska's *The Listening Landscape,* a critical performance of sustained and controlled devastation, but must content myself with the conclusion: "[Zaturenska's] pieces are like stage scenery, imposing and successful to the glance, coarse to a closer look: approximations. Poems like 'The White Dress' or 'Forest of Arden' show her at her rather disquieting best; they are rough and evitable successes—the work of a poet who has real talent, but not for words." What coolness and pith! Yet hardly has Jarrell dispatched "the country mouse," as he calls her, before he takes on her husband, "the town mouse," Horace Gregory: "A fortuitous collocation of the anti-poetic (plus, for emotion or profundity, the same old romantic and sentimental excesses)" is no way to express the modern world. For Gregory's tough-guy pose, like Hart Crane's, is ultimately as much of a romantic cliché as its opposite: "To the Muse of Poetry—a neutral monist from way back—Crane's burnt match skating in a urinal is just another primrose by the river's brim."

Jarrell is always willing to concede what is good in a mediocre artist, though his praise is often deadlier than his censure. But he passes the supreme test for critics: he sees the good in what he dislikes and the faults in what he reveres. Just consider the agonizingly judicious tributes, strictures, reversals, laments, and guarded exultations with which he followed Auden's later career, the decline from primacy into prestidigitation: "A little of the time Auden is essentially serious, and the rest of the time he's so witty, intelligent, and individual, so angelically skillful, that one reads with despairing enthusiasm. . . ." You may think that oxymoron a handsome thing, but there is better yet to come. Auden is that "most professional magician . . . the one who gets bored with magic, who at last has nothing up his sleeve, not even his arm. . . ." In the late poems "the Conscious and Moral Auden is, quite consciously and immorally, coming to terms with the Unconscious Auden by going along with it, letting it have its way—and not just in life, where we can do and gloss over anything, but in poems, which are held against us by us and everyone else. . . . Auden . . . lies back in himself as if he were an unmade bed, and every line in his sleepy, placid face seems to be saying: *But whoever makes beds?*"

Even more epigrammatic is this, from one of several pieces

about the Kipling Jarrell loved: "Illustration and conversation and description . . . have merged into a 'toothsome amalgam' which the child reads with a grown-up's ease, and the grown-up with a child's wonder." If we are bothered by Kipling's flaws, we must "consent to the fact that good writers just don't have good sense; that they are going to write in their way, not ours; that they are never going to have the objective impersonal rightness they should have, but only the subjective, personal wrongness from which we derived the idea of the rightness." Take that last statement as irony, and it wins the intellectuals over to Kipling; take it at face value, and it flatters and converts the nonintellectual objectors. Can criticism, any criticism, do more? Apothegm is brought to its peak in: "Everybody must have wished at some time that poetry were written by nice ordinary people instead of poets—and, in a better world, it may be; but in this world writers like Constance Carrier are the well oysters that don't have the pearls."

Only those incapable of it would call such criticism oversimplification. These sentences (in both the syntactical sense and the classical one of *sententiae*) fall into place with the snap of finality. But they are not snap judgments. They are distillations of scrupulous reading and thinking, of taste that developed gradually, genius that was there from the start. They are no more oversimplifications than was Columbus's egg: like it, they remain standing—for the eternal good or ill of their subjects.

Admirable, too, about Jarrell is his unshilly-shallying courage. Few other critics have dared to be so unequivocal: "Yeats's poetry—which seems to me far and away the best of our time"; "[Isaac] Rosenberg surely was a poet of no merit whatsoever." Or to name categorically "the best poetry critic of our time, T. S. Eliot," and "the best poet alive," Robert Frost. Even to dissenters, such gallant commitment must loom large and inspiring; and, of course, Jarrell backs up his judgments with cogent argumentation and soaring language. It may be that his uncommonly developed critical faculty hampered his poetic creativity; there is no doubt that his poetry lent wings to his criticism.

At this point the reader may expect an analysis of Jarrell's critical method. The best I can do in brief space is to quote Leslie Fiedler's remark from the memorial volume by various hands, *Randall Jarrell: 1914–1965*: "He is resolutely unsystematic, committed to no methodology or aesthetic theory . . . trusting to insight and depending on his feeling and talking self as a sufficient source of unity—he preferred stringing apothegms together to constructing logical sequences. . . ." But, *pace* Fiedler, Jarrell did construct logical sequences, except that nearly every sentence in the sequence was an apothegm. As I suggested earlier, though, and as Delmore Schwartz said earlier still, "His formulation may seem at first glance to be merely a piece of wit; but it is, in fact, an exact description and insight."

Jarrell, as poet and critic, criticized poetry simultaneously from within and without, which is to say thoroughly. (I disagree with him on only one major point: his overestimation of the very slight talent of Adrienne Rich.) Of course, there have been many poet critics. What has been rare, extremely rare, is the combination of such taste and such wit. Auden, for example, was a witty poet and man, but his criticism, albeit frequently shrewd and always intelligent, is not particularly epigrammatic and witty. Chesterton, conversely, was a wonderfully witty and gnomic critic, but his values, colored by his combative Catholicism, were often too eccentric. Now add to the rare combination of exceptional taste and epiphanic wit an absolute fearlessness, of the kind that the critic has to live in order to get it into his writing. As Robert Lowell said of Jarrell in the aforementioned volume, "He . . . often seemed tonedeaf to the amenities and dishonesties that make human relations tolerable. . . . Heads of colleges and English departments found his frankness more unsettling and unpredictable than the drunken explosions of some divine *enfant terrible,* such as Dylan Thomas." And join to this one more trait, finely observed by Lowell—exacerbated sensitivity: "You felt that even your choice in neckties wounded him." All that, I submit, is in a nutshell what made Jarrell the critic he was.

One can get from *Kipling, Auden & Co.* (the title is infelicitously exclusive) a whole magisterial course in poetry appreciation, and another in the practice of criticism unencumbered by theory. On any number of further subjects—music, fine arts, sports cars, sports, love, society, history (you name it)—there are nuggets of golden wisdom. For instance: "The people who live in a Golden Age usually go around complaining how yellow everything looks." There is additional delight in the many, various, unusual and unusually apt quotations that Jarrell's omnivorous reading and prodigious memory spew up with geyserlike dependability. Take that wonderful ad from 1910 that offers to keep car thieves away by means of "Bosco's collapsible rubber driver . . . so lifelike and terrifying that nobody a foot away can tell it isn't a real, live man. When not in use, this marvelous device is simply deflated and put under the seat. . . ."

Unlike Bosco's driver, Jarrell was the real thing from less than an inch away. I know of no other critic whose tastes were so catholic as to encompass with equal enthusiasm poets as antithetical as Whitman and Rilke, Frost and Laforgue. But he was, finally, deflated into suicide—I don't know whether by a sense of the world's insufficiency or of his own. Members of his family and friends who have tried to make his death appear an accident do him a disservice: they turn into a prosaic mishap what was a meting out of poetic, or at least critical, justice, mistakenly but gallantly applied.

[1980]

ABUSE OF PRIVILEGE
Robert Lowell as Translator

Two concepts of translation have flourished in the Western world. One, which we may call medieval (it earned Chaucer the title "great translatour"), consists of taking a story or poem by a "maker" in some foreign language and retelling it freely in your native tongue. The other, which we may call Renaissance, consists of transposing a piece of writing as faithfully as can be, word for word, into the other language. Except in the drama, it is the Renaissance mode of translating that has prevailed.[1] The explanation is not far to seek.

In the Middle Ages, for religious and political reasons, the concept of individualism was not highly developed. Writers were not particularly concerned with asserting their total originality. Culture was more truly international and there was a certain common stock of tales in prose and verse—the "matter" of Troy, for example—which poets considered their duty and privilege to pass on. With the rise in importance of the poet as individual, and with style becoming accordingly coequal in status with content, respect for one's own individuality made one as different and original as possible in one's writing, whereas respect for another's individuality kept one as true as possible to his manner and matter in one's translating.

[1] Renaissance translations were, to be sure, often very free by today's standards; nevertheless it is in them that respect for original authorship begins.

What Robert Lowell has done in his poetic translations, which he calls "imitations," is to return to the medieval mode: to retell a poem as though it came from some communal stock of plots or *topoi* in his own terms. One difficulty with this is immediately apparent. The medieval poet drew on stories that were vaguely but widely known, and his hearers or readers expected both a certain fidelity to and a certain variation on the themes. This poet-translator was dealing with stories in verse, and long story poems lend themselves to such "retelling": more or less following an outline while improving on some particular, embellishing a detail. But when poetry becomes predominantly lyrical and highly personalized, there is no story line to cleave to: everything is in the imagery, prosody, diction, sound. You render these—to the extent that you are able—or you render nothing.

Lowell's most important body of translations is the volume *Imitations*; let us begin by examining one of the pieces in it, a version of Rilke's famous "Orpheus. Eurydice. Hermes," whose title Lowell renders as "Orpheus, Eurydice and Hermes." Already by changing the quaint punctuation and adding the conjunction, Lowell loses the archaic, epigraphic quality Rilke is after. "Das war der Seelen wunderliches Bergwerk" ("That was the wondrous mine of souls"), Rilke begins; and Lowell: "That's the strange regalia of souls." Three things are clear at once. Lowell will not abide by the blank verse of the original, but will turn it into free verse; he will translate into a colloquial tone ("that's") antipodal to the austere elegance of the original; and he will change the imagery—*Bergwerk* ("mine") becomes, inexplicably, "regalia." The mineralogical image, souls in Hades that go like silver ores through the dark (and Rilke's line is all silvery *i*'s and short *e*'s—"Wie stille Silbererze gingen sie"), becomes sartorial: "regalia" made out of "platinum filaments." Poorer as this is in evoking the underground kingdom, it becomes confused as well: the filaments suddenly turn into what they are in the German, "arteries." But whereas metallic ores can be turned into arteries easily enough, especially in German where *Adern* means both veins and ores, the transition from garments to veins is unworkable. Rilke's image progresses from these veins to the underground blood that feeds the veins of living men. Lowell obtrudes with irrelevant references to powder beetles, otters, and an oak king, thus interrupting the flow of both the blood and Rilke's imagery.

Now Lowell inserts gratuitously, "The dark was heavier than Caesar's foot." What prompts him to stick Caesar's, not to mention his own, foot in it? Perhaps it is free association: *Porphyr* (which he doesn't translate) may suggest to him *porphyrogenetos,* and this, in turn, Caesar. But the result is as clumsy as it is irrelevant. Next, where Rilke is abstract as befits this lifeless realm, and speaks of "wesenlose Wälder. Brücken über Leeres" ("disembodied forests. Bridges over emptiness"), Lowell substitutes "distracted forests"—interesting, but what could it mean here?—and "bridges over air-pockets," which is too specific and more in keeping with the overworld of Pan Am than with the underworld of Pluto. Where Rilke's lake hangs over its distant bottom like rainy skies over a landscape, Lowell's "moaned over the background canals,/ like a bag of winds over the Caucasus." It is hard to see how a lake could be suspended over canals, and background ones at that; moreover, by making the lake moan, Lowell dispels the ghostly silence that hovers over this landscape. Even more perplexing is the presence here of that "bag of winds over the Caucasus," which I can explain only as Lowell's proleptic or prophetic reference to his then unwritten adaptation of *Prometheus Bound*. Where Rilke has "meadows, mellow and full of forbearance [*Langmut*]," Lowell has "terraced highlands, stocked with cattle and patience," which, quite absurdly, implies husbandry in Hades. Again, where Rilke's road is "laid out like a long paleness," which is appropriately mortuary, Lowell's is "unwinding like a bandage," which is merely out of the infirmary. Lowell is, apparently, mindful of the practical schoolboy precept that good writing is full of concrete, specific references and avoids abstraction (e.g., "paleness"); no less apparently, there are exceptions to this rule, exceptions that are called for here.

Rilke's Orpheus, "der stumm und ungeduldig vor sich aussah" ("who, silent and impatient, looked ahead"), undergoes a sad change: "He didn't say a thing. He counted his toes." Not only is this trivial and jocular without being original or funny, it is also preposterously inappropriate: why would—and how could—a man hurrying impatiently toward the world of the living and the return of his wife count his toes as he speeds ahead? The rest of the strophe is not without its minor inaccuracies, such as "His step ate up the road/ a yard at a time, without bruising a thistle," where Rilke has "Without chewing, his step devoured the path in great mouthfuls." Lowell's metaphor is mixed.

Then, however, Lowell mangles one of Rilke's finest images. Orpheus's senses are cleft in two: his gaze runs ahead like a dog, turns, comes back, and time and again stands waiting out there at the next turning ("vorauslief/ umkehrte, kam und immer wieder weit/ und wartend an der nächsten Wendung stand"—the rhythm, enjambment, and alliteration are noteworthy), while his hearing lingers on, like a scent, trailing backward toward her whom he must not look at. But what Lowell has "cut in two" is the "intelligence," so that the conflict of riven senses gets lost. Next, "gaze" becomes "outlook"—too abstract; and, worst of all, this outlook "worried like a dog behind him." The point is now good and killed: the gaze must look forward by Pluto's stipulation, also it is eager to get home and, like an impatient dog that finds its master too slow, it keeps running ahead. But when you have this dog "worrying" something (a bone?) and getting "behind" Orpheus, the image is ruined: sight is now permitted to stay behind at times and thus is not fully cut off from hearing. And when this hearing "breathed myrrh behind him" instead of simply "staying behind" as in Rilke (who pushes the prefix graphically all the way back: "blieb sein Gehör wie ein Geruch zurück"), the confusion is compounded.

The rest of the strophe in translation continues the diminu-
tion of the original. Thus Lowell's Orpheus has behind him
"the currents of air in his blue cloak," rather less effective than
the terse "seines Mantels Wind" ("the wind of his cloak"). At
the end of the strophe, Lowell seems plain ignorant of German. How else explain the reduction of "If he dared turn
around once . . . he would have to see them, the two quiet ones
who silently follow him" (the beauty of the German is chiefly
in the assonance: "die beiden Leisen, die ihm schweigend
nachgehn") to this prosy bit of garbling: "And as a matter of
fact,/ he knew he must now turn to them . . ." etc. On the
contrary, Orpheus is trying very hard not to look back. Where
I put an ellipsis Rilke has a parenthetic statement, characteristically displaced by Lowell, which drives home Orpheus's
aching awareness of the terms of the bargain. If you translate
"müsste er sie sehen" ("he would have to see them") as Lowell
does, "he knew he must now turn to them," the only charita-
ble interpretation is that you do not distinguish this from the
indicative *er musste sie sehen,* which would mean "he had to see
them." Lowell makes Orpheus irresponsible and weak—especially with that casual "as a matter of fact" dragged in out of
nowhere.

I have room here for only a few more of these egregious
distortions. Take another Rilkean master-image: Orpheus's
passionate lament for Eurydice has created "a world of griev-
ing, in which everything is once again present: woods and
valley, and path and borough, field and river and beast; and . . .
around his grief-world there revolved, exactly as around the
other earth, a sun and a starry, still sky, a grief-sky with
disfigured stars. . . ." Lowell imitates as follows: "out of this
sorrow came/ the fountainhead of the world: valleys, fields,/
towns, roads . . . acropolis,/ marble quarries, goats, vine-
yards./ And his sorrow-world circled about her,/ just as the
sun and stern stars/ circle the earth—/ a heaven of anxiety
ringed by the determined stars. . . ." Lowell muddies the clear
correspondence of the world and the grief-world (or sorrow-
world) created by the songs: "out of this sorrow came the

fountainhead of the world" does not identify the replica as Orpheus's grief-stricken poetry. Then, all those specificities— marble quarries, goats, even an anachronistic acropolis— sound more like a tourist folder than Rilke's poem. But the main point here is that in the sorrow-world the phenomena, like the stars, are *entstellt* (disfigured, contorted with pain), something completely muffed by Lowell's epithet "determined." Previously, he gave us "stern stars," which is good fractured German from *Stern* ("star") but hardly conveys Rilke's beautiful "gestirnter stiller Himmel," let alone the loveliness of the real world as opposed to its distorted mirror image in Orpheus's dirges.[2]

Again, Rilke says that Eurydice is so fulfilled with death that she has no desire to live again. In the text we get: "Like a fruit with sweetness and dark, so was she filled with her great death, which was so new that she fathomed nothing." In Lowell: "Like an apple full of sugar and darkness/ she was full of her decisive death,/ so green she couldn't bite into it." Plainly if death fills her with sugar like a ripe apple, that death cannot also be green, unripe, and not to be bitten into. Eurydice, next, is revealed in the "new maidenhood" of death, which Lowell's "marble maidenhead," for all its alliteration and funerary overtones, does not properly identify. Her sex "was shut, like a young flower toward evening," which Lowell mistranslates "Her sex had a closed house/ like a young flower rebuking the night air." That "closed house" is awkward enough, but "rebuking the night air" must be based on sheer unawareness that *gegen* means "toward" as well as "against." On the other hand, setting up an inapposite conflict between the flower and the night air might also be a bit of that characteristic Lowellian violence (as often the poet's downfall as his achievement) intruding uninvited.

Lowell can as easily become overabstract as overspecific. Thus where Rilke says, simply and concretely, that Eurydice was no longer "that blond woman who sometimes echoed in

---

[2] Punning translations like this one probably derive from Ezra Pound, about whose influence on Lowell see below.

the poet's songs," Lowell produces a bloodless abstraction: "that blond transcendence/ so often ornamenting the singer's meters." Rilke continues: "No longer the wide bed's fragrance and island, and that man's possession no longer." Lowell has: "nor a hanging garden in his double bed./ She had wearied of being the hero's one possession." This is a fiasco: who would want to have a hanging garden in his bed, even if it's double? An island in a wide bed is something else again: wide bed suggests ocean bed in which an island is appropriate. Moreover, the beloved's body in a bed, which would otherwise be a place in which to toss shipwrecked, does become a life-saving island. Further, it is wrong to make Orpheus, especially in this context, "the hero," rather than just a man. And Eurydice has not wearied of him; it is just that the magnificence of death is beyond the humble competition of life.

And now consider the end of the poem. In the German, Hermes looks at the backward-glancing Orpheus sorrowfully, and escorts back a Eurydice just as entranced and unconcerned as before, walking "uncertainly, gently, and without impatience." In Lowell, the god looks at Orpheus reproachfully, and "His caduceus was like a shotgun on his shoulder"—a final piece of anachronistic violence that does violence also to the meaning of the poem: it implies the cruelty of the gods, whereas Rilke had in mind merely the incommensurability of life and death.

In his introduction to *Imitations,* Lowell describes his aims as translator or adapter:

> I have tried to keep something equivalent to the fire and finish of my originals. This has forced me to do considerable rewriting. . . . I have been reckless with literal meaning, and labored hard to get the tone. Most often this has been *a* tone, for *the* tone is something that will always more or less escape transference. . . . I have tried to write live English and to do what my authors might have done if they were writing their poems now and in America.

Except for making one wonder why "a tone" should have required such hard labor ("the tone," of course, would), this sounds very fine. But, I am afraid, what Lowell has done with Rilke's poem is neither a decent translation nor a good original work, merely a disaster. Lowell goes on to say, "I believe that poetic translation—I would call it an imitation—must be expert and inspired, and needs at least as much technique, luck and rightness of hand as an original poem." I am not sure I know the difference between technique and rightness of hand, but I can affirm that the foregoing translation is as devoid of them as it is of luck. I cannot escape the feeling that Lowell translates when he is unable to write anything of his own, not so much out of love for the poem translated as out of love for the sound of his own poetic voice. As a result, he rationalizes the admittedly difficult and essentially thankless art of the translator into something grander and even more difficult than it is. In actual fact, a version such as this of "Orpheus" is all the more shocking a failure since Lowell was neither faced with rhyme nor willing to be bound by meter. There are, to be sure, slightly better performances in *Imitations,* but there are also quite a few just as bad. This sort of thing should not be inflicted on great poetry; indeed, it shouldn't happen to doggerel.

For one thing, although Lowell translates from many languages, the only one he admits to not knowing at all is Russian. Yet one is compelled to question his competence in others as well. One would assume him to be most at ease with French, yet he is guilty of howlers even there. Valéry's Helen of Troy (in "Hélène") returns to the world of the living and exclaims, "Azur! c'est moi . . ." ("O azure, it is I!"). Lowell, clearly mistaking this for *L'azur, c'est moi,* translates in his "Helen": "I am the blue!" Still, I suppose one can do good enough work from trots, if one will only abide by them. Yet questioned in connection with his Pasternak imitations whether he knew any Russian, Lowell told the *Paris Review* interviewer, "No, I have rewritten other English translations, and seldom even checked with Russian experts." This does not augur well.

Lest it be assumed that Lowell works better with strict,

rhymed forms, let us look at his imitation of Baudelaire's famous sonnet *"Recueillement,"* which he calls "Meditation." Take the rhymes of the octave: care, here, atmosphere, care/ bare, back, bazaar, back. Not only are there no feminine rhymes to provide diversity as in Baudelaire, but also the similarity of all the vowel sounds is oppressive. Worse yet is the recurrent use of identities (care—care; back—back), which is aurally distressing. Baudelaire, to be sure, has *ville* and *vile* followed by *servile,* but these are homonyms, which, like *rime riche,* are perfectly in keeping with French prosody. The very first thing that strikes us in the French is the cadence, which sets the mood: "Sois sage, ô ma Douleur, et tiens-toi plus tranquille./ Tu réclamais le Soir; il descend; le voici." Lowell has "Calm Down, my Sorrow, we must move with care./ You called for evening; it descends; it's here." In the first verse, Baudelaire makes the two main words the only polysyllables and places one at the end of each hemistich. Lowell has a disyllable in "Sorrow," but nothing to balance it. "Calm down," moreover, is much less affecting than "Sois sage" ("behave yourself," but with overtones of "get wise"), and "move with care" suggests some kind of stealthy maneuver, whereas Baudelaire is asking for dignified, stoical endurance. In the second verse, besides effects of vowel coloring that we can hardly expect the translator to get across, there is the dramatic progression from the long first hemistich to the quick staccato of the second; "le voici," without a verb, being even more brusque than "il descend." The change from nominative to accusative is particularly effective. Lowell does what comes naturally in English, which is fair enough, but here only some brilliant piece of strategy could have done the trick.

Baudelaire's crowd that, under the whip of pleasure, "Va cueillir des remords dans la fête servile," becomes one that "fights off anguish at the great bazaar"—no equivalent for gathering remorse at the slavish feast: Baudelaire's crowd is more than a bunch of revelers trying to forget mortality; it is mankind so cursed with a subaltern mentality that its very exaltation is supine, its most longed-for fruit the bitter one of remorse. Now Lowell proceeds to exhibit that lack of a sense of place (or, sometimes, time) that is so frequent in these adaptations. Thus Lowell's regret emerges from the "sea," although the locale is Paris and the waters those of the Seine as the *arche* further implies. But it is the last two lines in which the translation truly comes to grief. The shroud of night is *traînant* ("dragging"), in motion, not "strung out," which is static. "Entends, ma chère, entends la douce Nuit qui marche" is not conveyed by "listen, my Dearest, hear the sweet night march!" What informs the original is the stately and inexorable forward movement, to whose ineluctability the repetition of *entends* contributes, even while suggesting also the intimate persuasion of a repeated pat on the head. Switching from "listen" to "hear" jettisons both effects. In the second hemistich the sense of spacious progression is achieved by the rubato of *Nuit* refusing reduction to monosyllabicity, and by the open feminine ending of *marche* ("walks") continuing the disyllabic movement of the line. Lowell's monosyllables ending with the incorrect "march" (it should be something like "treading," "pacing," or "advancing"), both too military and too short, suggest a night that arrives like a platoon in close-order drill rather than a blessed solvent in which the poet and his pain can dissolve and cease to be.

But perhaps we should pay special attention to Lowell's versions from the Italian: in the *Paris Review* interview Lowell speaks of his work with that language as something "which I have studied closely." Let us look, then, at his rendition of Leopardi's "L'infinito." In the case of such a particularly famous poem, the translator's responsibility to the original is even greater than usual. Lowell ignores Leopardi's hendecasyllabics and substitutes free verse, not the ideal vehicle for this formally controlled, highly assonant, bittersweet reverie. Again Lowell's sense of place is faulty and plays havoc with the topography: "That hill pushed off by itself was always dear/ to me and the hedges near/ it that cut away so much of the final horizon." But Leopardi is himself on that lonely hill—"pushed off" implies that he is looking toward it; the hedge, too, is *on* the hill—"near it" is utterly mystifying, though "near" does, to be sure, rhyme with "dear." The poet on the hill cannot see much of the farthest horizon because the hedge excludes his gaze. This picture and its symbolic significance are neatly obfuscated by Lowell's circumlocutions.

Lowell now gives us "I reasoned" for "nel pensier mi fingo," which is conjuring up before the mind's eye or imagining— anything but reasoning. Thereupon we read, "I set about comparing my silence to those voices" (of the winds); but that is not at all what Leopardi is comparing: the silences of infinite space with the sound of the wind in the trees. And where Leopardi cherishes "the living season and its sounds," Lowell abstractively extols "things . . . and all their reasons and choices." Leopardi's conclusion, "So amid this immensity my thought is drowned; and shipwreck is sweet to me in this sea," turns into "It's sweet to destroy my mind/ and go down/ and wreck in this sea where I drown." That mind-destruction is irrelevant Lowellian violence, and "go down . . . wreck . . . drown" is clumsy tautology.

But Lowell is supposed to have performed an outstanding service to Montale; what about his translations of that poet? The same problems obtain here. Take "La casa dei doganieri," which Lowell translates as "The Coastguard House." Montale here recalls a visit to a shore-watchers' house (in no sense "a death-cell," as Lowell gratuitously suggests at the very outset) with a woman he loved and still loves. She, however, is not beside him now; she has forgotten that house. The poem is a night-piece; at a crucial point Montale observes, "but you remain alone and do not breathe here in the dark." The dark, significantly, is here, not there; the poet is in it and vainly yearns to share its intimacy with the woman. Lowell translates: "but you house alone/ and hold your hollow breath there in the dark." To transpose the dark and the breath elsewhere, into a house of the woman's, is to miss the sad immediacy of the unshared *here*. The derogatory and uncalled-for "hollow" is likewise detrimental. But not content with missing the place, Lowell promptly misses the time as well. The last stanza continues the nocturnal meditation: "Oh, the receding horizon, where the light of the tanker rarely flares" is changed by Lowell into "Oh the derelict horizon,/ sunless except for the/ orange hull of a lonely, drudging tanker." Derelict horizon is nice, but now the time turns into day: "sunless" and "orange hull" perceptible only by daylight. By splitting the poem into night and day, the actual contrast between past and present, between this moment and the erosion of time, is forfeited.

Elsewhere, too, Lowell takes unwarrantable liberties with Montale. In "L'anguilla," after evoking the life cycle of the eel, the poet asks the woman the climactic question, "puoi tu/ non crederla sorella?"—"can you consider her (the eel) not your sister?" Lowell stands this on its head: "can you call her *Sister*?" Nature, befriended by Montale (the woman cannot deny her kinship with the eel), is kept at arm's length by Lowell (the woman is suspected of inability to confess her closeness to the fish). Again, in "La primavera hitleriana," Montale concludes, after conjuring up the horrors of the occupation, with a hopeful gaze into the future. Lowell, however, omits almost all of that long last strophe in order to be able to end his version, "Hitlerian Spring," on a note of despair, which he heightens by rendering "Oh, the wounded spring is still a feast if it freezes this death to death" as "April's reopened wound is raw!" Of course, in the introduction of *Imitations* Lowell unabashedly proclaims that he has made all sorts of cuts, additions, transpositions, and seems to think it all quite justified. But does a translator—even if he calls himself by another name, such as "imitator," supposed to set him beyond the reach of criticism—have the right to change the entire mood, intention, import of a poem? Of a serious poem by a genuine poet? At what point does an act of "imitation" become an immoral act?

In the interview already quoted, Lowell speaks of the closeness and kinship he felt to the Rilke and Rimbaud poems he translated. We have already seen what he has done to his kinsman Rilke; how has he dealt with that other, no less major kinsman, Rimbaud? If, for instance, one reads Lowell's version of "Les Chercheuses de poux," whose title becomes "The Lice-Hunters" (though it should, of course, be "The Louse-Hunters"; thus one says "fox-hunters" in English, not "foxes-hunters"), one would never guess that Rimbaud wrote it in mingled gratitude and amusement for two maiden aunts of his friend Izembard. Upon emerging from a week's stay in jail, the young poet was deloused by these two Good Samaritans. The poem, irrespective of its autobiographical basis, evokes the mixture of relief and awkwardness a boy feels while lice are being crushed to death in his hair. Lowell's version seems to be about two wicked fairies that descend on a child, perhaps in his fever dream, and somehow cruelly torment him by—of all things—delousing him. That makes no sense and no poetry. As for "Bateau ivre," Lowell announces that he has cut out a third of it; he calls this procedure "unclotting," and the poem "some of the more obscure Rimbaud." What he does keep, however, does almost less justice to Rimbaud than what he omits. As if this were not enough, Lowell takes a couple of poems by Rilke and adds to them stanzas of his own.

I could cite endlessly. What, for example, could be more distasteful than Lowell's taking three poems from Heine's final sequence, *Aus der Matratzengruft,* written with irony, tenderness, and no mawkish self-pity from the very deathbed, and turning these immensely simple yet trenchant poems into maundering, anachronistic, rhythmless lucubrations? One quatrain must illustrate the whole shameful procedure. Heine writes: "My day was merry, happy was my night./ My people cheered me on whenever I smote/ The lyre of poetry. My song was joy and fire,/ It kindled many a lovely blaze." No great poetry in this particular stanza, only the prideful invocation of past happiness, and, in the German, a graceful movement: "Mein Tag war heiter, glücklich meine Nacht./ Mir jauchzte stets mein Volk, wenn ich die Leier/ Der Dichtkunst schlug. Mein Lied war Lust und Feuer,/ Hat manche schöne Gluten angefacht." Lowell comes up with this: "My zenith was luckily happier than my night:/ whenever I touched the lyre of inspiration, I smote/ the Chosen People. Often—all sex and thunder—/ I pierced those overblown and summer clouds. . . ." This is a painful mixture of deliberate and inadvertent misreading. To translate *Lust* as "sex" ("lust") is to perpetuate a traditional freshman boner; the rest may be willful distortion. Heine is happy that both his public life ("day") and his love life ("night") were fun; Lowell's pessimism has to change this to some kind of glum parabola (from zenith to night). Heine says that his poetry was beloved by his public; Lowell turns this into Heine's allegedly unrelenting attack on—whom? The Jews? The Germans? But Heine was never consistent in any of his likes or dislikes. He says his poetry was joyous and fierce (romance and satire), and that it stirred up some pretty passions (this could be taken both literally and ironically). Lowell has Heine somehow deflating his readers with sex and anger. Lowell's image does not work: if the readers are pompous, overblown clouds, why bring in "summer" with its positive connotations?

An imitation such as "Heine Dying in Paris" is not only an act of poetic vandalism, it is also a falsification of Heine's life and of Heine's evaluation of his life. Ostensibly rendering Heine's spirit though not his letter, Lowell is actually lessening the man's human stature (ambiguous as it was) as well as his poetic gifts. This, perpetrated on a dead and defenseless poet, is an act of double indecency. And such cavalier insouciance is rampant in *Imitations*. For example, Rilke's poem that Lowell translates as "Pigeons," and whose original he identifies as "Die Tauben," is not at all "Die Tauben," written in Paris in 1913, but the last of a series of verse letters to Erika Mitterer entitled "For Erika, on the Feast of Praise," dated Ragaz, 1926, only four months before the poet's death. But what are we to expect from Lowell, who says in the interview I have been quoting from that these imitations "were both a continuation of my own bias and a release from myself"? A curious contradiction that! And the introduction to *Imitations* begins: "This book is partly self-sufficient and separate from its sources, and should be first read as a sequence, one voice running through many personalities, contrasts and repetitions." Not only is this megalomania, it is also, worse yet, nonsense. A book made up of so many diverse ingredients can neither be a sequence nor tell us much about the translator beyond something about his translatorial taste and competence. And if one voice really runs through the whole enterprise, the enterprise must be biased and sick to the core. Finally, I doubt that anyone who "first" reads this book "as a sequence" can be expected to come back for a second helping of any kind.

The begetter of Lowell's imitations is, without question, Pound, and particularly the Pound of the versions from Propertius. But though I am no great admirer of Pound's Propertius (and even less of such jesuitical champions of Pound's Propertius as Hugh Kenner), I cannot be wholly unmoved by Propertius's Pound, that is to say, by what Propertius brought out in Pound. But it is precisely because Pound was able to ignore his original so sublimely, and because Pound is a great enough poet in his own right, that the damage to Sextus Propertius becomes an homage to Ezra Pound and English free verse. Lowell, however, is not that free from his models, nor has his free verse the energy and variety of Pound's. It is the neither-fish-nor-fowlness of Lowell's imitations, plus all the red herring they contain, that makes them perverse as translation and unpalatable as poetry. And though there may be only a tenuous connection between literature and morality, there seems to me to be a more demonstrable one between this kind of translation and immorality.

Yet the fault is not entirely that of the poet-translator who, puffed up with a mixture of merited and unmerited praise, loses his sense of judgment. Almost as much to blame are the critics who well-nigh unanimously acclaimed *Imitations* at its publication in 1961, and the critics who in the years since then have not dared to raise a dissenting voice. Typical of the less than enthusiastic reviews was that by Louis Simpson in *The Hudson Review,* which, after some well-taken strictures, nevertheless concluded that Lowell's "translations of Rimbaud and Rilke, for example, are interesting in poetic terms—that is, in every line difficulties of sound and meaning are resolved. To check his 'imitations' against the originals is to learn something about the tact of poetry." That last sentence is not only a gem of overstatement, it is even an inadvertent truth—if one can learn to identify something elusive by its total absence. Hugh B. Staples, in his *Robert Lowell: The First Twenty Years,* considers these imitations "more than translations." As Mies van der Rohe propounded a kind of architecture in which "less is more," Lowell may have produced a type of translation in which more is less.[3]

To turn now to Lowell's most recent dramatic version, *Prometheus Bound.* He calls it "derived from Aeschylus," and I am forced to conclude that Lowell's derivations are no better than his imitations. Modern dramatists have frequently retold Greek myths or Greek dramas, even Greek dramas about Greek myths. The aim of these versions has always been to find a contemporary interpretation or application of the time-honored, timeless originals, so that what emerged was a new

---

[3] Lowell's *Phaedra* is a dramatic imitation: it does to Racine's play what *Imitations* does to the poems it attacks. Two examples will have to suffice. "J'ai revu l'ennemi qui j'avais éloigné:/ Ma blessure trop vive aussitôt a saigné./ Ce n'est plus une ardeur dans mes veines cachée:/ C'est Vénus tout entière à sa proie attachée" becomes " . . . I saw Hippolytus/ each day, and felt my ancient, venomous/ passion tear my body limb from limb;/ naked Venus was clawing down her victim." No comment could be as damning as mere juxtaposition, and I offer none. (I cannot, however, help wondering whether Venus became naked by way of fractured French: *toute entière*—in the altogether.) And again: "O toi, qui vois la honte où je suis descendue,/ Implacable Vénus, suis-je assez confondue?/ Tu ne saurais plus loin pousser ta cruauté./ Ton triomphe est parfait; tous les traits ont porté" becomes "Implacable Aphrodite, now you see/ the depths to which your tireless cruelty/ has driven Phaedra—here is my bosom:/ every thrust and arrow has struck home." It will be noted that even where the meaning is more or less conveyed, the exquisite cadences of the original verge on, or indeed hurtle into, cacophony. What we are left with is (in a line of Hippolytus's perhaps significantly not translated by Lowell) "Cette indigne moitié d'une si belle histoire!"

work by Molière or Giraudoux, by Kleist or Hebbel, that was an integral part of its author's *oeuvre*. Lowell's *Prometheus Bound* sets out, likewise, to be "an unbinding of Prometheus for us." In the same program note, Lowell asserts that though "nothing is modernized . . . my own concerns and worries and those of the times seep in." Lowell also affirms that there are no tanks or cigarette lighters in the play. True. There are, however, microbes, phalanxes, wastes of the moon, and various references and allusions to atomic cataclysm, to the Freudian son cutting off (in Lowell's flavorsomely idiomatic language) "his father's balls," to the war in Vietnam. But that kind of seepage is only natural.

What is unnatural about this play is that it is not as a whole about anything identifiable. Of drama as such there is not a great deal in Aeschylus, but at least we know what the issue is: power and intellect join hands to rule the world, power usurps the throne and casts down intellect, power finds (this is only hinted at in this first play of the trilogy) that it needs intellect to save it from self-destruction. In Lowell there is only generalized violence; expatiation on a variety of muddy issues (and mud, as Francis Fergusson has noted, is a dominant presence in the play); and indulgence in a thick, clotted prose full of headstrong, runaway images. The language is something of a cross between Abraham Cowley and André Breton, but with a typically Lowellian savagery informing most of it. The violence of the diction and the limpness of the "action" form about the only notable conflict in this work, which does, in a way, manage the impossible—to be more static than Aeschylus's drama.

If one looks very hard, one may catch references—besides those already mentioned to the Bomb and the Vietnam War— to the plight of the powerless intellectual in the Great Society; worthy themes all, but none is developed, nothing goes deeper than surface ripples. There are felicitous lines and occasional forceful tropes. Thus Prometheus says of men, "I gave them hope, blind hopes! When one blind hope lifts, another drifts down to replace it. Men see much less surely now, but they suffer less—they can hardly draw breath now without taking hope." Or this, from Io about her growing up: "I could speak to the cattle. Later, I could speak to the herdsman. Later, I could speak to my father." But there is also an abundance of nonworking imagery, blindly drifting tropes: "When I close my eyes, I am able to think. I can almost move. In the darkness, the stars move down on us like burning metal." How do we get from closed eyes to stars? And if the stars shower us with sizzling metal, doesn't that interfere with our thinking? Again, Io says: "I seem to wade through my own heaviness, as if I were a pasture sinking back into a marsh." This conjures up a pasture wading through a marsh; moreover, wading through implies emergence, whereas sinking is submergence. But most typical is this from Prometheus to Io: "Water spiders will slow and clot on the thick syrup of your shadow." That is not metaphor, merely mucilage.

Whole paragraphs are murky. Thus Prometheus says, "I saw the head of Cronus was a slab of meat, and it seemed to me if I could cut through the slab of meat, I would find a silver ball. The ball was there, it cracked open, inside it another, and another and another, and then suddenly, the head of Cronus, my own head, and the heads of all the gods were broken spheres, all humming and vibrating with silver wires. The whole world was an infinite sphere of intelligence." This is an uneasy mixture of Andrew Marvell and René Magritte. But as for meaning: if Cronus is a fool, why are there all those silver balls of mind in him? Why should mind be a set of Chinese boxes, or balls? And what are silver wires doing *inside* those balls? And how do the spheres continue to hum and vibrate (i.e., function) when they are cracked open? Such imagery troubles one on the page; on the stage, it absolutely refuses to move forward.

One of the sources of confusion in the play is that it keeps contradicting itself. On the simplest level we get Ocean saying that one of his hands is paralyzed "from managing . . . this big bird" on which he rides. A few lines later he tells us "I guided him with my mind. No reins or bit." On a profounder level, Prometheus regrets: "I should have been more loyal to the idiocy of things," yet this is contradicted by what the *status quo* harbors: "The nothingness of our beginning is hard at work to bury us." These statements often sound wonderful until one starts to analyze them: "We have always wanted to escape with our lives from life"—upon scrutiny, this apparently penetrating paradox means either that we don't want to die or that we don't really want to live, probably true both ways but not very startling in either. Or again, "I know that I must suffer, because I suffer without grandeur or nobility"; this rings out like a giant aperçu, but proves to be only a medium-sized non sequitur. Perhaps, however, we should examine a longer sample; here is a fragment of Prometheus's interminable prophecy to Io: "You will run faster than you ever ran before, but more peacefully now, as if you know [sic] the flies would never catch up, that now you had only to fight off the death-stings of your own body, that hound-pack of affliction, closing in to kill you, poor bleeding hound, your tongue dripping, your teeth snapping, the fur of some animal darting before you, grizzled white mixed with the red hairs, like the beard of Zeus, but no face there, no flesh, only a force dragging you forward to your death, a power to empty, so tireless and so cruel, it could only come from God." One gets a sense of meaningless, luxuriating brutality; of metaphors that clash and collide and cancel one another out—unless they don't make sense to begin with. What sort of an animal could Io—poor, persecuted cow— possibly be hounding? And why?

The one episode that seems to exercise Lowell's imagination is the story of Io. In seemingly endless speeches, Io and Prometheus rehearse her seduction by Zeus, her frantic, tortured wanderings, and her ghastly death to come. In fact, it is as if Lowell described at least three separate death scenes for her, each more agonizing than the previous, yet, for all that, not very different. The attitudes toward women and sex in the play are about as horrified as those toward despotism and death. Thus there is a gratuitous attack on Prometheus's wife, on the female Seabirds (Lowell's version of the chorus of Oceanids) who are made even less appealing than in Aeschylus, and, in a way, on Io, whose sufferings are dwelt on with monstrous relish. And what is one to make of Io's account of the first results of impregnations by Zeus: "two flies, as big as . . . thumbs . . . had crawled from my swollen stomach, half-dead, and already beginning to mate," an event on which Hera commented, "When women are warm enough to make love, the gods send them flies. The flies rise from your sticky flesh, are warmed by your heat, and kept alive by the blood from your thighs[!] or the milk from your breasts." We have come a long way from Aeschylus, but in what direction?

I find it impossible to say what the meaning or purpose of Lowell's play is. During certain scenes when Prometheus staunchly resists direct or indirect blandishments to play ball with Zeus, I almost wonder whether the whole thing is not an allegory of Lowell's famous refusal to appear at a garden party on Lyndon Johnson's lawn. If not that, it is just an all-around scattering of animosities, some justifiable, many not even fathomable. Structured hatred has produced, among others, some of the great plays of Ibsen and Strindberg; promiscuous hostility can at best, as here, yield a few good but disconnected moments.

Such as it is, Lowell's play did not deserve the treatment meted out to it by Jonathan Miller, who directed it for the Yale Drama School last May [1967]. In a program note characteristically five times longer than the author's, Miller explained his method. Prometheus figures in a myth that has "mysterious and erratic power." We learn next that "speaking with strict accuracy, plays of this sort [Greek drama? Plays based on myth? Plays whose protagonist is chained to a rock?] are located in something which for want of a better word we might call antiquity." Traditional productions of them, we learn, don't work, "But the point about these plays is that in some mysterious way their dramatic thrust seems to survive and transcend the time and space in which they were originally set." For want of a better word, we might call such utterances fatuity of the most advanced sort. Next we read that "contextual dislocation" is required for these myths to "become renewed and invigorated." In other words, we must update the play, see "round the edges of the text," but be careful to avoid changing dates only "to create a chic shock." The great difficulty with *Prometheus* is, it seems, that it "takes place in a primeval limbo," has characters "little more than talking vapors" and that any "antique" or "literal" rendition "would be almost ludicrous and even a bit pansy." Particularly to be dreaded are the "mechanical constraints indicated by the stage directions."

So Miller picked the early seventeenth century to set his play in, because it was a cultural watershed, because classical forms were then being reprocessed, and because the period was "full of peculiarly horrible politics . . . The Thirty Years War, Regicide . . . military theocracy." As a result, the setting (beautifully designed by Michael Annals) represents the outer walls of a "shattered castle keep" with strong overtones of the inside of Piranesi's dungeons. Thus the set suggests both that Prometheus is inside a dungeon and that he romps around outside it on a platform across a moat; and, to create total confusion, Lowell's text repeatedly locates him in "the thin, disabling air of this mountain top." Hephaestus and his crew seem, in the dark, to chain him to something as he utters piercing cries. When the lights go on, he is unchained and his trousers are bloodied, which, as Francis Fergusson has pointed out, may mean that he has been castrated. Thereafter, he moves about quite freely, despite frequent references to his immobilizing chains (presumably those "mechanical constraints [of] the stage directions" by which no director worth his salt would be hamstrung or castrated). The costumes are shabby and seventeenth-century; Miller tells us they stem from engravings by Jacques Callot, and indeed the characters look like disbanded *lansquenets,* impoverished petty gentry, or, rather, like a bunch of impecunious strolling players imper- sonating them. Ocean, for example, appears in a battered admiral's hat and epaulets, and the Seabirds seem to be wear- ing the hand-me-downs of the lady of the manor. When the Seabirds harangue Prometheus, they often read from their schoolgirl slates; when Prometheus utters some of his homi- letic tirades, they take these down as dictation on the slates. Sometimes he goes too fast for them and is obliged to slow down or repeat a word or two. When Prometheus tells Io she will bear a child to Zeus, the three virtuous ladies of the chorus avert their eyes and cover their ears in mock, or perhaps real, horror—who is to say what in this production is mock, and what real? When Io—desperate, tormented Io—asks Pro- metheus, "Tell me where I must go," she playfully slaps his arm and pettishly stamps her foot. When Prometheus tells her that he need not describe all the monsters she'll encounter— "When you have seen one, you have seen them all"—every- thing stops while the entire cast enjoys a hearty laugh. At the end of Act One, where Io is heartrendingly beseeching Prom- etheus to help her, all go off merrily for an intermission: the supposedly chained Prometheus offers his arm to the allegedly fly-haunted Io, and they walk off together across the fosse followed by the Seabirds animatedly chattering away among themselves. As Act Two begins, they all come out in the same informal way, plainly a troupe of down-at-heel actors in that most horrible age of regicide, military theocracy, and Puritan shut down of the theaters.

It is clear that Miller does not believe in doing things by halves: why settle for being "almost ludicrous and a bit pansy" when you can be absolutely laughable and completely camp? On opening night, he also invoked Brechtian alienation, but that holds no water here, either: in Brecht there are full-bodied plots against which the alienation effect can pit itself; in Aeschylus, the very remoteness, superhumanness, and ele- vated tone make alienation redundant. No, in reducing *Pro-*

metheus Bound to the level of seeing "round the edge of the text," or, in other words, beyond the fringe, Jonathan Miller was simply using that directorial prerogative made famous in our time by Elia Kazan and especially Peter Brook, which consists of the director's virtually rewriting the play, and which corresponds on another plane to Lowell's imitations of Rilke, Rimbaud, and the rest.

There are two principles at work here. First, by adapting a celebrated poem or play, or by "dislocating" the play one is directing, one cashes in on the original's prestige while also exhibiting one's prowess in the alterations; at the same time, one can always blame the foreignness or intractability of the original for one's failures. Second, one uses this as a surrogate for whatever creativity one finds oneself lacking. A poet runs out of poetry of his own, so he makes it out of someone else's, rather like the fly that lays its eggs in the living body of a certain caterpillar for the larvae to feed on. A director wishes he were a playwright, and, by way of staging it, rewrites the play entrusted to him. It is all part of that most terrible contemporary phenomenon in the arts that mistakes for inspired innovation what is merely lack of respect.

[1967–1968]

CURSED AND BLESSED

Ian Hamilton, *Robert Lowell: A Biography*

A ONCE popular concept of the poet that still lingers on in some quarters perceives him as: (1) an eternal child, unable to look after himself and living by the grace and nurture of friends and sympathetic strangers; (2) a heavy drinker and womanizer—except when he is (2a) a drug addict or pederast; (3) capable of saying and doing the most outrageous things; and (4) mad as a hatter. The notion, though more often wrong than right, fits Robert Lowell with classic—or should we say romantic?—precision. Although three of his contemporaries curiously resembled him in this—John Berryman, Theodore Roethke, and Delmore Schwartz, all of them, at one time or other, his friends—Lowell, a more prominent poet and public figure, emerges as the foremost *poète maudit* of America's recent past.

Lowell's life, then, if you look kindly at the above schema, was an archetype; if you don't, a cliché. Either way, the biographer who would do it justice must possess extreme tact, lest he, too, fall into oversimplification. The ideal biographer, of course, would be a divinely dispassionate creature, presenting all the germane information, interpreting the facts as perceptively as the works, but leaving ultimate judgment to the reader. Yet the great virtue of impartiality does not generate the kind of energy needed for an arduous biography such as Ian

Hamilton's remarkable, nearly 500-page *Robert Lowell,* into which went extensive reading, tracking down, and interviewing. Such books can be motivated and sustained only by passion: usually love, but sometimes hate. That Hamilton's book, on such a recent and pitfall-surrounded subject, can cleave so close to calm sympathy rather than to rowdy partisanship, to critical appreciation rather than to worship or envious malice, is no small achievement in itself.

Hamilton began the job at a time when most of the major figures in the poet's life were still alive and atingle with memories that the biographer taped in extensive interviews. He also read all manner of correspondence, not only from and to, but also *around* Lowell. For not since Wilhelm Meister (and he, after all, was only a fiction) did anyone have such a concerned society of protectors in back of him, counseling one another on how best to be of help, and stepping forward—singly or in teams—whenever actual assistance was needed.

Moreover, as a poet and former editor of two distinguished journals, Hamilton is well equipped to deal not only with Lowell's writings, but also with their sundry revisions, for the poet had an "inability (and this lasted all his life) to read a page of his own work without rewriting it." Thus certain parts of *Robert Lowell*—and they are among the best—read like the beginnings of a variorum edition of Lowell's poetry. Furthermore, Hamilton has culled the writings of some of Lowell's literary friends, associates, and spouses (e.g., Peter Taylor, Norman Mailer, Jean Stafford—though, inexplicably, not Elizabeth Hardwick) for fictionalized but not unrevealing aspects of his subject's life and personality.

Robert Traill Spence Lowell IV (1917–1977) was the son of Robert Lowell III, an amiable but weak naval officer who later went into business, and his powerful, domineering wife, Charlotte, née Winslow. That Robert senior came from a lesser branch of the illustrious family and that he lacked ambition were unforgivable flaws to Charlotte; and the always uneasy marriage provided young Cal (as he was to be dubbed at St. Mark's, his fancy but unintellectual school, either after Caliban, whom he once played, or after Caligula, whom he often tried to emulate) with a background in infighting and manipulativeness. At St. Mark's, where he distinguished himself mostly for roughness and slovenliness, he acquired his first pair of lifelong friends, followers, and amanuenses, Frank Parker and Blair Clark, as well as his first literary mentor, the English teacher and poet Richard Eberhart, whom Lowell was later to surpass, criticize in turn, and finally condescend to.

After a couple of unsuccessful years at Harvard, then under the presidency of his cousin A. Lawrence Lowell—to whom Cal was to write, some years later, one of the most patronizing job applications in recorded history—the future poet was placed by his mother under the care of Merrill Moore, a poet-psychiatrist (and, subsequently, Charlotte's employer and lover) who was connected to the Fugitives, and it is by him that Lowell was directed southward, to become the disciple of Tate and Ransom at Vanderbilt, and thereafter of Ransom at Kenyon College, where he formed lasting friendships with Peter Taylor, Randall Jarrell, and John Thompson. Despite tremendous uncouthness and messiness, he ended up graduating with top honors in Classics, becoming the class valedictorian and, as it were, Ransom's poetic son and heir. At Kenyon, Cal had begun writing poetry more seriously, though at age twenty-one he could still commit verses such as "his sinewed eyes, wildish elliptic orbs, / compressed intensity in jellied meat" and "—O felly blank, O general review!"— perhaps the worst line of printed English poetry since the notorious "O Sophonisba! Sophonisba, O!"

There followed the marriage to the novelist Jean Stafford, whose face he smashed up in a car accident (he was the worst of drivers), and, after she underwent long and painful surgery, resmashed with his fists during one of his periodic rages; according to Blair Clark, she lost 25 percent of her good looks in the process. Jean was a Catholic, as were such friends as Mrs. Tate and Robert and Sally Fitzgerald, and Cal was converted, to become, as a friendly Jesuit put it, more Catholic than the Church. He used his faith, in verse and prose, as an

eminence from which to fulminate against enemies and terrorize friends. Later, when, as Stafford felt, Catholicism had
served his literary purpose, Cal began his gradual return to
Episcopalianism and rabid anti-Catholicism. During World
War II, Lowell refused an army commission, became a
conscientious objector—although he was jailed for one year
rather than the customary three, and at a minimum-security
prison—thus beginning his career as a public figure with the
much-publicized "Declaration of Personal Responsibility"
sent to FDR. Eventually, Cal and Jean acquired the first of the
poet's beloved New England houses, and began a life of assiduous drinking and boisterous entertaining. Meanwhile Lowell
had also started his career as teacher or poet in residence,
which he was to pursue intermittently, here and abroad, until
his death.

Then came the first major extramarital affair—with
Gertrude Buckman, the ex-wife of ex-friend Delmore
Schwartz—and the declaration that, reborn in this new love,
Cal was leaving Jean. Stafford agonized as Lowell, now Poetry
Consultant to the Library of Congress, was reborn yet again,
this time thanks to a Washington socialite, whom, during an
intimate evening at home, he almost strangled in a fury over
her inadequate reading of Shakespeare's plays. A pattern was
formed: about once a year Lowell's madness would come upon
him in concert with "a new life" through a grand passion
(though sometimes without), and leading, after some extraordinarily manic behavior, to confinement in an institution,
domestic or foreign, according to where he happened to be.

Meanwhile Lowell was rapidly making his literary reputation: first as our leading formalist poet with *Lord Weary's Castle*; then, after a slump with *The Mills of the Kavanaughs*
(deemed too obscure and long-winded), as our leading *vers
librist* (under the influence of a new mentor, William Carlos
Williams) with *Life Studies*. Divorced, Lowell had met Elizabeth Hardwick at Yaddo—where, in one of his bursts of anti-
Communist mania, he waged an ugly and unsuccessful

campaign against the allegedly fellow-traveling director of that artists' colony—and, in 1949, married her. Hardwick stood by him—lovingly, helpfully, heroically—through the annual outbursts of what, after many false diagnoses, was finally labeled manic-depressive psychosis; for twenty-three years she endured through the failures of psychotherapy, shock treatment, and Thorazine. Much later, lithium was, for four years, able to control Lowell, but by that time he was married to Lady Caroline Blackwood. When lithium and Blackwood also failed, and *that* marriage broke up, Lizzie let Cal stay with her for ever longer periods. Returning from a short visit with Caroline, Lowell died of a heart attack in the taxi arriving at Hardwick's door. Clutched in his hands was a parcel containing Blackwood's portrait.

We follow, too, the politicization of Robert Lowell: his anti-Vietnam War activism (fairly mild); his open letter to LBJ to refuse an invitation to the White House he had previously accepted; his association with and campaigning for Eugene McCarthy, which may have helped scuttle Honest Gene's unsanguine bid for the Presidency. There are the literary friendships (and virtually no enmities, unless with Auden) with older poets such as Frost, Eliot, and Pound; with contemporaries, such as Jarrell, Berryman, and Elizabeth Bishop; with students or disciples, such as W. D. Snodgrass, William Alfred, and Adrienne Rich, who was later to turn on him ferociously. There are brief but perspicacious evaluations of Lowell's poetic and dramatic output (the latter less important to Lowell: he found playwriting "so easy—it's a crime"), and fastidious excerpts from contemporary reviews of Lowell's works, not forgetting the adverse ones. Quite often Hamilton manages such lapidary insights as "it was probably harder for Lowell to discard rhymes than to invent them," and, by way of explaining the slackness of the later work, "The death of Randall Jarrell had removed the one critical voice Lowell was in fear of."

There are fine accounts of Cal's comradeships with men—

some literary, some not—who helped him variously: editing his poems, getting him in and out of hospitals, soothing his hurt or angry women, or just listening to him; and no less fine accounts of relations with mistresses and wives, who had happy periods ensconced or traveling with him; endured bouts of vehement infidelity or violent insanity; fumed at being abandoned by him, and yet often went on caring and wanting him back—sometimes even advising him about other women. What Hamilton cannot quite convey, however, is the reason for all this love and support lavished on this difficult, sometimes charming but as often inconsiderate and hurtful, man.

Was it his poetic eminence? The magic of the Lowell name? The large, strong, good-looking exterior that nevertheless betrayed vulnerability? The albatrosslike helplessness when not immersed in his own element, poetry? These and other reasons are adduced and illustrated with quotations and anecdotes, but the Lowell appeal does not become concrete and palpable. Perhaps it could not, in any biography. Hamilton evokes the fury of later composition—four pseudo-sonnets a week for a couple of years. He conveys the grimness of the years when, conversely, no poetry would come. He summons up the tragicomic ecstasy and horror of the manic phases, and the "dark, post-manic and pathological self-abasement" of those that followed. Yet out of tactfulness, or the modest wish to keep himself out even though he knew Lowell, we get something like a documentary whose voice-over narration has not yet been added to the soundtrack.

So we read Lowell's proposal, from one of his sanatoriums, to Elizabeth Hardwick:

> How would you like to be engaged? Like a debutant [sic]. WILL YOU? How happy we'll be together writing the world's masterpieces, swimming and washing dishes.
> P.S. Reading *The Idiot* again.

Was ever lady in such humor wooed—and won? Doesn't this call for a comment from the biographer? Did Lowell really think he and Lizzie would be united in masterpieces? Or was he joking? Or mad? Or just reading *The Idiot?* Again, Hamilton gives many instances of Lowell's truly atrocious spelling, even hints at dyslexia, and reproduces early drafts of poems crawling with spelling and grammatical errors. But he does not speculate on what this means psychically never mind psychiatrically.

Or Hamilton will quote in extensive and riveting passages the pleas of Lowell's American friends, who knew Lizzie and Harriet (Cal's daughter by her), not to publish in *The Dolphin* certain poems incorporating raw and embarrassing autobiographical data, such as excerpts from Hardwick's anguished letters and phone calls. He will then quote English friends, who did not know the persons and miseries involved, urging the poet to publish everything in the interest of art. And he records faithfully Lowell's own squirmings and tergiversations. But he never enters the fray himself. This is admirable. Yet why doesn't he bring in, for our enlightenment, how other poets have dealt with like problems—for example, George Meredith, in his very similiar quasi-sonnet sequence *Modern Love?*

And although Hamilton handles Lowell's madness excmplarily—without stinting, smirking, or glossing over—he is not always fair to those who feared or reprehended it. Thus he paraphrases "enemies" of Lowell's: "How was it, they could disingenuously wonder, that this renowned spokesman for correct liberal causes persistently 'revealed,' in mania, a fascination with tyrants and monsters of the right?" Why that "disingenously" and those quotation marks? There is no doubt, from Hamilton's own account, that Lowell was obsessed with Hitler—Jonathan Miller reports on Cal's keeping a copy of *Mein Kampf* on his shelf under a *Fleurs du mal* dust jacket—and that, as Blair Clark states, "an absolutely infallible indication of an impending manic episode was an interest in Hitler." At the University of Cincinnati, where many mistook Lowell's mania for the proper behavior of a famous poet, they were rewarded with a lecture in praise of Hitler just before the lecturer was carted off to the psychiatric ward. (In more benevolent accesses of frenzy, Cal, helped perhaps by lithium, would identify himself with Alexander the Great or Christ, not Hitler.) At an English clinic, Jonathan Raban found Lowell holding a piece of steel and declaring it was "the Totentanz. This is what Hitler used to eliminate the Jews." Yet Hamilton seems tacitly to censure Caroline for considering "the mere mention of Hitler . . . a danger sign." In view of the rages she had experienced, small wonder.

Even more unappealing—because not excusable by madness—was Lowell's snobbery. This meant "taking the . . . aristocracy and family tradition seriously," as Cal wrote his parents; going on the odd "little ancestor worshiping spree" and composing lists of antecedents, and growing ecstatic over a distant cousinship with Boswell; questioning everyone on a trip to the Orkneys about Traills and Spences; and even understatedly flaunting the sumptuous way in which he, like other Lowells, would be buried. At Milgate, Caroline's country house, Cal enjoyed playing the country squire, and was delighted to identify himself and his wife as "Robert and Lady Caroline Lowell." He was vastly overimpressed by his fleeting association with Jackie Kennedy, and announced in one of his crazier moments that "LBJ has asked me to be in his Cabinet." To Peter Taylor he recommended England as having "safe schools, no negroes." And with snobbery came arrogance: "Father, forgive me/ my injuries,/ as I forgive/ those I have injured." (Not those who injured me.) No comment on all this from Hamilton.

But even on the poetry, Hamilton sometimes allows himself a slight bias. Though hard on Lowell's poorer works, he will let slip a remark about "one of Lowell's most perfect [sic] and impenetrable" images, as if impenetrability were a virtue; he will gush about the line "The Lord survives the rainbow of His will," even though, as he says, no one has been able to explicate it. There is something show-offy even about Lowell's best poetry—a hunting for effect that Jonathan Raban was to describe as follows: "For almost every sentence that Cal ever wrote if he thought it made a better line he'd have put in a 'never' or a 'not' at the essential point." Raban also cites Cal's first quoting Mme Flaubert's line about her son, "Till the mania for phrases dried up his heart," in the poem on Flaubert, then blithely changing it to "enlarged his heart," thus reversing the meaning and rewriting history. Calvin Bedient cites Lowell's recasting "Often the player's outdistanced by the game," as "Often the player outdistances the game," which is better, but testifies to a lack of passionate conviction. No comment from Hamilton.

Still, the book is splendidly researched and documented, and its general knowledgeableness and subtlety are couched in a pleasingly perspicuous style. I found few factual errors: the poetess Louise Labé is transsexualized into "Louis Labe," the magazine *Commonweal* becomes *Commonwealth,* and Ted Roethke's fatal heart attack is said to have occurred on a tennis court rather than, as it did, in a swimming pool. This cancels the prophetic tone of Lowell's last letter to Roethke: ". . . to write we seem to have to go at it with such singleminded intensity that we are always on the point of drowning." Nicely put; indeed, much of Lowell's prose is most impressive. On the whole, I prefer it to his poetry, which, though full of powerful images and resonant lines, is a poetry of patches rather than of rounded poems.

And what a strange patchwork the life itself was: fraught with triumphs and exultation, beset with periods of humiliating sequestration and self-torment. All the same, when you consider how Lowell was taken care of by so many devoted hands, never obliged to do uncongenial work or left in serious financial straits, and recognized and exalted during his lifetime, you will agree with Elizabeth Bishop's remark to him: "In some ways you are the luckiest poet I know!"

[1982]

HIGH-CAMP CAMEOS

Frederic Prokosch, *Voices: A Memoir*

I HAVE read little of the poetry of Frederic Prokosch and less of his prose, but I would not be surprised if his new book, *Voices: A Memoir,* ended up among the most involving things this once highly regarded poet and novelist has written. Just who is Frederic Prokosch, now seventy-five and living in his villa near Grasse, the perfume capital of the South of France? Recent handbooks on American literature tend not to list him.

The son of an Austrian-Czech immigrant, Eduard Prokosch, a distinguished professor of philology who taught at the Universities of Wisconsin and Texas, then at Bryn Mawr and Yale, Frederic went to Haverford and got a doctorate from Yale with a thesis on Chaucerian apocrypha, abstruse enough to please his learned father. He combined in himself the cultivated, polyglot graces of his Slavic and Central European background and of his good Anglo-American training (he also attended Cambridge University), and was a young man of exceptional handsomeness, with "the dark good looks of an advertiser of razor blades," as the envious Harold Acton put it. Prokosch, Fritz to his friends, had all the advantages. As *sportif* as he was intellectual and artistic ("You look more like an athlete than an aesthete," Wallace Stevens told him), he was a fine tennis and outstanding squash player, enthusiastic driver of spiffy cars, early success as novelist (*The Asiatics,* 1935) and poet (*The Assassins*, 1936), and was published in both Geoffrey Grigson's *New Verse* and in Eliot's *The Criterion*. Prokosch had the further benefit of ready access to the international homosexual elite whom Auden—his master, nemesis, and object of fierce love-hate—wittily dubbed the Homintern.

Furthermore, Prokosch was an avid listener, fearless accoster of assorted celebrities, and a kind of intellectual agent provocateur, able to toss out with apparent innocence the most outrageously confession-begetting questions, as when he asked A. E. Housman why he picked the wretched poet Manilius to become an expert on, or inquired of Wallace Stevens, "But why did you take up insurance?" So Prokosch met and, as it were, audited more greats in literature and the other arts, society, and sports—and even espionage—than you and I meet tradesmen. With galloping pencil and tentacular memory, he gathered up their appearances, conversations, tics, and behavior, much as he collected butterflies, another of his ruling passions. There was no question of his writing ability; even a hostile critic such as Randall Jarrell (reviewing Prokosch's 1941 verse collection, *Death at Sea*) pronounced this "decerebrate Auden" to be "second-hand and second-rate—but oh, so effective!" A scarcely less distinguished arbiter, John Peale Bishop, proclaimed *The Assassins* "an impressive first book," and Prokosch "a poet to be watched" and "even now, a poet to be read." I know few memoirs more hilariously readable than *Voices,* in which Prokosch has collected, now that the sitters are safely dead, his sketches from life, enhanced with a little cross-hatching from memory and distortion from mischief.

How truthful are these portraits or cameos, etched in equal doses of acid and affection? Not so malicious as those by Fritz's "glittering friend" Gore Vidal, yet as unsparingly witty as they can be benignly graceful, these brief, sprightly, pungent evocations are a mite too chiseled and bejeweled, too minutious and self-consciously shapely, to be the mere jottings of even an unusually fluent pencil and well-schooled memory—the mere record of unvarnished truth. As early as 1941, the admiring

Francis Scarfe described Prokosch, in *Auden and After,* as one who "writes with an immaculate but somehow fatal ease"; and Dylan Thomas may have spoken truer than he knew in a 1937 letter to Vernon Watkins, deploring Prokosch's being known "only as a dilletante [sic]." For who but a dilettante—albeit a dilettante of distinction—would send hand-printed Christmas pamphlets of his work on fancy paper, year after year, "from Paris, Florence, Bangkok, Venice, and Singapore, bound in mauve, vermilion, violet, with labels of chromium, oak, and ambergris [how disgusting; but, of course, he means amber]" to become, in later years, "a trouvaille for bibliophiles and a triumph at Sotheby's"? And who but a most exquisite dilettante would collect stamps, but only those "that bore the portraits of butterflies or . . . reproductions of illustrious painters"?

Of a butterfly mounted on a wall, Prokosch says, "He looked vividly alive but too symmetrical to be alive." At a party for the Sitwells, Prokosch reflects about Sacheverell that "his very dilettantism gave him a special authenticity, just as a butterfly is authentic by grace of its frivolity." These are characteristics of the writing in *Voices*: a certain frivolity that confers more credibility on butterflies than on memorialists, and a teased stylistic symmetry that looks vividly alive, but is too good to be totally, breathingly true. It is a style reminiscent of Gertrude Stein, just back from Spain when Fritz and his college roommate visited her. We read:

> The Goyas were very nice and the El Grecos were more than adequate but I felt no rapport with the Murillos and Zurbaráns. Alice said that she profoundly distrusted the Zurbaráns but we trusted Mallorca when we came to Mallorca. We walked through the market and sniffed the melons. The melons of Mallorca are subtle and alluring, but the fish of Mallorca are unpretentious and naive.

This is very much the Stein style: the non sequiturs, the premeditated pseudonaiveté, the all too neatly balanced and refrain-laden sentences, and that perfectly Steinian anticlimax "we trusted Mallorca *when we came to Mallorca.*" But a clever and knowledgeable parodist could also have made it up. Certainly Miss Toklas could, as when, years later, with Gertrude dead and her own "moustache . . . turned from black to mottled gray," she told Fritz: "Gertrude's sense of severity never failed her when it came to artichokes."

Voices is, above all, an exercise in high camp. A mode that no one, not even Susan Sontag, has conclusively defined, it is a genre excelled in by homosexuals, though not exclusively theirs. It consists of taking the trivial seriously and vice versa, of saying shocking things with nonchalant elegance, of uttering dazzling paradoxes that contain piquant grains of truth, of keeping a straight face in the midst of an (often self-induced) shambles, of creating an artificial world of highly concentrated, style-besotted farce. It is the spirit of Boris, the homosexual child in Gide's *The Counterfeiters,* whose every yes is jostled by a no, and the reverse. It is not so much that high camp tramples on the truth as that it uses it as a trampoline for self-sufficient fancy.

Once more, then, how truthful are these memoirs? Clearly, the eight-or-nine-year-old Fritz (with a certain tendentiousness, dates are kept out of the reminiscences) could not have perceived the visiting Anna Pavlova like this: "She rolled her eyes luridly and glanced around the room, as though detecting a lurking threat in the bowl of roses and the bust of Mozart. Her sunlit fingernails danced about under her chin, capricious as fireflies." And it is questionable whether even a youth of high-school age could have spotted a "half-despairing search for truth" in the "groping little pauses of Thomas Mann." And are we to trust the college student who, meeting James Joyce at Sylvia Beach's Paris bookshop, quotes the master as follows:

> Good heavens, what did you say? The stream of consciousness? What's *that*? . . . Molly Bloom was a down-to-earth lady. She would never have indulged in anything so refined as a stream of consciousness. When I hear the word "stream" uttered with such revolting primness, what I think of is urine and not the contemporary novel.

Then Joyce proceeds to find this supposedly innovative device in Shakespeare, Sterne, and even Aeschylus. Well, self-contradictory as this sounds, some of it is believable as a display of cantankerous gamesmanship. But it is that solecistic genteelism, "lady" for "woman," that rather queers it all for me.

Yet the mature Prokosch often seems just as unreliable. Could Bernard Berenson really have used as the hallmark of good literature its ability to make him giggle? Thus Thackeray was good because he passed the giggle-meter test, but Austen and Dickens flunked it. Then: "Dostoevsky makes me giggle. Even Chekhov now and then. But Hardy—goodness me, who ever giggled at *Tess of the d'Urbervilles*?" Can we believe that Hannah Arendt, predicting the end of culture as we know it, "kept smiling with delight at the prospect of calamity"? (Well, maybe.) Or that Vladimir Nabokov, in luxurious and productive semiretirement in Montreux, could be fairly described as a "lonely and sad and disillusioned lepidopterist"—except perhaps by a fellow lepidopterist who, indeed, was disillusioned and sad at the disparity in their nonlepidopteric achievements?

Nevertheless, you want to believe at least some of it, and most of it is fun when read in the proper spirit. True, the method is somewhat sleazy, and was nicely pinpointed by Lady Emerald Cunard:

> How clever of you, Frederic. . . . You somehow coax people into saying not what they really *want* to say but into what they all of a sudden cannot help saying. You catch them on the wing. Maybe you have learned it from your butterflies. How wicked if you ever wrote it into a book, how very mischievous!

And that's how it works: Prokosch will ask Marianne Moore whether she doesn't really prefer things to people, and forthwith she admits to it, just as Isak Dinesen is made to confess her belief in ghosts, and Edith Sitwell is prodded into comparing herself with Pope.

He does, however, get his celebrated acquaintances to look

and sound credible. I can see Joyce having "the air of an embittered provincial surgeon," Virginia Woolf "sitting at a desk behind a waterfall of galley proofs," Cyril Connolly seeming "alarmed by the thought of an impending banality," Dylan Thomas being "not quarrelsomely . . . but gently and caressively tipsy," T. S. Eliot looking "pale and shy, with ears and fingers alert for pain," Edmund Wilson sporting a "babyish expression of benevolent implacability" as he drops a mayonnaised shrimp into Sitwell's coiffure, and this about Somerset Maugham—a landscape in a figure: "Two deep yellow slopes ran down past his nostrils and settled, like glaciers, over the chasms of his mouth." I can see and hear them: Wallace Stevens who "scratched his snowy chin and his face grew still more recondite" while he mused about tea sent to him in a diplomatic pouch: "I would love to sail in a pouch. If not in a diplomat's then perhaps in a kangaroo's." Thomas Wolfe, who struggled with chopsticks in a Chinese restaurant and exclaimed: "I'm incapable of discipline. I'm like the Mississippi River. Does the Mississippi have subtlety? Does the Mississippi use chopsticks?" And E. M. Forster being gently, dimly bitchy about D. H. Lawrence: "I am not referring to his accent, which at best was debatable. I am thinking of his outlook, which was highly *simpatico*. . . . Whatever he may have done in print, his private life was above suspicion."

This sort of thing tells us more about Forster than about Lawrence, and still more about Prokosch. Repeatedly, these celebrities condescend to, ridicule, or savage other celebrities, but while artistic or moral reputations collapse all around him, Prokosch's persona and stature remain wonderfully unscathed by the flying debris. Some of these essays contain more than one portrait each—either consecutively or encapsulated one within the other. Thus "The Martyr," a cool skewering of Frank and Queenie Leavis and their *Scrutiny* acolytes, Wilfrid Mellers (whom Prokosch spells "Wilfred Meller") and L. C. Knights, begins with a rapid sketch of Guy Burgess; both are brilliant, but the Leavis group portrait is satire at its most funnily mordant. And so "The Black Veil," a rather more amiable but not innocuous evocation of Edna Millay, has ensconced inside it, in Millay's words, an equally stunning anecdote about her fellow poet Elinor Wylie. But often the anecdotes are too trivial and trivializing, like those conversations with the famous or near-famous that Prokosch himself dismisses in a style that is the epitome of camp: "They meant nothing and they meant everything, they were true and yet false, they were brilliant yet ridiculous, they were profound but profoundly meaningless."

In his essay-review of *Voices* in *The New York Review of Books,* in which Gore Vidal pays homage to both the writer and the man, we read: "By and large, he has chosen not to praise himself. . . ." This is nonsense. Prokosch tells how, fully clothed, he dove into the Venetian lagoon to bring back the wallet Chagall had let fall in; and how, stark naked, he rescued from the treacherous ocean, at Guincho in Portugal, a young Frenchwoman whom no one else in that nocturnal beach-party crowd could save. We read about his kindness to beggars and contempt for the social elite. The great praise him: Housman remarks that "*The Asiatics* is a little masterpiece," Gide calls it "brilliant but at the same time peculiarly peasantlike" with an "unmistakable Slavic earthiness," Forster declares its fabrications "much too poetic to have been based on vulgar tourism." He is told by Lady Cunard, "If you hadn't been so handsome I might never have met you"; but he is also erudite as all getout, reading and rereading (in the original) Cervantes and Homer, translating Hölderlin and Goldoni, discussing music with Beecham and Gieseking, and art with Berenson and Peggy Guggenheim. But in the end he gives it all up, to become a recluse in his house near Grasse and, though winning prizes at the odd bridge tournament, seeing no one and mostly communing with nature. And writing. We could almost believe that he is as Tennessee Williams described him in a letter to Donald Windham, "much nicer than I expected and quite simple and kindly."

Yet even Williams in a later missive comments: "The South

of France is only good if you like to swim and gamble and consort with chic tourists, which Prokosch does"—the same Prokosch who writes Tennessee that "Florence is full of blue-eyed blonds that are very tender-hearted and not at all mercenary." Whether traveling the world over in search of truths about nature and art, or whether cruising about in more mundane pursuits, Prokosch does not strike me as especially simple and kindly. Particularly unpleasant is his frequent strategy of letting the great reveal themselves in physical or spiritual nakedness, vulnerability, or ludicrousness—even ugliness—to provoke a Prokoschian outburst of sudden, patronizing love for them in their absurdity—thus with Dylan Thomas, Eliot, Hannah Arendt, Edith Sitwell, among others.

Still, Vidal is roughly right when he says that Prokosch "tried to distill the essence of each voice rather than what might have been exactly said." The essence of each voice: the technique is summarized in Prokosch's charming and provocative meditation on Goldoni and the *commedia dell'arte,* where "the comical portraits descended into caricature":

> I was enthralled by this vision of a stage where human beings enhanced their humanity by putting on noses. Far from growing more artful they somehow deepened their naturality, and their foibles and eccentricities looked all the more convincing. Once at a carnival, where the dancers gathered in the Campo San Angelo and scampered about on the bumpy flagstones, I was amazed when they took off their masks at midnight, and instead of looking more human they looked insipid and expressionless. The mask had been discarded and a deeper vacancy was revealed.

Clearly, Prokosch believes in the truth of masks and caricatures. And read as *commedia dell'arte,* his memoir works. Yet the problem with masks is their provenance. Thus Prokosch describes Curzio Malaparte's appearance: "It looked as if a mask had been grafted on a face which has been profoundly and incurably mutilated. . . . I wondered whether the mask was the result of clumsy surgery or of a laceration of the spirit still deeper and more unfathomable. " So one wonders about these vignettes: are their caricatural distortions the pithy exteriorizations of spiritual quirks or are they imposed by the surgery, clumsy or wickedly clever, of our memorialist? Often enough, however, Prokosch convinces me of his telling, if not the truth, what Anatole France called *une histoire plus vraie que la vérité.*

When the style is not excessively affected and clockwork-like—which it fairly often is—it can be quite winning, as in this passage from a visit to Stein and Toklas during their wartime exile at Bilignin in the French Alps: "Gertrude and Alice crossed the lawn to look at the radishes. All I saw was their behinds—that of Gertrude broad and imponderable, that of Alice very narrow and anxious and vulnerable. I was touched and reassured by the sight of their behinds." So you can add to the not-to-be-underestimated gossip value of *Voices* its mock-soulful cheekiness, especially apt when dealing with such vaguely camp figures as Gertrude Stein and Norman Douglas, or even, on a higher level, E. M. Forster.

And there is an added attraction: the autobiographical elements that, in a dotted line, trace the life story of a many-faceted, much-traveled man, whose activities stretch from chasing butterflies to speculating about the relationship of landscape and people, from struggling with the writing of fiction (no less fascinating for the results' mediocrity) to being an American agent in wartime Portugal and Sweden. If Prokosch is sometimes cavalier about other people, even to getting their names wrong ("Katya" for Katia Mann, "Lucchino" for Luchino Visconti, "Caillaux" for Roger Caillois), he is fastidious enough about F. P., recording even comments and situations unflattering to himself. A fascinating subplot is the history of his curious involvement with W. H. Auden. This does not appear to have been a sexual one, but Prokosch began with intense feelings for Auden, the poet whom, above all others, he emulated, learned from, and desperately tried to equal, if not surpass. His name for it is a metaphysical rather than physical infatuation.

Accordingly, Auden keeps popping up throughout *Voices,*

either in person or in conversations. The more Auden slights or waxes ironic with Prokosch, the more Prokosch belittles his later work (which was, indeed, poorer) and portrays him as petty, ravaged, forsaken by the Muse—satanic rather than, as once, Luciferian. Animal imagery proliferates: "His iguana-like eyes had grown jaded and suspicious and the creases in his neck looked like the folds in a dead balloon . . . and his hands, cracked and swollen, lay on the table like lobsters." At their last meeting, "the wrinkles were deepening, the pouches were thickening. The eyelids looked scaly and shifty, reptilian." The piece about Arendt is even called "The Monster," referring not to Hannah (many chapters have archly oblique titles) but to Geoffrey Grigson's having called Auden a monster, which elicits Arendt's feeble defense: "Our Wystan is often monstrous but he is never quite a monster." Finally, in the section on Malraux, who, along with Mann and Santayana, is pronounced one of the three most intelligent men Prokosch knew (the three most intelligent women, in a parallel piece of campy list-making, are Stein, Arendt, and Marguerite Yourcenar), Auden figures as a model of "intuitive intelligence . . . dissipated when he started to distrust his intuition." Absorbing account, this, of a doomed, one-sided, "metaphysical" love affair: vindictive, but not without its truths.

Literary loves and hates, *Voices* abounds in them. Also in racy anecdotes, true or trueish Also in conjurings-up of people and places, which, when they don't miss the mark, dart straight to the core of one's memory. And, toward the end, as Prokosch grows old and reclusive but content amid nature and memories and continuing work, there is even a bittersweet tenderness. There are lumps of ungraciousness in this book. There is also finespun delight.

[1983]

ENGLISH
LITERATURE

SIMPLE BUT NOT SIMPLISTIC

Stevie Smith, *Collected Poems*

STEVIE SMITH was a most curious poet. Small and little-girlish-looking to her dying day (in 1971, when she was sixty-eight), she worked for a magazine-publishing company and lived in remote North London, unmarried and taking care, most of her life, of an aunt who had helped raise her. For Stevie and her sister had had a sickly mother, and their father kept dashing off to sea ever since the poet was a tiny child. From her wise investments, though not from her writing—which included three novels and much book reviewing along with her poetry—Stevie was able to live cozily in her unfashionable Palmers Green house, even if getting to the parties she loved in the chicer parts of town was a bit of a problem. She wrote steadily and published in sundry magazines; her first collection of verse, *A Good Time Was Had by All,* dates from 1937, when she was thirty-four; a fiction, *Novel on Yellow Paper,* had come out the year before.

Slowly, steadfastly her reputation grew; particularly popular were her poetry readings. She was finally able to resign from her office job; after years at it, she also gave up as regular book reviewer for the *Observer.* Almost equally prized as her poems were her whimsical line drawings with pencil or ball-point pen, some of which were published as a book. They seemed to be illustrations for her poems, yet they were mostly doodles that the poet appended more or less appositely to her verses when these would come out in book form. Most of her life she seems to have been an enemy of religions without quite breaking away from the Church of England; though she perpetually contemplated suicide, she also managed to enjoy her life quite considerably. In 1969, she won the Queen's medal for poetry; in 1971, she died of a brain tumor. Her last poem was the second one to be entitled "Come Death." As James Mac-Gibbon writes in the preface to her *Collected Poems,* "Although she had lost her power of speech . . . she made it clear that she did not wish her life to be prolonged, handing me the typescript of that poem with the word 'death' encircled."

Shortly after her death, the poet's celebrity was boosted by Kay Dick's book *Ivy and Stevie,* a double portrait of Smith and I. Compton-Burnett. Now (1976) we get *The Collected Poems of Stevie Smith,* edited by James MacGibbon with Linda Stearns, a beautiful piece of bookmaking. The last collection included here, *Scorpion and Other Poems,* was not published as a book till after the poet's death. Although the present 591-page tome calls itself *collected,* it should really be titled *complete,* for it brings together all of Smith's discoverable poems in, as nearly as ascertainable, chronological order, along with all the available drawings. There is much to be said for this inclusiveness, for Smith's very particular, peculiar, pointed yet personable tone is present even in many of her weaker poems; still, there are others (like "The Ride," "The Crown of Gold," or "A King in Funeral Procession," for instance) that I doubt whether Smith would have wanted preserved. So selectivity might also have been justified. It is not the only contradiction, as we shall see, that adheres to the poet's work.

Smith went to a good girls' school, but never attended university; she falls somewhere in the middle between a sophisticated, cultivated autodidact and a naive artist with a yearning for the primitive. This is one of the governing dualities in her work; the other is her agitated fluctuation between love of life and longing for death, further complicated by the fact that "life" was as often as not a purely imaginary construct, and death appeared vari-

ously as absolute obliteration or some ineffable form of survival. These dichotomies seem to be responsible for the stylistic
and ideological duality that affects most of her poems: one cannot be sure whether they are capriccios, diversions, jests content
to suggest in passing something provocative and serious, or, on
the contrary, outbursts of despair seeking solace by turning to
playfulness. A playfulness, by the way, that can be rather acrid at
times.

"She had no view, only views," writes Calvin Bedient in the
chapter on Stevie Smith in his *Eight Contemporary Poets*. Except
for certain verbal excesses and one or two questionable assertions, this essay is so fine that it must be the despair of all of us
who write about Smith after Bedient. Still, there remain some
elaborations, clarifications, and discriminations to be made.
Thus it is significant to observe that most of Stevie Smith was
already there in *A Good Time Was Had by All*: she is one of those
poets who ripen early and whose poems do not yield up their
chronological order to inference. Consider the third piece in *A
Good Time* etc. (and, accordingly, in the *Collected Poems*), the
very autobiographical "Papa Love Baby":

My mother was a romantic girl
So she had to marry a man with his hair in curl
Who subsequently became my unrespected papa,
But that was a long time ago now.

What a folly it is that daughters are always supposed to be
In love with papa. It wasn't the case with me
I couldn't take to him at all
But he took to me
What a sad fate to befall
A child of three.

I sat upright in my baby carriage
And wished mama hadn't made such a foolish marriage.
I tried to hide it, but it showed in my eyes unfortunately
And a fortnight later papa ran away to sea.

He used to come home on leave
It always was the same
I could not grieve
But I think I was somewhat to blame.

This poem exhibits all the characteristics of Smith's most mature versification. Her poems are often written in a latter-day adaptation of the medieval *prosimetrum,* a mixture of verse and prose. In certain other poems of hers this is even more apparent, yet note here, too, how the first three lines, though irregular, are iambic-anapestic in character, whereas the fourth defiantly refuses to scan. Lines five and six (and this, too, is typical: Smith seldom writes in stanzas of fixed length, preferring instead strophes of whatever number of lines suit her need, rather like prose paragraphs) are quite flat and prosaic, but seven through ten are an almost strict quatrain in alternating trimeter and dimeter. The effect in the next four lines is achieved by variations in rhyme: the abundant feminine rhymes of lines eleven and twelve, whose euphony somehow makes more absurd the alleged precocity of the child Stevie. The following couplet, with its exiguous rhyme, makes deliberately matter-of-fact, even offhanded, the reporting of a crucial and drastic turn of events. In the last quatrain, the effect depends on the prolonged final line with its typically unsettling Smithian ambiguity: is it serious or mocking, humble or arrogant, factual observation or preposterous exaggeration?

For the tone shifts with quicksilver impudence from didactic ("What a folly it is . . .") to colloquial ("I couldn't take to him at all . . ."), from mock-tragic ("What a sad fate to befall/ A child of three") to drawing-room comedy ("And wished mama hadn't made such a foolish marriage . . .") to that pensively confessional—or, for a child of three, perhaps rather self-aggrandizing—last line. In between, there is even the worldly-wise, "But that was a long time ago now," and the world-weary, "It always was the same." The result is disturbing: we feel like mourners at a funeral where the coffin is dropped and the corpse rolls out. We are torn between horror and mad giggles. It is one of Smith's basic strategies: to tell a sad story banteringly, to couch the elegiac in *vers de société* or even children's verse. The childlike badinage can rise to the heights of outright cruelty, however, as in a much later poem, "The Wedding Photograph," where, at the very moment the nuptial picture is taken, the bride is already meditating about how her hunter husband will die: "The old lion on his slow toe/ Will eat you up, that is the way you will go." Yet all this malice is couched in something approaching baby talk.

The sixth piece in *Collected Poems* is the first of Stevie's many epigrams, a genre in which she achieved many fine successes, but which also can reveal her at her most self-indulgent. "Alfred the Great" runs: "Honour and magnify this man of men/ Who keeps a wife and seven children on £2 10/ Paid weekly in an envelope/ And yet he never abandoned hope." The wit lies in rhyming a grandiloquent honorific, "man of men," with a mere numeral; and in that almost irrelevant weekly envelope, which tragicomically rhymes with the grand, life-giving abstraction, *hope*. The subject of Smith's epigrams may become almost lofty, as in the much later "Man Is a Spirit": "Man is a spirit. This the poor flesh knows,/ Yet serves him well for host when the wind blows,/ Why should this guest go wrinkling up his nose?" Or the epigram may be traditionally caustic: "The Englishwoman is so refined/ She has no bosom and no behind." Often, to be sure, Stevie's epigrams become mere doodles: "All things pass/ Love and mankind is grass." But sometimes they reach the classic purity of the late "Some Are Born," a serene miniature elegy worthy of the Greek Anthology:

> Some are born to peace and joy
> And some are born to sorrow
> But only for a day as we
> Shall not be here tomorrow.

Notice how beautifully the suspension at the end of line three works: "as we . . ." As we—what? The previous lines were end-stopped, and so this *we* floating out there, suspended and suspenseful, is disquieting by contrast. Yet we hope for the best: we have been promised a chagrin that lasts but a day, after all; presently we learn that it is our very life that is transient, that the cure for sorrow, death, may be worse than the malady. But not so for Stevie Smith, the friend and lover of death, who makes the soothing lilt of her last line an act of perfect reconciliation to its idea.

We are forced to wonder, however, how the same epigrammatist can concoct something so silly as "Come": "Venez vite/ Avec moi/ To the street/ Of the Cow." This may have some private significance, but why put it into even the most ephemeral kind of print? Smith often writes macaronic verse—the other language being usually French, occasionally German, once or twice Latin—but it never works. Sometimes she even ruins a perfectly good piece of work by this means, such as the late poem "On Walking Slowly After an Accident," which ends, after nineteen good English lines, with this accident: "*Ni le chagrin de* dandelion seed"—bilingual for no conceivable reason. When macaronics are not funny or appropriate to a situation, one must assume that they represent some personal aberration, here presumably the autodidact's need to show off her culture.

Continuing with the early work, we come upon "Progression," a fine example of how an outwardly humorous poem can soak up biting acidity in the witch's caldron of Smith's art, an art that, as she put it in "The New Age," "is wild as a cat and quite separate from civilization." Conversely, "To the Tune of the Coventry Carol" shows the poet at her most liltingly lyrical, writing in strictly formal sestets, but with a touch of tart didacticism supplying a counterweight to all that melodiousness. The last stanza runs:

> O lovers true
> And others too
> Whose best is only better
> Take my advice
> Shun compromise
> Forget him and forget her.

Such a poem has clearly earned the right to dispense with commas, and so look more rapid to the eye, more open and spilling over into the world that surrounds it.

Or take the initial quatrain of the much looser "Spanish School":

> The painters of Spain
> Dipped their brushes in pain
> By grief on a gallipot
> Was Spanish tint begot.

Here the childlike, tripping movement of the verse is strangely, disturbingly belied by the somberness of the subject. The sound, too, has an obsessive insistence: the syllable *pain* is prefigured in *painters* and *Spain;* the hard *g* of *grief* is echoed in *gallipot* and *begot.* This light verse hides a sonorous punch, as numbing as the dark, ponderous pigments of the Spanish painters. *Gallipot* is particularly apt, meaning here the tiny receptacle in which colors are mixed, without losing its bleak primary meaning of medicine jar.

"Night-Time in the Cemetery" shows Smith in one of her antihumanist moods, but still preserving her charm: "These people are not familiar/ But strange and stranger than strange peculiar/ They have that look of a cheese do you know sour-sweet/ You can smell their feet." In "Up and Down," the poet, again in a misanthropic disposition, displays her tonal brilliance; the last tercet reads: "I shall be glad when there's an end/ Of all the noise that doth offend/ My soul. Still Night, don cloak, descend." After a pair of rather too perfect tetrameter lines, lulled by the singsong, we are hit with a verse whose two middle feet are spondaic: "Still Night, don cloak." The thud is overpowering. Smith was to repeat this effect in her very last poem, "Come, Death (2)." And the effect is heightened by the apt change of coloration: the tonally bright "Still Night" is followed by the dark vowels of "don cloak," suggesting the tenebrosity she wants and gets from the night. There is some archaism here, in the *doth* and in the capitalization of

Night, but archaism is a device Smith often uses effectively to give her poems Biblical, Elizabethan, or other desired overtones.

Stevie Smith was a great one for doing odd things with her last lines. Thus, in the somewhat later "For a Dead Vole," she will end a strictly cadenced and rhymed poem with a totally prosaic line, conveying that the hitherto very alive vole is now thoroughly dead. A similarly effective use of the prose closing line occurs in one of her last poems, "Oblivion." Explaining this change from verse to prose, Calvin Bedient writes, "Smith sometimes uses meter as a foil, to show where we have been or would like to be before showing where we are." But whereas an uncadenced—or, as it were, anticadenced—passage can be telling by way of contrast, to allow an entire poem to slip into prose is a different matter. "Major Macroo," for example, continually teeters on the edge of prose and sometimes falls in, as in the four closing lines: "Such men as these, such selfish cruel men/ Hurting what most they love what most loves them,/ Never make a mistake when it comes to choosing a woman/ To cherish them and be neglected and not think it inhuman." That is very well put, but it is put well in prose, not verse, terms. There is something too nakedly declamatory, too sensibly pedagogic, direct, and unresonant about it; poetry, even at its simplest, works more subterraneously, elusively—even insidiously—than this. Among Smith's later works, there are entire "poems" that, despite all their good sentiments (or perhaps because of them), are sheer prose. Take, for instance, the piece that begins: "Of all the disgraceful and abominable things/ Making animals perform for the amusement of human beings is/ Utterly disgraceful and abominable. . . ." Poetry can be a lot of things, but it can never be that foursquare. There are not even those morsels of meter to act, in Bedient's phrase, as a foil.

"Numbers" is the first (though, as we shall see, anomalous) example of a Smith poem from which signs—respectfully outstretched arms or mockingly pointing fingers—direct us toward other poets' work. Stevie was a fine parodist and a no less fine echoer by way of homage; here, however, we have a case of pure coincidence (or prolepsis): the poem prefigures in concept and mood Jacques Prévert's much more considerable "Inventaire." This rapprochement is thought-provoking, for although Smith has not, to my knowledge, been compared with Prévert, there are distinct similarities between them in subject matter, technique, and ideology (e.g., the satirical antireligious poems). Into the realm of parody, or at least that of allusive persiflage, falls a piece like "To the Dog Belvoir" (title) "Whom I Saw in a Dream Push Baby N. from under a Brewer's Dray and Die in His Place" (subtitle): "The stricken Belvoir raised a paw and said:/ I die a perfect gentle quadruped" [poem in its entirety]. Aside from the joke of a poem shorter than its full title, and the fun of a quasi-heroic title referring to a mere idle dream, there is the parodic allusion to Chaucer's "parfit gentil knight," which is funny because of a slight inherent ridiculousness in the very word *quadruped,* and because a knight on his horse really is a sort of quadruped, and because the very idea of a knighted dog is ludicrous.

All through this first collection of Smith's, *A Good Time Was Had by All,* I repeat, the distinguishing characteristics of her oeuvre are present and, for the most part, fully developed. Thus "The Parklands" is one of those quasi-Blakian protoballads, with overtones of Rossetti and Poe, that crop up throughout the *Collected Poems,* although in this particular mode Smith did get better with time. But not even she could improve on the perfection of "Road Up," a kind of poem that was to become a specialty of hers. In it, a strange person is caught in an unusual act, and the whole thing is depicted with exemplary concision and sharpness, while the deeper implications are left to us to decipher. Here the technique is the reverse of what we observed in some previous instances; it is now a switch from looser, more prosaic lines to a concluding couplet of greater lyrical intensity and in stricter versification. In six lines, the poem describes a derelict sleeping in the middle of the busy Euston Road rather than on the more appropriate Thames Embankment; occasionally, he tosses in his sleep and gives the road a thwack. The poem then ends: "Was he dowser tapping for water I wonder,/ Or was it a sudden spasm of rage that split his dreams asunder?" Notice how the absurdity of the penultimate line—this sleeping bum is clearly no dowser— makes the last, more plausible but still highly fanciful, line seem to be the soul of believability. More important, however, is the image of rages ripping a dream apart and hitting the pavement; what more perfect emblem of urban despair, of poverty in a megalopolitan setting? Contrasted with the jocular dowser, the bereft, angry dreamer becomes virtually a tragic–heroic figure.

Yet the many-sided Stevie Smith sees not only the horrors but also the consolations of city life; Palmers Green, her habitat, is transformed in "Suburb" into something at least tolerable by nightfall. Again and again, Smith finds powerful ways of saying ordinary things, which would not be especially unusual in any poet; what is unusual is that the power is achieved through ambiguity: is this utterance mocking or sad, pathetic or hilarious? When a rejected mistress describes how not being looked at by her lover feels, she exclaims: "O never castle in the hills of Spain/ Was half so much of nothing as thy Jane. . . ." Castles in Spain, of course, we all know about, but there is something wonderfully crazy about specifying the topography of such a nonexistent castle: "in the hills of Spain." True, castles are often on hills, and the exigencies of meter demand a few extra syllables here; still, to describe a landscape whose *sine qua non* is its nonexistence! And then to make Jane not "half so much of nothing," as if nothing were subdivisible! And what does "half so much" mean here? Less of nothing or more? In the realm of nothing, less is indeed more, but in the momentary tailspin into which this reckoning with imaginary numbers, or non-numbers, throws us, Jane's situation becomes even more . . . what? Heartbreaking? Laughable? Impossible to say. Stevie Smith is *simultane-ously* mocking and sad, pathetic and hilarious, and therein lies her genius.

There are, in the later collections, marvelous examples of Smith's slipping into the idiom of other poets. Thus "O Happy Dogs of England" is perfect Chesterton, and parts of "A Shooting Incident" are true Belloc—as when an adoring, overdependent dog elicits the reflection "The human heart is not at ease/ With animals that look like these." Sometimes, though, along with deliberate parody, we get inadvertent pastiche. Even this need not be bad: "Little Boy Sick" is a nice, quaint crossbreeding of Blake and Belloc, and there is a fine Shakespearian-Metaphysical ring to a final couplet like this from "The Friend": "But thou of present depth and former height/ Has highest height attained and needst no flight." (I assume that *has* for *hast* is a typo or *lapsus calami*.) And consider this, from a much later poem, "I had a dream . . ." greatly and justly admired by Bedient, where the poet dreams that she is Helen of Troy:

Well, nine years there had been of it, and now
The heavy weather, and the smells
From the battlefield, when the wind was in that direction,
And the spirit of the men, too, on both sides,
This was substantial enough; it seemed to me
Like the spirit of all armies, on all plains, in all wars, the men
No longer thinking why they were there
Or caring, but going on . . .

Doesn't this pleasantly remind you of Eliot's "Journey of the Magi"— " 'A cold coming we had of it . . .'" and the rest?

Much more interesting, though, are the cases where memories of earlier poetry elicit a different, but still remotely indebted, kind of poem, as with the very fine "Now Pine-Needles" that clearly echoes George Meredith's famous "Dirge in Woods." Meredith was stoical about the symbolic death of the pine needles, which, where all is "still as the mosses that glow . . . are quiet as under the sea." Overhead, in the cloud-fretted sky, "rushes life in a race," but we are like the needles: "And we go,/ And we drop like the fruits of the tree,/ Even we,/ Even so." This is meant to incorporate death in a natural cycle: reconcile us to dropping out of the exciting but tiring race ("As the clouds the clouds chase") and place us in harmony with nature as we gently sink to the mossy flooring like the pine needles, to find peace there as at the bottom of the sea.

Not so Stevie Smith. She addresses her dead pine needles in an almost gloating tone: "You are not brown because the sun has touched you/ You are brown because you are dead." Even the parent tree sighs not for sadness but "Only because the wind blows." She refuses to grieve for these needles that did not know they were alive and do not know they are dead. Rather, "I will sleep on you pine-needles,/ Then I shall be/ No more than the pine-tree/ No more than the pine-tree's needles." Human beings are not so blissfully ignorant as pines and their needles, but they can merge with them in sleep—and, by implication, death—and then they, too, can become unknowing and unfeeling. This is the first significant salute to death in Smith's poetry, a death not accepted, as in Meredith's poem, but sought after: "I *will* sleep" rather than 'I shall sleep'; then, however, "I shall be/ No more. . . ." After the act of the will, inevitability takes over.

No poet was more in love with death than Stevie Smith, not even those melancholy Romantics such as Alphonse Rabbe and Leopardi. To her, death is usually a friend, sometimes a lover; sometimes it is eagerly awaited and rushed toward, sometimes a fulfillment not to be hastened (by suicide or otherwise) but savored after a lifetime of ripening for it. The latter attitude is expressed in such a poem as "Study to Deserve Death," which ends: "Prate not to me of suicide,/ Faint heart in battle, not for pride/ I say Endure, but that such end denied/ Makes welcomer yet the death that's to be died." Even God, who is basically rejected by Smith, gets a left-handed compliment in "My Heart Goes Out": "My heart goes out to my Creator in love/ Who gave me Death, as end and remedy./ All living creatures come to quiet Death/ For him to eat up their activity/ And give them nothing, which is what they want although/ When they are living they do not think so." Here again the poem becomes prosy at the end, almost, I would like to think, out of indignation—disgust with those foolish people who would prefer to live forever.

In a late poem, "The Donkey," Smith concludes with "the thought that keeps my heart up/ That at last, in Death's odder anarchy,/ Our pattern will be broken all up./ Though precious we are momentarily, donkey,/ I aspire to be broken up." Observe how the dogged repetition of "broken *up*," which evolves from "keeps my heart *up*," drives home the stubborn yearning. There is, however, a much more curious and complex tribute to death in "Pretty," where a series of ever more destructive animals and dour landscapes is described as pretty. The word changes from description to exclamation, to become, at the end, a steady ecstasy:

> Cry pretty, pretty, pretty and you'll be able
> Very soon not even to cry pretty
> And so be delivered entirely from humanity
> This is prettiest of all, it is very pretty.

About this ending Bedient remarks that it "bites deeply into the inhuman; it chills." True enough, if you take that "delivered entirely from humanity" as an achievement *this* side of death. But it seems more plausible to assume that what Smith had in mind was a bantering, ironic, and finally impassive assent to all the harsh, arid, painful, and unpretty facts of life until you die with sarcastic approval on your freezing lips, and cease to be—which is prettiest of all. In that case, the poet, though still not painting a pretty picture, is at least not an out-and-out misanthrope.

The latter may, however, be the case in "Scorpion," where the poet equates herself with that venomous creature, and is in love with inhuman purities of which the ultimate is death. And so, in the end, the poet-scorpion humbly sues: "O Lord God please come/ And require the soul of thy Scorpion// Scorpion so wishes to be gone." There is something almost heartrending about that *so*: the voice of a sad, cajoling child issuing from the mouth of a cynically poisonous creature. And, most moving of all, there is that final plea to death, from the poet's deathbed, "Come, Death (2)":

> I feel ill. What can the matter be?
> I'd ask God to have pity on me,
> But I turn to the one I know, and say:
> Come, Death, and carry me away.
>
> Ah me, sweet Death, you are the only god
> Who comes as a servant when he is called, you know.
> Listen then to this sound I make, it is sharp,
> Come Death. Do not be slow.

Clearly only someone who had lived on intimate terms with death could speak to it in such an unaffectedly friendly tone. Writing from her last agony, Smith is careless about rhyming: the rhymes are either very obvious (me—be) or missing (god—sharp). It might even look as if fillers had been shoved in—that "you know," for instance—for the sake of the rhyme, and that the meter remains conventional from haste or despondency. But, on closer inspection, that "you know" is right: it establishes the mood of chatty conviviality. There are other subtleties: the "sharp sound" is both the wheezing breath of the moribund and the intense cry for deliverance; "the only god," perched at the end of a line, is not just the only god who comes as a servant, but also, by the implication fostered by that enjambment, the only god there is. To be *carried away* is also to be beside oneself with ecstasy. The last line is reduced to six syllables, of which, however no fewer than five are accented. This short, heavy line has all the gravity and urgency, all the weight and simplicity, of someone speaking with his last breath. After such utterance, the rest must be silence.

Yet counterposed to this death-as-dissolution-and-deliverance theme is another one: death as some sort of fulfillment that is more than annihilation. This theme appears in three poems that Bedient justly numbers among Stevie's finest; I would go further and say that, along with "Not Waving but Drowning," they constitute her very best. The last of these chronologically is "Black March," one of those short-line poems in which Smith displays her mastery of that by no means easy form of versification. Death appears as "A breath of fresh air,/ A change for you," which suggests something more than pure cessation. In a middle-period masterwork, "The Blue from Heaven," King Arthur leaves behind the queen, the knights, the world, and "has gone to ride in the blue light/ Of the peculiar towering cornflowers." That unearthly blue, the color of hope, again seems to promise something beyond absolute nothingness.

And then there is that extraordinary late poem, perhaps the most beautiful of all, "The Ass," in which a silly girl, Eugenia, somehow protected by her innocent abstractedness, manages, even though she is considered an ass by all, to overcome the powers of evil. A witch releases her after years of slavery because the stupid girl remained so happy; a fiend tempts her to sink into a morass, "But she said, No./ She was not such an ass. . . ." Finally, after the enchanted wood and the long, narrow causeway, she runs into the great waves of the sea: "Now she is gone. I thought/ Into her tomb."

> Yet often as I walk that sandy shore
> And think the seas
> Have long since combed her out that lies
> Beneath, I hear the sweet ass singing still with joy as if
> She had won some great prize, as if
> All her best wish had come to pass.

The movement of the verse itself is highly evocative here, but, expressed with utmost economy, there is much more. What are we to make of that "combed her out" that stands for decomposition? That death is a tidying up, a smoothing out that wears the person away to nothingness? But Eugenia, who was the friend of briar and bramble, of beetles, gnats, and mosquitoes, who sang "Baa-baa-ba-bay" for seven happy years along the causeway, is not one to be smoothed over, combed away into neat oblivion. Her song continues. Is it merely a poet's song that outlives her body? Or is it something more quintessentially indestructible, a joy death cannot extirpate? True, there are those *as ifs* to cast doubt on the significance of the singing; but there is no *as if* about the singing itself—that is there. And note the curious singular in "all her best wish," suggesting that all her best wishes were only one wish—this. There is also the Biblical tone of "come to pass," noted by Bedient; it suggests a miraculous fulfillment, and somehow detaches the *as ifs* from Eugenia and transfers them to the poet. It is Smith who can only *hope* that the song is one of joy and fulfillment; Eugenia may very well possess them with nary an *as if* about them.

But Smith is too complex a soul to come to a simple conclusion about death; in "The Crown of Bays" it seems to be a dubious commodity, and in Smith's most famous poem, "Not Waving but Drowning," both life and death appear as an agony of fright and pain:

> Nobody heard him, the dead man,
> But still he lay moaning:
> I was much further out than you thought
> And not waving but drowning.
>
> Poor chap, he always loved larking
> And now he's dead
> It must have been too cold for him his heart gave way,
> They said.

Oh, no no no, it was too cold always
(Still the dead one lay moaning)
I was much too far out all my life
And not waving but drowning.

This poem sums up two other dominant themes of Smith's
poetry: the lack of love, and the lack of genuine companion-
ship. And when this dead man keeps complaining in death,
we have no doubt that the complaint is leveled against both
the friendless, loveless life he had to endure, and the loveless, friendless death that befell him. Even death can disap-
point.

Calvin Bedient sharply perceives the duality in Stevie
Smith. "Few so skillful," he writes, "at opening a crevasse
between two truths. Is it wise to abandon hope wholly? 'No,
it is not wise.' Is it wise to endure when Death's a prize
easy to carry? 'No, it is not wise.' Certainty of this kind is
worse than the uncertainty it resembles; it is wisdom past
cure." But this doubleness of hers clearly extends beyond considerations of life and death, to views of death itself, which,
old friend though it be, does not yield an unambiguous answer. And, to complicate matters further, it is possible that
the real Stevie Smith—or a sizable, cheerful part of her—
is not to be found in the poetry at all: "When I am happy I
live and despise writing," she says in one poem, and, in
another, "Nobody writes or wishes to/ Who is one with their
desire."

Be that as it may, it would be a great pity if Smith were to be
neglected and ultimately forgotten because what she wrote
was—undeniably—not major poetry. The bulk of the verse in
the more than 500 pieces that make up the *Collected Poems* is
an excellent source of what Lionel Trilling has called "the
pleasures of poetry of low intensity," something, he thought,
"we are not enough aware of" nowadays. Yet Stevie's best
poems are not even lacking in intensity—and may, indeed, be
"major"—as witness, for instance, "To Carry the Child," in

which she movingly yet without any false pathos describes the painful duality of the adult who carries a child within him or her, and the suffering this causes for both of them. Here are the concluding stanzas:

> You would say a man had the upper hand
> Of the child, if a child survive,
> I say the child has fingers of strength
> To strangle the man alive.
>
> Oh it is not happy, it is never happy,
> To carry the child into adulthood,
> Let children lie down before full growth
> And die in their infanthood
> And be guilty of no man's blood.
>
> But oh the poor child, the poor child, what can he do
> Trapped in a grown-up carapace,
> But peer outside of his prison room
> With the eye of an anarchist?

Not only is the handling of slant rhyme masterly here, not only is the use of synecdoche most artful ("fingers of strength," "grown-up carapace"), there is also that extraordinary, ambiguous image of the child being urged to die in infancy. Is this to be taken literally? Not really, of course, but there is a certain ambivalence that suffuses the poem: maybe it is not only such an inner child that is meant, but any child; for does not a real child—growing into a man, and man being mortal—cause a man's death? Even without these overtones, however, the poem is horrifying enough, as when the child strangles "the man alive," suggesting (correctly) that the man is not strangled to death, but strangled without being killed, which may be worse. And there is the horror of that child within, the sweetest part of a human being, turning into a creature of hate.

Well, this is hardly an example of the poetry of low intensity. Possibly a poem such as "I Remember" would be nearer the mark:

> It was my bridal night I remember,
> An old man of seventy-three
> I lay with my young bride in my arms,
> A girl with t.b.
> It was wartime, and overhead
> The Germans were making a particularly heavy raid on
>   Hampstead.
> What rendered the confusion worse, perversely,
> Our bombers had chosen that moment to set out for
>   Germany.
> Harry, do they ever collide?
> I do not think it has ever happened,
> Oh my bride, my bride.

This, you might well say, is poetry of low intensity or, simply, minor poetry. And yet, and yet! Why should a young girl marry an old man of seventy-three? Because she is dying of consumption, and because it is wartime. The younger men are off to war, and may never come back. Even the old bridegroom and the tubercular bride may not live out their short remaining terms: the bombs may kill them first. The two of them may even desire such an ending; they have refused the relative safety of an air-raid shelter. True, it is their bridal night. But what sort of bridal night? Can the old man satisfy this young girl whom, as we have read in Thomas Mann and elsewhere, tuberculosis must have made even more avid sexually?

Just as "perverse" as this earthly mating is the confusion in the sky: bombers coming, bombers going. We hear the girl ask timidly whether these enemy craft ever collide. A curious question from someone who ought to be either scared for herself or immersed in lovemaking. And why, reminiscing later, should this by then very old man—left a widower, we infer—recall that awkward, almost foolish, question? And then dissolve in well-nigh audible tears: "Oh my bride, my bride"? Because something bigger—or smaller, and more personal—is implied by the question: Are there perversely preposterous collisions in the sky? Can there be between our own so unalike selves so unlikely a collision, explosion, orgasm? The doomed young bride would not consciously intend such an allusion, but the ancient bridegroom, then as now, would take it as such. "I do not think it has ever happened," he said. Still, he must have hoped that it might. We don't know whether it did, we know only that a lonely old man misses what is gone, even if it was in wartime, amid a deadly downpour.

Perhaps I am misreading this poem; perhaps the correct scenario is different. No matter; it is intensely suggestive, and bound to elicit speculation in any dedicated reader. And here, to end on an unquestionably minor note, is an even smaller poem, one so minuscule that, at first, it seems no more than a squiggle or two-finger exercise. From the late period, and seemingly written just before the powerful "Pretty," it is called "Piggy to Joey":

> Piggy to Joey
> Piggy to Joey
> Yes, that's what I was—
> Piggy to Joe.
>
> Will he come back again?
> Oh no, no, no.
> Oh how I wish I hadn't been
> Piggy to Joe.

This is a true miniature that must be examined under a magnifying glass. Piggy is obviously the nickname of the heroine, typical enough for a young girl a little stouter and pinker than most. Joey, her boyfriend—or, since the ages are indeterminate, perhaps just her little friend—grows into Joe; but the girl remains to him what she was: a pal, a tease perhaps, someone no closer than her unromantic nickname implies. Now, much later, she longs for the boy she spurned: here is the same triple *no* as in "Not Waving but Drowning," preceded by the same *oh*. How much hopelessness crouches in that fourfold staccato O, followed by yet another: "Oh how I wish. . . ." When the refrain "Piggy to Joe" returns, it is manifestly no longer carefree roseate chubbiness that "Piggy" stands for; it does not even mean "Piggy" anymore. It now means "Piggish to Joe," swinish to the one who loved me.

This is poetic minimalism, but out of such minimal effects Stevie Smith constructed her longer, larger, more complex and powerful poems—poems still written, perhaps, by the child in man, but with the strength to strangle the man alive. Or to move him. Or elate him. Or both.

[1977]

THE LIMITS OF INTELLIGENCE

George Bernard Shaw, *Collected Plays with Their Prefaces* (Definitive Edition)

To review the "Definitive Edition" of Bernard Shaw's plays means to reread his oeuvre of fifty-two stage works and rethink Shaw's place in today's theater and letters—which, in turn, means confronting one of the more curious cases in modern literature. For Shaw has, after enormous success, neither proceeded to a peaceful place in the pantheon of continued popularity and respect, nor fallen into the blatant eclipse that sometimes unjustly overtakes celebrity before patricide is duly superseded by ancestor worship. With Shaw, it is not just a case of his reputation having reached that uncertain age—too old to be loved, too young to be venerated; rather, the animus of some of his most brilliant contemporaries continues to hound him a quarter-century after his death, even as legions of solid citizens maintain his flame burning at medium-high. Emblematically, our Canadian neighbors have a thriving Shaw Festival while our own most vociferous drama critic persists in considering Neil Simon more entertaining than Shaw.

The list of Shaw's illustrious detractors is impressive, with poets in particular tending to disparage his alleged prosaism. Eliot spotted a poet in Shaw, but one that was "stillborn"; to Pound, he was "fundamentally trivial—a fake." D. H. Lawrence considered his characters "fleshless, bloodless, and cold," and shocked Cynthia Asquith by finding Augustus John's portrait of Shaw with his eyes closed "very true symbolism." Aldous Huxley wondered whether Shaw "ever [knew] anything about human beings": Gide was put off by what he considered the man's arrogance, and Orwell opined that Shaw's "only function is to console fat women who yearn to be highbrows." Joyce patronized him as "a born preacher": for Robert Graves, the plays were Lucianesque dialogues by a "philosopher turned demagogue." Most horribly, Shaw appeared to Yeats in a dream as "a sewing-machine that clicked and shone . . . [and] smiled, smiled perpetually."

But Shaw could summon up as dazzling an array of champions. Pirandello insisted that "there is a truly great poet in him," whom Shaw, out of Anglo-Irish combativeness, was "often willing to forget." Brecht, who may have gotten his "epic theater" from him, lauded his casual-contemptuous approach as permitting "complete concentration and real alertness," and said that he gave the theater "as much fun as it can stand." Playwrights as mutually antagonistic as O'Casey and Coward were alike in their respect for him; in a tempered but essentially admiring obituary, Thomas Mann called attention to his "wit-inspired poetry"; and Borges concludes a perceptive tribute with the remark that Shaw's works leave "an aftertaste of liberation."

The question is whether one views Shaw's sociopolitical philosophizing as devouring his dramaturgy, his didacticism and horseplay as fatal to his poetry, his melioristic preaching and debating as the opposite of profound innovation, genuine artistic idiosyncrasy, and a tragic vision of life. But for anyone willing to look, not merely prosecute, both poles are present in Shaw, who once confessed he would never have written plays had he not been "a chaos of contradictions." And as Edmund Wilson noted in a finely balanced appraisal that finally comes out for Shaw's artistry, though not for his ideology, "given genius—the more violent the contraries, the greater the work of art."

The contraries in Shaw are certainly violent. A cheerfully committed socialist all his adult life, Shaw was nevertheless so shaken by World War I as to find himself drawn to monarchy, dictatorship, even despair. Almost ascetically abstemious in sex, he nonetheless had a period of indulgence he dramatized in *The Philanderer.* Though the scourge of the middle class, he proudly declared that he could turn cheese merchant without having to change one aspect of his daily existence. The sworn enemy of money, he was also one of its most inspired collectors. In a letter to the impecunious O'Casey, forced to sell some author's rights for a pittance, Shaw warned uncompromisingly, "Let wife and child perish, and lay bricks for your last crust, rather than part with an iota of your rights," but generously enclosed a hundred pounds. A champion of simplified, modernized spelling, he fiercely clung to the archaism "shew" for "show." His plays perceived women as predators, but also as basically healthier and more sensible than men. He wanted to change society reasonably and kindly but radically; still, after some daring schemes for improvement, his plays end, as like as not, on a question mark, or on something that strongly resembles the status quo.

Just as for his compatriot and colleague Oscar Wilde, the basic dramatic ingredient for Shaw was the paradox. But whereas Wilde kept it at the level of the epigram, Shaw, both consciously and otherwise, let it permeate every aspect of his drama. For him the most truly brave officer was to be the least heroic, even as his Saint Joan was to be chiefly a commonsensical peasant girl. So a patient's death could move a ludicrously complacent doctor to a touching outburst of misquoted poetry, as, indeed, the leader of a band of robbers in the Sierra Nevada proves to be an eccentric bard. An impoverished dentist emerges as a great "sexual duelist," whereas the renowned duelist, Don Juan Tenorio, is merely a stumbling but lucky swordsman. Little Private Meek proves a giant among soldiers, but the giant Ferrovius is mild as a lamb. A bishop keeps demanding that the devil be given his due, and the Devil himself holds forth with compassionate eloquence about human misery. Even stranger things happen: old captain Shotover drinks not to dream but to stay awake; when, by willing it, some people begin to live three centuries, longevity comes to those to whom the idea never occurred.

Paradoxes are in order for a man who was himself a paradox, and some of the best definitions of Shaw have borrowed the device. Thus Robert Brustein sees Shaw as "a rebel in search of a community"; Harry Levin as "that unconventional master of convention"; and G. K. Chesterton, with a double-barreled salvo, as "full of dry magnanimity" and "inhumane humanity." It must hinge on Shaw's going from wise child directly to pawky old man—from living with, and mostly off, his mother until he was over forty, and then heading straight for a platonic marriage with a rich woman who looked after her aging, crotchety sage with discreet devotion, while Shaw indulged in avuncular epistolary love affairs. That skipping over central manhood is mirrored in the plays by two quintessential taboos: the fear of love and the fear of death. For these, Shaw devised the twin remedies of the Life Force, the power of creative evolution that carries mankind willy-nilly ahead, subsuming and neutralizing the chicanery of romantic love; and willed longevity, gradually leading toward immortality a mankind that has learned how to harness the Life Force. The traditional battle between Eros and Thanatos shifts in Shaw to Logos taking on the combined forces of Eros and Thanatos— but from such a largely dialectical contest it is hard to wrest tragedy.

Yet tragedy is indispensable to the vision of even a major comic dramatist; its lurking in the background contributes to the ultimate greatness of, say, *The Tempest, Volpone, The Misanthrope,* and *Leonce and Lena.* Shaw labeled two of his works as tragedies, but neither *The Doctor's Dilemma,* good as it is, nor the fourth part of *Back to Methuselah,* dreary (like the rest of the play) as it is, is tragic. But tragedy does skulk around *Heartbreak House* and *Saint Joan,* two of his best plays, even if in the end he cannot but fudge it. Still, there is a way in which even the desperate evasion of the great poetic themes of love and death, by its very desperateness, creates a seriocomic intensity that rises to the heights of a poetry of the prosaic: of sense, rather than the senses, passionately embraced.

This takes various forms in the plays. It can be a duel of ideas—old and new, appealing or otherwise—flashing across the stage like the clash of sabers; or it can be some unlikely, prosy personage, like the very proper lawyer M'Comas, pleading with the estranged Mrs. Clandon for her uncouth husband, one of those "people whose touch hurts," in *You Never Can Tell*; or it can be crazed old Shotover inveighing against an even madder, and morally flabbier, humanity in *Heartbreak House;* or it may be Bagot, the gentleman-thief and clandestine clergyman of *Too True to Be Good,* preaching like some Sartrean existentialist into empty space. It can, of course, be the country girl, Joan, choosing the stake over being locked away from nature; but it can also be, not of course, the Inquisitor pushing a steady, pervasive, forbidding conviction past mere rhetoric into an icy poetry.

It is usually a poetry of pleading, of rational persuasion backed up with bounties of wit or dignified self-assertion—as in Caesar's nocturnal salute to the Sphinx, or Jennifer Dubedat's defense of her unworthy husband, to which the acquiescence of those who know better lends a beautifully absurd pathos. The only thing it never manages to be is a window on the absolute, on something beyond what can be apprehended by mere intelligence, however sensitized. Thus when Mrs. George, in *Getting Married,* vaticinates about the essence of Woman and the vision becomes a mass of self-contradictions, when Major Barbara's compromise with Undershaft is to be elevated to a paradoxical victory, when the Old Gentleman in *Back to Methuselah* opts for death over banality, Shaw's art is not up to the complexity, grandeur, or transcendence of the situation.

But one of the triumphs of Shaw's drama is that it reads as

dramatically as it plays—just as it plays as intelligently as it reads. There is something irresistible about a dramatist who can write with equal ease "That boy will make his way in this country. He has no sense of humor" and "This world [is] a place where men and women torture one another in the name of love." If Shakespeare had his infinite variety, Shaw, who mistakenly believed himself his superior, knew how to make his finitude look almost infinitely various. So pick up this new edition of *Collected Plays with Their Prefaces,* to which Dan H. Laurence, that exemplary Shavian, has appended relevant and racy articles, letters to the editor, and interviews granted by GBS. You will find the text definitive, the typography pleasing and as free of typos as humanly possible, the format a delight for eye and hand, even the binding and jacket design a rare surprise. Start reading with *Arms and the Man* and *You Never Can Tell,* then skip ahead to *Man and Superman* and *Heartbreak House,* and you'll be hooked and ready to roam backward and forward through these seven volumes, ad libitum and *ad majorem hominis gloriam.*

[1975]

A LEGACY FROM OUR TENANT

Rupert Hart-Davis, ed., *The Letters of Oscar Wilde*

"YOUR idea of the grand perverts is excellent," wrote D. H. Lawrence to Aldous Huxley, encouraging him about a book on men like St. Francis, Leonardo, Goethe, Byron, Baudelaire, Wilde, and Proust. "They all did . . . or tried to . . . kick off, or . . . intellectualise and so utterly falsify the phallic consciousness, which is the basic consciousness, and the thing we mean, in the best sense, by common sense." Lawrence was perfectly right to label Oscar Wilde a man not distinguished for his common sense. Neither, for that matter, was Lawrence. But this did not prevent either of them from being deeply sensible about certain things, and Wilde's ideal of a life in beauty makes at least as much sense as Lawrence's phallic consciousness. The concept of Wilde as a grand pervert, however, makes no sense at all, though Lawrence here accidentally accords him artistic justice by ranking him with a group of men whose peer—in some respects, though not all—Wilde clearly was. He is, for one thing, the author of one of the greatest correspondences in the English language, the epistolary equal of Keats, Byron, and Lawrence himself.

The publication in the same year of these two vast and magnificent collections of letters, Lawrence's and Wilde's, allows for absorbing comparisons. Indeed, as one reads the twelve hundred and sixty pages of Lawrence and the eight hundred and sixty pages of Wilde, one might come to the conclusion that if either of these equally spectacular epistolarians could be called a "grand pervert," Wilde is not the one. Wilde, as nearly as anybody in our time, was a true tragic hero; his was a real-life Greek tragedy, conforming closely to the Aristotelian tenets: "pity and terror" in the downfall of a man "highly renowned and prosperous, who is not eminently good and just, yet whose misfortune is brought about not by vice or depravity, but by some error or frailty." And his life also had that quality of all great tragedies of being both infinitely sad and ultimately ennobling and, therefore, joyous.

It may well be that Wilde was not "eminently good and just," though he was generous to a fault, incapable of hatred and unkindness or vindictiveness, free from any fanaticism other than his pursuit of beauty, utterly delightful in prosperity and, for the most part, cheerful in adversity—none of which can be said of that grand man of health, Lawrence. (But Wilde would never have dreamed of calling Lawrence perverted.) And we can now concede that there was in Wilde no "vice or depravity," for his homosexuality was, as Hesketh Pearson notes, something "that hurt no one but himself." But there was in Wilde both "frailty" and "error." Frailty, to have fallen completely under Lord Alfred Douglas's baleful spell; error, to have courted, indeed demanded, disaster. And no one had been more "highly renowned and prosperous" than Wilde, which he, with his customary immodesty, was first to admit.

The Letters of Oscar Wilde is the perfect way of apprehending the tragedy of the man, and if his famous epigram is accepted as the truth—that he put his genius into his life and only his talent into his work—then the tragedy, or, more accurately, tragicomedy contained in *The Letters* is, in fact, a work of genius. I am inclined to consider it as such. And with the help of Rupert Hart-Davis, the impeccable and inspired editor of the book, we can follow the phases of the drama not only in the letters, but also in the excellent footnotes—neither too abundant nor too sparse—through its glittering and awesome parabola. And nature, which, as Wilde astutely observed, imitates art, has so arranged it that the climactic letter, the eighty-page missive to Douglas from Reading Gaol, should come at the exact center of the book. Everything else, too, is in its proper place: the rising action, the triumph, the fall, the pathetic dénouement. There is also wit and humor galore in these letters, humor which, as Wilde wrote to the actress Marie Prescott, "does not destroy terror, but, by relieving it, aids it."

Not that these letters preponderantly produce an effect of terror. On the contrary, they display chiefly serenity, charm, unmalicious satire, wit; also, love of beauty, mankind, and—first and last—self. But this love of self, though it is full of histrionics and ostentation, is always saved from vulgarity either by good nature or by good writing, or by a combination of the two. And though the style is not infrequently showy and sometimes, inevitably, trivial, this book is unquestionably the best biography of Oscar Wilde to be had;[1] first, because it was written by a better writer than any of the others, and, second, because anything Wilde omitted is so neatly, knowingly, and self-effacingly filled in by the editor.

Here, to begin with, are the student days at Oxford in letters that reveal an alert young man, full of prankishness and *sensiblerie,* but neither particularly witty nor otherwise extraordinary—although to some readers his protracted flirtation with the Church of Rome may come as a surprise. But soon Oscar is in London, and the aestheticism and epigrams begin: "Nowadays the selection of colours and furniture has quite taken the place of the cases of conscience of the middle ages, and usually involves quite as much remorse." And the graciousness: to John Gielgud's grandmother he writes, "I am filled with delight at the beauty of your name—Aniela! It has an exquisite forest simplicity about it, and sounds most sweetly out of tune

---

[1] Written well before Richard Ellmann's magisterial biography appeared.

with this fiery-coloured artificial world of ours—rather like a daisy on a railway bank!"

Presently, Wilde is off on his American lecture tour, and now at last we can read a full account of this episode which ranges from high comedy to outrageous burlesque. He has three secretaries, the "third whose hair resembles mine is obliged to send off locks of his own hair to the myriad maidens of [New York], and so is rapidly becoming bald." He meets Indians: "They are really in appearance very like Colvin [the Slade Professor of Fine Arts at Cambridge], when he is wearing his professorial robes. . . . Their conversation was most interesting as long as it was unintelligible," but when translated, it reminded him unpleasantly of that of a certain Scottish judge. When he drank Horace Tabor's silver miners under the table deep down in the Matchless Mine, "they unanimously pronounced me in their grand simple way 'a bully boy with no glass eye'—artless and spontaneous praise which touched me more than the pompous panegyrics of literary critics. . . . Then I had to open a new vein, or lode, which with a silver drill I brilliantly performed, amidst unanimous applause. The silver drill was presented to me and the lode named 'The Oscar.' I had hoped that in their simple grand way they would have offered me shares in 'The Oscar,' but in their artless untutored fashion they did not."

Next, Oscar is back in London, and this large portion of the letters Hart-Davis divides into two sections: before Douglas and after. Here come, besides a proliferation of wit, remarkable insights into the nature of art, splendid vignettes of London society—a whole social history of the period—and a sort of theatrical, literary, and cultural chronicle of the late eighties and early nineties. Then, with the entrance of that evil genius "Bosie" Douglas, there ensues an eloquent account of excess and abandon, of impossibly high living, of Wilde's sexual and emotional *Hörigkeit* where Douglas was concerned, and of the little tremors leading up to the disaster.

The following section consists of the letters from prison, and contains for the first time the full text of *De Profundis,* as that extraordinary document has come to be called. It is a devastating analysis of a calamitous relationship, an often revolutionary meditation on life, art, and the human spirit, and a violently moving piece of self-condemnation and revelation. It is packed with shattering insights: "The gods are strange. It is not of our vices only they make instruments to scourge us. They bring us to ruin through what in us is good, gentle, humane, loving." Or: "Morality does not help me. . . . But while I see that there is nothing wrong in what one does, I see that there is something wrong in what one becomes." Or again: "Everything to be true must become a religion. And agnosticism should have its ritual no less than faith. It has sown its martyrs, it should reap its saints. . . ." And yet again: "I am advised to try on my release to forget that I have ever been in a prison at all. . . . To reject one's own experiences is to arrest one's own development. To deny one's own experience is to put a lie into the lips of one's own life. It is no less than a denial of the Soul."

But probably the most fascinating and touching part of the book is the final quarter, dealing with the three last years of Wilde's life. The letters of these years of sometimes merry, sometimes pathetic and even penurious exile—one moment ludicrous, the next heartbreaking, and the next full of benign wisdom—shed considerable light on the least known and most intensely human phase of Wilde's existence. Here he realized that he could no longer create and truly poured his genius into conversation and correspondence. "Come any time you like," he writes a friend. "I am not responsible for the architecture of the chalet: all that I am responsible for at Berneval are the sunsets and the sea." Of *The Ballad of Reading Gaol,* he writes: "The popularity of the poem will be largely increased by the author's painful death by starvation. The public loves poets to die in this way. It seems to them dramatically right. Perhaps it is." His badinage, in these difficult times, is irrepressible: "The English are very unpopular in Paris now, as all those who are over here, under Cook's direction, are thoroughly respectable. There is much indignation on the Boulevards. I try to convince them that they are our worst specimens, but it is a difficult task." Or: "Paris is terrible in its heat. . . . Even the criminal classes have gone to the seaside, and the *gendarmes* yawn and regret their enforced idleness. Giving wrong directions to the English tourists is the only thing that consoles them." Such harmless jibes were Wilde's only revenge for all the dreadful injustice England had done him and continued to do him to the end.

If in this little appreciation I have given the word mostly to Wilde himself, it is because I don't know whose words— certainly not mine—would be the equal of his. But at the end I must quote three words by a simple Paris landlord of Wilde's, one Jean Dupoirier, "whose devotion and generosity," as Pearson summarizes it all, "went so far that he never mentioned to Ross the sums Wilde owed him, and [who] even bought champagne and other luxuries without once revealing the fact that the cost came out of his own pocket." Let us stop to consider what sort of a man Wilde must have been to have inspired such devotion, and inspired it—though I do not wish to detract from Dupoirier's personal glory—in a member of the parsimonious and xenophobic Parisian middle class. But I am particularly haunted by the image of the faithful Dupoirier trudging after Wilde's hearse, which (I imagine) carried also the good hotel-keeper's wreath made of beads—how tasteless and how beautiful!—with its three-word inscription: "A mon locataire."

"To my tenant"—what charming pride of possession, and again, what discreet, shy humility in these three words! More than that: they are symbolic of Wilde's relationship to the world. He was its enchanting, irresponsible tenant, living on credit in one sense, repaying it a thousandfold in another. As we read the almost nine hundred pages of *The Letters of Oscar Wilde,* we realize again, and perhaps more clearly than ever, how much the host is indebted to this tenant's wisdom, wit, and incomparable grace.

[1963]

THE PRINCE OF PARADOX

Rupert Hart-Davis, ed., *More Letters of Oscar Wilde*

IT is virtually impossible to write about Oscar Wilde without invoking his quintessential self-critique spoken (note: not written) to André Gide: "Would you like to know the great drama of my life? It is that I've put my genius into my life; I've only put my talent into my works." If this is so, and many who knew him have corroborated it—though Wilde would have been pleased, I'm sure, to hear it contradicted—we must be doubly grateful for *More Letters of Oscar Wilde,* a supplement to Rupert Hart-Davis's marvelous edition of the *Letters of Oscar Wilde,* published in 1962 and now regrettably out of print.

For if the spontaneous Wilde is to be preferred to the premeditated or literary Wilde, a new collection of his correspondence should be particularly welcome. (Not that such a distinction, as Richard Ellmann warns, "could . . . be so finely drawn; his writings plagiarized from his conversation, and his conversation from his writing.") The letter writer, after all, is closer to the talker than to the author, especially when you consider that no conversationalist ever became famous without being a great monologuist. In his recollections, Sir William Rothenstein, the painter and friend of Wilde, notes:

The great talkers I have heard—Whistler, Oscar Wilde, Henry James, George Moore, Bernard Shaw, Yeats, James Stephens, Ralph Hodgson—have been monologuists. It is right they should be so . . . there is a kind of creative talk which should not be interrupted.

More Letters comprises only 215 loosely filled pages, of which no more than 160 are taken up with letters (although the two short essays in the appendix, nineteen pages in all, are remarkable in their own right). It is a mere pittance compared to the feast of the *Letters*. But a toothsome pittance it is, even if these letters cannot be called major, with the single exception of the one to the actor-manager George Alexander, shrewdly instructing him on how to stage some parts of *Lady Windermere's Fan*.

A fascinating aspect of this collection is that it cuts swiftly across all phases of Wilde's life save the very earliest, permitting us to follow the revolution of the wheel of fortune in a cinematic, speeded-up motion. But what prevents the letters from reading like a mere postscript to *A Myrrour for Magistrates* is their almost unfailing good humor. Barring the odd gripe and passing fulmination (usually at Smithers, the publisher, for not sending a promised check), everything, even the cadging, is done with forthrightness and grace. Besides, as Evelyn Waugh remarked apropos of the *Letters,* "The reviewers complain there are too many pleas for money, but the poor beast was penniless."

The first, and briefest, section (1875–78) contains letters from Oxford. The next section (1879–81) spans the early London years in which Wilde was slowly making his journalistic reputation. Here, as throughout the book, Rupert Hart-Davis's notes tactfully provide just the right amount of information. We find Wilde gushing about Greats (i.e., Classics), in which he took a first at "the only fine school at Oxford . . . where one can be, *simultaneously,* brilliant and unreasonable. . . ." This anticipates the future publisher George Macmillan's appraisal of Oscar as both nonsensical and sensible. Indeed, Wilde was at no time of his life only one or the other, but always an enchanting and exasperating mixture of the two.

Next comes the lecture tour of America in 1882, where Oscar dazzled, provoked, and, by and large, charmed the colonials. He would appear in "black velvet with lace," attire "suitable for . . . the last century," arousing with word and deed "the excitement of some strong people at the colour of my necktie, the fear of the [American] eagle that I have come to cut his barbaric claws with the scissors of culture, the impotent rage of the ink-stained, the noble and glorious homage of the respectable"—the latter going so far as to name a school of design in Philadelphia for him. Too bad the adventures among the miners of Colorado do not figure here, but all in all, we get a good enough picture of the fellow whom Eleanor Marx, Karl's daughter, described at this time as "that very limp and very nasty young man . . . who has been making such a d.d ass of himself in America."

In the 1883–90 section Wilde continues his lectures on literature, art, and aesthetics in England, publishes poetry and more literary journalism, edits a women's magazine, and rises to fame. He is now consulted on literary matters, and dispenses sound advice. He compliments one writer on perfectly combining "simplicity and strangeness," and warns another that parody requires, "oddly enough, a love of the poet whom it caricatures." The wit, too, is in full swing.

It is between 1891 and 1895 that Wilde's letters, reflecting their author's career in its apogee, become most Wildean. The style now achieves that wittiness based on the most serious treatment of the absurd and the most prankish juggling of paradox. Wilde explains to the princess of Monaco why he missed her soirée: "I am still almost without voice, and without voice one cannot even listen with appreciation." In a letter to Smithers from the final period in France (c. December 28, 1898), Wilde complains about Robert Ross, his friend, first lover, and literary executor: "I am always rebuking him for his idleness, which I attribute entirely to his early hours." In the same month he writes Laurence Housman from La Napoule about the local fishermen. They "have beautiful eyes, crisp hair of a hyacinth colour, and no morals: an ideal race. I have two special friends . . . both quite perfect, except that they can read and write." And this advice concerning Housman's young lover, who has fallen sick: "I think a little want of sympathy would make him well: it has a wonderful effect on invalids."

We have, then, examples of both varieties of epigrams G. K. Chesterton perceived in his 1909 review of Wilde's works:

> One might go through his swift and sparkling plays with a red and blue pencil marking two kinds of epigrams; the real epigram which he wrote to please his own wild intellect, and the sham epigram which he wrote to thrill the very tamest part of our tame civilization.

Chesterton distinguishes between such sayings as "Nothing survives being thought of," which he considers an example of the nobler sort of nonsense with an idea in it, and others such as "A well-tied tie is the first serious step in life," which he calls rubbish spoken by a charlatan.

The Wildean epigram, first of all, is a form of exaggeration. In one of his last letters here, we find Wilde telling Ross: "I am now *neurasthenic*. My doctor says I have all the symptoms. It is comforting to have them *all*, it makes one a perfect type." An exaggeration, however, that subverts the established and the customary. So, too, illiteracy becomes a form of perfection if, as Chesterton all but concurs, thinking is destructive—at the very least of unclouded beauty not meant to be sicklied over by the pale cast of thought. And what of Ross's idleness stemming from his "early hours"? Chesterton would surely have blue-penciled that one. Yet isn't living an orderly, early-rising, workaday life precisely what militates against the creation of nonchalant, mischievous, Wildean art?

But what exactly is the epigram, or paradox, this thing that James Joyce, in a 1909 Italian newspaper article on Wilde, called "his restless thought that proceeds by sophisms rather than syllogisms"? It is a mode of subversion by an inversion of values that seems to be ultimately connected to another form of inversion: homosexuality. With the paradoxical epigram, the homosexual tweaks the establishment's nose, turns the heterosexual world arsy-varsy with a vengeance, and, once upside down, the top man is less high than the bottom dog. In his *Recollections of Oscar Wilde* (1932), the painter Charles Ricketts explains the Wildean propensity for epigrams as "the recoil of one who had met with hostility or derision when he had wished to charm." That is oversimplification, but the retaliatory aspect is undeniable, and the clever inversion of values can be found in the works of such homosexual writers as Norman Douglas and Ronald Firbank, Joe Orton and Terrence McNally, Roland Barthes and Michel Foucault.

Why is this kind of subversion so resonant? I doubt that it has much to do with Joyce's explanation that it represents "the truth inherent in the soul of Catholicism: that man cannot reach the divine heart except through that sense of separation and loss called sin." Two other factors seem more relevant. First, in a relativized universe, we are compelled to perceive some truth in the opposite of everything. "He was an ingenious man," Borges wrote about Wilde in *Other Inquisitions,* "who was also right." Once we have become committed, for better or worse, to seeing the other side of every question, Wilde's minority view—that loyal opposition—must also be taken into account, and may be found to contain, as Chesterton argued, some useful truth.

Second, as Borges noted, "the fundamental spirit of [Wilde's] works is joy." It is the joy of exaggeration, which Wilde described so seductively in his glowing review of Pater's *Appreciations* (March 22, 1890):

It is possible, of course, that I may exaggerate about [the essays]. I certainly hope that I do; for where there is no exag-

geration there is no love, and where there is no love there is no
understanding. It is only about the things that do not interest
one, that one can give a really unbiassed opinion; and this is no
doubt the reason why an unbiassed opinion is always absolutely
valueless.

Here is the paradox enlisted in defense of the paradox, the
epigram as its own epigrammatic justification.

The last significant letter from the prelapsarian period of
Wilde's life is the one to Ross from Algiers (c. January 25,
1895), where Oscar had gone with "Bosie" Douglas on a
flagrantly homosexual escapade involving Arab boys. Wilde
writes:

> There is a great deal of beauty here. The Kabyle boys are
> quite lovely. At first we had some difficulty in procuring a
> proper civilised guide, but now it is all right and Bosie and I
> have taken to haschish: it is quite exquisite: three puffs of smoke
> and then peace and love. Bosie wakes up at night and cries like a
> child for the best haschish.
>
> We have been [on] an excursion into the mountains of
> Kabylia—full of villages peopled by fauns. Several shepherds
> fluted on reeds for us. We were followed by lovely brown things
> from forest to forest. The beggars here have profiles, so the
> problem of poverty is easily solved. . . .
>
> The most beautiful boy is said by the guide to be "deceitful":
> isn't it sad? Bosie and I are awfully upset about it.

This little prose poem in the style of Wilde's later *Poems in Prose*
could serve as the starting point for both a stylistic analysis and
a psycho-philosophical study of Wilde's life. Suffice it to note
that it is the obverse of the epigram: though equally manipulative, it inverts existence not into ironic paradox but into poetic
fantasy, into a bittersweetly sentimental fairy tale.

The next section, "Reading, 1895–97," shows that Wilde's
good humor and wit did not forsake him even in jail. Thus
Wilde writes his solicitor that he would rather not have to sign
a document while still in prison "as 'residing in Reading Gaol,'

an address, which, however admirable from an ethical point of view, will not, I trust, be permanent. . . ." In 1905 Max Beerbohm observed of Wilde, "Even 'from the depths' he condescended," and "enjoyed the greater luxury of condescending to himself." And condescend to himself he does when he writes, "I don't know what to do with my money except to throw it away," and refers to "my halcyon days, which did me, I dare say, a lot of harm." Always there was Wilde's generosity: a letter from a kindly warden relates how Wilde refused offers of contraband food because its smuggling in might imperil the benefactor.

The book's three final sections—"Berneval," "Naples," "Paris"—exhibit self-criticism ("I feel that while there is much that I have lost, still there was much that was not worth keeping"), incurable romanticism in his persistent love for the unworthy Lord Alfred ("our souls touch in myriad ways through the estranging air"), and above all, the old wit. When Wilde accidentally smudges one of the copies of *The Importance of Being Ernest* he has autographed, he declares, "As I have initialled the smudge, it must count as a *remarque*. You might ask one and sixpence extra for that copy." (In 1981, the smudged copy was to fetch 8,500 dollars at auction.)

Still, for all their good humor, these last letters are saddening. The man who was generous enough to pay half the two hundred pounds' fine incurred by an obscure anarchist poet ("Whatever I did was merely what you would have done for me. . . .") was obliged to panhandle relative strangers for fifty francs. His own generosity—and recklessness—continued unabated. When in 1898 Wilfred Hugh Chesson mentioned Emile Verhaeren to him, Wilde exclaimed, "Oh! now you mention the greatest living poet." And well he might praise the Belgian who wrote that "to live is to take and give with joy," and also, "Il faut aimer pour découvrir avec génie." Certainly Wilde had given gladly and was taking equally gladly now that he was, in his own words, dying as he had lived: beyond his means. But he had also loved intensely enough to discover with genius. He indignantly responded to Chesson's attempt to console him with "the life of the spirit": "There is no hell but this: a body without a soul, or a soul without a body." It is right that he died before he was quite reduced to either alternative—before we could have applied to him what he said of one of his revered masters: "Poor dear Pater has lived to disprove everything he has written."

[1986]

DR. JOHNSON IN MIDDLE AGE

James L. Clifford, ed., *Dictionary Johnson:
Samuel Johnson's Middle Years*

WHAT a rare creature is a great critic! English literature has a
plethora of matchless poets, novelists, and playwrights, but
until this century, which is too new for the process of sifting to
have been completed, there have been only four unquestionably major critics: Coleridge, Hazlitt, Arnold, and the subject
of the present study, Samuel Johnson. Three of these critical
giants also wrote poetry, and all of them were essayists in a
broader sense as well; otherwise, however, the four had little in
common beyond their genius and rarity. To be a member of a
string quartet is in some ways more glorious even than to be
the concertmaster of—let alone a mere player in—a philhar-
monic orchestra.

In many respects the most astonishing and imposing, both
in his achievement and in the contradictory beliefs and attitudes from which it sprung, was the first member of this
critical foursome, Dr. Johnson, as he came to be known—
though he was no doctor, and even his M.A. from Oxford,
which he left early because of poverty, was only a belated
honorific. The late James L. Clifford, who taught at Columbia
University and was one of the most distinguished Johnson
scholars, was perhaps best known for his *Young Sam Johnson*

(1955), an essential book for our knowledge and understanding of Johnson's beginnings. Now, with *Dictionary Johnson: Samuel Johnson's Middle Years,* Clifford covers the years between 1749, when Johnson's tragedy *Irene* was produced by Sam's former pupil David Garrick, to a respectful but mixed reception, and 1763, when Johnson met and gradually warmed up to a young Scot named James Boswell.

Three lustrums, then, during which Johnson produced most of his perdurable essays (the *Rambler, Adventurer,* and *Idler* series); compiled his epoch-making dictionary virtually single-handed; turned out his philosophic novel *Rasselas*; and also published (in 1749, though Clifford does not here deal with it) his greatest poetic achievement, the Juvenalian satire *The Vanity of Human Wishes.* The Shakespearian commentaries, the account of the Scottish tour, and *The Lives of the Poets* were to come afterward.

Two major problems dogged Johnson through most of these fifteen years: poverty and ill health. The life of a Grub Street hack was grubby indeed, and the rent on Johnson's Gough Square residence was often in arrears, eventually leading to eviction and a not inconsiderable period when Johnson had no fixed abode. His furniture was so paltry and decrepit, the dirt so assertive, that it was fortunate that Johnson's nearsightedness verged on purblindness and that Miss Williams, the trusty housekeeper, was totally blind. Johnson sometimes went for two days without really eating; his best attire was so shabby that a housemaid very nearly evicted him from an elegant party to which he had been invited. As to his health, Johnson asserted that he did not know a single day entirely free from pain; a childhood sickness had left him forever a bundle of tics and tremors, odd foot stampings and fist clenchings, so that William Hogarth, for instance, thought at first that he was meeting an idiot—until the idiot started to talk inspiredly; a host showing Johnson around his house and disturbed by the fancy footwork Johnson indulged in informed him that he believed the floor to be quite firm.

The incidents of those fifteen central years are all here. The death of Tetty, Johnson's much older wife, whom Sam loved even though she had long since stopped sleeping with him; the demise of his mother, whom Johnson had not seen for eighteen years while still claiming to care for her; the passing of Miss Boothby, the pious bluestocking who was the chief of several women Johnson considered for his second wife—but there was to be no remarriage, only the letter "M" accruing in his diaries, to indicate a solitary, and to Johnson sinful, substitute for sex. Here are the clubs he started, the friendships he made and often kept against improbable odds, the late rising and dilatory work habits, the endless cups of tea consumed (at a hostess who demurred after the seventeenth, Johnson growled, "You are rude, Madam!"), the magazine and newspaper jobs lost because of unpopular political opinions, particularly Johnson's bitter opposition to the war with France.

We follow in great detail the literary journalism—Johnson could turn out an essay in no time amid a noisy gathering; the desultory but often feverish work on the dictionary; the literary alliances and enmities. Sometimes Johnson is bailed out of debtors' prison by friends like Samuel Richardson; sometimes Johnson is thus rescuing Oliver Goldsmith. Whenever he can avoid working, Johnson does so: the sole reason he undertakes the dictionary is "not love or desire of fame but the want of money, which is the only motive to writing that I know of." He makes frequent resolves to put an end to idleness—especially in the many prayers he composes on a variety of occasions—yet, even as he remains a practicing Christian, he continues as a practicing idler. His generosity to the poor and maltreated is great and various, whether he works hard on starting a hostel for reformed prostitutes or gives his last half-guinea to a visiting student whose father was once kind to him. He writes one of his most moving essays in behalf of French prisoners of war, even though he dislikes the French: let "no man be longer deemed an enemy than while his sword is drawn against us." Finally Johnson obtains a yearly pension of three hundred pounds—thus his worst worries are over, although his enemies mercilessly lampoon the man who, in his dictionary, defined "pensioner" as "a slave of state hired by a stipend to obey his master." Despite the jeers, Johnson does not change the definition, nor does he assist in any way the government of Lord Bute that granted the stipend.

Clifford gives us a clear view of a man peculiarly divided: a Tory in many ways too liberal for his times, an authoritarian hating most existing forms of authority, a Christian wholly uncharitable to those who depart from orthodoxy, a man of huge intellectual curiosity and accomplishment wasting much time hobnobbing with and debating mental inferiors, a great lover of feminine company staying curiously clear of relationships with women (on the murky area of Johnson's sexuality Clifford is much less explicit than on the Doctor's toilet habits), a champion of mankind often boorish to individual men, and a great believer in the critical judgment of the public who nonetheless would have kept hoi polloi out of art exhibitions where they became "idle and tumultuous." There were certain directions in which Johnson's otherwise agile intellect could not be budged—he cared little for music and art; was it that, as Bernard Shaw suggested, savage schoolmasterly beatings had somehow lamed young Sam's mind?

Dictionary Johnson is a worthy book that nevertheless falls among many stools. In this day of critical biographies it is an unreconstructedly uncritical biography in both senses of that epithet: it does not go much deeper into Johnson's writings than, say, "*Rasselas* [is] worth reading over and over again"—something Hilaire Belloc noted a good fifty years ago; and, for all its accumulation of quotable opinions, it does not cite such famous but damaging comments as Garrick's later remark on *Irene*: "When Johnson writes tragedy, 'declamation roars, and passion sleeps.' . . ." Although one can form one's own opinion of the Johnsonian style from the many splendid specimens included (e.g., "Surely life, if it be not long, is tedious, since we are forced to call in the assistance of so many trifles to rid us of our time, of that time which never can return"), the book never undertakes a definition of it such as we can get, even if we don't have time to read W. K. Wimsatt's magisterial study (*The Prose Style of Samuel Johnson*), from so concise a contribution as James Sutherland's to the *Festschrift* for D. Nichol Smith, *Essays on the Eighteenth Century*. And though Clifford tells us repeatedly that talk became more important to the aging Johnson than writing, this talk is not compellingly analyzed, despite many a witty example (e.g., "I like the man too well to read his book" or this, to a sycophant roaring at everything Johnson uttered: "I hope I have not said anything that *you* can comprehend").

Still, the undoubted merit of Professor Clifford's book is its prodigious inclusiveness. The author has gathered from the obscurest sources a bouquet of flowers that ran the risk of blushing unseen, and there are things here that even the conscientious reader of much finer books on Johnson—such as John Wain's more idiosyncratic and lively, or W. Jackson Bate's more speculative and far-reaching, *Life*—would not have encountered elsewhere. Occasionally, though, Clifford gives us too much: do we need a lengthy meditation on the exact nature, number, and locations (all putative) of the commodes in Johnson's Gough Square house; must we have a detailed description of Joshua Reynolds's father's house merely because the painter once showed it to Johnson? Conversely, an essential detail is sometimes missing: though Clifford provides a full account of the Lauder affair, wherein Johnson for a while supported a fraud who accused Milton of plagiarism, nowhere does he explain exactly what Lauder did, i.e., take some lines from an obscure Latin translation of *Paradise Lost* by one William Hogg and claim that they were an unacknowledged source Milton stole from.

My greatest quarrel with *Dictionary Johnson*, however, is that it never pulls together those excellent but scattered ingredients that, juxtaposed and duly commented on, would make clear what it means to be a critic such as Johnson was, from finger-tips to marrow. We get incidents—Johnson's insulting a kindly host's house for combining modern sash windows with antiquated thatching, attacking the famed marine view from another host's windows because one could espy land on the far side of the water, or throwing himself fiercely, albeit inexpertly, into a controversy over whether Battersea Bridge should have a round or elliptical arch. But we do not get an indelible overview of Johnson's critical compulsion, his inability to subordinate moral or aesthetic indignation to social amenities, his approaching even such impersonal activities as dictionary-making with outbursts of critical subjectivity. And yet Johnson never glibly set himself above what he evaluated; with sound modesty and sense of humor he wrote, "Criticism is a study by which men grow important and formidable at very small expense." Truly he was both the "great Cham of Literature," as Smollett dubbed him, and, as Boswell accidentally misread it, the "great Chum of Literature."

[1979]

MARLOWE, REMEMBERED AND DISMEMBERED

A. L. Rowse, *Christopher Marlowe:*
A Biography
J. B. Steane, *Marlowe*

As if Christopher Marlowe's short and turbulent life had not been punishment enough for both his sins and his genius, he had also to be penalized posthumously for being born in the same year as Shakespeare. This has meant—besides invidious comparisons—considerable neglect by centenary celebrations, whether in the form of fashionable dramatic festivals or of highly publicized literary tributes. It does remain, however, an open question whether even oblivion is not preferable to such a memorial as A. L. Rowse's biography. Luckily there is also J. B. Steane's critical study, which provides, among other things, an effective antidote to Rowse.

Professor Rowse, who will leave no tombstone unturned, has already wrought considerable havoc in Shakespearian studies with a brace of quatrocentenary memorials to the Bard; he now undertakes to dispose of Marlowe at one fell swoop. The book is called *Christopher Marlowe: A Biography,* and a modest amount of marvel is due the title itself: how does one write a book-length biography of a man whose life survives as a handful of facts and perhaps two handfuls of more or less plausible conjectures? But Dr. Rowse is a historian and has found that problems of literary history have "worked themselves out . . . by following proper historical method." This presumably means that where the literary historian sadly lacks information, the historical literarian (to coin a phrase) blithely manufactures it. And in his preface, Dr. Rowse appropriately quotes a tribute to himself from the author of a *two*-volume biography of Marlowe.

How does this proper historical method function? It pronounces as unimpeachable texts of Marlowe's works about which, with good right, scholars continue to be profoundly uncertain. It identifies, on the flimsiest internal evidence, Marlowe as Shakespeare's rival for the affection of Mr. W. H.—himself scarcely more convincingly identified as Southampton. It arbitrarily assigns works whose conclusive dating is impossible to periods where they most suit Dr. Rowse's imaginary life of Marlowe. And it accepts without question the identity of Marlowe's views with those of his unsavory protagonists—the murderous Guise and the demoniacal Barabas.

Here is the historical method at work. If Robin, an illiterate but presumptuous clown in *Dr. Faustus,* is portrayed as having difficulties reading a magic invocation, one may deduce from this "a touch of disgust" in Marlowe with his academic training: "no doubt he had more than enough of it." From this and similar evidence one concludes that the translations of Lucan and Ovid must have been done at Cambridge, to get away from the curriculum. If the protagonist of *Edward II* has a minion, and if the latter part of *The Massacre at Paris* contains references to Henry III's minions, *Edward II* must have been written just after *The Massacre.* And if the murderer of Edward is called Lightborn (Lucifer), then, obviously, *Dr. Faustus,* in which Lucifer appears, must have been written shortly after *Edward II.* Even if this were logic, it could just as easily prove the opposite chronology.

What doubts the historical method might still leave in our

minds are then squelched by handily hammered-in superlatives and absolutes, which might be called the hysterical method. By practicing up on Ovid, Marlowe "laid the foundation" for *Hero and Leander,* "the most perfect and classic of Elizabethan poems." "No writer was ever more autobiographical," we are told summarily, and "no writer thrilled more electrically" to contemporary discoveries, which last may constitute the scientific method: applying the Electric Thrill Meter to Marlowe's verse.

Unfortunately, none of these methods seems to protect Dr. Rowse from self-contradiction. Thus we are told that "Marlowe was not much influenced by anyone" and that being "of a daring and aggressive originality . . . he did not accept anything from anyone." But in the very next sentence we learn that he "was a bookish, intellectual dramatist" for the understanding of whose plays "the reading that went into them" is of great importance. On page 149 we read that *Dr. Faustus* is "a most original work," though by page 152 it has become "not far removed from the traditional moralities," in fact, "very traditional." Dr. Rowse specializes in instant self-contradiction, which is not to say that some of his contradictions don't extend slowly and capaciously over the whole book.

Rowse misreads freely. He claims that in *Tamburlaine* the challenges to divine retribution result in no reaction from above, though, in fact, they do—albeit perhaps less obviously than the most literal-minded reader might wish. He speaks of Marlowe's showing up where "a passage [of Holy Writ] is at variance with Christian teaching," when Marlowe is merely showing up Faustus's sophistry in quoting only half-statements. When Barabas echoes Aristotle, this strikes Rowse as strangely Marlovian, as if it were not perfectly in character for the Jew of Malta to be influenced by the Mediterranean Jewish Artistotelians. The text of *Faustus* seems perfect to Rowse, and the play indubitably Marlowe's last, when the very scholars on whose findings Rowse relies (while continually jeering at them) are at loggerheads about these matters. He ridicules what he calls the squeamishness and unhistoricity of scholars who judge *Faustus* to be a collaboration because of the lack of delicacy in the comic scenes—when, actually, doubts about single authorship are based simply on the lack of quality in some of the writing.

Factual mistakes abound in Rowse's book, most of them founded on plain ignorance of literature. Thus, for example, the conventions of Elizabethan sonneteering are taken at face value and absurd biographical data extrapolated from them. Grand pronouncements are erected on missing pedestals: we are told of "a dominant theme in all Kyd's work," though, aside from a translation, only one play by Kyd survives. More important, Dr. Rowse exhibits lack of understanding of either poetry or drama. For he can say that "the spontaneity of alliteration would indicate how much the poet was moved"— as if a reiterated rhetorical device were a mere accident and, if it were such, a sign of overwhelming emotion rather than of carefree playfulness. And "plays centered upon one towering character" are of relatively "primitive dramatic type," which neatly takes care of *Oedipus Rex, The Misanthrope,* and *Hamlet.*

But there is worse yet: Rowse seems unable to think logically. Thus we are told that the use of a phrase from Ovid in *Dr. Faustus* "is effective, for Marlowe himself has made it so very famous." Or that "it is appropriate that the Book of Job should be to the fore in [*The Jew of Malta*], since Barabas . . . thinks himself worse persecuted [than Job]." Which means that something is effective because it is used effectively.

As for Dr. Rowse's style, grammar, and syntax, they have to be seen to be believed, and even then they are hardly believable. "We now know that Shakespeare's 'small Latin' was not so small as was thought: he knew quite enough Latin for his purposes, and his inspirations, as a poet; while he knew even less Greek. While Marlowe knew more of both . . ." ". . . He had much in common with Ralegh; like him there was a rift in his personality. . . ." "Of the authors . . . in Greene's pamphlet, two of them took offence. . . ." "In the last months of

Marlowe's life . . . Kentish associations surrounded him at the end of his life as at the beginning. . . ." And here is a typical Rowsian sentence: "To the Elizabethans, he was their idea of a poet; as to us in our time—and a hardly dissimilar fate, a kind of self-murder—was Dylan Thomas."

But Dr. Rowse saves his finest *coup* for the end, when—after grandly patronizing most other Marlovians and then superbly presenting his own platitudes and fabrications as spectacular discoveries—he proceeds to tell us exactly what Marlowe would have written had he lived longer. This opens up fascinating new possibilities for the historical method: biographies of unlived lives.

By contrast, J. B. Steane's *Marlowe* is a critical study, which, above all, avoids falling into any biographical fallacies. It contents itself with relating briefly and clearly the known biographical facts, and then goes on to examine closely, searchingly, and with discrimination the texts and meanings of the plays and poems. Mr. Steane's method is scrupulous and modest, and so his findings are often tentative. He has no ax to grind or particularly new approach to display, hence the book has a certain unspectacular straightforwardness that may leave jaded palates untickled. One may quarrel also with some of Mr. Steane's interpretations, though these quarrels are apt to be minor, and there is a slight amateurishness in some attempted parallels.

What is important, however, is that Mr. Steane does interpret: that his thoughtful analyses make sensible use of existing scholarship and criticism, and that he provides us with judicious aperçus over and above his sound general surveying. Though his style is a trifle pale, it is not without specific felicities, and one feels oneself addressed by a good mind and a refined sensibility. In a few words, Steane can tell us more—and tell it more correctly—than Rowse in a whole chapter. Thus of *Tamburlaine*: "The dramatic effect is to compel a justification of bloodshed and tyranny in the name of genius, magnificence and power." Of *Edward II*: "The dominant spirit is one of belittlement, where dignity is undermined, nobility turned to pettiness, and man made abject, thwarted and humiliated. The scene is never transcended by poetic life or breadth of reference or positive values felt in any counterpoint. The nature of the achievement is depressing." On the danger of writing Marlowe's biography from the few available facts: "The glimpses may be as clear as crystal, and generalising from them as futile as crystal-gazing."

Steane is particularly good at analyzing Marlowe's non-dramatic poetry and verse translations, and at showing the development of Marlowe's versification and its place in the history of English poetry. And the book contains the most cogent assessment yet of *Hero and Leander,* revealing it to be neither exquisite jewelry nor a mocking piece of nastiness, but a troubled hovering between extremes and as rich in intense poetry as in disturbing psychological revelations. Even as biography, which it does not purport to be, Steane's book far surpasses Rowse's; it belongs—along with the works of Boas, Levin, F. P. Wilson, and (with serious reservations) Cole—on the small shelf of essential studies of Marlowe.

[1965]

FRENCH
LITERATURE

BETWEEN MEANING AND NONSENSE

Roland Barthes, *New Critical Essays*

FOR the reader unmoved by the heady publicity that clings to the name of Roland Barthes like overinsistent perfume to a passing exhibitionist, three things become immediately clear upon reading him. (1) There is real intelligence at work here. (2) The intelligence wastes itself on efforts to make the criticism more important than the thing criticized. (3) The stuff is, finally, unreadable.

This is not the place for an overview of Barthes's triumphant career as one of several popes of structuralism, whose competing seats are not just in Rome and Avignon, but also in a number of institutions of higher learning from Paris to New Haven and beyond. Still less is it suitable for an all-out attack on structuralism and semiotics, imperative as such an enterprise may be. Yet merely by attending to the dense, almost impenetrable, pages of *New Critical Essays,* Barthes's not so new book now posthumously published over here, one can begin to convey the limitations of this approach.

French critical thought, once more or less Cartesian, has become largely Barthesian regardless of its many brand names—the most picturesque being "deconstructionism," the brainchild of Jacques Derrida. The essential problem with structuralism and semiotics is that they don't belong in the arts. It was doubtless useful for Claude Lévi-Strauss to be structural about anthropology, and for Ferdinand de Saussure to be semiotic about sociology; but when these disciplines invade literary criticism, the effect is rather as if Monaco tried to switch the source of its income from roulette to agriculture.

The eight essays in the present volume were originally published in France as an appendage to *Le Degré zéro de l'écriture* (*Writing Degree Zero*) in 1972. They are structural analyses of works by or aspects of La Rochefoucauld, Chateaubriand, Proust, Flaubert, Eugène Fromentin, and Pierre Loti, as well as a structuralist interpretation of the illustrations for Diderot's *Encyclopédie,* and a propaedeutic essay on how "to undertake the structural analysis of a literary work," entitled "Where to Begin?"

Let *me* begin with a relatively simple example of what Barthes is up to, a passage from his essay on Loti's *Aziyade*. He has just tracked down a certain bisexuality in this ostensibly straightforward piece of romantic exoticism, the story of a British officer and a Turkish odalisque who die for their clandestine love affair. Barthes perceives in the espousal of Oriental clothes by the hero (likewise named Pierre Loti) a kind of transvestism—or, rather, a device that legitimizes the wearing of flowing, feminine attire. By assuming this Oriental disguise, moreover, the person becomes "a pictorial being" in an exotic tableau.

And now we read: "The goal of transvestism is finally (once the illusion of being is exhausted) to transform oneself into a describable object—and not into an introspectible subject." Already we are on shaky ground. Why is the protagonist—or, indeed, the writer, for Loti is manifestly playing at partial autobiography—any more an object as a transvestite than as Lieutenant Loti in his British officer's uniform? The uniformed Westerner is a standard literary and pictorial feature of the Eastern scene. Note, by the way, that parenthesis; throughout, Barthes uses parenthetic remarks to introduce grandiose, often irrelevant, and frequently incomprehensible asides that raise, or even pretend to answer, vast psychological or philosophical questions. The need to close a parenthesis in fairly short order allows him to hurry on, like jesting Pilate, without staying for elucidation. What illusion, exactly, has been exhausted? And how?

To continue: "The consecration of the disguise (what belies it by dint of its success [can you follow this parenthetic remark?]) is pictorial integration, the passage from the body into a collective writing, in a word (if we are to take it literally), *transcription*: dressed exactly (i.e., in a garment from which the excess of exactitude is banished), the subject dissolves himself, not by intoxication, but by Apollinism, by participation in a proportion, in a combination system." Not so fast, please! How does "dressed exactly" get to be glossed as "from which excess of exactitude is banished"? And how does one dissolve oneself in Apollonianism (the translator, Richard Howard, should know there is no such English word as "Apollinism") in a combination system? And why is it Apollonian to disguise oneself as an old Arab? And how is that a "combination system"—what, in fact, does that scientific-sounding term mean? Is it a way of mingling with the natives? Then why not say so?

To go on: "Hence a minor author, outdated and evidently unconcerned with theory (though a contemporary of Mallarmé, of Proust), brings to light the most complex of writing's logics: for wanting to be 'the one who belongs to the tableau' is to write only insofar as one is written: that abolition of passive and active, of expresser and expressed, of subject and statement, in which modern writing is seeking to discover itself." First, how many "logics" does writing have, and how do they get to be more or less complex? Shouldn't everything logical be equally perspicuous? Next, what is the meaning of "write only insofar as one is written"? How does this abolish the categories enumerated? And who says that modern writ-

ing is seeking to discover itself in those categories? But suppose that is what modern writing is doing; has then Loti—this
outdated, untheoretical, minor writer—ushered in modern
writing? That would make him pretty major, I should think.

Perhaps Loti has not consciously done anything; his writing
has merely "brought to light" these things; or, more precisely,
Barthes's analysis of his writing has ushered in modern writing. Or perhaps it is not so much a matter of ushering in
modern writing as destroying (or deconstructing) all accepted
views on writing. Not surprising from someone who, in *The
Pleasure of the Text,* attempts to queer the essence of writing,
the sentence, by dismissing the writer as "a Sentence-Thinker,
i.e., not altogether a thinker." In the present volume, in the
essay on Chateaubriand, Barthes writes, "We find ourselves
dreaming of a pure writer who does not write"; in his *Writing
Degree Zero,* he speculated about "that Orphean dream—a
writer without Literature." And to think that he has to drag
poor blameless Orpheus into that shabby transaction!

Orpheus, incidentally, keeps getting it. At one point Barthes
claims that Orpheus loves Eurydice only because she is lost,
"in accordance with the old myth . . . which defines love." But
the myth does not necessarily define love, and certainly not in
that way. Barthes may interpret as he wishes, but he cannot
claim that his interpretation *is* the old myth. Presently, however, things get hairier yet: ". . . like Orpheus, who loses
Eurydice by turning back to look at her, *nothing* loses a little of
its meaning each time it is set forth (set back)." How inept to
use Orpheus and Eurydice to make a point about the difficulty
of describing "nothing." There is no parallel between an eager
husband looking back at his beloved wife returning from the
dead and a structural critic worrying the problem of how to
describe nonexistence. One does not look *back* at nothing, in
any case, and what is that parenthetic "set back," except a
further setback for the reader?

Let us look at another passage, this one from an examination
of Chateaubriand's *Life of Rancé,* a pious biography the old

writer undertook at the behest of his confessor, the Abbé Séguin. Barthes writes:

> The Abbé Séguin had a yellow cat. Perhaps this yellow cat is literature itself, for if the notation doubtless refers to the idea that a yellow cat is an ill-favored, probably stray cat and thereby combines with other details of the Abbé's life, all attesting to his kindness and poverty, this yellow is also quite simply yellow, it leads not only to a sublime—in short, intellectual—meaning, it stubbornly remains on the level of colors (opposing, for example, the *black* of the old housekeeper and that of the crucifix): to say a *yellow cat* and not a *stray cat* is in a way the act which separates writer from mere scribe, not because the yellow "creates an image," but because it casts a certain enchantment on the intentional meaning, returns speech to a kind of *asymptote* of meaning; the *yellow cat* says the Abbé Séguin's kindness, but also it says *less,* and it is here that there appears the scandal of literary speech. [Also the scandal of translatorese: surely, "it is here that the scandal of literary speech appears" is called for.] This speech is somehow endowed with a double wavelength; the longer one is that of meaning (the Abbé Séguin is a holy man, he lives in poverty accompanied by a stray cat); the shorter one transmits no information, if not literature itself: this is the more mysterious one, for because of it we cannot reduce literature to an entirely decipherable system: reading, criticism are not pure hermeneutics.

Where to begin? Consider only the impossible second sentence that rambles on relentlessly with rudimentary punctuation and stretches well beyond syntactical cohesion and psychological endurance. Next, how can Barthes assume that just because the cat is yellow, it must also be ill-favored and probably a stray—later in the paragraph, the "probably" is dropped, and the cat becomes an apodictic stray. Suppose some noble lady had given her worthy confessor an adorable calico kitten, the pride of the litter? What would be left of that typical Barthesian strategy, elaborate superstructure erected on arrant supposition? And how in God's name does "yellow cat" make you a writer rather than a mere scribe "because it casts a certain enchantment on the intentional meaning"? This enchantment, mark it well, has nothing to do with creating an image—that would be too simple for a critic of Barthes's superhuman subtlety. Rather, it "returns speech to a kind of asymptote of meaning," and is remarkable because it says *less*. That "asymptote" is a good example of science dragged into criticism in order to make it more impenetrable and imposing—a way for the critic to say less and make it sound like more. "This yellow is also quite simply yellow"—here we have the scandal, not of literary speech but of pseudoliterary criticism.

Then Barthes hits upon an idea of genius: a second, shorter wavelength (more science) that "transmits no information, if not literature itself." How, if it transmits no information, do we know it is there? Maybe it is not a wavelength at all, but an invisible papaya that transmits no taste if not fruitiness itself? How does "literature itself" get transmitted except by performance, by function, even if the means is suggestion, indirection, understatement? Literature will indeed not become decipherable by such an investigation; as for criticism of this kind, far from being pure hermeneutics, it is pure mystification.

Barthes never explains how this short wavelength operates; he tells us merely, with Pythian opacity, that it "suspends speech between meaning and nonsense." Later, we find him proclaiming that "The modern writer . . . must be at once outside the ethical and within language, he must create the general with the irreducible, rediscover the amorality of his existence through the moral generality of language: it is this *hazardous* passage which is literature." Now, there are evidently people who find this sort of thing impressive, and there may even be some who can make sense of it. For me, it is a curious combination of scientism (asymptotes, wavelengths) and some sort of Zen (transmitting no information, if not literature itself), and so perfectly otiose.

As I have pointed out elsewhere concerning Michel Foucault, there exists an affinity between homosexual writers and the paradox. In Barthes, paradox is everywhere, ranging from the clever epigram to flagrant, and quite unabashed, self-contradiction. Consider the following passage from the quasi-autobiography *Roland Barthes*:

> . . . the world, as a literary object, escapes: knowledge deserts literature, which can no longer be either *Mimesis* or *Mathesis* [an order, a system] but merely *Semiosis,* the adventure of what is impossible to language, in a word *Text* (it is wrong to say that the notion of "text" repeats the notion of "literature": literature *represents* a finite world, the text *figures* the infinite of language: without knowledge, without rationale, without intelligence).

Literature as the adventure of what is impossible to language, text as a figuring of language without intelligence, semiology as the only remaining option! And yet a little further on in the same book we read: "What has attracted him [Barthes] is less the sign than the signal, the poster: the science he desired was not a semiology but a *signaletics.*" From the frying pan into the fire: even the only remaining choice is finally inadequate to so deep and far-reaching an intellect—condemned, moreover, to accept (however ungraciously) being a Sentence-Thinker.

Gore Vidal has observed in *Matters of Fact and of Fiction*: "Like so many of today's academic critics, Barthes resorts to formulas, diagrams; the result, no doubt, of teaching in classrooms equipped with blackboards and chalk. Envious of the half-erased theorems—the prestigious *signs*—of the physicists, [teachers of literature] now compete by chalking up theorems and theories of their own, words having failed them yet again." True enough, and in *New Critical Essays,* Barthes demonstrates how "a sudden dissymmetry disturbs" a maxim by La Rochefoucauld "and consequently makes the entire series of surrounding symmetries signify" by "simply casting the maxim as an equation . . . a b c^1. ^{3}/c^2b a." And what is the maxim thus simplified? "Philosophy triumphs readily over past evils and evils to come, but present evils triumph over it."

What has invaded literary criticism here is not only science but also linguistics; in a sense, one could say that Barthes represents the vengeance of linguistics on literature and literary scholarship, which have long relegated linguistics to an ancillary position. But most important to Barthes is paradox: proving the truth of the opposite of what is traditionally and commonly held true. Thus the point of the La Rochefoucauld essay is that the *Maxims* are not, as generally believed, moral and psychological insights, but verbal games. The plates of the *Encyclopédie* are not sane, rational diagrams, but constant attempts at "impious fragmention of the world."

Again, Chateaubriand's *Life of Rancé,* so far from being a pious pensum in response to priestly exhortation, is in fact "a work of sovereign irony . . . a nascent schizophrenia, prudently formed in a homeopathic quantity . . . a certain 'detachment' applied by excess of words . . . to the tenacious will to suffer." Proust is by no means attempting to record the shifting values of his era; rather, he wants to construct a mythic perspective. Flaubert's exhausting stylistic efforts were directed to freeing the writer from the rhetorician (so far, so good), only to subject him to the "master of linguistics" (nonsense). Fromentin's *Dominique* is not a pioneer novel of psychological analysis but a subversive, "illegal" book that "invites us to idleness, to irresponsibility."

Though there is usually some marginal insight in Barthes's lucubrations, they seem to me neither central nor lucid enough to be of major critical interest. Most revealing is the essay "Where to Begin?" which proposes to demonstrate how to perform structural analysis, and uses for its subject Jules Verne's trashy *The Mysterious Island.* The intention seems to be to prove the importance of structural analysis by showing what wonders it can wrest even from works of negligible literary merit. The result, however, is the opposite: by making the critical method more important than the work it comments on, it reduces first literature, then criticism, to insignificance.

[1980]

EPISTEMOLOGICAL FLIP-FLOP

Jean-Paul Sartre, *Saint Genet, Actor and Martyr*

THE only person who has an even harder task than the reader confronted with Jean-Paul Sartre's remarkable study *Saint Genet, Actor and Martyr* is the reviewer. It is his problem to determine whether this book is about Jean Genet or about existentialism; whether it is a work of literary criticism, existential psychoanalysis, or metaphysics; whether one should conceive of it as a defense of Genet or as an attack on our bourgeois society. Or whether the whole thing is an outcry— sometimes contemptuously sardonic, sometimes passionately lamenting—against the human condition. By turns, and even simultaneously, the book is all of these things, and the wealth of its suggestivity, sharpness, and insight makes up—or almost—for its excessive difficulty, diffuseness, repetitiousness, and sheer length.

One of the great difficulties with *Saint Genet* is that it is almost impossible to tell when Sartre is paraphrasing Genet, when he is explicating and elaborating him, when he is interpreting him rather freely, and when he is actually disagreeing. Often he offers long and seemingly sympathetic interpretations of Genet's psyche only to disassociate himself suddenly from the ideas and values involved. At other times, however, he makes no bones about agreeing with Genet, if only to use him as a stick to beat the middle classes with. Are we, then, in the realm of contradiction? Perhaps. But to Genet and, largely, to Sartre, contradiction is the stuff of life.

Paradox rather than the sentence or the paragraph is the basic unit of this work, as it is also of Genet's worldview. Though it is never stated in so many words, the fundamental concept of *Saint Genet* is: everything is as much its opposite as itself. Throughout the book appearance is a reality, while reality proves illusory. The most important terms are the being of nonbeing and the nonbeing of being. Evil becomes a kind of good—at least by contrast with what is commonly accepted as such and what Genet-Who-Is-Sartre (or Sartre-Who-Is-Genet) reveals in all its insufficiency and hypocrisy.

It is, unfortunately, impossible to summarize a book that traces Genet's development according to a curious dialectical sequence that only roughly coincides with anything as mundane as chronology, and uses biographical data with cavalier, indeed sovereign, nonchalance.

Briefly, the argument proceeds from Genet's illegitimacy and childhood with peasant foster parents and his first petty crime, which elicited the hurling of the word "thief" at him. With these two coordinates, bastard and thief, Sartre constructs his system, showing with a logic that is more ingenious than inexorable how Genet becomes a juvenile delinquent, a homosexual, an enemy of society, a pimp, a burglar, a jailbird, an oblate of pure Evil, an aesthete, a writer of genius, a social and literary lion. The six hundred pages in which this development is traced form a brilliant metaphysic of evil and *esthétique du mal* with which one often quarrels, but which no less often elicits one's clenched admiration and shamefaced agreement. Always, however, it makes one question accepted values— social, religious, political, and ethical—and always it plays, as do Genet's novels and dramas, the role of devil's advocate with greater conviction and coruscation than it has perhaps ever been played before.

The three main points of Sartre's thesis are scarcely original. That Genet's ascesis of evil is a kind of sainthood in some ways preferable to orthodox sainthood—or, in other words, that white is black—is an idea whose roots go back as far as Anaxagoras. That under stress of deprivation it is possible to invent one's own upside-down sense of values (but in the outer spaces of being is there up and down?) has been maintained succinctly by Milton's Satan:

> So farewell Hope, and with Hope farewell fear,
> Farewell Remorse: all Good to me is lost;
> Evil, be thou my Good. . . .

Lastly, the notion that by writing out his problems the writer gets rid of them—literature as therapy—goes back at least as far as Goethe. But Sartre's contribution is that, while applying these propositions to Genet's life and work, he gives us not only an absorbing spiritual biography of Genet, but also a working model of the Sartrian universe.

In a sense, *Saint Genet, Actor and Martyr* can be viewed as a fictionalization of Sartre's major philosophical treatise, *Being and Nothingness.* I say fictionalization because the liberties taken with strict fact, the discursiveness of the approach, the elaborate and often poetic style, the frequent invention of illustrative anecdotes, the healthy vulgarity, the marvelous excursions into social irony (as in that magisterial disquisition on the bourgeois attitude to Nature, or another on consumers versus producers) place *Saint Genet* very nearly in the realm of modern philosophical fiction, which, in turn, is a sort of existentialist-absurdist prose poetry flourishing nowadays under the name of "antinovel."

The first quarter of the book is heavy going. Here Genet must become the vehicle for Sartre's higher philosophizing—for example, about the "being-in-itself" and the "being-for-itself." Here, too, a good deal of Husserlian phenomenology, Heideggerism, and Sartre's existential psychoanalysis is concentrated. But as we read on, the language becomes less opaque, and Genet the man and, eventually, writer emerges more and more compellingly. There are, to be sure, periodic relapses; I find it hard to be enlightened by statements such as this:

> Jean's soul, which has drifted out of the world, and Genet's consciousness, which was cast in the mud, are symmetrical: their absences correspond on both sides of the mirror: looking at himself in the glass, Genet, the living corpse, sees Jean who sees Genet, his image. The dead Jean becomes the reflection in eternity, in nonbeing, of the Death that Genet lives in being from day to day. Genet and Jean are, for each other, *all* by virtue of being *nothing*: Genet is transformed into all by a rejection of all, he the All-Evil; Jean *who no longer is,* is in all the Absence of All.

But Sartre is able to come out with stunning insights often far transcending his subject. "We are not natural beings, our modest and tenacious defenses against death define us as much as does the progress of death in our organs." Or: "If you are *common,* you can dress up as a woman, show your behind or write poems: there's nothing offensive about a naked behind if it's everybody's; each person will be mirrored in it." Or again, "To speak is to pass over words in silence." Or, no less pregnant, but more directly relevant to Genet: "The consciousness of the word is a local awakening within the fantasy: he awakes without ceasing to dream." Genet's credo defined: "It is in culture that he wants to make holes and contrive dizzying falls." Genet's achievement: "He is the secret bad conscience of the good consciences."

It is unfortunate that this study of Genet, published in 1952 as the introduction to his collected works, could not address itself to his later plays for which he is best known here. But in calling meticulous attention to Genet's novels, the publication of *Saint Genet* undoubtedly ushers in the appearance in English of these novels, only one of which was hitherto available in an expensive, limited, under-the-counter edition. These staggering, baroque fictions eminently deserve to be known, and Sartre's book is, despite its excesses, a good preparation for them. Bernard Frechtman's translation, barring a few misplaced accusatives and popular solecisms, as well as an occasional archaism such as "channelize," is highly competent. Why, however, does he give the title of Genet's *L'Enfant criminel* correctly as *The Criminal Child* and then incorrectly as *The Child Criminal*?

Sartre would also have done much better juxtaposing Genet with Lautréamont and Sade, both of whom he surpasses, than with Mallarmé, whom he cannot begin to equal. And certainly much of the argument has nothing to do with Genet. Still, if we get illuminations such as "Genius is not a gift but the way out one invents in desperate cases" or "Unless one is a god, one cannot make oneself happy without the help of the universe; to make oneself unhappy, one needs only oneself," are we going to look such admirable gift horse-sense in the mouth? Let us concede that Sartre's study is an uneven book about its subject. It is a powerful book about a good many other things.

[1963]

FROM ODD NUGGETS, A GOLDEN MEAN

Albert Camus, *Notebooks: 1942–1951*

ONCE, as a boy, I was taken up to a peak in the Julian Alps from which one could see three countries. I recall my disappointment at their not being, as on maps, differently colored, but placidly alike. Today, I would have rejoiced in this fact, as I rejoice in the worldview of Albert Camus, who achieved that arduous elevation from which psychology, politics, metaphysics, and art all look like the selfsame country.

As those familiar with the first and much less consequential volume, *Notebooks: 1935–1942,* will know, "notebooks" is the *mot juste* here. Like their predecessor, these *Notebooks: 1942–1951* are not a journal in the gossipy sense of the Goncourts', in the poetically playful sense of Jules Renard's, or in the highly developed literary sense of Gide's. Neither, however, are they anything like Valéry's *A Poet's Notebook,* in which questions of craft and theory are single-mindedly pursued. Camus's notebooks are a catchall: thoughts caught on the wing, words caught on the lips (the author's or someone else's), silent outcries caught in the depths of one's being. Also aphorisms—one's own or other people's, for this is also a commonplace book—and, above all, jottings of ideas, perceptions, conversations, incidents, plot outlines or details of future works, most of them never executed.

This promptly raises the question of readership. If a body of notes is an honest *aide-mémoire* for its author, and not, like the diary of Wilde's Cecily Worthing, "simply a very young girl's record of her own thoughts and impressions, and consequently meant for publication," does it justify itself as a book; and, if so, whom does it concern? It concerns all those who loved Camus the writer, and all those, more numerous perhaps, who respected Camus the man. My own recollections of him include only a glimpse in Harvard Yard, where he wore that light-colored, Humphrey Bogartish raincoat (he did, in fact, have the odd good looks and oblique charm of a subtilized Bogart), and, later, a spirited lecture, after which he answered our earnest student questions with fervent serenity and a commitment greatly and quietly exceeding that of the questioners.

Those who look for the writer Camus in these notebooks that accompany his life from its twenty-eighth to its thirty-seventh year will find considerable light shed on the making of the works of that period, notably *The Plague, The Just Assassins,* and *The Rebel*. Now, it is doubtful whether these works, in their respective genres, have the striking power of earlier achievements: *The Stranger, Caligula,* and *The Myth of Sisyphus*. It is even arguable whether any of Camus's imaginative writings are indisputably first-rate, though *The Stranger* should survive as one of the best expressions of a world mood that, if anything, is more evident now than a quarter century ago. What is more important is that all three works stem from a noteworthy mind and sensibility, and that these setting-up exercises and by-products, prolegomena and paralipomena, are the operational procedures of a dedicated writer, to be followed with interest and, frequently, delight. Readers able to savor the similarities and differences between first insights and final embodiments will find themselves rewarded; better yet, anyone who can share in the frustrations, agonies, and slowly unfurling pleasures of creation will become thrillingly involved. There are notes as simple and touching as "Rise early. Shower *before* breakfast. No cigarettes before noon"; and others, more elaborately probing: "I took ten years to win what seems to me priceless: a heart without bitterness. And as often happens, once I had gone beyond the bitterness, I incorporated it in one or two books. Thus I shall be forever judged on that bitterness which has ceased to mean anything to me. But that is just. It's the price one must pay."

For those whose main interest is the man Camus, there is even richer ore to be mined. He can be seen here loving and learning, fighting his tuberculosis, enduring the war as a writer for the Resistance (he was disqualified from active combat), reacting keenly to postwar upheavals, fostering friendships and replying to criticism; in short, living. We read: "Nostalgia for the life of others. This is because, seen from the outside, another's life forms a unit. Whereas ours, seen from the inside, seems broken up. We are still chasing after an illusion of unity." Or, "Greatness consists in trying to be great. There is no other kind." (The translator, mistakenly, gives "no other way.") Again, "Whoever has not insisted upon absolute virginity in people and the world, and screamed with nostalgia and impotence of achieving it, whoever has not been destroyed through trying to love, halfheartedly, a face that cannot invent love and merely repeats it, cannot understand the reality of revolt and its rage to destroy." The last passage, by the way, was incorporated almost verbatim into *The Rebel*.

But the book can be appreciated on a more general level, as a sovereign attempt to make order out of chaos, bit by bit; it shows the process of fusion of art and metaphysics, psychology and politics, not from the Olympian heights of a finished work, but out of the helter-skelter of total immersion in nature, books, daily routines, cataclysms, passionate meditations, history in the making. What gives special meaning to Camus's progress as reflected here is his admirable philosophical position and his superb temperament.

The universe, to Camus, is absurd, because God does not

exist but death does; because we want immortality but must
make it out of mortality; because the heart cries out, and the
world, unreasonably, remains silent. Humanism is insufficient, and Christianity and Marxism are only the two faces of
the same worn coin whose purchasing power is nil. Out of
this, to me, most accurately sized-up human predicament,
Camus emerges with solutions that are partial, but the best
possible. "Pessimistic as to the human condition," Camus says
in the *Notebooks,* "I am optimistic as to mankind." And again,
"We have but one way of creating God, which is to become
him." (The English in both these quotations is shaky, but we'll
come to the translation in a moment.)

The very reason for which Camus is now in eclipse should,
in time, make him more valuable to us—when the extremist
positions of the Christian and Marxist existentialists have had
their overlong day. For it is now held against him that he strove
to discover a *via media,* a middle course between individualistic
self-centeredness and self-sacrificing altruism, between too
rigorous justice and self-indulgent anarchy, between Hellenis-
tic sun-worship and post-doctrinal despair. But what makes
this middle path significant and charismatic is that it is not a
flabby compromise, but a hard-won reconciliation of impassioned opposites; that it is, for example, against violence, but
for an exacting indignation.

Camus accomplished his difficult synthesis by being an
inspired eclectic. Thus we find him in the *Notebooks* as recep-
tive to Constant and Stendhal as to Tolstoy and Dostoevsky, as
able to learn from Schopenhauer and Nietzsche as from Pascal
and Simone Weil. His subjects are various: the sea, his mother,
suicide, Greece, Algeria, the controlling of passion, the correction of the created world. Everything is grist for his slow
militancy, from a sweet little old woman who brought her own
faggot to add to the stake on which Jan Huss was being
burned, to the man who gave up cigarettes but, when the
H-bomb was invented, took them up again. Sometimes the
result is frisky jottings, sometimes soul-shaking horror, some-

times a fine bit of prose poetry about trees and sky and water, sometimes a perfect maxim: "He who despairs of events is a coward, but he who hopes for the human lot is a fool"; "Love is an injustice, but justice is not enough"; and this, on which the book ends: "Any achievement is a bondage. It obliges one to a higher achievement."

Germaine Brée and Susan Sontag have shown how poor Philip Thody's translation of the first volume of the *Notebooks* was; Justin O'Brien's Englishing of the second is no better. I have no space here for the numerous offenses against grammar and tone, the minor bowdlerizations or overexplicitness, the padding out of knife-edge concision or the trampling on exquisite cadences. But there is worse. A sacrificial cake becomes an artificial cake; a small jug, a duckling (*canette* can mean either, but it takes a kind of perverse genius to think that the child Camus measured out his poverty in pet ducklings!); the portrait of a woman, S., becomes, through the ignoring of gender, the portrait of a man. When Camus writes of Communism that "C'est une histoire de Chrétiens," he means that it is a Christian mess, not that "It is a history of Christians"; when he writes of renunciation of oneself, he surely does not mean "yielding to oneself." And so on.

Much is lost, but not all. As an epigraph to his *Lettres à un ami allemand,* Camus appended a thought from Pascal: "One does not show one's greatness by being at one extreme, but by touching both at once." *Notebooks: 1942–1951,* this warm-hearted and spine-chilling book, remains, even in Professor O'Brien's rendering, at home at both extremes.

[1965]

A WOMAN OF PARTS
Arthur Gold and Robert Fizdale, *Misia*

MISIA GODEBSKA was not just a fascinating woman. She was also an institution—perhaps, successively, three institutions—and, beyond that, the epitome of an age. Descended from a cello virtuoso grandfather and a father who was a highly successful although pedestrianly academic sculptor, the young, motherless Polish girl grew up, first, with warm relatives in Belgium, then in a cold Paris girls' school poorly run by nuns. She was to have no learning or intellectual bent, but an uncanny feeling for the arts, especially for music and painting.

When still quite small, she once sat in Liszt's lap and played Beethoven for him on the piano; the pianist-composer exclaimed: "If I could only play like that!" When, years later, Misia announced to her teacher Gabriel Fauré that she was giving up her pianistic career to get married, the great master tearfully begged her to persevere. By that time she had absorbed much artistic talk at the house of her unloving father, Cyprien Godebski, and lived for a while in London, either alone or, more likely, as the mistress of Félicien Rops, the artist and illustrator specializing in sadism and diabolism, who must have taught her the ropes. Even as a tyke, she may have spied on the meetings in Cyprien's house of the League of the Rose, a group that acted out sexual fantasies; yet Cyprien also insisted

that the nuns give her a weekly bath—something revolutionary for France in those days, though by now it may have
become the norm.

The gentle Fauré, the satanic Rops; the hygienic bath (to be
taken modestly in one's petticoat), exposure to orgies—contrary demons watched over Misia's development. But no one
watched with the same concern as Arthur Gold and Robert
Fizdale, the well-known duo pianists and until now authors
only of a few articles on cookery, who have just come out with
their first book, *Misia*. This is a deeply sympathetic and thoroughly enjoyable popular biography of the remarkable Marie
Sophie Olga Zénaïde Godebska, nicknamed Misia (1872–
1950). Her three marriages (of which none gave her lasting
happiness and only the third turned gradually into a strange,
perverse, stubbornly enduring love) were ideally suited to
establish her in the circles that made her one of the great
salonnières of all time—if not the most important hostess, at
least a most desired guest, most prized contact, most diversely
inspiring muse, and most awesome puller of strings in the
world of the arts.

Married first to the comfortably-off dilettante Thadée Natanson, cofounder and editor-in-chief of the leading avant-
garde publication, *La Revue Blanche,* she became the friend,
protectress, platonic beloved, inspiration of numerous outstanding writers, poets, painters, composers, and other artists
who published in or gravitated toward that periodical. Then
and later, she was repeatedly painted by Renoir, Toulouse-
Lautrec, Vuillard, Bonnard, Valloton (to name only the most
significant), and was the friend of many other artists, notably
Picasso, who was apparently more than a little smitten with
her. The literary figures in her life included over the years
Verlaine, Mallarmé, Apollinaire, Valéry, Gide, Proust,
Claudel, Cocteau, Colette, Jarry, St.-John Perse, Morand,
Max Jacob, Reverdy, and a host of lesser lights. She appears
prominently in plays and novels by Proust (as both the noble
Princess Yourbeletieff and the pushy Mme Verdurin of *A la*

Recherche), Cocteau, Octave Mirbeau, and Alfred Savoir. In music, she was close to Fauré, Satie, Debussy, Ravel, Stravinsky, Poulenc, Milhaud, Auric, and more, many of whom dedicated works to her.

It was the crass Anglo-Turkish millionaire Alfred Edwards, however, who, after bombarding her with passion, expensive gifts, and relentless persistence until she first lived with and then married him, made it possible for Misia to become a Maecenas. She was to be the only woman whom Diaghilev could envision as his wife, but, of course, preferred to consider his sister. More important, the great despot recognized that her taste in music was better than his and actually took her advice on musical matters. This led to her becoming wildly sought after by those who wanted to be produced by the supreme impresario. It was during the Edwards years that even aristocrats who had considered Misia a parvenu opened their doors to her; it was through Edwards, too, that she got to know the dicier layers of bohemia.

When Edwards finally abandoned her to pursue and eventually marry the bisexual prostitute-turned-actress Geneviève Lantelme (this stunning young creature was mysteriously drowned a couple of years later; according to one rumor, killed by Edwards himself), Misia married the grandiose and mediocre painter and stage designer José-Maria Sert. A rich, pretentious, yet knowledgeable and enthusiastic Spaniard, this society artist, womanizer, and sexual athlete was, though three years younger than Misia, a perfect father image. Like Diaghilev, Sert was to become an international figure, painting murals in rich people's houses all over the world; accordingly, Mme Sert's social sphere was extended even farther. Thus Misia was instrumental in the rise to world fame of Gabrielle "Coco" Chanel, with whom she remained in a lifelong mixture of intimacy, competition, and enmity. As for the many celebrated figures in the theatrical, concert, dance, and social worlds with whom Misia was involved, their number is too great for enumeration.

What exactly were her endowments? Beauty? The countless paintings and photographs offer contradictory evidence: in some she appears alluring or at least appealing; in others one sees merely a healthy Slavic peasant. The written evocations are equally conflicting. Proust, in his last letter to Misia (when he was too close to death for flattery), refers to her "cruel and beautiful face." In *Stravinsky in Pictures and Documents,* Robert Craft, no doubt basing himself on his coauthor, Vera Stravinsky, who knew her well, refers to Misia as a virago, and as the "plain-looking, busy-bodying, insufferably snobbish tyrant of Parisian society," but grants her "an extraordinary gift of musical perceptiveness." Many artists were in love with her: Renoir, Toulouse-Lautrec, Vuillard, Bonnard, Reverdy certainly; Mallarmé and St.-John Perse probably. Colette's affection may have had passionate lesbian overtones; Chanel was suspected of having an affair with Misia.

Yet she seems to have had sexual problems. She was never in love with Natanson, and though she affirmed that Edwards was a great lover, she confessed to planning the next day's menu while he made love to her. To the American heiress Hoytie Wiborg, the only woman to whose insistent advances she admitted yielding (albeit only once), she said after the act, "Is that all you know how to do?" She did come around to loving Sert passionately, but only after she began to lose him to the very young and pretty Roussy Mdivani—with whom she fell in love, too. A crazy triangle evolved, giving rise to, among other things, the aforementioned works by Cocteau and Savoir. When, at thirty-two, Roussy, whom Sert had married, was dying of tuberculosis, it was Misia who lovingly sat up with her night after night while Sert slept next door. After Roussy's death, Misia and Sert drifted back into an uneasy, quasi-marital relationship, but maintained separate domiciles. Perhaps Mme Simone, the actress who portrayed Misia in Savoir's play, was right when she imparted, at the age of ninety-eight, a bit of old theatrical gossip to Gold and Fizdale: "Misia was never any good in bed."

It was certainly not her intellect that charmed people. Misia herself boasted of not reading books, merely leafing through them to get their gist. We cannot tell how good her literary taste was—whether, for example, she appreciated Mallarmé for his poetry or merely for his attentions to her. Certainly she allowed most of the gift fans that he inscribed with poems to her to disappear; when she was advised not to reprint Renoir's love letters in her autobiography, these too got lost. She once amazed some friends with batches of letters from Proust, many of which she had not even bothered to open, and allowed these friends to help themselves to them. (They vanished as well.) Yet, when she and Sert proved unable to save Max Jacob from the Nazis, every year, on the anniversary of Jacob's death, she reread his poems to her.

She was particularly good, though, at recognizing the best new musical works. She grasped (not immediately) the greatness of *Pelléas et Mélisande,* and (immediately) of *Boris Godunov, Le Sacre du printemps, Les Noces,* and various works by Satie and Ravel, while she also enjoyed the charm of Poulenc and certain others of talent. She was astute about painting, too, except about that of Sert, where closeness blinded her. Still, she was unsophisticated enough to refuse baring her breasts for Renoir to paint, much as the old painter entreated her. And she would not even consider posing for Maillol in the nude.

Misia's outspokenness was certainly in her favor. She dared to write Stravinsky that she hated one of his works, and refused to accept any of Picasso's later paintings as a gift, thereby obviously hurting the painter's feelings. Yet for all its honesty and quickness, her mind was, I think, also trivial; she described the Nazis marching into Paris as "overgrown homosexual boyscouts," and commented on the first performance of *Jeanne d'Arc au bûcher*: "This brings together the three biggest bores in the world: Claudel, Honegger, and Joan of Arc." She could, however, write vividly on occasion, as certain passages from her memoirs attest. We must assume that she had an indefinable sexual appeal as well as a swiftness of perception and saltiness of expression that anecdotes and recollections only partly convey, and that photographs do not capture at all.

What makes Misia so compelling is the way her life acts as the focal point or objective correlative of an era; an age wherein the aristocracy, the more enterprising part of the bourgeoisie, the artists, and the demimonde mingled with an *éclat* and reverberations unmatched before or since. This, in a sense, is the subject of Proust's masterpiece, and Misia and her circle were indeed a large part of Proust's source material. There was such upward and downward mobility in these bustling, brilliant, exhibitionistic worlds, such play of what Fizdale and Gold call "unbelievable coincidence and startling revelation," that our authors rightly wonder whether Proust was imitating life or vice versa. They write:

> Who could have foretold that Misia, who had once been assured that society would never receive her, would now reign as one of the queens of Paris? Or that Chanel, whom Misia had not been permitted to bring to the Beaumonts' a few years earlier, would soon employ [Count de] Beaumont to design jewelry for her? Or that this peasant girl from the provinces would refuse to marry the Duke of Westminster? Or that Léon Blum, the *fin de siècle* dandy of Misia's *Revue Blanche* days, would become the Socialist leader of France? Or that Picasso, so courageous in his art, would not have the guts to help his dear friend Max Jacob when Jacob was on his way to certain death in a Nazi concentration camp? Or that the Catholic Rightist Sert would save Colette's Jewish husband Maurice Goudeket from the same fate? Or that the dying Jewish composer Darius Milhaud, nostalgic for his youth, would tell his wife he would like to see his old friend Paul Morand, an arch-collaborationist, even though they had not spoken for years? Or that Proust himself, the amateur who dabbled in literature, would write the greatest French novel of the twentieth century? . . .

Misia moves along rapidly and absorbingly; it is a laudable piece of work, coming from the hands of virtual amateurs. Nevertheless, amateurishness will out. That the biography is

not fully documented (the sources are not always clearly indicated, and their trustworthiness is often not evaluated) is of
small importance in a popular treatment; surely Misia herself
would not have wished it to be more scholarly and less readable. But certain errors and omissions could have been
avoided. Thus Natanson disappears from the book after his
divorce from Misia, though we want to know a little about his
later life (he outlived her by a year). A passage from Baudelaire's *Peintre de la vie moderne* about dandyism purports to be
an exact translation, though it is in fact an abridgment and
oversimplification.

The authors, who fancy themselves capable of offering verse
translations of French poetry, always come to grief with them.
For the sake of rhyme, they will stoop to something like
"Toulouse Lautreek" (a low trick); or they may simply mis-
translate, as they do the couplet from Mallarmé concluding
their tale: "Each other flower cannot help but [sic] know/ That
Misia has been born, and sweetly so." The distich actually
translates: "Every other flower cannot fail to realize/ That
Misia did something charming by being born."

There are grave problems of style. The worst is the stance of
omniscience, that hallmark of biographical vulgarization, as in
"One eyebrow raised in a circumflex, Thadée screwed his
monocle into place, took a closer look—and fell in love." Or:
"In his imploring eyes there was an unexpressed question."
There is redundancy, as in "a quiet peace"; cliche, as in Edwards's being "a diamond in the rough"; inept imagery, as
when newspapers "lick their tabloid jaws" (not even lips). Or
take this sentence: "The music's abstract power, like the tip of
an iceberg, was barely visible to the general public." Even to
the most enlightened public, music and its abstract power are
only *audible* (or perhaps sensible); as for the tip of the iceberg (if
that tired image must be trotted out yet again), that is precisely
the part fully visible to all.

Simple English grammar is often beyond our authors (and
their copy editors), resulting in such things as "two men

whom she imagined would give her" and "large amounts of roses." So it is not surprising to find them unattuned to connotations, which leads them to grotesque gaffes. They will record the coprophiliac Edwards's "penchant for excrement," and inadvertently begin the next sentence with "[Misia] gushed"; then compound the faux pas by citing her opinion that Edwards's infatuation with Lantelme "was all *merde.*"

Despite highly commendable research—both in perusing written materials and in interviewing every conceivable surviving informant—there are factual errors. The child Misia is described as listening to the conversation of the Goncourt brothers even though one of them, Jules, had died two years before she was born. Gustave Kahn is identified as the inventor of the prose poem—which existed for a good half century before Kahn invented *vers libre*. Apollinaire is said to have coined the term "surrealism" for the program notes of Cocteau and Satie's ballet *Parade,* although he had used it a couple of months earlier in conjunction with his own play, *Les Mamelles de Tirésias* (see his letter to Paul Dermée of March 1917).

Even so, Gold and Fizdale have written a hugely diverting, variously informative, and ultimately moving book. The account of the declining years, after Sert's death, when everything began to abandon Misia—society, wealth, the new arts, even her eyesight (it started to fail, ironically, at Lourdes, where she had gone to pray for Roussy's recovery)—is both shattering and restrainedly rendered. As Misia becomes lonelier and weaker, the writing turns purer and stronger, and the authors' love for their heroine shines forth with compassion and dignity. One wonders how Gold and Fizdale wrote the book: on one typewriter keyboard with four hands, or on facing typewriters in close harmony?

[1980]

DUAL TO THE DEATH

Francis Steegmuller, ed. and trans.,
The Letters of Gustave Flaubert,
1830–1857

ARE there any great artists not in the grip of some form of dualism? The true writer is nearly always divided, riven into warring halves. At its mildest, this means an inner dialogue rising into a debate; more often, though, a set of contradictions at snarling odds with one another, which only the supreme effort at control, the reconcilement through art, brings into delicate but lasting balance. In no author I can think of are more kinds of dualism more startlingly manifest than in Gustave Flaubert (1821–1880), and nowhere in his work are they more patently exhibited and analyzed than in his letters.

Flaubert's letters are acknowledged to be among the finest written in French, arguably *the* finest. Among modern English epistolarians, only Byron and D. H. Lawrence can compete with Flaubert in immediacy, variety, intensity, and un–publication-oriented perceptivity. It is, therefore, a major literary event to have available at last a substantial part of his correspondence, translated and edited by Francis Steegmuller, even if *The Letters of Gustave Flaubert, 1830–1857* is only the first of two volumes, and although both together will represent only a

fraction, however sizable, of an output that, for all its copious-
ness, never palls.

Modernism in the novel—whatever it is or may have been—
has produced a good many bastards; even more numerous are
its putative fathers. Its paternity was most cogently assigned
by Théodore de Banville to Flaubert's two great fictions of
"modern life": *Madame Bovary* and *L'Education sentimentale*. Yet
if Banville had not been a friend of the Flaubert who claimed he
could not understand Stendhal, he might have more fairly
granted Beyle copaternity. Flaubert, then, preoccupies us as a
writer and—because of the relationship that existed between
them despite his frequent denials—man; together these two,
author and human being, constitute one of the fountainheads
of the modern novel. Whether art imitates nature or vice versa,
we would be fools not to be interested in our origins, in the
sources of a sensibility that, despite modifications, is still very
much our own.

What characterizes Flaubert's attitudes to art as to life is their
duality: he loved and hated them both. In 1846, aged twenty-
five, Gustave compares an early presentiment he had of life to
"a nauseating smell of cooking escaping through a ventilator:
you don't have to eat it to know it would make you vomit."
Five years later, he writes: "I hate life . . . and everything that
reminds me that life must be borne. It bores me to eat, to dress,
to stand on my feet, etc." He has no sense of being young: at
twenty-four he is already fed up with sex, women, masturbation; he "no longer feel[s] the glowing enthusiasm of youth"
and, by the next year, has "the sensation of being inordinately
aged, older than an obelisk."

But such passages can be matched with contrary ones:
accounts of merry escapades, notably on the long journey to
the Orient; ecstatic moments of friendship or physical love;
communings with nature; above all, transcendent experiences
with literature, whether in reading or in writing. He can
"derive almost voluptuous sensations from the mere act of
seeing." And, the day before his thirty-second birthday, he

writes his mistress, Louise Colet: "Today I am overflowing with serenity. I feel calm and radiant. My entire youth has passed unmarred, unsapped by weakness. From my childhood to this very hour it has followed a single straight line. . . . I am like springtime. I have a great, flowing river in me, something that keeps churning and never ceases."

Thus about life; but what about art? (Or "the god of Art," to whom, as the fourteen-year-old Gustave already tells his friend Chevalier, they must devote themselves.) The fear of never really succeeding as an artist, never becoming a master, never even getting published, runs through these letters as a melancholy refrain; often it turns into downright hate. "Style is achieved only by dint of atrocious labor, fanatical and unremitting stubbornness." Flaubert evokes the "agonies of art" (the untranslatable *affres* means anguish, dread, horror, pangs, spasms); he speaks of "[us] poor devils, writers of prose, who are forbidden . . . any expression of personal feelings—think of all the bitterness that remains in our souls, all the moral mucus we gag on." One scene in *Madame Bovary* takes him five months to write; he laments, "If at least I enjoyed doing it!" Elsewhere he thinks he might "die of vexation and impatience . . . were it not for the fury that sustains" him.

Antithetically, he also ardently loves his work. At twenty-four, he tells his beloved friend Alfred Le Poittevin: "The only way not to be unhappy is to shut yourself up in Art and count all the rest as nothing." A year later, he "cannot imagine how people unconcerned with art can spend their time." In 1851, "Only the habit of persistent work can make one continually content; it produces an opium that numbs the soul." In 1853, after finishing part II, chapter 9 of *Bovary,* he rhapsodizes: "It is a delicious thing to write, to be no longer yourself but to move in an entire universe of your own creating. Today, for instance, as man and woman, both lover and mistress, I rode in a forest on an autumn afternoon under the yellow leaves, and I was also the horses, the wind, the words my people uttered, even the red sun that made them almost close their love-drained eyes."

There is a nonstop ambivalence about a love that is a numbing opium and a hate that is, at least, a sustaining fury. Indeed, the most frequent tone is one of duality, of love-hate, of an impassioned yea-and-nay: "I love my work with a love that is frantic and perverted, as an ascetic loves the hair shirt that scratches his belly." Two years later (1854), he expresses it even more powerfully: "What an atrociously delicious thing . . . writing is—since we keep slaving this way, enduring such tortures and not wanting things otherwise." For Flaubert, obviously, art is a secular asceticism, both positive and negative. At nineteen he had thought of castrating himself, he tells Louise, "and later spent two entire years without touching a woman." There are moments "when one needs to make oneself suffer, needs to loathe one's flesh . . . so hideous does it seem." This piteous state of affairs almost drove him into a monastery, "perhaps [to have become] a great mystic." But, as it happens, his "love of form"—art, writing, style—deflected the asceticism into secular channels. To the extent it produced works of art, this was, of course, beneficial; but to the extent Flaubert used it as an escape from life and love, it was also, alas, sterile.

The correspondence is the perfect peephole—no, picture window—into the man who, in turn, holds the clues to the writer, and is the standard-bearer of art for art's sake. Two aspects of this chary, inconsistent, odd, indeed perverse lover become manifest in these letters: homosexuality and sadomasochism. They, too, strike me as forms of ambivalence, of duality—at least as Flaubert indulged, or did not indulge, in them. On the homosexuality, Steegmuller is reticent; at most, he permits himself a veiled suggestion or two. Yet there is no doubt that the letters to the dearest male friends, Ernest Chevalier and Maxime Du Camp, and especially Alfred Le Poittevin and Louis Bouilhet, are more intimate, tender, rapturous than all but a very few passages in the missives to Louise. On these matters, the late Enid Starkie is most explicit, in *Flaubert: The Making of a Master*, though it must be remembered that, as a lesbian, she may have been arguing *pro domo*. Still, she is judicious enough to speak only of "some homosexual practices" (some of them confirmed by the letters here available for the first time in English), and she prudently adds that "nothing positive can be proved" with any but, perhaps, Louis Bouilhet.

More interesting than either these speculations or the descriptions of some pederastic encounters with Arab catamites are what I would call secondary homosexual characteristics: adoration of and dependence on one's mother, whom one also slightly patronizes and resents; preference for older women, i.e., mother figures such as the lifelong platonic beloved Mme Elisa Schlesinger, twenty-six when the fourteen-year-old Flaubert fell deeply in love with her, and Louise Colet, Flaubert's only mistress of significant duration, ten years his senior; the striving to make men out of one's women: "I was addressing myself to your virile intellect," and, again, "I treat you like a man and not like a woman"; and, though here I am on shakier ground, a sadomasochistic relation with Louise, which Steegmuller perceives only in mental terms, although it seems to have been physical enough.

Soon after he has become involved with Louise (1846), our longtime admirer of Sade and Lacenaire brings back some mementos of their Paris dalliance to his nest in Croisset; one of them is Louise's handkerchief, on which "I see your blood. I wish it were completely red with it." No menstrual blood, this; we soon learn that the other chief keepsake, Louise's slippers, also display bloodstains. Gustave has "the cravings of a wild beast . . . a love that is carnivorous, capable of tearing flesh to pieces." In another letter: "I bite your lip: is the little red spot still there?" Elsewhere we read of "violent caresses. . . . I made you cry out two or three times." In the first year of the liaison he speaks of his embraces as those of cats that draw their females' blood; near the end of the affair, the image recurs, heightened: "I am like the tiger, who has bristles . . . at the tip of his glans, which lacerate the female."

The homosexuality seems to have been largely or wholly repressed—hence a form of dividedness; could not the heterosexuality, then, out of spite and frustration, turn sadomasochistic—another form of rivenness? From these incertitudes and contradictions, Flaubert escapes into art (often with a capital A), which appears to him a sure refuge from life. The writer, by the very peace-requiring nature of his work, "must live alone and seal [his] windows lest the air of the world seep in." A few years later, the image changes, but the spirit remains the same: "The way to live serenely, in clean, fresh air, is to install yourself atop some pyramid, no matter which, provided it be lofty and have a solid foundation. Ah! It isn't always 'amusing' up there, and you are utterly alone; but there is consolation to be taken in spitting from so high a place."

Unfortunately—or perhaps fortunately—the ambivalences of life and love one tries to flee from into literature have a way of following one even into an airtight room or onto the top of a pyramid. Most blatantly, Flaubert tergiversated between such statements as "*Madame Bovary* has nothing 'true' in it . . . into it I put none of my own feelings and nothing from my own life" and the celebrated remark "Madame Bovary, *c'est moi.*" Yet the ambivalence was, in many ways, creative. *Bovary,* as he correctly perceived, was to be the first book to make fun of its heroine and hero in such a way that the irony, instead of detracting from the pathos, intensified it. (Elsewhere he writes that the greatest artists are both pitiless and tender.) Later he explains that he abhorred ordinary existence, the bourgeois world of Emma and her men, but that "aesthetically, I wanted this once—and only this once—to plumb its depths." It was, of course, not to be only once: Flaubert's fictions shuttled, with perfect regularity, between exotic, historic, heroic themes, and modern, mundane, even petty ones.

In *Madame Bovary* we can see this duality settle into the very form and style, as Flaubert contrives "to give prose the rhythm of verse (keeping it distinctly prose, however) and to write of ordinary life as one writes history or epic (but without falsifying the subject)." No wonder critics found it hard to classify Flaubert: was he a romantic, a realist, a naturalist? A Parnassian in prose, perhaps, or a Decadent? Yet even if the form had its ambiguities, the dedication with which Flaubert pursued his art became ever more single-minded, fanatical, and prolonged: *Bovary* took almost five years, *Salammbô* and *L'Education sentimentale* six each, and death cut off *Bouvard et Pécuchet* at seven. This sublime intransigence is everywhere in the letters: "Perish the United States rather than a principle! May I die like a dog rather than hurry by a single second a sentence that isn't ripe!" Flaubert preferred a risky lawsuit by the imperial censorship against *Bovary* to making changes in the text: "I will not make a correction, not a cut; I will not suppress a comma; nothing, nothing!" he wrote to the work's first publishers.

He recognized the difficulties of a style that was meant to resolve contradictions and fuse opposites better than anyone, however. It is easy, he writes, "to chatter about the Beautiful. But it takes more genius to say, in proper style, 'close the door' or 'he wanted to sleep' than to give all the literature courses in the world." Still, he managed to "walk straight ahead on a hair, balanced above two abysses of lyricism and vulgarity" and even to blend them; to convey the effects of a symphony in a book; and, indeed, to anticipate that art of the future he foresaw as "something halfway between algebra and music." He was able, as R. A. Sayce demonstrated in *Style in French Prose,* "to pack more meaning into a word, a phrase, a sentence, a paragraph, than perhaps any other writer. . . ."

Francis Steegmuller, who has translated and written about Flaubert often and well, has again done a splendid job of selection from the correspondence, as well as of providing connecting texts and notes. But his translation, though able, is not brilliant. Two examples at random. Young Flaubert wants to write a book worthy of Bruegel's *Temptation of St. Anthony,* "mais cela demandait un autre gaillard que moi." The raciness of *autre gaillard* is not conveyed by "someone very different." Gustave writes to Bouilhet, "Quand nous nous reverrons il aura passé beaucoup de jours, je veux dire beaucoup de choses." This is a kind of zeugma: "many days, I mean many things, will have passed." Steegmuller flattens it into "Many days will have passed—I mean many things will have happened." *Collège,* in French, is not college but high school; simple Mme Flaubert would say "dried-up," not "desiccated."

There are also curious lapses of diction and grammar, which I would have expected the Harvard University Press to catch. I am not pleased with such anachronisms as *ploy, nymphet, clobbering,* and *where are you at?* But I am unhappier yet about *further away, as though I'm, a few less hours, neither you nor I are, I wrack my brain, horses who, where art thou, luxurious locks?* and several more like them.

Still, we have here, in mainly good English, some of the greatest insights into the making of art. Let me close with two. "If you participate actively in life you don't see it clearly; you suffer from it too much or enjoy it too much. The artist, to my way of thinking, is a monstrosity, something outside nature." And: "An author in his book must be like God in the universe, present everywhere and visible nowhere." Even that greatest dichotomy—between monster and God—Flaubert could, if not resolve, at least put to immortal use.

[1980]

A RESTIVE SPIRIT

Restif de la Bretonne, *Monsieur Nicolas*

THE typical eighteenth-century man may have been psychologically split, but believed himself to be whole. Not until the nineteenth century did it become fashionable to be openly torn apart and secretly proud of it. In this, as in many other respects, Restif de la Bretonne (1734–1806) was ahead of his times. For a bifurcated writer and paradoxical human being, the apogee of Romanticism could scarcely provide one better; Restif was peasant and Parisian, moralist and immoralist, obsessed by the truth yet compelled to embroider it. A polygrapher who poured out some 240 (mostly indifferent) volumes, he produced one eccentric but thoroughgoing masterpiece. There was hardly a book of his without revolutionary social or scientific ideas to be realized by the future, or without passages of penetrating forthrightness, whose worth also remained largely for the future to realize.

The son of a prosperous farmer and winegrower, Nicolas Edmé Rétif (he later archaized the spelling and added the name of the paternal estate, La Bretonne) was briefly educated at two Jansenist seminaries run by his half brothers. One school was closed down, the other closed its doors to him for having written a licentious poem. His boyhood was spent mostly around his native Sacy in enjoying the works and pastimes of the country. He would have gladly followed in his father's footsteps, but was deemed too intelligent for farming. Whether to save or ruin this plowboy, his father apprenticed him at sixteen to the printer Fournier in Auxerre. This was a useful position from which to undertake one's education, not to mention one's sentimental education, paying fervent homage to the promiscuous printer's virtuous, unhappy wife while wreaking havoc among the town's available young girls.

Restif became a hardworking journeyman printer and hard-playing womanizer. As he wrote later, "It is this ability to get back to work after a meal, an amusement, or a business deal which has set me apart from my fellow printers all my life." But the interest in Mme Fournier, whom he attempted unsuccessfully to possess, eventually cost him his job with his boorish employer. This entire section of Restif's life reads like an episode from *The Red and the Black.*

At not quite twenty-one, Restif arrived in Paris, which, except for two or three quite short periods, he was never again to leave. He worked long hours, often close to starvation, but, capable printer that he was, he survived, even if lacking the money to go home for his father's funeral. Repeatedly running away from potentially right women ("I always fled from everything which could give me happiness or peace of mind"), he ended up marrying in 1760 Agnès Lebègue, a shrew with literary pretensions, who may or may not have been the whorish termagant Restif depicted her as, but who, in any case, was the wrong woman for this difficult Don Juan. Many years, separations, and acrimonious clashes later, the two were divorced (1794). Their surviving offspring were the daughters Agnès and Marion, alternatingly the bane and balm of Restif's life: sometimes it is they who fished him out of his poverty, overwork, and prostration from venereal and other diseases. Agnès married a sadist, Augé, with whom Restif was continually on the warpath and who, under the Revolution, almost got his father-in-law guillotined.

Meanwhile, Restif had decided that some of the fiction he

had to print for a living was so poor that he could surely do as well or better. In 1767 his first novel came out; in 1775 his first success, *The Perverted Peasant*. Like most of his fiction, it is autobiographical, the story of a country boy's corruption by the City, its immoral sophisticates and venal courtesans. Restif was now a writer and wencher, associating with cheap prostitutes when impoverished, with fancier ones when his books paid off, and occasionally having the requisite luck and leisure for a genuine love affair, which, however, always managed to end unhappily.

Restif's writings would easily occupy a forty-foot shelf. They cover the fields of fiction, drama, biography, autobiography, sociology, science, politics, not to mention the verses of his youth. In his various works he predicted the disasters of the Revolution, aerial warfare, modern city planning, collective farms, and much more. He has been called the true father of socialism whose ideas Fournier plagiarized, and certainly Restif was a good Christian communist all his life, generously sharing what little he had. His tracts concerned themselves with extensive sociopolitical reforms, covering everything from theater to prostitution. His fictions and nonfictions interpenetrate; both tell a great deal about eighteenth-century life, particularly its lesser-known byways. Restif's masterpiece is his autobiography, *Monsieur Nicolas,* now translated by Robert Baldick and published in a hefty one-volume edition.

Should we be grateful for this? The translator's liminal note implies that the omissions of this edition, except for the final episode, the story of Sara, are unimportant: "attempts at verse . . . sentimental effusions . . . tediously repetitive accounts of . . . sexual prowess." But the story of Sara is a Proustian gem, the chronicle of Restif's Swann-Odette relationship with the daughter of his landlady. The writer, well into his forties and enjoying a brief period of prosperity, is bled dry by a faithless and mercenary teenager with whom he is obsessed. As for the verses, effusions, sexual exploits, they are what constitutes the bizarreness, uniqueness, and lovable psychosexual bric-a-brac of this book: they are Restif. The best modern French edition of *Monsieur Nicolas* comes in six sizable volumes; cutting these down to one is not to be passed over with Baldick's laconic note, ending on the upbeat assertion that none of the omissions has been dictated by "prudery or 'good taste.' " True, but not good enough.

There are whole episodes missing from this abridgment, just as there are others reduced to dangling, barely comprehensible bits. Nor is Baldick above howlers, as when he translates *envie* as "envy," *crapuleux* (low or sordid) as "crapulous" (in English, only inebriated), or *deux jumelles* (female twins) redundantly as "two twin sisters." His English is sometimes independently inadequate, as when he uses "fulsome" or the verb "intrigue" in a positive sense, or falls into syntactic clumsiness. Not that Restif's French is the pinnacle of elegance; but it is, except for his quirkily Shavian simplified spelling, correct. On the other hand, we do now have some idea in English of this remarkable autobiography, conceived along the same lines as Rousseau's but, apparently, before Rousseau's; a work of greater outspokenness and zest than the *Confessions* and one that no less a critic than Paul Valéry placed far above the latter. Maybe we ought to be grateful.

Monsieur Nicolas is somewhat of a problem because we cannot always tell what is fiction in it, what truth. The peasant in Restif wanted fantastic tales that might yet, somehow, be true; the Parisian in him craved truths stranger than fiction. What he came up with was a fictionalized autobiography, or a pre-Capotean nonfiction novel. "It can be called his fiction," wrote Wilhelm von Humboldt, "but the real inner truth is truer to nature than art, forever idealized."

The autobiography covers not only what I have already related of Restif's life; it continues through many upheavals to the final period of indigence, when Restif had to become his own printer, indeed to save paper by setting this book directly into type without the mediation of a manuscript. The support or admiration of Beaumarchais, Bernardin de Saint-Pierre,

Crébillon *fils,* the Encyclopedist Mercier, and Benjamin
Franklin, recognition beyond the border from Goethe and
Schiller, occasional invitations into high society were slender
compensations for the penury of one who lost his last money in
the Revolution. Though the Institut rejected him, his funeral
was a grand affair, attended in quantity and by quality.

What makes *Monsieur Nicolas* invaluable is the luminous
evocation of country living and the searchlight thrown on the
murkier corners of life in the city. Better yet, perhaps, is the
sharpness of psychological insight into the author's and other
souls; occasionally he is enmeshed in self-delusion, but self-
delusion so honestly narrated that what the writer failed to
grasp, the reader can seize upon with pleasure and profit.
There are fascinating revelations from this man who had his
first coition aged not quite eleven and who draws up (in an
omitted section of the book) a list of 700 named amours—not
counting the totally fly-by-night ones. Here are anecdotes of
voracious sexual appetite, a frank account of foot and shoe
fetishism, a curious urge for pure, platonic relationships in the
midst of carnality. And other absorbing ambivalences: the man
who seriously believes that he has "never enjoyed as much as
half a day of unalloyed happiness" can as earnestly declare that
he has been sublimely happy, until her premature death, with a
twelve-year-old whom he considered, like many another of his
mistresses, his natural daughter. Recurrent incest fantasies are
revealingly spelled out, as are rationalizations for not finding a
satisfactory lasting relationship.

Even stranger than his odd involvements are some of Restif's
peculiar renunciations. But through every kind of deprivation
there shines in this book a sense of self-confidence: "I try not to
fail myself as others have failed me." Restif comes up with the
extremely modern argument that his amatory misadventures
constituted research for his writings, in which he depicts
"man as he is, and not as he should be." What he offers here is a
scientific examination of "a man's complete life . . . a useful
supplement to Buffon." It may be that, as his first English

critical biographer, C. R. Dawes, has claimed, Restif lacked a
sense of humor, yet it is hard to read unamused an episode such
as the one of the boardinghouse where the lodgers had to pass
performance tests before being gradually advanced by the
landlady from the favors of her mother, through her own, to
those of her elder daughter of nineteen, then to the final
prize—those of her younger one. Restif comments, "You had
to be the epitome of virtue and decency to get as far as the child
of fifteen." Whether such humor is deliberate or accidental
scarcely matters.

But Restif, the great rival and enemy of the Marquis de
Sade, was also a fine human being. "I have always loved with
delicacy, and often platonically," he writes, and goes on to
announce one of his many psychological discoveries, that "the
source of tenderness of heart lies in the organs of physical
love." He can even be extremely poetic—in his prose, if not in
his verse—as when he speaks of sleep with its "hairy fingers."
His influence on Balzac and Stendhal has been demonstrated,
and Marc Chadourne, in his excellent monograph, has pointed
out parallels with Chateaubriand, the Romantics, Zola, and
Proust. Constant, Nerval, and Baudelaire were among Restif's
early admirers; in our time, the *Restiviste* revival is gaining
momentum. Born on the border of Burgundy and Champagne, Restif combines the virtues of their respective brews:
the full-bodied aroma of the one with the aphrodisiac sparkle
of the other.

[1968]

GERMAN
AND AUSTRIAN
LITERATURE

A VERY ABSTRACT CONCRETE

Thomas Bernhard, *Concrete* (translated by David McLintock)

AN Austrian who detests Austria and Austrians, a human being who confronts humanity with the greatest mistrust, a writer who puts his faith in writing even while his every sentence attests to his doubt of its efficacy, a man for whom life is at best grotesque and the grave is the goal cannot help attracting the brighter children of a century that flirts with torment and skirts doom. Such a writer is Thomas Bernhard, the 53-year-old poet, playwright, novelist, and storyteller, whose following among literati, intellectuals, and cultural fellow travelers grows steadily while the rest of the world blithely ignores him.

Three of his novels—*Gargoyles* (whose German title, *Verstörung,* a word coined by Bernhard, is bleaker but untranslatable), *The Lime Works,* and *Correction*—have been available in English translations. Now so is the novella *Concrete* (meaning the building material, not the opposite of "abstract"), first published in German in 1982. Bernhard's literary models include Kafka, whose despairing nightmare vision is also his, down to certain surreal elements presented as if they were utterly commonplace; Beckett, whose minimalist landscape and reductionist narrative are also Bernhard's; and Kleist, the rush and fatality of whose sentences Bernhard strives for— not, like Kleist, with structures whose tautness barely contains their frenzy, but with agglomerations of clauses and phrases sometimes a page or two long, with commas taking over for periods.

But Bernhard deals with a world more recognizably ours than that of his models. Incursions of the surreal are sparser than in Kafka, the cozy bourgeois appurtenances are not nearly so stripped down as in Beckett, and Kleist's manic breathlessness becomes an airlessness in which the lungs struggle for difficult breath. This airlessness is best conveyed by Bernhard's prose, which, in his later works, is one unbroken paragraph from first page to last. The device is more distressing than one might think. Only after reading Bernhard's work (or late Beckett, from which it derives) does one realize how much those little breathing spaces at the left margin mean; they not only provide rest for the eye and mind, but also give shape to the text and enable us to find our bearings.

The endless paragraph of Bernhard is a dark, stifling corridor along which we are propelled by a running band of words whose monomaniacal destination is the end of the tale, cessation, death. But the running band is in the haunted house of a dour amusement park; freewheeling sentences—there is no punctilious subordination as in Proust or Thomas Mann—that run on, stagger, tumble across commas, with periods coming when they are no longer expected, a surcease arriving too late for relief. Discomfiture and unrelief are the stuff of Bernhard's, as it were, predeconstructed prose. And, to change metaphors, what surf, what undertow to buffet us—a sentence, or quasi-sentence, is promptly reconsidered by the next, sometimes revoked, more often restated and infinitesimally revised. Instead of resuming, the next sentence retraces, kneads, worries, tautologizes the foregoing.

Concrete, which is easier going than some of Bernhard's work, has minimal action. Rudolf, a well-to-do but always unwell musicologist, has been working for ten years on his magnum opus, a study of Mendelssohn, but, unable to think up the lead sentence, he hasn't written a word. Nothing but notes. He has published little—he considers publishing a crime—and is, clearly, a hypochondriac. His sarcoidosis is not that serious an illness and responds to prednisolone. Rudolf lives in a country house in a village, Peiskam, where, apart from visits from his housekeeper, he receives only Elizabeth, his hated sister. At first, she is represented as the bane of Rudolf's life; she seems to brutalize and terrorize him. A fancy real-estate agent, she makes few but hugely lucrative deals and lives stylishly in Vienna, except when she comes—at his invitation—for protracted stays with her brother, apparently to make his life unendurable. "What good has it done you to study all that rubbish?" she jeers and paralyzes Rudolf.

Even as an adolescent she would enjoy physically destroying some essay of his. Now she usurps his house, her smell haunting the rooms long after she is finally gone. "She treats me just like a madman," Rudolf reflects, and "she had recently taken a liking to saying over and over again, *You'll die*." It should be noted that Bernhard loves italics; he'll use them for quotations, for emphasis, or as an alienation effect—as he will also use the pluperfect, the subjunctive, and deliberately self-referential narrative devices that remind the reader he is looking at fiction. But gradually, as Rudolf ruminates—the novel is a set of his notes—the hatred for his sister yields to love-hate, and, finally, to a symbiosis very much like love. Her involvement with the Catholic clergy, her sexual activities, her wheeling and dealing are viewed with a kind of admiring scorn; eventually she is even granted a considerable intellect. The bond is one of "being impossible, erratic, capricious and vacillating," which "always got on other people's nerves and yet has never ceased to fascinate them and make them seek our company [there's the standard Bernhardian paradox]—fundamentally because we're capricious, erratic, vacillating and unreliable [there's the not-quite-repetition]."

Otherwise *Concrete* records Rudolf's meditations on work, intensive but nonproductive; society, omnipresent but mad, stupid and cruel; and life, minimal and mostly pointless. A year and a half ago, Rudolf traveled to Majorca, where he has some rich friends. Now he is trying to work up the strength to return there and escape winter. His chief existential problem is whether he can pack his needed belongings, which include source material and notes for the Mendelssohn work, some of them essential, some only nearly so. While working up to this giant task, he gives us his animadversions. They sound, at times, like a Beckett parody: "I don't associate with a living soul. I've even given up all contact with the neighbours. Unless I have to shop for groceries I no longer leave the house at all. And I hardly get mail because I no longer write letters. When I go out for a meal I flee from the restaurant almost before I've entered it or eaten my nauseating food. The result is that I hardly speak at all, that I've forgotten how to. Incredulously I practice speaking, to see whether I can still produce a sound," and so on, in David McLintock's able translation.

There are spectacular fulminations against Austria, its government, its church, everybody. "Ninety percent of the time today we are up against subtle exploiters, ten percent of the time against unpardonable idiots." Even St. Francis has to take his lumps; even Schopenhauer, in one of the rare amusing passages, takes a drubbing: "People keep a dog and are ruled by this dog, and even Schopenhauer was ruled in the end not by his head, but by his dog. Fundamentally it was not Schopenhauer's head that determined his thought, but Schopenhauer's dog. I don't have to be demented to assert that Schopenhauer had a dog on his shoulders and not a head." Only one thing still cheers Rudolf, but "apart from music everything else was worthless." Eventually even the musical life of Vienna palls: "I always had the impression—and still have—that the same orchestras always play the same things, even though in fact they always played different things—and still do."

After pages of tergiversation, Rudolf finally makes it to Palma, Majorca, in one sentence: "At two o'clock when the car came to collect me, it was still eleven degrees below zero in Peiskam, but on my arrival in Palma, where I am writing these notes, the thermometer showed eighteen degrees above." Do you expect the next sentence to start with "however"? Right you are. "However, this naturally did not improve my condition—quite the contrary." In Palma, Rudolf finally confronts real misery. The last time he was there, he met Anna Hardtl, a young compatriot who told him a heartrending story of destitution and her husband's death. On this trip, he discovers the tale's shattering epilogue. And this suffering of poor people is encased in concrete—in their streets, in their rows of shabby hotels, in the seven-tiered cemetery walls whose pigeon-holes hold their remains. And Rudolf experiences "extreme anxiety."

Is Rudolf one of the walking dead? Bernhard's characters are drawn to death, either jaggedly harrying themselves toward it or helplessly drifting into it. There is no actual talk of suicide in *Concrete,* but the hero of *Correction* writes, "We're a nation of suicides. . . . but only a small percentage actually kill themselves . . . even though we hold the world's record for suicide." In *Gargoyles* a character remarks, "Everything is suicide. What we live, what we read, what we think: training for suicide." But in what may be Bernhard's finest work to date, three short autobiographical volumes not yet available in English, he says, "I absolutely had the feeling of being saved when I recognized the possibilities of complete aloneness and took possession of them." Does Rudolf have this chance? Or can he at least claim what the hero of Bernhard's short story "Jauregg" avers, "So every evening . . . something sets in that does not let me despair, although I would *have* to despair, although in truth I *am* desperate."

No wonder Rudolf favors Mendelssohn, of whom Schumann wrote, "He is the most radiant musician, the one who most clearly saw through the contradictions of our age and first reconciled them." But can Rudolf write his book? "Time," he feels, "destroys everything we do, whatever it is." And in Palma, "instead of starting to work on Mendelssohn . . . all I could think of when I woke was Anna Hardtl." In a speech he gave accepting the Anton Wildgans literary prize, Bernhard said, "When we're on the traces of the truth without knowing what this truth is, which has nothing in common with reality save that truth we do not know, then it is foundering, it is death on whose traces we are." Yet Wildgans, the Austrian poet-playwright in whose name the prize is given, was an optimist. Not so Bernhard, the narrator of whose first novel, *Frost,* reports on "expeditions into the jungles of aloneness." *Concrete* is such an expedition—a small one, through a small jungle. But the aloneness is enormous.

[1984]

THE DRUMMER OF DANZIG

Günter Grass, *The Tin Drum* (translated by Ralph Manheim)

FROM time to time we must reexamine the meaning of the concepts "classical" and "romantic," which, like the works of Homer or Dante, need to be retranslated or, in this case, redefined for every age. As we look at twentieth-century fiction, we see one kind of writing whose ideal is omission, whose unit is the vignette that yearns to compress itself into an aphorism. This is our classicism. And there is another writing whose aim is inclusion, whose basic form is the catalogue striving to heighten itself into a prose poem. This is our romanticism. To draw examples from France, where they have a way of being more exemplary, there is the classicism of Gide, Radiguet, Camus confronting the romanticism of, say, Proust, Montherlant, and Genet. The greater writers try to bridge the gap: Gide had to write *The Counterfeiters*; the work of Proust is shot through with maxims.

In *The Tin Drum*, Günter Grass has written a novel without equal so far in postwar Germany—let no one mention in the same breath the lucubrations of an Uwe Johnson. Grass's book is a major romantic novel that, in its carefully designed structure and economical use of a welter of incidents, approaches classicism.

Duality runs through the book. Even the provenance of *The Tin Drum* is dual, just as its hero, Oskar Matzerath, has two putative fathers. For the novel derives, first, from a French tradition—Grass lived for a long time in Paris—represented by writers such as Jarry, Apollinaire (particularly the Apollinaire of *Les onze mille Verges*), and Céline, writers in whom furibund sexuality and Rabelaisian humor, sadism, and stylistic experimentation and innovation proceeded *pari passu*. There is in Günter Grass a great, metaphysical anger. But the anger comes at us in trappings of humor, eroticism, absurdity, poker-facedness—it is, in short, a Mardi-Gras anger—and is not readily recognizable for what it is. But its impact on sensitive readers is all the greater for that.

While adopting this French orientation, *The Tin Drum* manages to improve on its models. Explaining German Romanticism to French readers, Heine wrote: "A French madness is nowhere near so mad as a German one; for in the latter there is, as Polonius would say, method. With unrivaled pedantry, with terrifying conscientiousness, with thoroughness such as a French lunatic cannot even conceive of, this German frenzy was practiced." *The Tin Drum* is also nourished by German Romanticism. Oskar is the obverse of E. T. A. Hoffmann's *Klein Zaches,* another mischievous dwarf. Zaches has the magic gift of receiving the reward due any great action performed by anyone in his presence; conversely, Oskar has genuine talents of sorts, but they are sinister, and, directly or indirectly, lead those around him to disaster. The stealing of the Good complements the palming off of Evil. But whereas in *Klein Zaches* justice triumphs, in *The Tin Drum* injustice goes its merry way. It does not exactly triumph—there are no more triumphs in our day, not even triumphs of injustice—but it does go on.

The Tin Drum is the story of Oskar Matzerath, born in the twenties, whose mother was a Danzig woman, and whose father was either her German husband or her Polish lover. The infant is gifted with an adult brain at birth, and resolves not to grow up to be a shopkeeper like the elder Matzerath. Aged three, Oskar throws himself down some stairs and arrests his growth; he refuses to go to school or talk properly but becomes a fiendish artist on the toy drums his mother keeps him supplied with. When a new drum is not forthcoming, he discovers that he can shout glass to pieces even at great distances, which proves a useful method of petty blackmail and, later, of other mischief-making. As Oskar grows older, he becomes the cause of the deaths of his mother and both presumptive fathers, and of several other people to boot. Not so much the cause of death as its catalyst, and who can assess the responsibility of a catalyst? So Oskar gets away with murder.

The story covers the rise of Nazism, the war, the collapse of Germany, but all only as reflected in Oskar's existence. He has many picaresque and demonic adventures: he becomes an "artiste" entertaining troops in Normandy, a "reincarnation" of Jesus who leads a gang of likable JDs into destruction, his brother's father if not his keeper (by having a child by his stepmother), and so forth. After the war, he sees fit to grow a little, but in so doing develops a hump. He is relocated to Düsseldorf, where he becomes by turns a carver of funeral monuments, a nude model for crazy artists, a drummer in a jazz trio, and, finally, a famous and rich concert-drummer who, in solo recitals throughout Germany, drums elderly people back into their youth—a kind of faith healer, in short. Accused, at last, of the one crime he did not commit, he is found guilty of murder but reprieved to a mental institution. Though he finds happiness there, it looks as if he will soon be released. And then what? He is thirty, and he is afraid.

Such an outline does no justice whatever to the plot, let alone to the work of art. Günter Grass is also a poet, painter, sculptor, stage designer, dramatist, literary critic, and genuine eccentric; all these occupations have helped him fill his long novel with a splendid *mélange adultère de tout*. Grass calls himself a realist, but this is true only to the extent that he can describe with equal verisimilitude plain things such as the contents of a grocery, more abstruse things such as the work of a stone-carver or waiter in a ferocious harbor canteen, and fantastic things that can pass for minor miracles. Always, however, the romantic poet is eager to take over. Thus we read of the child Oskar, in a garret, disturbed in his drumming by noises from the courtyard: "A hundred carpet-beating females can storm the very heavens, can blunt the wing tips of young swallows; with a few strokes, they tumbled the tiny temple that Oskar had drummed into the April air." The world is too much with Oskar, but the expression is not that of the worldly realist. Consider Oskar's words about how his mother, after four days' painful vomiting and dying, gave up "that bit of breath which everyone must cough up in order to obtain his death certificate." Whereupon, Oskar goes on, "we all breathed easy again. . . ."[1]

The novel is distinguished by its blend of dreary reality and spectacular fantasy, of wit and toughness, of lyricism and amorality. If Grass's vision is realistic, it is the realism of someone who does not allow for optical illusions, who does not know or does not care to know the laws of causality, who has no visual or moral perspective: a sharp observer, but an observer from Mars. Thus Oskar watches a neighbor woman carrying a carpet rolled up and slung across her shoulder "exactly as she might have carried a drunken man; but her man was no longer living." And thus Oskar wonders upon seeing the toy soldiers abandoned in Danzig by a little Polish escapee, "Perhaps he had stuffed a few uhlans into his trouser pocket and they might later, during the battle for the fortress of Modlin, reinforce the Polish cavalry." Thus, too, Oskar notes that at his father's funeral "it decidedly smelled of dead Matzerath."

The salient feature is irony, but an irony that, for all its immensity, is not savage. It is indifferent rather than angry,

---

[1] Ralph Manheim, the translator, renders this as "the bit of breath which each of us must give up if he is to be honored with a death certificate. We all sighed with relief. . . ." This loses not only Oskar's tone of almost innocent callousness, but also the terrible yet pregnant play on "bit of breath" and "breathed." Since Mr. Manheim's translation is persistently inept, I am obliged to make up my own versions.

and the reader's own indignation must rush in to fill the moral vacuum left by the protagonist's nonchalance. Grass is a master of all ironies: simple, complex, multilateral. Simple: " . . . films in which Maria Schell, as a nurse, wept, and Borsche, as a chief surgeon close upon a most difficult operation, played Beethoven sonatas through the French windows and displayed his sense of responsibility." Complex—because it can do double duty, as when it not only lets the absurdity of a situation dawn on us slowly, but also affords a gruesome insight into Oskar's nonhuman reaction to a severed ring finger which he picks up with a collector's zeal: "Oskar . . . realized that the inside of the finger was marked high up to the third joint with lines attesting to its diligence, determination, and ambitious perseverance." (The translation, with its pluperfect tense, misses the horrible, matter-of-fact disregard of reality, couched in a syntactical construction that treats the dead finger as a living being; Manheim translates: "this had been a hardworking finger with a relentless sense of duty.") And multilateral irony—when Oskar's tiny son, already somewhat taller than his father, strikes Oskar down and makes him muse: "Could he, too, express childlike affection such as is supposedly worth striving for between fathers and sons, only in homicide?" Note that the homicidal scene takes place at Matzerath Senior's funeral, caused by Oskar, hence the "too," i.e., filial hatred as something basic and inherited, viewed by Oskar as "affection" but of a "childlike" sort, a term suited to "sons" but here, as a zeugma, referring also to the feelings of "fathers." Yet, in the face of all this, such "affection" is still supposed to be "worth striving for."

In a perceptive essay, Hans Magnus Enzensberger has examined Grass's style and found in it everything from syntactic ballets to imitations of the Litany, from rondos and fugatos to the language of case histories, from legal jargon to underworld slang, from dialect to gibberish. To this list should be added the technique of film montage, with all kinds of superimposition and cross-cutting, and certain devices of parody (e.g., the history of Danzig told as a cabaret monologue); also such stratagems as describing something that, it turns out, did not happen, then blithely going on to what did; or enumerating several possibilities of how something might have been; or getting at an important point only by way of the longest verbal retards. Add to this anticlimaxes and non sequiturs, and you begin to have an image of Grass's style. But then, out of nowhere, a whole prose poem, or a mere lyrical cadenza: "Stillness, maybe a fly, the clock as usual, very softly the radio." (Which Manheim prosifies into: "It was quiet, maybe the buzzing of a fly, the clock as usual, the radio turned very low.")

What makes *The Tin Drum* spellbinding, however, is something beyond story and style; it is the hauntedness of its author, and the personal myths he creates, full of urgency and driving power. There are a number of continually recurring motifs in Grass's work. Thus the play *Ten Minutes to Buffalo* deals with a fantastic trip to Buffalo, in which the destination is not reached. In *The Tin Drum,* Oskar's arsonist grandfather may or may not have escaped to Buffalo; Oskar himself tries to escape there, but never makes it. Another play, *The Wicked Cooks,* displays a horde of viciously intriguing ladle-wielders. These same cooks with their ladles recur in a poem in *Triangle of Rails (Gleisdreick),* Grass's volume of verse. In *The Tin Drum,* the unloved and killed father is a passionate cook, and Oskar's final bogey, the only fear he cannot shake, is *die Schwarze Köchin,* a black female cook, whom Manheim foolishly turns into "the Black Witch," just so as to rhyme with "pitch"!

From the garb of cooks it is not far to that of nurses and nuns. Grass has publicly stated that nuns fascinate him; his private obsession with them is manifest in his fantasy world. As a painter, he has exhibited whole series of paintings of nuns, which is exactly what the painter Lankes does in *The Tin Drum*. Compulsively, almost all of Oskar's passions are for nuns—or nurses. The nurse is the secular replica of the nun, and her uniform is the photographic positive of the nun's negative. She, too, wears a cross, albeit a red one, and, in

German, she, too, is called *Schwester.* Nuns are the subject of a poem sequence in *Triangle of Rails* that reiterates, almost verbatim, certain passages of *The Tin Drum.* In the novel, nuns and nurses are repeatedly adored, longed for, made love to unsuccessfully, assaulted, raped, shot, deferred to, exalted.

Other obsessive motifs include the firebug, doves and seagulls, physical malformation. Now, various commentators—including the blurb writer—have perceived Oskar as a symbol of the alienated artist, of guilty Germany, of corrupt mankind, to say nothing of diverse religious allegories. Some of these identifications may be in order, but they beg the underlying issue: Grass's unrelenting need to write the biography of his unconscious. Which is, of course, both the most and the least respectable reason for writing: it accounts for the best of Goethe, as for the worst of Sade.

This is not the time or place for an analysis of Grass's personal mythology, even if I were competent to undertake it. But something can be cautiously hinted at, something to which the polarity nun-nurse points, and that brings us back to the problem of duality with which we began. For *The Tin Drum* is fundamentally about duality. Its very narration shuttles, at the drop of a comma, between present and past, even as the narrator, sometimes within the same sentence, shifts from "I" to "he, Oskar." Oskar has two putative fathers: the solid burgher and amateur cook, Matzerath, who could "express sentiments only in soups," and the dreamy, dandified, sentimental Bronski—Germany and Poland, West and East, action and idea. Oskar's mother is hopelessly partitioned between two men; Matzerath is caught in the crossfire of scowls exchanged by the two pictures in his bedroom: Beethoven and Hitler, genius and madman. Oskar's two favorite books—almost his only ones—are the Dionysianly orgiastic memoirs of Rasputin, and Goethe's Apollonianly transfigured *Elective Affinities.* And, above all, the plot thrashes about between two poles. There is Oskar's insistent striving backward into the womb: as a boy, he keeps trying to hide under his grandmother's skirts; as a young adult, he still shuts himself into the clothes cupboard of the nurse he covets; at thirty, he finds the insane asylum's bed insufficiently criblike. But there is also life moving forward and pushing Oskar before it: out of every asylum, lunatic or otherwise, and, ultimately, into death.

It is here that the couple, Nurse and Nun, becomes relevant. The Nurse stands for the return to the womb: Oskar cherishes a youthful picture of his mother as an auxiliary nurse; throughout the various maladies of his later life, nurses take care of him; often they hover over him while he enters a coma that is like the dark of the womb. At the other extreme stands the Nun, the black sister who succors the dying and prays for the dead. Oskar, significantly, craves both the Nurse who stands for earthiness (she is presumed to be of loose morality), and the Nun, immaculate Bride of Christ, who points to the Beyond.

Our tragedy is that we fail in both directions: life can neither retreat into the embryo nor pass on through death. The main nurse in the novel cannot be possessed by an Oskar suddenly struck with impotence; the principal nun is, with Oskar's help, raped by someone else. The nurse is subsequently murdered; the nun, apparently, commits suicide. Fulfillment is not to be had. Oskar's friend Herbert Truczinski tries to copulate with a wooden figurehead in the shape of a naked girl, which would bridge the gap between transient flesh and enduring wood. He dies in the attempt. Oskar interfoliates his Rasputin with his Goethe, but the resulting mixture is a trick and delusion: life knows no idyll in which "Ottilie docilely strolls on Rasputin's arm through the gardens of central Germany, while Goethe sits in a sleigh by the side of some dissolutely aristocratic Olga, as they glide along through wintry St. Petersburg." Indeed, in the end, even Goethe becomes a bogey for Oskar and merges with "the Black Cook": in death, to be sure, there is fusion, but what avails fusion then?

It is to be deplored that *The Tin Drum* comes to English readers diminished by Ralph Manheim's translation: in length, by well over a hundred pages; in quality, inestimably. Much that was either too difficult, or seemed too elaborate or obscene, has been flattened out, abridged, or omitted. On almost every page constructions, jokes, meanings are weakened, disregarded, or missed. None of which, however, has kept the translation from being extolled by literary and academic reviewers alike.

This is profoundly regrettable, because *The Tin Drum,* with its linguistic superabundance, its mythopoeic nature, its uncannily loving and palpable evocation of a city as it was but never again will be, its exploration of sex both bitter and humorous, its scatology, its dwelling on the father-son relationship while doing true obeisance to the eternal feminine, its religious coloring, its esoteric lore, its inextricable blend of reality and hallucination, its split between sensuality and spirituality, its wealth of magnificently grotesque invention, is a German approximation of—you guessed it—*Ulysses.* Approximation only, not equivalent; but a spectacular achievement all the same. *The Tin Drum* pursues, dazzles, sinks its claws into the mind. Whether it can also ambush the future remains to be seen.

[1963]

AN UNPLEASANT CHARMER
Ronald Hayman, *Brecht: A Biography*

THE paradigm of the artist as monster has been Richard Wagner. This dubious honor should by now have been transferred to Bertolt Brecht, whom, if I didn't like pigs, I would call the perfect swine. Most artists are characterized by dualism in the form of either a split or a fluctuation between high-mindedness and egoism. In Brecht, too, there was a dualism, but, rather unusually, both of its poles were equally reprehensible. At one extreme was the utterly self-indulgent, antirational, immoral hedonist, exemplified by the hero of his first full-length play, *Baal*; at the other was the omnipotent commissar, exemplified by Stalin, whom Brecht often praised, only rarely and clandestinely criticized, and never repudiated.

For the truth is—as emerges, even if not quite clearly and forcefully enough, from Ronald Hayman's study—that Brecht was always after self-aggrandizement and power and lording it over the hated bourgeoisie he stemmed from; he merely veered from a lawless individualism that threatened to run amok to a self-discipline imposed by Communism (without ever explicitly declaring himself), where he could hide his selfish drives behind ostensible service to the masses. But he almost never showed disinterested concern for other people. Typically, during the East German workers' uprising of 1953, he had no sympathy for the justly indignant strikers, and instead sent

supporting letters to the heads of the government and their
Russian adviser. Yet he hedged his bet with a certain ambiguity in a sentence or two, for there must always be an escape
hatch in self-contradiction. While other artists were riven by
duality, Brecht reveled in duplicity.

The Brechtian double negative (which does not, however,
make a positive) can repeatedly be found in his works. Take the
ballet with song *The Seven Deadly Sins* (1933), whose heroine is
characteristically split into two women, Anna I and Anna II.
Anna I is conventional and practical, even coldly opportunistic; Anna II is romantic, unbridled, passionately self-
indulgent. Critics have generally failed to notice that the values
of both Annas are made out to be contemptible. Or take the
poem "Changing Tires" (1953), which I translate:

> I sit on the shoulder of the road.
> The driver is changing tires.
> I don't like it where I come from.
> I don't like it where I'm going.
> Why do I watch the changing of tires
> with impatience?

Again, the alternatives are equally unsatisfactory; the one
overriding need is continual change, to satiate the restlessness
of this smug yet tormented man. It is the same restlessness that
made him often have two or three mistresses—and, later, a
wife as well—simultaneously. It is the restlessness that never
let him consider one of his plays finished: *Mann ist Mann*
underwent eleven major revisions and some minor alterations
before it left Brecht's hands, and no play was ever safe from
complete overhauling years later, so as to conform to the
author's changed political views. Then there were those
numerous projects, a number of them at an advanced stage,
left unfinished.

There is something distasteful about this perpetual, frenzied
tinkering, especially since the "definitive" versions of the plays

that get printed and reprinted are in several cases markedly inferior to inaccessible earlier ones. But this, too, was a form of self-assertion, if only at the expense of one's former selves.

Hayman shows how Brecht, practically from his birth in Augsburg in 1898, managed to dominate his family, particularly his mother and younger brother, while being a physical coward in confrontations with neighborhood boys. From the sway over his mother, who died when he was twenty-two, Brecht learned how to boss, first schoolmates, then teachers, girls, and professors at the University of Munich, where he enrolled in medicine to keep out of the army during World War I or, if drafted, to assure his assignment to duty as a medical orderly. The only medical lectures he attended dealt with venereal disease, a constant worry; otherwise, he fitfully attended literature classes. He got his first journalistic job, as a critic on the Augsburg paper, by writing a disingenuous encomium of a piece of junk, and he indeed did avoid fighting at the front by getting the army to assign him to a medic's post in Augsburg. Emboldened by sexual successes, he started evolving a style that was partly based on his mother's beloved Lutheran Bible, partly on his rebellious urge to undermine the solemnities of Teutonic syntax.

Early literary influences were Villon, Büchner, Rimbaud, Verlaine, and, above all, Wedekind; lyric poetry, often sung to the guitar to tunes of his own making or borrowing, preceded drama. Brecht's first full-length play, *Baal,* was devised, characteristically, as a revision of, or counterstatement to, a play by Hans Johst he despised. *Baal,* as Hayman puts it, "represents the apotheosis of sexual appetite," yet also reveals a contempt for women and a latent homosexual element Hayman is good at calling attention to in Brecht's life and work. In New York during World War II (though Hayman doesn't quote this), Brecht amazed Klaus Mann and Frederic Prokosch by declaring *Baal* his favorite play because of its "deep emotional validity for me," as well as "subtlety" and "a touch of the homoerotic." When his companions, both homosexual, asked whether he had ever been "a homoerotic," Brecht answered (if Prokosch, an unreliable source, is to be trusted), "Never in the flesh, but my mind runs riot occasionally."

Meanwhile young Brecht was seriously involved with at least three women, by two of whom he was to have illegitimate children. Paula Banholzer, whom Brecht called Paul, was gentle and pliable; Marianne Zoff, a minor opera singer, was capricious and willful, and involved also with a man called Recht. As Hayman demonstrates, Brecht was, in a sense, conducting through Marianne a complex and bizarre love-hate relationship with Recht. Such relationships appear in Brecht's work, too—between Garga and Schlink, for example, in the play *In the Jungle of Cities.* Eventually, the two young women jointly confronted Brecht and asked him to choose between them. He said he wanted both, and afterward told Paula he would marry Marianne to legitimize that baby, then secure a divorce and marry her.

Note, though, how Brecht, who didn't want babies ("there's so little one can do with children, except be photographed with them") reacted when Marianne had a miscarriage that he chose to misperceive as an abortion: "I could strangle her. . . . That's how a pregnant whore unloads it! And to think that I wanted to have this leaky pot, trickling with liquid efflux from various men, installed in my room!"

Why did women go crazy about Brecht throughout his life, leaving husbands, homes, their countries to share his exile and—in all ways save sexually and as literary collaborators—play second fiddle to his tough, efficient, unprepossessing wife, the actress Helene Weigel? What attracted them to this man who was homely, smelly, with dirty collars and fingernails, as well as forever surrounded by smoke clouds from his Virginia cigars? Albert Maltz observed that "the stench of [Brecht's] unwashed body made it an ordeal to sit beside him."

Well, the man had insidious charm. Moreover, he radiated absolute, insane self-assurance, was unmistakably marked by genius, and was hard to get. This charming ruthlessness, or really predatoriness, he also applied to his work. As Brecht once reminded the critic Alfred Kerr, "Obviously, the basis of just about every great age in literature is the force and innocence of its plagiarism." Accordingly, some of his best plays, e.g., *Mr. Puntila and His Servant Matti* and *The Caucasian Chalk Circle,* are based on other people's plays; *Edward II, The Mother, Schweyk in the Second World War,* and *Coriolan* are mere revisions of other people's drama or fiction; and many plays are full of forceful but not particularly innocent borrowings, say, from Villon in *The Threepenny Opera* (based, of course, on John Gay) or Kipling in *Mann ist Mann.* Some plays attributed to him actually were not his work; though she denied it, Elisabeth Hauptmann, his mistress, wrote all of *Happy End* except the songs. In various instances, his stage ideas come from sundry collaborators, several of them women he was sleeping with.

In theory, Brecht encouraged others to take liberties with his plays; in fact, he wanted to direct or codirect them himself, in the latter case invariably wresting the reins from his codirector's hands. Failing that, the plays had to be staged by persons he trusted, frequently his disciples or factotums. When G. W. Pabst altered *Threepenny Opera* in the movie version, Brecht sued him and his producer; as the producer's lawyer cited Brecht's borrowing and changing the Ammer translations of Villon, an enraged Brecht stormed out of the courtroom. So, too, with his women: Brecht would check up on them telephonically early in the evening and late at night. If one of them so much as seemed to have had sex with another man, she was likely to be dropped. When the aging Brecht fell for the young Isot Kilian, married to the philosopher Wolfgang Harich, among his chief protectors during the final East Berlin years, he simply told Harich: "Divorce her now. You can marry her again in about two years' time." Worthy of Caligula!

Politically, Brecht was equally disreputable. As a boy, he adored Karl May, whose supreme hero was Old Shatterhand, a great German hunter in America's Wild West, and a favorite of Adolf Hitler, whom Brecht, incidentally, did not oppose until he himself had to flee the Nazis. With his conversion to Karl Marx (even the names are similar!), the superman yielded to the supermass. Not exactly, though, because Brecht's heroes and heroines had a way of remaining idiosyncratic individuals whom, in revisions of the plays, he tried to make less sympathetic—notably Mother Courage and Galileo. Yet they continued to be quirkily likable, whereas the plays featuring collective heroes, such as *Days of the Commune,* proved failures.

Brecht's relations with the Soviet and East German governments were occasionally strained—particularly when the Germans banned or forced him to rewrite some of his works—but he never openly rebelled. The closest he came to that was guilefully negotiating for and acquiring Austrian citizenship while maneuvering to get his own theater in East Berlin, where he lived high off the hog when most others were starving. Ultimately he did get the Theater am Schiffbauerdamm, where his Berliner Ensemble, under him and Weigel, became one of the world's finest companies.

Hayman is right to argue that in Marx, Lenin, Stalin—in short, in Communism—Brecht sought and found the strong father figure that kept him from dissolving into Baal; in Weigel, who looked after his interests and creature comforts in any number of self-abnegating ways, he got himself a mother surrogate. He could thus maintain the role of the greedy child, playing off woman against woman, collaborator against collaborator, political allegiance against another (fake) political allegiance, the expedient lie being one of the favorite tools of this man who advocated greater truth in art. He was particularly adept at negotiating simultaneously with several producers, translators, and actors for the same thing, keeping each rigorously in the dark about his dealings with the competition. Sometimes, however, he outsmarted himself, especially during his years in America, where more than one important production fell through owing to his Machiavellianism or intransigence.

Hayman is good at tracing Brecht's motley career through early successes in Berlin and elsewhere in Germany; then through the seesaw years of exile in Denmark, Sweden, Finland, and the United States; and, finally, through the period of slightly tarnished triumph in Germany and the world up to his death from heart disease in 1956. Into 388 pages, the author packs a wealth of biographical material, plus a tidy sum of Brecht's political, theatrical, social, and literary ideas. There are, in addition, not very detailed or profound but useful discussions of the plays, fiction, and theoretical writings. What gets shortchanged is the poetry, despite our growing sense that it may surpass the drama. To be sure, several of Brecht's plays will remain staples of the repertoire, with others popping up intermittently. Still, the ten volumes of poetry contain some of the best verse written anywhere in the first half of our century. Unfortunately, Hayman quotes the verse only when it serves his biographical purposes, and then in his own sometimes inaccurate, always unpoetic, translations.

Although the writing is mostly clean and fluent, Hayman is no stylist, nor does he often hit on those happy formulations that bring a subject alive and become lastingly portable in the reader's memory. Similarly, his literary connections are not compelling enough, and he is better on the anecdotal and gossipy aspects of this life than on any others. There are lapses of diction, e.g., "consensus of opinion," and the odd ambiguity as in "Surrounded by admiring friends, he found it easy to seduce girls." Brecht could sink pretty low, but he did not put on live sex shows.

Sloppinesses are present in all sizes, from tiny to huge. A serpent becomes "she," merely because the German *Schlange* is feminine; the Swede Selma Lagerlöf is called a "Norwegian writer"; the character Andrea Arti, in *Galileo,* becomes Andrea del Sarto, even though he's no painter; the composer Jerome Moross turns into Maross; the set designer Howard Bay is donkeyfied into Bray; in the cast of *Arturo Ui* we find "Ciceronian vegetable dealers," without their being particularly golden-tongued, merely inhabitants of Cicero, Illinois; the actor-director Gustaf Gründgens becomes Gustav; and, most shockingly, the by then long-dead bourgeois Stefan Zweig is resurrected as a speaker in Communist East Berlin— a confusion with his brother, Arnold. Hayman loves to overaccentuate: Karin Michaelis, the Danish novelist, becomes Michaëlis; Mackie Messer (Mack the Knife) turns into Mäckie; and we get *oratio obliquà,* although there are no accents in Latin and, in any case, "indirect discourse" would do fine. As celebrated a line as "Erst kommt das Fressen [gorging], dann kommt die Moral" is misquoted and diluted into "Erst kommt das Essen [eating] und dann die Moral."

The system of bibliographical references is confusing: it is hard to figure out where a quotation comes from when several are lumped together in the same back-of-the-book note. And if you track one down, it may prove misleading. We read, for instance, that "Brecht wanted to avoid 'the kind of gag that endeared the audience to humanity in a generalizing way.' " Certainly, I thought, that must read "endeared humanity to the audience." Checking page 42 of *Theaterarbeit,* I found that the passage, deploring the loss of social content from humor, actually reads (I translate): "The pratfall appears as something sheerly biological, as something comical among all men in all situations." What Hayman offers as quotation is at best a faulty paraphrase. Further, *Brecht: A Biography* leans rather heavily on previous Brecht biographies, such as Klaus Völker's, which in English bears the same title, and James K. Lyon's *Bertolt Brecht in America.* This is understandable; the trouble is that Hayman's very wording is at times too close for comfort to that of his sources.

Hayman's basic literary sensibility is not above suspicion either. He speaks of "*Die Jungfrau von Orléans . . .* written in sub-Shakespearian blank verse," and, later, of "*Wallenstein . . .* a sub-Shakespearian history play." What is the point of this sniping at Schiller? Rare indeed is the blank verse that can match Shakespeare's, and a history play that can't equal Shakespeare's histories can nevertheless be well above the ordinary. But Hayman does know how to quote the right things. How pricelessly revealing is this statement of Brecht's: "Nothing is more important than learning to think crudely. Crude thinking is the thinking of great men." What a wonderfully, almost lovably, absurd argument *pro domo*. Too bad that it is separated by 175 pages from this description of Brecht directing the Berliner Ensemble:

> Both in selecting from ideas proffered by the actors and in interpolating details of his own, Brecht would work for internal variety and contradiction in each sequence. He no more liked a scene to sit still than he liked sitting still himself while writing or thinking. . . . Though the political thinking behind the productions was simplistic, the blending of contradictory impulses made the resultant performances subtler than any others to be seen in Berlin. While the working-class audience stayed away, intellectuals from East and West flocked to his productions.

There you have the fundamental duality: simplistically crude thinking buttressed by infinitely finicky complexity in presentation. Brecht's rivenness translated into action, even as so many of his characters either lead double lives (Puntila, the two Annas, the female Shen Te who is also the "male" Shui Ta) or are scoundrels and weaklings who nonetheless do good, brave, or just things (Galileo, Mother Courage, Azdak). His own double-dealing enabled Brecht to empathize with the rascal and the split personality, and to make him or her the kind of racy antihero that, much more than epic theater, is Brecht's true dramatic achievement.

Yet although the writer will live, there is no redeeming the man. In a final act of cowardice, Brecht requested that he be buried in a steel coffin to keep the worms out, and that, to ensure death, his heart be pierced with a stiletto. A wooden stake would have been more appropriate.

[1983]

A MARXIST AMONG THE CAPITALISTS

James K. Lyon, *Bertolt Brecht in America*

BERTOLT BRECHT'S six-year exile in America is a tale of mutual misunderstanding. Neither Hollywood, where Brecht lived, nor Broadway, to which he came frequently, made any real use of his genius; the House Un-American Activities Committee (happily) never grasped his true political orientation. For his part, Brecht, after five years in the hated capitalist U.S., could write: "No wonder that something ignoble, loathsome, undignified attends all associations between people and has been transferred to all objects, dwellings, tools, even the landscape itself." The unorthodox but hard-bitten Marxist still saw this country as he had visualized it in his works *Mahagonny* and *The Seven Deadly Sins*. "He was," as James K. Lyon puts it, "not examining life in America to adjust his model of it, but to confirm it."

It would be nice if geniuses, particularly those in the arts, were nice fellows. We may disregard Peter Shaffer's vulgarized Mozart in *Amadeus,* but we cannot ignore the deep unpleasantness of the historic Beethoven, the monstrosity of the real Wagner. Wherever exactly Brecht fits in on that scale, there is little doubt that he was well hated by many and well loved by a few. Thomas Mann, a fellow "exile in Paradise" (i.e., Los

Angeles), considered Brecht a party-liner and a monster, but "very gifted, unfortunately." W. H. Auden, his most illustrious collaborator and translator, called him one of the few people on whom a death sentence might be justifiably carried out, and added, "In fact, I can imagine doing it to him myself." Another important fellow exile, the philosopher-critic Theodor Adorno, claimed that Brecht spent two hours a day pushing dirt under his fingernails to make himself look proletarian; George Sklar called him a "real Hitler," who reflected the very Germany he had reacted against.

Make no mistake, however: James K. Lyon's fascinating study, *Bertolt Brecht in America,* is written with empathy and reverence; it is just that Professor Lyon is scrupulously honest in reporting the bad news along with the good. Actually, the tragicomedy of Brecht's American sojourn (July 1941 to October 1947) is preceded by a prologue. In 1935, the New York Theatre Union, a "workers' theater," decided to stage *The Mother,* Brecht's free adaptation of Gorky's novel, and agreed to bring over the author in an advisory capacity; he was then living as a refugee from Hitler's Germany near the Danish island town of Svendborg. Nobody in America knew about "epic theater," and Brecht was going to show the Theatre Union how to achieve it. As he wrote his wife, the actress Helene Weigel, back in Denmark, he established "a nice little dictatorship"—which meant that he terrorized the director, actors, and executive board with repeated shouts of "*Das ist Scheisse! Das ist Dreck!*" and by bullying demands for endless discussion meetings. Eventually, he and his henchman and composer, Hanns Eisler, were thrown out of rehearsals.

Although most of the people who met Brecht then found him, as did Albert Maltz, contentiously arrogant and made more repulsive by his bodily stench (he disliked bathing), he did acquire some important champions in Mordecai Gorelik, Joseph Losey, John Houseman, and Marc Blitzstein. In New York, Brecht saw plays by Odets (loved one, loathed the other), caught nearly every gangster movie in town, and returned with a suitcase full of clippings about the murder of Dutch Schultz and other horrors of capitalist life—Q.E.D.

As Hitler was getting too close for comfort, Brecht—who, like the heroes of most of his plays, was no hero—began to bestir himself about moving to America. Many American and refugee notables helped him with money and affidavits, yet there were numerous setbacks and a long wait for the visas; finally, the Brechts, their two children, and the two main odalisques of Brecht's harem were ready to depart. Over the years, that harem consisted of intelligent women who adored Brecht, helped him with his work (he tended to write his plays with a collective of writers, at least one of them a woman), and shared his bed. Along with cheap cigars and English-language detective fiction, they were his "means of production," as he graciously, or Marxianly, referred to them.

Brecht, who in Losey's words "ate very little, drank very little, and fornicated a great deal," was seldom without this often meddlesome retinue, which once elicited from Eric Bentley, Brecht's foremost American supporter and popularizer, the cry "I've had enough of Brecht and his female followers!" But Weigel, in Professor Lyon's phrase "a Marxist lady in proletarian garb," tolerated them and accepted Ruth Berlau, a Danish actress, and Margarete Steffin, a German proletarian writer, as traveling companions to America. En route, Steffin died of consumption in Moscow, and Brecht, who, because of hesitations about leaving without her, almost missed the last boat available to him, arrived from Vladivostok in San Pedro disconsolate, to grieve for the next year or two in equal measure over losing Margarete and getting America.

Dante himself could not have found an apter inferno for Brecht than Southern California, "this Tahiti in metropolitan form" with its "cheap prettiness [that] depraves everything," where his hatreds extended from the flimsy architecture to the store-bought bread, where the air was unbreathable and there was nothing to smell. America, as he complained in poems and letters, was all marketplace, all selling. The drugstore sells you a sandwich, and also vitamins to supplement its insufficient nutritive value. The President sells the people on the war as writers must sell their plays and scenarios. According to a particularly bitter maxim (not quoted by Professor Lyon), "One is forever buying or selling; one sells, one might say, one's urine to the urinal." And again: "The intellectual isolation here is enormous. Compared to Hollywood, Svendborg was a world center."

Of course, there is a good deal of Brecht's perennial opposition, his ingrained adversary attitude, in all this. As the actress Elsa Lanchester was to observe, "He was anti-everything, so that the moment he became part of a country, he was anti–that country." Brecht's personality is explained by Professor Lyon as a stance that helped him keep alive his righteous indignation about social injustice. But that hardly explains his never overtly coming out against Stalin's atrocities (indeed, often defending them) and never really criticizing East Germany, where he finally settled (though, cagily, with an Austrian citizenship—just as he deposited his Stalin Prize money in a Swiss bank) and where he did not come to the aid of the workers' uprising or of fellow authors abused by the state. It does not explain, either, Brecht's hideous utterances, such as "We have fraternized too long with ignorant decency," or "Now and then I catch a glimmer of the agony of the ungifted," or (about those not accepting his political views) "They have to be shot" and, more specific, the comment about Hanns Eisler's overtly anti-Stalinist sister, "The swine has to be shot." And it does not explain why Brecht never spoke out in behalf of suffering Jewry, even though his wife was Jewish.

Contradictory attitudes characterize all of Brecht's behavior. In his dealings with people, he tended to be opportunistic and manipulative, repeatedly playing off one translator or collaborator against another, one potential star or director of his plays against one or several others. Often, though, he did not bother to answer letters or even telegrams with various offers, thus incurring severe financial losses; during their early California period, the Brechts had to subsist on 120 dollars a month, mostly the gift of fellow refugees. To those in political power, however, Brecht would be deferential, throwing the beloved works of Lenin overboard lest the U.S. immigration authorities object, strictly obeying the curfew laws for enemy aliens, and soothing HUAC (before which he appeared in 1947) with half-truths, when not bedeviling it by acting the ignorant foreigner. But if Brecht played Azdak, Galileo, and Schweik in his political life and literary politics, he was fiercely uncompromising on the rare occasions when something of his reached the American screen or stage.

In the movies, despite numerous aborted efforts, this amounted to being co-scenarist on Fritz Lang's *Hangmen Also Die,* for which, after unjust arbitration, John Wexley ended up getting sole writing credit. In the theater, except for some very minor productions, this meant only *The Private Life of the Master Race* and *Galileo* off-Broadway (the latter also in Los Angeles) and the adaptation, with Auden, of Webster's *The Duchess of Malfi* for Broadway. That none of these succeeded had something to do with Brecht's either refusing to work with famous directors such as Max Reinhardt and Erwin Piscator, because he felt he could not control them, or forcing his actual directors, such as Berthold Viertel and Joseph Losey, into subordinate positions. Since, by and large, circumstances did not permit his implementing his notions of epic theater, he often, directly or indirectly, sabotaged his own productions, just as, for reasons of fanatic perfectionism, he stopped most translations of his works from reaching print. As ferociously as he craved success in America, it had to be on his own unbending terms.

None of these frustrations, however, impeded the creative output of the forty-three-to-forty-nine-year-old Brecht in America: the revised version of *Galileo, The Caucasian Chalk Circle, The Visions of Simone Machard, Schweyk in the Second World War,* the ideas if not the writing of *The Short Organum for the Theater,* and numerous fine poems had their genesis here. Perhaps William Dieterle, the refugee movie director who helped bring Brecht to the U.S., was right in insisting afterward that "success in Hollywood would have harmed Brecht immeasurably." It may well be that the mutual misunderstanding between Brecht and America was salutary at least for him.

Professor Lyon's book has three shortcomings. First, its subdivision into Brechtian topics rather than being one continuous narrative causes overlapping, repetitions, confusions in chronology. Second, it is not well versed in show-business matters: Eva Le Gallienne, for instance, is called a method actress; Paul Muni (rather than Cornel Wilde) is named as Chopin in *A Song to Remember;* Rod Geiger (the producer) is called the director of *Salt to the Devil,* an Edward Dmytryk film; and any number of notables have their names misspelled. Third, it is not particularly well written, being short on insight and heavy on cliché, and rather weak in the grammar and syntax department. It even stoops to ignorant spellings such as "hari-kari" and words not existing in English such as "niveau."

But *Bertolt Brecht in America* is saved by two things: its exhaustive and immensely rewarding research and the sheer fascination of its subject. Page after page affords glimpses of a spellbinding genius behaving oddly, shrewdly, shockingly— with unexpected generosity or with seeming self-destructiveness that proves ultimately advantageous. A typical example is Brecht's exchange with Abe Burrows, who was supposed to do an English version of the street singer's ballad in *Galileo:*

> *Burrows:* Tell me, Bert, how does this street singer feel about Galileo?
> *Brecht:* He feels nothing.
> *Burrows:* (hesitantly) I mean . . . is he praising Galileo?
> *Brecht:* No.
> *Burrows:* Is he against Galileo?
> *Brecht:* No.

Burrows: What do the pamphlets that he's selling say about Galileo?

Brecht: They just tell about him.

Burrows: (puzzled) Are they for him or against him?

Brecht: It doesn't matter.

Burrows: Well, just tell me one thing, Bert. Why is the man singing a song?

Brecht: Because I want him to.

Brecht's will was always the final arbiter; if it could not triumph over America, neither was it sucked into the American habit of compromise.

[1981]

A MONSTER OF SENSITIVITY

Ronald Hayman, *Kafka: A Biography*

FRANZ KAFKA is the writer par excellence who is all things to all men. Proust and Joyce have exerted as great an influence on other writers, but for a great many twentieth-century men and women Kafka's world view has become both archetypal and seminal. It is to each interpreter the face of his particular fear or desire. To Hermann Broch, a Joycean novelist, Kafka— not Joyce—was the one who did justice to our "condition of utmost helplessness." For Albert Camus, the absurd in Kafka's work was "recognized, accepted," and, through this resigna- tion, "no longer the absurd." For Thomas Mann, Kafka was essentially "a religious humorist"; for Vladimir Nabokov, no "religious implication can be read into Kafka's genius." "The Kafka hero," said Samuel Beckett, is "not spiritually precar- ious"; "the Kafka hero," wrote W. H. Auden, "is convinced from the start that he is doomed to fail." And so on and, contradictorily, on.

Kafka's literary constructs have concrete shapes and hard edges, but they are so diaphanous that every reader can see his own world framed, indeed focused and magnified, by them. There are three main interpretations of Kafka's work. There is the Freudian, according to which fear of an overbearing, vul- gar, crassly physical, and commercially successful father col- ored all of Kafka's work (and, perhaps, life); the political, usually Marxist, according to which Kafka's existence under the crumbling, capitalistic Austro-Hungarian monarchy and his employment by the imperially corrupt Workers' Accident Insurance Institute (where injured workers were often cheated out of compensation) made the Kafkan oeuvre essentially an attack on bourgeois bureaucracy; and the religious-mystical, which perceives Kafka's life and work as a steady gravitation toward Judaism and its religious and secular lore, with perhaps a dash of Gnostic demonology added.

Though there is much hostility among the rival schools of hermeneutics, the three interpretations are by no means mutually exclusive: the father, emperor or supreme bureaucrat, and God figures may represent concentric menaces, coexistent in the already mentioned transparency, and the petty demons are just as tormenting whether they are psychological, bureaucratic, or infernal. I concur with Paul Rosenfeld's estimate:

> There is no other modern writer whose subject matter—for all that Kafka's talent has been called a narrow one—is so broad, or whose symbols, whatever their partial explanation, are so clearly articulated in a statement that embraces and gives the quality of so much of modern experience.

Since the pioneering biography by Max Brod, Kafka's friend and literary executor (1937), many others have been written and some translated into English. But Ronald Hayman's *Kafka* is the first authoritative and comprehensive biography written in English, and possibly the most exhaustive in any language. It is certainly most exhausting to read, though, given the subject, this must be taken not as derogation but as a compliment. It is curious that two of the greatest virtuosos of feeling in modern literature—veritable monsters of sensitivity—were both German-speaking citizens of Prague: Rainer Maria Rilke, born in 1875, and Kafka, in 1883. Of these two exacerbated sensibilities, Rilke's could at least draw sustenance from a better childhood; Kafka, of a lower social class, was also Jewish.

Hayman shows us compellingly Kafka's troubled family background, the flare-ups of anti-German and anti-Semitic violence in the Prague of the period, the ruthlessness with which Kafka's father, Hermann, chugged away at assimilation and material success. Though a boor himself, Hermann wanted his son to be both refined and virile; he never read to the boy, but tried to teach him army songs, marching, and the like. Often he severely berated or punished him, with mother Julie taking his defense only feebly, if at all. This large, gruff man, who cared not a rap for his son's writing ("Put it on my bedside table" was the only comment on Franz's most important nonposthumous book), haunted Kafka all his life. "Arguably he never wrote about anything else," Hayman concludes.

Almost from the very beginning, Hayman constructs his biography predominantly out of the words of Kafka himself (his fiction, diaries, letters, conversations) and of those who knew him. I would guess that four-fifths of *Kafka* is in quotation marks, so that reading the book is like looking at a mosaic from a few inches away, almost tessera by tessera. This is tiring in itself, and a hundred times more so when you consider how much anguish each little piece can contain. Yet we need this fatigue if we are to begin to appreciate Kafka's miseries, terrible even—or especially—if self-inflicted. From the outset, the boy blamed himself for the deaths in infancy of two brothers, and for begrudging his three surviving sisters the little time their mother could take from the family dry-goods store. Scolding servants and mostly unsympathetic teachers aggravated the child's sense of isolation. Inadequate food—along with insufficient heating, a constant feature in the apartments the family kept steadily changing—may have prepared the ground for the tuberculosis that, after torturing Franz for seven years, was to finish him off, not yet forty-one, in 1924.

It could be claimed that all of Kafka's problems were based on ambivalence—or, more precisely, quadrivalence or some still higher valence. As Hayman writes, "Though unable to concentrate on other people, he dreaded being alone in a room; though plagued by insomnia, he found sleep was no better, for dreams were delirious." Yet this being drawn and quartered by contrary pulls is fundamental to Kafka, who in one of his letters sketches a man being put to death by a four-way pulling contraption. He started out as a student of German literature, but got his degree in law; after some literarily useful drudgery in the law courts, he ended up with a lifetime position at the Workers' Accident Insurance Institute, a civil service job he characteristically hated and enjoyed. Though the work was strenuous and boring, he could unearth issues that might have remained buried, and sometimes help workers to monies that would have been denied them. Also, the neutrality he had to maintain in reports about injuries may have given him pleasure, Hayman contends, as "an extraversion of the masochistic gratification he had in thinking about damage done to his own body or its destruction or degeneration."

Hayman perceives "Kafka's whole life as a series of hesitations in the process of condemning himself and carrying out the execution." But the hesitations allowed for intervals of merriment and even fleeting joy. There were the friendships with young men such as Max Brod, there were the more or less serious (but sparse) involvements with women, and there was, above all, the writing. Yet ambivalence seeps into almost everything, and the Kafkan laughter is no ordinary laughter. Thus Franz apologizes to Brod for mistakenly addressing to another friend a card meant for him:

> Please be angry about it and don't speak to me any more. My future's not rosy and I'll surely—this much I can see—die like a dog. I too would be glad to avoid myself, but since that's impossible, I can at least be glad to have no self-pity.

There is, surely, an element of irony in this declaration by a twenty-year-old, but not of a funny kind. To another friend,

Oskar Pollak, he writes: "We human beings ought to confront one another as reverently, as thoughtfully and as lovingly as we'd confront the entrance of hell." Thirteen years later, Kafka will write the third of his fiancées, "No one sings so purely as those who are in deepest hell; what we take to be the song of angels is their song." (Hayman translates the end too laconically as "that's what sounds angelic.") When Kafka kept breaking up while reading from *The Trial* to his friends, we may assume that that laughter, too, was hellish. And pure.

Yet the greatest scope for ambivalence was offered by women. Kafka was torn between visions of himself as husband and father and the overriding sense that this was never to be his destiny—not to mention his reluctance to join the "adult conspiracy" against children. There were four fiancées of sorts. First Felice, to whom he got engaged twice, only to get disengaged twice, and to whom he wrote some six hundred pages' worth of letters. She seems not to have aroused him physically, only epistolarily. There was, apparently, no sex, and very little physical contact; but a good excuse for producing fiction, which came in spurts: roughly one major frenzied burst of several weeks or months, followed by three fallow years. Felice also made the diaries grow, the only place where he felt he could hold on to himself; yet, of course, he also viewed the diaries as a confession of failure to write fiction reaffirmed daily. The second fiancée, Julie, a simple, earthy creature, was done in partly by paternal dismissal (Hermann called her one of those "Prague Jewesses" who entrap men with special blouses and "give themselves to anybody"), and partly by the loss of a wretched apartment Franz and she had chosen for themselves.

The third fiancée, Milena, Kafka's Czech translator, was more literary-intellectual and physically satisfying (though, again, there is no record of more than four sexual encounters), but there were other problems: Franz was already in the tightening grip of consumption, Milena was Christian (anathema to the Kafka family), and she had an unworthy husband whom she nevertheless could not leave. Another great correspondence, more cerebral than the one with Felice, to whom he had written: "I'm lying on the ground in front of you and beg you to kick me aside, or we'll both be destroyed." With Milena, he could sound even more complicated: "Perhaps it isn't really love when I say you're what I love most; love is that to me you're the knife with which I rummage inside myself." (Hayman translates "the knife I turn inside myself," which is less revealing.) Although Milena seems to have been the first woman with whom sex did not hold "a quite specific vileness . . . slightly repulsive, painful, filthy . . . some sulphur, some hell," the relationship still couldn't work because "I can love only what I can place so high above me that it's out of reach."

This did not prevent the occasional brief liaison with a shopgirl or a fellow patient at the many sanatoriums, hotels, or pensions Kafka visited in several countries in search of cures for a variety of lesser ailments first, for tuberculosis later. Toward that final illness he again managed to be ambivalent. It seemed to him psychic, simultaneously a reprieve from marriage and the ultimate defeat, but also, for a while at least, something enabling him to sleep much better. Hayman notes: "He had constantly been asking himself whether he was not unworthy to stay alive. Tuberculosis must have seemed like an answer from outside, a judgment written on his body"—an allusion to "In the Penal Colony." "It's not really illness," Kafka wrote, "but certainly it isn't health. Certainly it's the lungs, but then again it isn't the lungs." Typically, he who before becoming tubercular thought nothing of going to a sanatorium now frequently begrudged the money for treatment.

Even his writing, that which he was most dedicated to, could not escape his overarching ambivalence. It was not the disease but writing that was killing him, he explained to Brod; to Gustav Janouch he disparaged his work: "If one can give no help, one should remain silent." Only twice did he seem to become unambiguous about matters of moment. During a slight remission in the last stages of laryngeal tuberculosis, he decided unequivocally to marry Dora Dymant, the nineteen-year-old who lived with and nursed him in his terminal year. And he firmly instructed Brod to burn all his unpublished manuscripts, among them his three novels. But Brod had told him he would not comply with such a demand; and even while writing Dora's father for permission to marry his daughter (a request the father's rabbi promptly vetoed), Kafka must have known that he was moribund. Perhaps the only unalloyed pleasure in his life had been his friendship with his youngest sister, Ottla; she usually understood him and made no demands. Like her elder sisters, she was to perish in the Nazi death camps.

In his youth, Kafka was estranged from Judaism, let alone Zionism. Indeed, a Jewish school chum feared Franz might convert him to atheism. But, later, a group of traveling Yiddish actors so fascinated him with their personalities and performances that he became entangled in their work and lives; from Yiddish drama, he progressed to Hassidic tales, the Talmud, the Kabbalah, and other Jewish lore, traces of which show up in his writing. Toward the end of his life he was ardently reading the Bible and studying Hebrew, as well as considering emigration to Palestine. But about this, too, he had serious doubts. There is no evidence that the God he periodically invoked was an orthodox one; sometimes he was distant and inaccessible, sometimes cruel and vindictive, condemning Kafka to writing as a punishment. Near death, Kafka thought not of God but of the demons he felt were lurking in his fiction, which must, therefore, be destroyed. Perhaps his most telling—because most ambiguous— utterance was (in refutation of Gnosticism) "I don't think we're such a serious lapse on God's part—just one of his bad moods, a bad day." Was there hope outside our world then? "Plenty of hope—for God. . . . Only not for us."

The last pages of *Kafka* are almost unbearably sad. But at least Franz had a loving woman, Dora, and a devoted young medical friend, Robert Klopstock, faithfully tending him. Not until he was thirty-two had he moved out of his family home, where he had no privacy, heard his parents' lovemaking through a thin partition, and could have his letters and diaries pried into at any time. And not till his fortieth year had he finally got away from Prague for good, which he considered his greatest achievement, but only to come near death in Berlin and to die outside Vienna. Final irony: when his already celebrated friend Franz Werfel wrote to the chief physician of the Wiener Wald Sanatorium for a private room for Kafka, Professor Hayek refused: "A certain Werfel has written to say I should do something for a certain Kafka. Kafka I know. He's the patient in No. 13. But who's Werfel?" And the final paradox: racked by the last, terrible pains, Kafka implored the doctor who was giving him antidotes: "Don't cheat me. . . . Kill me, or you're a murderer." The parents did not come to their son's deathbed, and, at the funeral in Prague, Hermann Kafka turned away in disgust from Dora, who had collapsed on Franz's grave.

Ronald Hayman has sifted all the available information for his book, chosen the matter for inclusion aptly, and put it together conscientiously and concisely. I find no factual errors except for a few misplaced accent marks and a reference to the poet Detlev von Liliencron as Gustav. Stylistically, Hayman is no world-beater, and there are occasional lapses in grammar, syntax, and imagery. We get things such as "he could talk to both Minze, to Tile and to Dora"; "the lecturers were authoritarians, authorized by the university authorities"; "Most often the restlessness could be unleashed only in the evening. Still at its peak during the night it leaked all over his sleep without fueling any work"; and, most curiously, "Kierkegaard's reaction to Freud's remark." The reasoning is sometimes circular and naive, as in:

> If Kafka had spent more of his life in possession of a space that was indubitably his, he would have been a happier man but would have been without one of his tensions that needed to find release in his work.

Some readers may also object to Hayman's easy Freudianizing, as when he traces Kafka's vegetarianism and identification with animals to a grandfather who was a Jewish ritual slaughterer. Conversely, Kafka's horror at seeing his parents'

288 German and Austrian Literature

soiled nightclothes spread out on their bed is worth more speculation than Hayman accords it. But I agree with his judgment that Kafka's guilt feelings and "the need to feel authoritatively condemned made it impossible for him to remain agnostic." What I do object to is the plethora of comparisons to and contrastings with other writers and even painters—always superficial, and sometimes (when involving minor writers) insulting.

But, on the credit side, Hayman has the guts to challenge Walter Benjamin's revered but obfuscatory essay on Kafka, offers a pretty fair panorama of Kafka's major and minor writings (even if his interpretations sometimes seem questionable), and has drawn an indelible picture, physical and psychic, of this tortured being, indecisive and self-flagellating and hard to take, yet also dignified and controlled, often tender and generous, and by no means wholly joyless. *Kafka* is a full-length portrait worth hanging alongside the writings; it is not, however, a key to hidden locks or an epiphany of genius. For that, we have to go to greater writers and critics. To Erich Heller: "Never before has absolute darkness been represented with so much clarity, and the very madness of desperation with so much composure and sobriety." To Randall Jarrell: "In Kafka there is an unexampled extension of the methods of comedy to the material of tragedy." To Robert Musil: ". . . a friendly gentleness, as in the hours of a suicide between decision and deed. . . ."

It is Borges who pointed out that it required Kafka to make us aware of a trait in some earlier writers that is definitely Kafkan. And let us recall that the patient in No. 13 has become cosmically eponymous: there is a Johnsonian style, a Byronic hero, but *kafkaesque* is the only word derived from a writer's name that can be applied to anything and everything.

[1982]

THE PATIENT IN NUMBER 13

Ernest Pawel, *The Nightmare of Reason:*
A Life of Franz Kafka

TURN-OF-THE-CENTURY Prague was, despite some relatively liberal policies of the imperial Austrian government, no
easy time and place to be a Jew. Though assimilation to Aus-
trianness was partially possible, most of the better jobs were
not available to Jews, and the empire itself, on foundations
getting ever shakier, was less than a safe bet. The Czech
nationalists, as yet fiercely repressed, held out little promise,
being even more anti-Semitic than the Austrians. All it took
was an alleged ritual murder of a Christian by a Jew, and a sub-
Russian but vicious enough pogrom was on. So Jews were
torn between assimilation to creaky Austria or unfriendly
Czech nationalism—unless they risked embracing a Zionism
reprehended by both.

It was in this atmosphere that a burly, hustling, upward-
mobile country peddler named Hermann Kafka married—
lovelessly—Julie Löwy, the daughter of a thriving Prague
brewer. At twenty-six, she was close to spinsterhood and
proceeded to make Hermann—lovelessly—a hardworking,
dutiful, and caring wife. Of their four children the eldest alone
was male: Franz, born July 3, 1883, and named after the
emperor Franz Joseph. (Surprisingly, no critic I know has

found in this the explanation for the given name of the hero of *The Trial:* Franz's other half.) Among his father's ancestry, Franz could have found to boast of merely a butcher able to lift a sack of potatoes with his teeth; he preferred to acknowledge only his mother's forebears, who included some renownedly learned, mystical, even saintly, Jews. On the historical, political, social, and family background, Ernest Pawel's new biography, *The Nightmare of Reason: A Life of Franz Kafka,* is especially good.

As Pawel points out in the bibliography, "the literature dealing with Kafka and his work currently comprises an estimated 15,000 titles in most of the world's major languages." Book-length biographies (some of them translations) are no rarity in English, yet the one close competitor to Pawel's book in recent years is Ronald Hayman's *Kafka* (1982), a worthy effort in its own way. Two major differences are perspicuous. First, Hayman's text covers 304 pages; Pawel's, 448. Second, Hayman adverts fairly consistently to Kafka's fictional writings, and draws biographical inferences; Pawel restricts himself to discussing the major fictions, and those briefly and unbiographically.

The extra space allows Pawel to dig deeper into the background, to give ample sketches of some of Kafka's significant friends and contemporaries, to write in many respects a history of ideas. And by refraining from rummaging in the texts, he avoids the trap of oversimplification that Hayman falls into. In a biography, literary criticism is perforce condemned to an ancillary role; this is particularly dangerous in the case of Kafka, whose writings are open to so many interpretations that just listing—or refuting—them could by itself fill a bigger book than Pawel's. Besides, there is plenty of Kafka criticism in English, most notably Erich Heller's *Franz Kafka,* and his essay on Kafka in *The Disinherited Mind.* Of solid interest, too, are the writings of Martin Greenberg, Walter Sokel, Marthe Robert, and the symposium *The World of Franz Kafka,* edited by J. P. Stern. If one does not mind too much idiosyncrasy or obfuscation, there are also Walter Benjamin, Nabokov, and Roland Barthes to consider. It is to Pawel's credit, therefore, that he largely stays off textual explication and extrapolation: the life, the autobiographical writings, the reminiscences of contemporaries are more than sufficient.

The Nightmare of Reason—the title itself, focusing on the Jew beneath the Goya, is not unsuggestive—covers mostly familiar ground but in a spirited, graphic, incisive manner, lacking neither wit nor compassion. It is all there: agonizing friction with the formidable yet also collapsible father; unrequited yearning for a full, perhaps excessive, motherly love; squalid living conditions and ambivalent relations with the siblings, of whom only the youngest, the magnanimous Ottla, became a real friend; problems with teachers, some of whom were actually good, and fears of not graduating; comradeships with several students, most of whom became well-known, and even a platonically homoerotic crush on one of them; changes of fields in university study, to settle uneasily on the law Kafka was never to practice.

Then come the stirrings, rather late, of sex, toward which Kafka retained a lifelong deeply troubled attitude, involving few compunctions with whores and semiprofessionals but much fear of "nice girls." We are given the relevant family, ethnic, and social background of the neurosis along with its specific, individual symptoms. In a later diary entry, Kafka was to write: "Coitus is the punishment for the happiness of being together." Pawel sums up Kafka's first real intercourse, at twenty, with a shopgirl: "As always he passed the test, and found the experience exactly as he had expected he would—dirty, degrading, depressing; hence stirring and tremendously exciting."

After some floundering and one disastrous employment, Kafka managed—through connections—to obtain a relatively prestigious job at the Workers' Accident Insurance Institute, where there were practically no Jews. He was beloved by his coworkers from top to bottom; did excellent services to injured workingmen (if necessary, against the company); wrote up safety measures that were to save lives and limbs; and traveled across the country and familiarized himself with lowly existences, which elicited the sympathy for the underdog that informs much of his writing. The management regularly promoted him (though his pay, to the end, was far from lavish) and granted him generous vacations and leaves of absence when his health or hypochondria required them. Considered indispensable, he was kept out of World War I against his own wishes, and when, upon the inauguration of the Czech republic, most top employees were replaced, Kafka was one of the very few to be respectfully kept on.

Pawel traces admirably Kafka's literary and other friendships, notably with Max Brod, Oskar Baum, Franz Werfel, and a few others. Compared to them, Kafka came to writing belatedly, as he did to sex, and was at first highly secretive about it. But being a person who "was constitutionally incapable of tackling any task, no matter how trivial, with . . . indifference," he naturally threw himself into writing with utmost fanaticism. "What I need for my writing," he was to apprise Felice, the first of his four fiancées or quasi-fiancées, "is seclusion, not 'like a hermit,' that would not be sufficient, but like the dead. . . . Just as one could not and would not drag a corpse out of his grave, I cannot be made to leave my desk at night, either."

"The *only* way to write [is] with . . . total opening of body and soul," he wrote another time. Elsewhere he noted how hard this was: "The sentences literally crumble in my hands; I see their insides and have to stop quickly." To Brod he confided that writing "is a reward for serving the devil . . . [a] descent to the dark powers," and added, movingly, "Perhaps there are also different ways of writing, but I only know this one; at night, when fear keeps me from sleeping, I only know this one." And, with lacerating eloquence, on another occasion: "If [the writer] wants to escape madness, he really should never leave his desk. He must cling to it by his teeth."

Yet writing was not the only thing that tyrannized Kafka.

All his life, well before tuberculosis took over and drove him into hospitals, he spent sojourns of various length in pensions or sanatoriums (or even, happily, in his sister Ottla's village), recuperating from various forms of fatigue, illness, or phantasms. Here, too, he had minor affairs with fellow patients (whether platonic or not is difficult to determine), and here he met one or two of his fiancées. A faddist in matters of health (embracing such alienating doctrines as Müllerism and Fletcherizing), a vegetarian who drank large quantities of raw milk (which may have caused his TB), Kafka was continually undergoing cures that usually benefited him little and sometimes actively harmed him.

Next, Pawel gives us Kafka's political, ideological, religious development: his interest in Czech matters, yet siding with Austria during the war; his at first sporadic then intensive involvement in Judaism, though never officially joining the Zionists for all his sympathy with their cause. As Pawel says, "Kafka's true ancestors, the substance of his flesh and spirit, were an unruly crowd of Talmudists, Cabalists, medieval mystics . . . seekers in search of reason for their faith. He was their child, last in a long line of disbelieving believers, wild visionaries with split vision who found two answers to every question and four new questions to every answer in seeking to probe the ultimate riddle of God."

Pawel further observes, "This tension between faith and reason, the dynamic, ever-precarious balance between essentially irreconcilable opposites, is at the heart of Jewish tradition"—and, he claims, of Kafka's oeuvre. Certainly Kafka hurled himself in later life (if someone who died just under forty-one had such a thing!) into the study of Jewish lore and the Hebrew language, and harbored hopes of emigrating to Palestine with the woman he loved (not always the same), there to start a restaurant with her as cook and himself as waiter. But for the synagogue and orthodoxy Kafka never had any use, rejecting ultimately all fathers, heavenly or earthly. Or so Pawel would have it; Hayman's conclusion is different.

Kafka is most fascinating as neurotic genius: wise child and perpetual patient. Pawel explains the endless cures and refusals to shoulder responsibility—Kafka did not move out of the paternal dwelling till very late in life—partly as a reversion to childhood as the pampered patient or looked-after son, and partly as Jewish and Kafkaesque self-hatred: "He displayed all the classic symptoms of an overweening aggression turned inward, suicidal self-hatred, agonizing indecision, hypo-chondria, manipulative self-pity, insatiable demands for love beyond any hope of satisfaction, and, in addition, the perennial somatic complaints, from chronic headaches and insomnia to lassitude and digestive disturbances." He was, in fact, a prime candidate for suicide, except that, as he told himself, "If you were capable of killing yourself, you would no longer have to do it, so to speak." In another letter he said, "It also occurred to me that my death would interrupt my writing more decisively than if I remained alive."

Ernst Pawel does justice, too, to the four main women in Kafka's life, as well as to some of the lesser ones; similarly, the upsurges of hope and positive action are given equal play with the dejection and accidie. Perhaps only the last months of painful dying from a tuberculosis that had attacked the larynx and made mere swallowing an unbearable pain receive less than their full due. I miss particularly one emblematic episode (recorded by Hayman), in which the already renowned Franz Werfel tried to obtain for the still little-known, moribund Kafka a private room in the Wiener Wald Sanatorium, and the chief physician responded: "A certain Werfel has written to say I should do something for a certain Kafka. Kafka I know. He's the patient in No. 13. But who's Werfel?" Poor Kafka—all his life he was the patient in No. 13, yet the final irony, as Pawel points out, is that "the would-be suicide of long ago had become a model patient who desperately wanted to live." No contradiction, I suppose, for the father of paradoxes.

A biography of Kafka today is not likely to dig up much new material. Pawel has, for instance, interviewed in Israel the octogenarian Dr. Puah Menczel, who, as a young girl, taught

Kafka Hebrew. But this intelligent woman has nothing much previously unsaid to say. Although on some bibliographical problems—the lacunae in the *Letters to Milena,* the roadblocks in bringing out the critical edition of Kafka's works—Pawel has fresh things to report, these are peripheral matters.

What Pawel has done mainly is to sift the enormous available material (the *Letters to Felice* alone are 600 jam-packed, sticky pages that test a biographer's extracting aptitude) and organize the key insights. He has also provided the necessary setting and background—and is particularly good on the ambivalent way the current regime plays up Kafka for the tourist trade but bans his books. Finally, he does not shy away from drawing certain risky but worthwhile conclusions.

Some weaknesses, mostly stylistic, remain. The author has, commendably, tried to make *The Nightmare of Reason* a work of literature in itself. On the whole, his writing is accomplished, sometimes elegant. But there are serious flaws, and I don't mean trifles like the reference to the great actress Gertrud Eysoldt as "Eyesoldt." On the lowest level, there are slips of grammar, e.g., "Each following their own routine," and a clumsy back-formation such as "adolescing." One level up comes an unfortunate trendiness, with references to "the public sector" and the Russian eagle as "the big bird," not to mention repeated use of the buzzword "basically."

On the next-higher level, we get painful clichés: "What he felt in his bones was a reality beyond appearances"; "The war was over. Peace had broken out." But worst of all are the occasional bits of portentousness and just plain overwriting. Thus when, at the non-end of *Amerika* the hero takes off on a train for parts unknown, Pawel comments: "Unknown to Karl Rossmann, alias Franz Kafka, that is; we have since found out where those trains ended up, some forty years later." Or this: "Open to question—wide open, with blood oozing out of the gaps—was only whether he would squander these gifts. . . ."

There is one additional problem. For non-German-speaking readers, the biographer feels rightly compelled to make up his own translations. Though he clearly knows his German and English, there are some strange lapses, as when the *Saale* (halls) of a castle become "chambers," or playing billiards is Americanized into "shooting pool." Or consider the question the unworldly young Kafka addressed to the urbane Brod, as Pawel translates: "If . . . eight people take part in a conversation, when do you speak up in order not to be considered taciturn? It surely cannot be done deliberately. . . ." Hayman is better: "If . . . eight people are sitting on the fringes [*am Horizont*] of a conversation, when and how is one to take the floor in order not to be considered uncommunicative? For heaven's sake, it surely can't be done at random. . . ." But even Hayman's rendering of *willkürlich* as "at random" should more properly read "arbitrarily."

Let us end, however, on a deservedly positive note. Pawel's book offers eminently sensible critical insights, much too rare these days. Thus we get such fine lapidary formulations as "If writing alone justified his life, it also justified his not living his life." There are many extended passages of sound sense, too. For example: "But even the most sane and sensitive reading [of "The Judgment"] is necessarily tied to the subjective bias of the interpreter and, at best, can only illuminate whichever side he happens to be on. For what a critic like Walter Benjamin sees as 'the unmaking of the corrupt and parasitical world of the fathers' is also the oedipal conflict, the struggle between freedom and authority, and the confrontation between God and man."

And this wrap-up to a fine biography: "His work is subversive, not because he found the truth, but because, being human and therefore having failed to find it, he refused to settle for half-truth and compromise solutions. In visions wrested from his innermost self, and in language of crystalline purity, he gave shape to the anguish of being human." Too bad about that overworked "crystalline," but otherwise exemplary.

[1984]

MUSIL ASCENDING

Afterword to *Young Törless*

I

WHATEVER Robert Musil, the great Austrian writer, touched, was or became difficult. Simplicity was not for him: in style, thought, or life. But the Musil touch, which turns everything into subtlety, complexity, ambiguity, is not, like the Midas touch, a curse. It is an honest awareness that life is difficult—or, as we read in Rilke, whom Musil revered, "There are no classes for beginners in life"—and that a mere simplistic acceptance of that fact will not lessen the difficulty.

But the fascination of what is difficult does not, as Yeats would have it in an early poem, dry the sap out of the veins, whatever it may do to spontaneous joy. Besides, difficulty in Musil is always both there and not there. He is not like the phony weight lifter who grunts and snarls as he lifts a weight which may be heavy, but not all that heavy; he is rather like the master juggler who would make us forget how hard his cavalierly performed feats are if we did not notice with anxiety the fearful swelling of his jugular vein. In the later Joyce, difficulty is, for the most part, awesomely there and not to be sophisticated away; in Kafka, difficulty is often deceptively self-effacing

This Afterword appeared in the New American Library edition of *Young Törless*, 1964.

298 German and Austrian Literature

and the reader may, in his artlessness, think it not there at all. These are perfectly good ways of being difficult, but they are not Musil's way. In him, difficulty and seeming simplicity tend to be simultaneously manifest as in that juggler and his jugular. Or, rather, as in those trick drawings of cubes where what palpably protrudes becomes forthwith concave—and, concave to the extent of receding into infinity, Musil's meanings will not stand still. It is a method that has its advantages: it encourages and urges us on even while slowing us down and forcing us to spare no imaginative effort. Reading Musil, we must balance our surging fascination with painstaking unraveling— we must, ourselves, become jugglers.

II

Robert Musil was born in 1880, the only child of an engineer who was to rise to not inconsiderable heights under the Austro-Hungarian monarchy. For working at various government jobs and eventually teaching with distinction, Musil Senior was knighted and died a respected old man. He was essentially scholarly, mild, and pliable; Robert's mother, however, was a tempestuous woman, presumably frustrated by marriage to the point of not even showing particular love for her son, who, nonetheless, cared much more for her than for the meek father who carefully softened the rod with which, at his wife's insistence, he would give the boy a caning. Before Robert was born, the Musils had had a little girl, who died before she was a year old. The image of what this sister might have been, added to that of what the mother should have been, was to haunt Robert's thought and work forever.

Of Musil's childhood be it said only that it was lonesome, that he exhibited considerable physical prowess during it, and that it contained the curious episode of an innocent "abduction" of a very young schoolgirl. The girl-child was to be one of Musil's emotional magnets: a sudden enthusiasm, much later on, for a twelve-year-old girl observed during a streetcar ride and never seen again was to be included in his main work, the sixteen-hundred-page unfinished novel *The Man Without Qualities*. And in *Young Törless,* the catamite Basini's body, "lacking almost any sign of male development, was of a chaste, slender willowiness, like that of a young girl."

Young Robert was in due time sent off to military schools in what is today Czechoslovakia, the second of which—a diabolic place, he called it—supplied the matter for his first published work, the short novel *Young Törless.* But a military career soon ceased to interest the youth, and he next turned, under his father's influence, to engineering.

Though he did very well at it, and was later to become even a minor inventor, Musil was unable to fulfill himself through engineering. He did, however, retain an abiding interest in physics and mathematics. Drawn next to philosophy and psychology, he was enabled by paternal support to acquire a second higher education in these fields. Subsequently, it was to be said—not entirely without justification—that Musil the writer became "isolated in a no-man's-land between science and literature." He was, at any rate, already writing *Törless,* begun when he was twenty-two and published in 1906 when he was twenty-six; the book, though it scandalized some people, had a fair success. It is with considerable interest that we note another publication in 1906: that of the *Cornet,* the first work to bring true recognition to a fellow Austrian, Rainer Maria Rilke.

It now became evident to Musil that he was meant to be a writer, and though he was to hold, out of financial necessity, a variety of jobs from librarian to something that might be called civilian-instruction coordinator at officers' training school, these jobs never lasted long, and it was chiefly as journalist and author that Musil made his often precarious living. In 1907 he met Martha Marcovaldi, a Jewish woman seven years his senior, estranged from her second husband, mother of two children, unattractive, freethinking, highly intelligent, and a talented painter. A few years later they were able to marry. Martha gave up her painting and became a dedicated handmaiden to the impractical genius she had married, and the two remained happy with each other to the end.

World War I found Musil distinguishing himself first as a front-line officer, then as the brilliant editor of various military newspapers. He was demobilized as a captain with numerous citations and decorations. Something military remained in him, consolidating an anterior aristocratic-snobbish streak. However poor the Musils were to be—and they were at times not a jump but a mere hop ahead of pennilessness—Musil's clothes had to be expensive and immaculate, and the sight of an unpolished pair of shoes hurt him physically.

The Musils kept shuttling between Berlin and Vienna, and Robert published short stories, plays, criticism, and articles on a variety of subjects, including sports, at which he was always extremely good; in fact, he died at the age of sixty-two from having overtaxed himself, despite a weak heart, at his daily gymnastics. In installments, Musil was also publishing his lifework, the endless, unfinishable, and unfinished *roman-fleuve* titled *The Man Without Qualities.* Though these works contributed to making him famous among a small elite, they achieved scarcely more than a *succès d'estime,* and the larger public has remained to this day, even in his own Vienna, ignorant of Musil.

With the rise of Nazism, the Musils, by then living mainly off a Musil Society, moved first back to Vienna, then, by way of Italy, to Zurich and, eventually, Geneva, where Musil died in near-poverty and almost total obscurity in 1942. Various attempts by men like Thomas Mann and Hermann Broch to interest American foundations in Musil's work, and so enable him and his wife to come to the United States, failed abjectly. Martha survived Robert, faithfully publishing at her own expense further parts of his work; she died in 1949 in Rome, where unpublished Musiliana remain to this day. But the collected works of Robert Musil already comprise, in German, three huge volumes, well edited and printed, published by

Rowohlt Verlag. There is more to come, and the customary doctoral dissertations and critical studies, as might be expected, proliferate.

III

Musil was a man of contraries, not to say contrarieties. It was Ovid who first formulated the dilemma of the modern artist, whether he be *poète maudit* or merely bedeviled novelist: *Video meliora proboque, deteriora sequor* ("I see the better and approve of it, but follow the worse"); this fits Baudelaire or Verlaine as well as it does, for example, Montherlant, who applied it to his autobiographical hero, Costals, in *The Young Girls*. But Musil's attitude is different, almost the opposite: "The world is not good," he seems to be saying, "but I understand and accept it; and yet I would make it, and myself with it, better."

The first pair of antinomies is life and work. Musil's was a lifelong struggle to find time and means for writing his one work, *The Man Without Qualities*; almost all of his output, *Törless* included, is, consciously or unconsciously, a preliminary sketch for it or a variation on some of its themes. So thoroughly is he intertwined with that novel, so significantly is its protagonist, Ulrich, a somewhat transfigured Musil, that it is hard to say whether Musil lived his writing or wrote his life.

Though his parents were strict nonbelievers, Musil came to be more and more concerned with the question of God (wondering, for instance, if God intended spirit to perish from the earth: "that would explain why he is not treating Robert Musil better"); but his English translators, Wilkins and Kaiser, are probably right to find in Musil "the interim method of a believer who simply doesn't happen to be believing in anything." Characteristically, Musil describes his attitude as "active passivism," and his fictional alter ego is "passionate and compassionless." Most critics have noted what Musil himself has told them, that he fluctuated between a sense of reality and a sense of potentiality, that he was a citizen both of a world of actuality and of a world of possibility. As Marie Luise Roth put it, a critical, analytical spirit in him confronted a constructive faith, a belief in Utopia. But what strove within him to become a synthesis was as likely to remain a conflict. "I have from science the habit of regular work hours," wrote Musil in his journals, "from poetry, that of waiting to be inundated; that is one of the causes of my difficulties."

Even the titles of some of his works attest to a deep-seated duality that often found irony to be its appropriate expression. There is the *Posthumous Writings from My Lifetime,* or the *Stories Which Aren't Stories,* and, of course, *The Man Without Qualities,* whose hero actually has plenty of them. Musil's attitudes toward life are "concave and convex," or "egocentric, as if one carried one's person in one's middle" and "allocentric, that is, not having any midpoint, but participating restlessly in the whole without putting aside anything for oneself." And "without qualities" does not mean lacking in aptitudes and even excellence, but being utterly free and uncommitted to any of the ways of the world, and thus, from the world's standpoint, a nonentity.

But most revealing of all is the fact that Musil could not finish his masterpiece, his life's work. He had been at it for some thirty-seven years and it was approaching page 2000. Scholars wrangle over whether Ulrich and his twin sister, Agathe, were to find their final ecstasy in full-fledged incest or in some abstinent otherworldly rapture. It is a question that, I am sure, Musil himself, who rewrote every chapter at least five times, could not answer—there lies the ultimate dichotomy. The only way out was to die.

IV

Austrian fiction reached its peak with Stifter's *Indian Summer (Der Nachsommer),* 1857. This is patently a novel written in a strong and safe empire: conservatively humane, nobly poised, and long-winded, it harks back to Goethe. If Stifter knew that the previous year had seen the publication of a book called *Madame Bovary,* his novel shows no sign of it. After Stifter, however, Austrian fiction, unlike poetry and drama, went into a decline. At the turn of the century, though, the dying Hapsburg era summoned up a final flowering of all branches of literature.

The two most brilliant writers who wrote, among other things, fiction were Hugo von Hofmannsthal and Arthur Schnitzler. In 1905, the year before *Törless,* Hofmannsthal brought out a dazzling volume of stories that were, however, tales rather than short stories; and although, several years later, the poet-dramatist-essayist was to make his one attempt at more sustained fiction with *Andreas,* this work remained a fragment. By 1906, Schnitzler had published one novella and one novel, and several short stories (not to mention his plays); but the shattering novella, *Dying (Sterben),* was essentially naturalistic, and *Frau Bertha Garlan,* however penetrant in psychological observation and social critique, was ultimately a conventional novel of unhappy love. In the story "Leutnant Gustl" (1901), Schnitzler had indeed created, besides a study of decadent manners, a spectacular stream-of-consciousness character sketch, but he was to follow this up only much later and then only once. The prevalent tone, thus, in serious fiction was the psychoanalytically tinged naturalism of the earlier Schnitzler, and the lyrical-fantastical heightening of reality in the young Hofmannsthal.

But the ironically profound, tragicomically probing, psychologically hypersensitive mode of Robert Musil was already dimly heralded in the admittedly minor writings of Peter Altenberg, a sandal-wearing, bohemian café-poet-in-prose who occasionally attained genuine poetic heights. In one of his little sketches, a young officer whom he envies for his immense luck with women replies, "Look here, Peter, look here; there's no such thing as luck. Those women with whom one has luck, it isn't luck any more. Those one has anyway. It would be luck only where one hasn't any luck. And that's just

304   German and Austrian Literature

where one has no luck at all!" In another little sketch, Altenberg wrote: "There are only 'spiritual relations.' The sexual
then is only the release of overwhelmingly pent-up accumulated life-energies of the spirit." This last was published in
1906, the year of *Young Törless,* and might have served as its
second epigraph. Musil, we know, was influenced by Altenberg.

V

What exactly is *Young Törless?* It may, to begin with, help to
establish what it is not. It is not one of the countless novels,
stories, or films about boys or girls sequestered in schools and
being sad, wild, pathetic, or pathological, or just jolly. It is no
more *Stalky and Co.* than it is *Mädchen in Uniform*; you will not
find its like in Jules Romains or Rosamond Lehmann, in Erich
Kästner, Ferenc Molnár, or Calder Willingham. Least of all, in
fact, is it an *End as a Man.* It is as unique in our day as it was
sixty years ago. The only work I can think of with which it has
a genuine kinship is Rilke's little sketch "The Gym Period"
("Die Turnstunde"), whose final draft dates from 1902, the
year Musil started working on *Törless,* but Rilke's short-short
story, for all its poignant perfection, provides only a whiff of
the world of *Törless.*

True, there is in this short novel homosexuality and sadism,
but we are, for all that, miles above, beyond, and even below
the world of Jocko de Paris. The German title of the work is
significant: *Die Verwirrungen des Zöglings Törless,* which is to
say the perplexities (or confusions) of the boarding- (or mili-
tary-) school student Törless. This emphasizes the state of
being cut off from the world, on which Musil puts much of the
blame, but it also, and more importantly, faces us with the not
merely psychological but also metaphysical problem: the perplexities, tearing uncertainties, self-dividedness attendant on
growing up.

But, again, that is not quite it. For growing pains, however much seen *sub specie aeternitatis,* are not the prime concern. Musil was as well aware as Wordsworth and Baudelaire that it is in childhood that we find "the seed of the strange reveries of the grown man and, better yet, of his genius," as Baudelaire put it. An adolescent enclave, especially if it contains a future writer of genius, becomes a compact model of the adult world and its concerns. It is true that Musil seems to particularize when he speaks of the "dangerously soft spiritual ground" of the young years that has somehow to be traversed, but we soon find the same image applied to mathematical speculation, where "our thinking has no even, solid, safe basis, but goes along, as it were, over holes in the ground—shutting its eyes, ceasing to exist for a moment, and yet arriving safely at the other side." Indeed, Törless finds imaginary numbers "like a bridge where the piles are there only at the beginning and at the end, with none in the middle, and yet one crosses it just as safely as if the whole of it were there." Another time, Törless feels "the urge to search unceasingly for some bridge . . . between himself and the wordless thing confronting his spirit." Not unrelatedly, Musil observes that the characters of *The Man Without Qualities* "are unable to make the leap across to another human being." In adolescence, maturity, abstract speculation, the problem is everywhere the same: how to get across the gaps—by bridges, leaps, desperate acts of the will. Törless's "institution" is the microcosm which, pursued to Musilian depths, assumes the dimensions and other characteristics of the infinite universe.

Homosexuality as such is unimportant here. It is significant only as a swampy ground in which the sickness of delusion can thrive. In a note dating from 1906 Musil insists that Basini could just as easily have been replaced by a woman and that instead of bisexuality there could have been any other perversion. Circumstances have much to do with such aberrations, and, in any case, Musil says, "I do not want to offer psychology in all its fine details . . . . I do not want to make things understandable but, rather, tangible. That, I think . . . is the difference between psychological science and psychological art." Elsewhere he says that he is not interested in representing a sick soul, but in rendering its distorted worldview through impressions of an excessive sensibility to things.

Growing to manhood, then, is a strange and morbid, fabulously hallucinated, but also emblematic human state for Musil—more than a mere atypical interlude of hovering between poetry and death, which Giraudoux's heroines must perilously negotiate as they move toward womanhood. Törless traverses various stages of doubt, loss, and despair, his sensitivity making the experiences more searing but also more fructifying. There is a painful spiraling in his attitude toward his family, although it is finally an upward spiral. The young prince represents an ideal, presexual friendship that, however, crumbles under the assertion of a more masculine selfhood. Now come the first stirrings of sexuality, and the notion of it as a dark and guilty thing finds perfect objectification in the coarse, dilapidated Božena who, disquietingly, becomes associated with the Mother.

There arises before Törless a series of upsetting double views such as that of woman as whore and mother. There is Beineberg, the friend who is both attractive and repellent; there is Basini, who is one of the boys and yet so alarmingly different; there is the secret room with its clandestine world both heady and horrible. There are mathematics, philosophy (Kant), and the very sky above, all of which can be so close and dependable and protective at one moment, and so cold, far, meaningless the next. Writing, too, whether in letters to one's family or in a proposed treatise on the nature of man, is an elusive, evanescent consolation. As Törless discovers in various contexts, there are two worlds within him corresponding to two worlds without him: a quotidian existence of rational, routine activity and ultimate soothing inertia; and also a dark, exciting realm of violent, often destructive, probably forbidden, impulses and adventures. Which is more real? Which is to be espoused? Or can the two be reconciled?

The central problem of the novel finds Törless in the field of three forces: Beineberg, who represents a mystical view of life, all too ready to renounce that very intellect with which he advocates the nebulous quantity, Soul; Reiting (probably so named after Reiter, the constant companion of Musil's parents, hated by the boy, who saw in him his mother's lover), who embodies ruthless activism backed up by shrewd intriguing— Napoléon is his idol; and Basini, who stands for the dark, seductive power of weakness and perversion, but accompanied by the ability to give. And that is what makes the book absorbing: that all these evils have a part of wisdom and good in them, and that all these evils are part of Törless himself. He, too, can dominate and bully Basini, at times in the sheer physical way of Reiting, at others in the more sinister mental way of Beineberg. And there is always the danger that he himself may become the older boys' victim through something in his nature that is Basini.

"All the evil in me is parts of good people. Create them!" Musil reminds himself in his journal; elsewhere he says he can re-create and feel within himself every abnormality with equal ease. Perhaps it was V. S. Pritchett who put his finger on it most deftly: "Consciousness is Musil's real subject, not the 'stream' but the architecture, the process of building, stylizing and demolishing what goes on in the mind."

VI

Philippe Jacottet, the gifted Swiss poet, explains that what induced him to spend four years of his life on translating Musil's work into French was a special quality: "the poetic, poetry, that is to say the struggle with a perhaps forever insoluble enigma, which is, nevertheless, to him who would approach it, illuminating and fertilizing." And indeed poetry is omnipresent in Musil's prose: there is scarcely a page of his prose fiction that could not, properly excerpted, pass for a prose poem.

One of the ways in which this poetry manifests itself in *Törless* is in the commanding use of imagery. Let me give here merely two examples: the use of the window as a recurrent motif that finally becomes a symbol, and the use of the worm as a metaphor that eventually becomes a philosophical utterance. Thus Törless is repeatedly seen, in the earlier part of the work, gazing in or out of windows. First he is looking into the windows of peasant dwellings and discovering there a troubling world of sensual earthiness. Next, however, at the cake shop, he is looking out of the window, in an effort to escape the physical fascination of Beineberg; later, he duplicates this maneuver, for similar reasons, at Božena's. It becomes apparent that a window is both a source of revelation, partially disturbing, and an avenue of evasion, disturbingly partial. In one case, one is confronted with the darknesses of human nature; in the other, with the promise of being taken out of one's troublesome humanity. But, of course, there can be no flight from human nature: *tamen usque recurret*; and non-human nature—whether in the shape of the threatening presence of trees closing in on a small child, or as a sky that cruelly withdraws from a boy's reach—is all too inhuman. (The latter scene curiously prefigures Roquentin's insight into his estrangement from nature in the famous passage from Sartre's *Nausea*.)

There was a moment in childhood, however, when the window did negotiate a peace between inside and outside—a significantly *open* window, this—when the child Törless listened to an unseen opera singer in an unknown language. But the language of art needs neither the immediate gratification of the senses nor the endorsement of intellectual cognition; it operates on a higher level by "transform[ing something] into something else." But when Törless wishes simply to remove his thoughts from Basini in the near-empty classroom, the bleakness outside is no more helpful than the darkness within. And the last time a window makes its appearance is in the faculty-investigation episode (a kind of comic variation on the comic-frightening scene in Wedekind's *The Awakening of Spring*), where the window reveals only a vast white plain and one black crow, a vision of yet starker despair.

But in between all these window images there comes, pointedly and relatedly, the image of "the narrow gateway where all that ever happens, the images of things, must throng together and shrink so that they can enter into man." This happens at "the invisible frontier" that lies "between the life one lives and the life one feels"; the solution, then, is not an outside window but a narrow inner gateway: the ability to reduce the magnitudes of life to a size fit for human consumption, and to keep that gateway open for continuous intercourse between the outer and inner worlds.

More imposing yet are the permutations of the worm, or insect, image. It first crops up as an emphatically didactic but still somehow remote simile: a reference to the sudden revelation of evil in Basini, which is exposed "like the worm-holes . . . when a piece of lumber splits open." The image reappears when Törless expects his parents to be disgusted by Basini's presence at school and muster up "something like the flick of the finger-tips with which one brushes off an unclean insect." But, evidently, the unclean insect is accepted by the world. Presently, Beineberg spells it out: Basini, the evil person, is no more than a worm in the road, one of those things "you never know whether to walk round or step on." Its purpose may be small, or it may be nil; it is just that one cannot be sure which. But hardly has Beineberg finished his great mystical-moral sermon, when already he himself looks like "a great, weird spider lurking in its web." Could it be that he who sits in judgment over evil embodies worse evil? Forthwith, however, Beineberg says: "I can overtake him with one stride, just as if he were a worm," and the reference is not to Basini but to Reiting. Slowly everyone is sucked into the worm-insect image. The necessary consequence follows: the ground under Törless appears as "fantastic lurking-places for slugs and snails" and in the wall behind him there is "a faint rustling . . .

of uncanny life awakening in the bricks and mortar." Worms, insects everywhere. And when, witness and accessory to the rape of Basini, Törless experiences a strange urge to get down on the ground and crawl, he, too, is engulfed by wormhood.

At this point the worm image becomes more terrifying yet: the blood on the assaulted and beaten Basini's mouth and chin forms "a red, wriggling line, like a worm." The ignoble, even in their suffering, fail to achieve tragic dignity: their very wounds are worms. Next, at night, the cord of a window shade hangs down "hideously twisted, and its shadow crept like a worm across the bright rectangle of the floor." Here the window and worm images intersect: the very brightness of the moon, which should enter one's bedroom like a blessing, is sicklied over by some man-made evil. But there is worse to come: in a dream, a mathematical theorem appears to Törless as a worm (the translators, unaware of the importance of the metaphor, unfortunately translate the German *Bandwurm,* tapeworm, as a "long skein"). Science itself has become vile. After this, there is once more a very plain and almost top-heavy comparison of the private life of a group of students to "that of the spiders and centipedes in the cellars and attics." Lastly, as "the hours crept on toward dusk" and the ticking of Törless's pocket watch is "like a little tail wagging on the sluggish body of the creeping hours," time itself has become a grotesque, absurd worm—an indefinable, repellent, all-encompassing insect.

For his handling of imagery alone, Musil has earned Ernst Blass's commendation as "the true poet of the new psychology." But there is also the sheer use of language: his choice of words, his syntax, his style. In the March 1964 issue of *Merkur,* Armin Kesser writes of Musil: "His language eschews the jutting and the overexplicit, it has divested itself equally of naturalistic devices as of the tension of finer psychological stimulants. It strives toward an equipoise in which objects are always allowed just so much space and silence around them as is needed to body forth pure form." I realize that this is a metaphor rather than a definition, but if there is anything that defies scientific definition, it is surely a great writer's language, the essence of his poetry. Readers with even a superficial knowledge of German are urged to examine the original of *Törless*; the translators, though they have battled heroically, and often with no small measure of success, fall far short of the inimitable quiddity of what Musil has written.

VII

Is there not, however, a succinct way of defining what *Törless* is about, someone will ask. Or, more precisely, what solution has the author for the perplexities he has narrated? An attempt at an answer in philosophical terms is to be found in an essay by Johannes Loebenstein:

> In the novella, every state of being attained, isolated, and determined to be essential is canceled out by another one similarly isolated. Now it is one position, now the other that appears as essential being. From the position currently determined to be essential, the other one is determined to be a not-quite-being, a relative nullity.
>
> But from the mutual relativization of all existences temporarily come to the fore, an essence could be deduced that would have to extend beyond all existence, an essence that we merely could not grasp with our thinking. Proceeding from this negatively circumscribed essence, however, one should be able to designate all these foreground-existences as a not-yet-being.

This terminology—existential, epistemological, or merely Teutonic—may not be to everyone's taste. Readers may prefer to turn to the text to find whatever tentative answer it yields.

That answer comes from a sort of flash-forward, in which Musil digresses into the future, where Törless-Musil discovers that the experience of evil has left behind "that small admixture of a toxic substance which is needed to rid the soul of its overconfident, complacent healthiness, and to give it instead a sort of health that is more acute, and subtler, and wiser." This is the acceptance that one must absorb a little existential evil for the sake of an essential equilibrium. Young Törless puts it in cruder words: "Things just happen: that's the sum total of wisdom." And Musil couches even this interim view of life in a lovely image: "One phase of his development was at the end; the soul had formed another annual ring, as a young tree does."

The end of the novella provides an objective correlative. As Törless and his parents drive past Božena's house, a quiet reconciliation occurs: the house is no longer a hulking, mysterious evil; and the mother is no longer a great, mysterious holiness. A common denominator has been found for prostitute and progenitress in the perfume all women exude.

VIII

There remains the very great problem of structure, which some think Musil deficient in. Certainly, leaving one's major work unfinished, even for the excellent reason that it was unfinishable, is a kind of formlessness. As the distinguished critic Erich Heller remarked in a conversation, Musil had plenty of genius but was rather short on talent. With much the same thing in mind, Frank Kermode says of Musil, "He was a great man, and everybody should find out why; but his is also the interesting limiting case, for if ever . . . we supposed that there was no limit to looseness and bagginess in the novel, this protean and apparently boundless monster, Musil proves the contrary. There *is* a point at which a novel turns into something else: a metaphysician's miscellany, interspersed with subtle *exempla*." But, addressing himself to the very same aspect of *The Man Without Qualities*, V. S. Pritchett finds in the book that "the habit of intellectual analysis is not stultifying to drama, movement or invention, but enhances them." Who is right?

Musil's writings contain some forestalling replies. He looked forward to a time when there would be "not much 'good,' but some 'better'; when no talent survives, only genius." Thus Musil might answer Heller: a little bit of genius exempts us from a large amount of talent. To Kermode, Musil might have addressed this entry from his journal: "Now, of course, one has to be able to tell a story if one arrogates the privilege of not wanting to; and I am, indeed, able to do it passably; but, to this day, the story I am telling is of secondary importance to me." True enough: the one time Musil let his narrative gain the upper hand, in the novella *Tonka,* the result, though respectable, was rather less than extraordinary.

In *Törless,* vastly shorter though it is than Musil's magnum opus, some looseness and bagginess is still, in lesser measure, noticeable. But if Musil's form were seriously flawed, it would be cold comfort that Denis de Rougemont considers Musil's compass greater than Proust's. And what avails it then for Thomas Mann to write in a letter to Rudolf Olden that Musil's work is "nothing less than a saving of face for our epoch, so amply compromised in the eyes of history"? For in a work of art, form comes first.

But Musil's form, loose as it may be, is right for his purpose. This purpose I take to be to show that the world is, at the very least, a double-bottomed box. Whatever solution is found is not the ultimate one: hidden beneath it is another layer of reality or truth, which may not be the last bottom, either. And that is not all. Upward, heavenward, there is no single roof: the box is also double- or multiple-lidded. There is metaphysical truth beyond metaphysical truth just as there is psychic reality within psychic reality. Musil's form enables him to set out in search of the ultimate truth and, even without bringing back a final answer, go a long way in the direction—in *all* the directions—that might, conceivably, lead to one. Let us not worry whether Musil stands above Proust or below, whether he is to be rated higher or less high than Joyce. Let us rather remember Musil's own words in an admirable commemorative talk about Rilke: "The heights of literary achievement are not a summit that continues to rise, but a circle inside which there are only dissimilar similarities, uniquenesses, irreplaceables: a noble anarchy and an Order of Brotherhood."

SCHNITZLER: POET OF THE UNFULFILLED

THERE is a kind of intense delicacy that a culture achieves only in a declining, dying social order. In America, the prime example of this is the passing of the Old South, given a death blow by the Civil War and then slowly, exquisitely perishing away. Of these protracted death throes came Faulkner and Flannery O'Connor, Tennessee Williams and Truman Capote, Carson McCullers and Eudora Welty. Such a dying culture is characterized by world-weariness and a concomitant desperate hunger for living, philosophy scattering itself in bittersweet epigrams, wit suffused with a cynicism no less melancholy than biting, sensuality propelled into perversity. There is a frenzied concern with sex as the last possible panacea, along with the excruciating awareness of the instability, indeed impossibility, of loving.

Such preeminently was the character of late Hapsburg Vienna, and of the writer who most incisively comprehended and least eradicably expressed it: Arthur Schnitzler (1862–1931). If I had to sum up in two words Schnitzler's literary contribution, I'd opt for the oxymoron "poetic naturalism." For he was the novelist, short-story writer, and playwright who accomplished the extraordinary wedding of naturalism

This essay first appeared as a program note for the Hartford Stage Company production of *Anatol*, 1984.

and poetry, i.e., the couching of trivial, tantalizing, or grimy truths in language fraught with a lyricism usually reserved for the summits of ecstasy and tragedy. But this marriage would have been meaningless if it had not stuck—if the incommensurateness of the partners had yielded an unstable union that, under scrutiny or the passage of time, fell apart. Instead, Schnitzler's works work: they cohere, create human beings and situations in all their vertiginous complexity and mystery, raise and shed light on the right unanswerable questions, and survive as enormously witty and heartbreaking tributes to the phosphorescent morass in which we live.

Schnitzler himself modestly wrote, "I am aware of the fact that I am not an artist of the highest caliber." Yet he accomplished the exceptional fusion of Ibsen's plots and characterizations that perfectly embody a relentlessly observed reality with eruptions of lyricism and a style worthy of that most poetic of playwrights, Hugo von Hofmannsthal, his close friend and author of the verse introduction to *Anatol.* This places Schnitzler, if not necessarily on the topmost rung, at least securely in that category for which the only suitable designation is genius.

Arthur Schnitzler was the son of a distinguished physician who, for all his love of the arts, insisted that his son follow in his medical footsteps, and of a mother who never presumed to disagree with her husband. Though Arthur would have preferred the artistic and bohemian life (which, to some extent, he espoused anyway), medicine it had to be, and for a good many years he was a laryngologist at a hospital, in the army, and, finally, in private practice. Nevertheless, his most daring medical—and not merely medical—experiments were in the psychological field of hypnosis. He and Freud met as assistants in the clinic of the famous Dr. Maynert and were friends until Freud decided that he had to avoid Schnitzler, whom he perceived as his *Doppelgänger,* his ghostly double. This did not, however, prevent Freud from corresponding with Schnitzler and sending him epistolary tributes. In 1906 he wrote, "I often asked myself in amazement where you could have gotten this or that secret knowledge I had to acquire through painstaking investigation of the subject, and I eventually got to the point of envying the poet whom I otherwise admired." And in 1922, on Schnitzler's sixtieth birthday, "At the root of your being, you are a psychological depth explorer as honestly unprejudiced and unafraid as anyone ever. . . ."

After the death of Schnitzler Senior and the growing success of the son's drama and fiction, medicine faded into the background and was eventually abandoned. But the doctor's scientific experience and methodology were not relinquished, nor was his unblinking perception of mortality. The year 1893 saw the publication of *Anatol,* Schnitzler's first major stage work (written between 1888 and 1891); the following year brought his first prose masterpiece, *Sterben (Dying).* The latter strikes me as the last word, in fiction that could not seem less fictitious, on the process of dying and its effect on a healthy beloved. A young woman has promised her tubercular lover that she will voluntarily follow him into death. With scrupulous objectivity that nevertheless depends on a vividly inventive style, Schnitzler evokes the dying man's ever more pathetic clinging to his diminishing life and, conversely, his growingly frantic attempts to drag his healthy young girlfriend down with him into death. At the same time, the thirty-one-year-old author renders with merciless clarity the woman's revulsion, her brutal but sane rejection of her moribund lover, and her panicky flight into life. *Sterben* is a novella of terrifying magnificence, and the other side of the coin from—and thus clearly related to—*Anatol.*

This is not the place to summarize, or even list, Schnitzler's numerous dramatic and fictional achievements in prose and verse comedies and dramas, both short and long; and in short stories, novellas, and novels. The closest thing to a complete edition we have—not including the unfinished, censored, or unperformed works from the Schnitzler archives, many of which have since been published and even mounted—runs to two thick volumes each of fiction and drama, or some 4,100 pages. Little of this has been brought out in English, still less remains in print, and hardly any of it has been adequately translated. Let me mention only that Schnitzler created an interior monologue well in advance of James Joyce, and that he was the first to deal incisively in fiction and drama with the problem of anti-Semitism.

What are Schnitzler's main themes? The passing of pleasure, fleetingness of love, shortness of life; our ignorance about the meaning of existence; the losing battles of goodness against the way of the world; and the failure of any and all means to transcend our mortality. This repertoire would be a bitter pill indeed, especially since the poetry and wit in which so much of it is couched refuse to function as sugarcoating—if anything, they make the sadness sadder, the absurdity more absurd. But there is a distinct compensation in finding that someone has captured our most tragic and tragicomic realities with such finesse, such sharp focus, such lapidariness. It is the triumph of intelligence and art—of language itself—over a sorrow for which no physician has a cure. It is the rejection of all religion, occultism, philosophizing in favor of accepting total cessation with consummate grace.

What could be more wrenching than this lament of the innocent young officer, Felix, in *The Lonely Way*: "But something that, out of a living happiness or living ache, was at all worthy of becoming remembrance—surely such a thing should not be able to lose its significance ever again." Yet as Schnitzler knew already at the time of *Anatol,* it can and does. In *The Lonely Way,* the middle-aged hero, Herr von Sala, answers the question of the young girl who loves him about why he keeps talking of death with "Is there a decent human being who in any one of his cozy hours thinks, in his deepest soul, about something else?" But the girl, Johanna, understands that "an existence without sorrow would be as impoverished as an existence without bliss." And, later in the play, Sala wonders: "The present. . . . What does that really mean? Isn't the word that has just been uttered already a memory?

Isn't the note with which a melody began memory before the song is ended?"

There is one palliative for the ache of living: play-acting, the confounding of semblance and reality, and most of us use it to some extent. Thus in the novella *Casanova's Homecoming,* the aging seducer starting to lose his power over men and even women, is able to hold forth "so eloquently in defense of his preposterous theories that . . . he [begins] to believe all the nonsense he [is] talking." Complementarily, he cries out "somewhat theatrically, as was his wont when a genuine passion burrowed inside him." And that supreme play-actor, the playwright, in the person of the dramatist Karl Bern—a character in Schnitzler's last, not quite finished, play, *Zug der Schatten (Procession of Shadows)*—exclaims: "My plays—you're not, for heaven's sake, going to take them seriously? At that rate, why not me?" Yet Bern's dismissal of his work as make-believe may be only another, more prideful, form of play-acting.

Any other sort of acting—action—is difficult to undertake. Beginnings are hard, and seeing things through is even harder. In a letter to the great director Otto Brahm (October 31, 1904), Schnitzler wrote, "For completion I seem indeed to have a lesser talent." The German word *Vollendung* means both completion and perfection; Schnitzler perceived himself as the artist—and man—of the uncompleted, the imperfect. Of an aristocratic family in *Countess Mitzi or The Family Reunion,* we are told, "They always remained strong in their faith. It was only their faith that changed." That way lies the solution, jejune though it be: assiduous dilettantism and persistent promiscuity can look determined and exhaustive. Impassioned change is the perseverance of unstable souls.

What better way for a comfortably off young man in a disillusioned, decadent society to pass his time than by womanizing? The raw material of *Anatol* as well as of other early works can be found in Schnitzler's autobiography, *My Youth in Vienna,* which, though begun in 1915 and fiddled with for some years, was left incomplete and imperfect; it stops with the year 1889, before Schnitzler's literary career took off. Still, here we find a record of Schnitzler's attempted and (more rarely) successful dalliances with a number of women and of his live-in affair with Jeanette Heger, a needleworker and prototype of that Viennese speciality the *süsse Mädel* (sweet young girl). These sweet young things were working-class girls who would have flings or longer relationships with young gentlemen not yet financially or emotionally ready to settle down; cast off or roving, the girls ended up marrying someone of their own class or becoming spinsters.

Here is Arthur with one such girl: "I could not seem to be completely happy with her. I don't think I am wrong in ascribing the blame for this to the hypochondriac element in my nature and the capital of mistrust that went with it, which paid dividends in the form of self-torture and the desire to torture others; but I was also irked that I was wasting my time, my thoughts, my finest emotions on a creature who was basically insignificant. . . ." And here he is with Jeanette: "Now we were together evening after evening, yet somehow couldn't be happy. I tormented her incessantly with my jealousy, strangely enough not in connection with the months just gone by but with the more distant past. She wept, kissed my hands humbly, yet couldn't assuage me. Sometimes, and not under the influence of some groundless hypochondriac mood or other, I felt that I was on the verge of despair and was filled with dread as I realized the futility and irrevocable passing of the years."

In these two passages we have, as it were, the essence of *Anatol*. What, however, was the origin of the rather unusual form of seven very loosely related, short one-acters? Schnitzler wrote the plays separately and not in the final order he gave them. Some, I suppose, are based on actual events; others are projections of certain Schnitzlerian traits onto Anatol, who both is and isn't the author. Together, these sketches attempt to show all the principal aspects of the insufficiency of amatory relations—a *summa erotica* for *fin-de-siècle* Vienna. With fine

320 German and Austrian Literature

intuition Schnitzler rejected an earlier concluding playlet, *Anatol's Megalomania,* and did not even bother to finish one called *The Sweet Young Girl.* Still, there are good things in both pieces. In *Anatol's Megalomania,* our hero is aptly characterized as "a virtuoso of jealousy," an instrument from which he wrests every conceivable sonority. And it is in this play that Anatol utters an epigram that (as Schnitzler admits in one of his notebooks) comes from Oscar Wilde: "We [men] always want to be their [women's] first love, they always our last." That sums up the difference in expectation between men, who, in love, pursue an impossible ideal (the absolute purity of the woman), and women, who, more practical, are willing to settle for a compromise (if not the past, at least the future). But whereas burrowing into a woman's past is totally fruitless, trying to hold on to a man may be only slightly more rewarding. There is, however, besides the agony of jealousy, the pleasure of forgiving. So we get the following in *The Sweet Young Girl*: "*Anatol*: It's a wonderful thing, forgiveness, only it uses up the spirit, and there is no more painful virtue. *Fritzi*: Besides, it's nonsense. Truly forgive—that's something you can never do, right? *Anatol*: I guess not."

These, then, are the overarching concerns of *Anatol*: jealousy, a fatal difference between male and female aspirations, and the inability to forgive. Notice how perfectly the schema is worked out in the seven playlets. *The Crucial Question* is an ironic undercutting of everything that follows: Anatol is shown lying to himself, for he really does not want to get at the truth about Cora's past once he finds in hypnosis a surefire means of obtaining it. Thus all the subsequent plays in which he seems to pursue the truth are given a prefatory lie to. In *Christmas Shopping,* we see Gabriele, the respectable young wife, consumed with curiosity about the sweet young girl who is Anatol's mistress. No doubt Anatol would be only too glad to have Gabriele step into that role, but no—this is the married woman who did not dare, and the play ends in shared frustration. The sixth play, *Agony,* which positionally balances the second, will take up Gabriele's opposite: the young wife who did dare, but even she won't give up her unhappy marriage when Anatol challenges her to do so (does he really want it, or is he merely testing her?), and the result is just as frustrating. Also the end of the affair.

But before we get to this complaisant yet respectable married woman, there are three variations on the not so respectable sweet young girl. First, Bianca, the circus artiste. The gallivanting Anatol, despite the mementos he casually hoards, has all but forgotten his past women. Nevertheless, he expects this one, Bianca, to have been permanently affected by their brief encounter. To his dismay, he discovers that she has forgotten him more thoroughly even than he has her. This third playlet, *Episode,* is reflected in the fifth, *The Farewell Supper,* in which Anatol has been deceiving his dancer-lover Annie with a rather sweeter young girl in the outer city; he pretends that compassion kept him from coming clean. When he finally brings himself to confess, he is beaten to it by Annie's candid admission that she has fallen for a fellow dancer. Though Annie is far from noble, Anatol is farther, yet his indignation is boundless. The double standard is rampant also in *Souvenirs,* where Anatol cannot accept that Emilie, who loves him, should also want to preserve (as we have seen him doing in *Episode*) quite harmless souvenirs of a past love: a ruby that spilled from her medallion during her defloration and a black diamond that is extremely valuable. But when she allows him to drag out of her the explanation for her refusal to discard them, she learns what Schnitzler expressed in one of his posthumously published aphorisms: "How hard, how thankless it is to be wholly truthful with a human being whom we are in danger of losing even through half the truth."

Finally, in *The Morning of Anatol's Wedding,* a skit that Schnitzler came to loathe in later life, both man and woman reach the nadir. Wising up to what's going on, Ilona, with whom Anatol resumed his affair the night before his wedding to another, threatens to break up the ceremony. When this proves impracticable, she proposes to come back to wreck the marriage. As for the bride, she gave Anatol a cold good-night kiss after the wedding-eve party to which she invited one of her former beaus—not very promising. Anatol experiences this as "the last night of freedom, adventure . . . perhaps even love." He declares, "I am decidedly not in a marrying mood today. I'd like to cancel." And, with regard to Ilona, "Well, yes, one always marries *another* woman." The past, in the opening play, concealed a torturing enigma; the future, in this closing one, cradles a depressing near-certainty.

In *Anatol,* Schnitzler mockingly laid bare the double standard. In the posthumous *Aphorismen und Betrachtungen (Aphorisms and Observations),* we read: "Someone to his beloved: There is metaphysical proof that the unfaithfulness of women is to be taken more gravely than that of men. Had I to chalk up an unfaithfulness to me, I could without hesitation forgive myself. But never you." This is your simple, basic double standard; the one in *Anatol,* however, is more complicated. Anatol wants the pure—other men's faithful wives and sweethearts—to become impure by becoming his; he also wants the impure—the sweet young girls and demimondaines—to become pure for him. In other words, a double standard heightened by narcissism. Characteristically, someone like Anatol must be both happy and unhappy in love to be truly excited ("*Max*: Surely she loves you? *Anatol*: Infinitely. . . . But that's beside the point. She is unfaithful to me"), and that way lies madness. He even realizes that women are fundamentally the same as men, yet would have them different. And he does what he accuses Gabriele of doing: he wants someone he doesn't want if someone else is getting her.

Still, Anatol is aware of not being one of the great ones, but that may be the very reason he wishes to be, impossibly, a woman's god. To achieve this, he must first make the woman, however insignificant, "worthy" of him (*Max*: I didn't overlook something; rather, you saw something in her that wasn't there"); but by so inflating the partner, he becomes inordinately vulnerable to her. Friend Max's customary sensible advice—"Nothing is sadder than warmed-up magic. . . . One should not want to relive anything"—goes steadily unheeded. If Anatol has a point when he tells Emilie, "We believe everything women tell us, from the first lie that entrances us," she has an even better one, "How lucky are those women who can lie. . . . You men cannot bear the truth." But men have a gift for self-delusion (women do, too) that allows them, however burned by one woman, to think the next one different, unique. "Well, yes," is Max's sage rejoinder, "one discovers the type only toward the end of the affair." And *there* is the explanation of *Anatol's* structure: we must have several playlets involving different women in order to be shown how seemingly different hopes turn to identical ashes; only toward the end of the cycle do we see the thematic correspondences, the condemnation of individuality to typicalness.

"Happily I have no illusions," says Anatol, who reeks of them. But Max may indeed not have them; he, clearly, is above the fray. He is rational, witty, amiable though somewhat cynical, a good friend not taken in by either Anatol or Anatol's women. But what price wisdom? The only way to rise above the sexual melee is not to be part of it at all. As far as we can tell, Max has no involvements; Bianca is the only female with whom he has a nexus, but a strictly platonic one. I have no doubt that Schnitzler, who saw his quasi–alter ego sharply and pitilessly ("I am in possession of a sure means of not being hurt by a reproach: I know myself," he wrote Else Singer in 1895), nevertheless did not advocate Max's alternative of detachment. And it is not as if Anatol did not have his moments of lucid self-recognition: "I have always been a hypochondriac in love." There is something honest also about his awareness of masculine guilt toward women—"Did we not have the obligation to squeeze the eternity we promised them into the few years or hours during which we loved them? And we never succeeded, never"—embellished, indeed aggrandized, as it is. At least it isn't wholesale self-vindication, and it is better than Max's patronizing "What a mystery *we* would be to women if they were rational enough to speculate about us." Yet condemnation comes easier to Anatol than generosity; in the end, he calls Emilie a whore and implies much the same about Bianca, Annie, Else. Perhaps the clinching insight is Max's when he tells Ilona, "Now you think yourself a demon, but you are only a woman. Still, that too is quite enough."

We are not demonic; we are only women—or men. But that is enough for us to make life hell for one another. This is what *Anatol* documents, what most of Schnitzler's plays and fictions are about. Hence all endings are less than happy. In *Professor Bernhardi,* a young woman dies wretchedly of the consequences of a clumsy abortion, without perhaps even knowing the name of her seducer. Remarks the eponymous doctor hero, "And such a thing too was once called happy loving." The fundamental problem may be one Dr. Schnitzler diagnosed in himself in a letter to the distinguished scholar-critic Georg Brandes (March 2, 1897): "I think that every human being has a great existential flaw that prevents him from bringing his being to possible perfection [*Vollendung* again!]; my sin may be that I do not understand how to live something out all the way." Anatol has no stated profession, so that Schnitzler can show him as nothing but a perennial dabbler in love. Charming, seemingly frivolous, and whimsically melancholy as *Anatol* is, it is nevertheless a serious critique of emotional dilettantism. It may be that the hero could have been happy, or at least happier, with any of these women if only he had not stopped short for a whim, for an obsession, for another woman. The soul, too, has its coitus interruptus.

AN ABYSS DEEP ENOUGH

Philip B. Miller, ed., *An Abyss Deep Enough: Letters of Heinrich von Kleist*

HEINRICH VON KLEIST (1777–1811) was one of Germany's greatest and most original writers of short fiction and drama. Why, then, is he so little read and performed in non-Germanic countries? Although his themes—the desperate need to find oneself, the hardships of the journey to the center of one's being, the near impossibility of coming back alive and having anything to show for it—are as modern as can be, nothing outside of great lyric poetry so defies translation as Kleist's prose. The German sentence lends itself notoriously to extension, but Kleist has stretched and tautened its bow to the point where one is almost afraid that it will end not with a period but with an arrow in one's throat. Yet the content of the sentence, heightening the tension, is likely to be some simple, intimate truth looked straight in the eye. It is, as H. H. Holz has noted, the syntax of a poet who demands of language the ultimates of sobriety and frenzy.

In the drama—and Kleist's short life and even shorter writing career were good for eight plays, of which five are immortal—this tempest-tossed genius undertakes the superhuman: as Rolf Michaelis remarks, "The impossible is attempted: to represent the failure of language in spoken dialogue." That applies even to such fictions as "Michael Kohlhaas" and "The Marquise of O . . ." and certainly to such plays as *Penthesilea* and *The Prince of Homburg*. These and other works have been available in English translations of varying veracity, but it remained for Philip B. Miller to bring us a generous selection from Kleist's letters, essays, and anecdotes (understandably admired by Kafka) entitled *An Abyss Deep Enough*.

The letters become, as supplemented by Miller's notes and comments, a foreshortened but highly suggestive account of Kleist's matchlessly painful, heroic life. That life—after failure in military, diplomatic, civil-service, literary, and amatory careers—ended, at age thirty-four, in a double suicide with an incurably ill young married woman. As Kleist said in one of his suicide notes, "The truth is, there was no help for me on earth." (How much better even that spare, stark utterance sounds in the more solemnly cadenced German!) But there is insight and help for all of us in these letters by a literary master, written in large part before or after nurturing any hope of success as a writer, so that they reach out for present communication rather than posthumous publication.

Set forth with unique honesty and acuity is the struggle of a spirit that could find peace neither in Kantian idealism nor in Romantic irrationalism, neither in science nor in art, neither at home nor abroad, neither in friendship nor in hetero- or homosexual love. This brilliant, maddened man's failures read like a reverse *Bildungsroman*—more exactly, the story of an education in despair. "My fate is to live and die a student," the young Kleist perceives, but of what? He tells his patient fiancée that in five . . . no, six . . . no, ten years he will be able to marry her; all he needs to be happy is freedom, a home of his own, a wife. This trinity changes, next, to tilling a field, planting a tree, begetting a child. Then two grander elements sneak in: Kleist will gladly die after achieving "a child, a beautiful piece of writing, and a great deed." By 1803, upon laboring 500 "consecutive days, with most of the nights thrown in" on a never-to-be-finished play, his wishes are down to a modest *one*: to complete the play, after which heaven may do with him as it will.

Terrible are his outcries: "Ah, how empty and desolate and sad to have outlived one's own heart!" "Ah, this inborn vice of mine never to be able to seize the moment, and always to live in a place where I am not, and in a time that is either past or not yet come." He concludes, "I am some sort of a failed genius, but failed not in their sense, but in my own." Or: "It was hell that gave me this half-talent . . . heaven grants a whole one or none at all." "I write only because I cannot stop," he laments. For he cannot express his inner world: "We have no medium for such expression. . . . Language, the means we do have . . . cannot limn the soul." Finally, "Life holds nothing nobler than this: to be able to throw it away with a noble gesture." He rebukes one friend with "Who would wish to be happy in this world! Fie! You should be ashamed," and consoles another with "Not even the best is worth the regretting!"

His magazine and newspaper publishing ventures fail, his published fiction has little reverberation, his plays flop and he doesn't even see them done. But, to the end, he keeps writing his dazzling anecdotes and essays, in one of which he elaborates superbly on the Horatian theme that stylistic virtues "would best have proved their value if you had failed to notice them at all." In another, he defends the paradox that puppets are greater dancers than ballet stars. In a third, he argues provocatively that the artistry of an experienced old singer more than makes up for the decline of his voice. Kleist did not live to acquire such experience, but his young voice is among the most penetrating, moving, and revealing—even if language is only that "something more coarse" with which "like certain volatile . . . chemical substances" thought must be combined "in order to appear."

[1982]

SLAVIC
LITERATURE

PROMOTER OF MEANING

Joseph Brodsky, *Less Than One*

ON the evidence of *Less Than One,* a collection of essays by the
poet Joseph Brodsky, there exists such a thing as poet's prose.
Despite a slight overlapping, this is not the same as poetic
prose, a somewhat dubious proposition, often no more than
bejeweled verbiage and clangorous rhythms. Poet's prose,
however, is rather like Rimbaud's definition of poetry: a prolonged, immense, systematic derangement of all the senses.
Or something like the pushing aside of molecules to enter into
the heart of matter, into the mind of the universe. It is a
deliberate skewing of perception, so as to see around appearances into truth.

Brodsky is remarkable in many ways. He is one of that small
band of foreign-born writers who have mastered English as
well as native artists, even if perhaps slightly differently. But
he came to English relatively late, and is the only such writer of
major significance in verse, even if he first writes it in Russian
and then translates it into an English that in no way feels like a
translation. First jailed, then expelled by the Soviets—at age
thirty-two in 1972—he has been teaching literature at several
distinguished American institutions, as well as teaching himself how to write English prose as good as his already
renowned Russian poetry. Thus he has achieved a small personal bridge across the world's widest, most ominous abyss.

Not that Brodsky is a mediator in any political sense: his hatred of Communist Russia—which, among its other crimes, disallowed his aging and dying parents any reunion with their only child—is matched only by his fanatical love of poetry. This love of poetry is what rattles around imperiously in the condescended-to cage of prose of this collection. It should be noted that the quality of the essays varies according to their type. Those dealing with biography and autobiography—notably the first, about Brodsky's early years, and the last, about his parents—are incomparably moving in their blend of rough-hewn truthfulness and boundless love. A similar intensity and intelligence inform the pieces about poets Brodsky has known personally, but here friendship can cloud judgment, and the ones about writers known from their work only tend to be better. But even there tendentiousness crops up: Brodsky must defend his admiration against potentially less favorable judgments. He regains his control in essays about ideas (e.g., "On Tyranny," where the Soviet system is skewered with a kind of sardonic lyricism) and places (e.g., Leningrad/St. Petersburg, which he loves, and Istanbul/ Byzantium, which he hates, and where the geographical, historical, cultural ruminations stimulate even as they ramble on).

The first quality of this poet's prose is brilliance, which freely commits grand assertions and paradoxical idiosyncrasies in the hope of breaking up the solidified commonplaces of established wisdom and making a new world from the re-shuffled shards. Take this, from the essay on Mandelstam: "A poet gets into trouble because of his linguistic, and, by implication, his psychological superiority, rather than because of his politics. A song is a form of linguistic disobedience, and its sound casts a doubt on a lot more than a concrete political system: It questions the entire existential order. And the number of its adversaries grows proportionally." Such aperçus are too grandiose; they border on a Rimbaldian, or more ordinary, derangement. But they also contain a smidgen of genius, a sliver of cutting truth.

This poetic mode of perception depends on—its second

salient quality—the arrogant yet awesome faith in the absolute superiority of poetry to prose and, by implication, anything else this world can come up with. A recurrent thought, it is most baldly stated in the essay on the prose of Marina Tsvetaeva: "The poet, in principle, is higher than the prose writer." As elaborated in the essay on Auden, it reads: "Unlike fiction writers, poets tell us the whole story; not only in terms of their actual experiences and sentiments but . . . of language itself, in terms of the words they finally choose." What takes some of the curse—though none of the edge—off such brutal statements is Brodsky's downright mystical belief in the superiority of poetry to any poet, and in the sacred primacy of language above, or at least prior to, poetry itself. Again and again he restates and refines his notion that the structures of the language fashion the writer, that the word that chooses him (rather than vice versa) determines the flow of his thought, the shape of his verse or prose. Call it the verbal equivalent of Michelangelo's assertion that the statue is in the stone, and the sculptor merely disengages it from the marble.

Whether or not we agree with this, as it were, religion, it is inspiring to observe it guiding and fulfilling Brodsky's thinking, disengaging from the poet-essayist his most sculptured utterances. "A poem," he says in the fine essay on Montale, "is a form of the closest possible interplay between ethics and aesthetics." Still, as we gather from the essay on Tsvetaeva's prose, "a reader can be taken by the hand by prose and delivered to where he would otherwise be shoved by a poem."

This leads us to another characteristic: Brodsky's fierce partisanship and concomitant purblindness. Whichever favorite poet he is writing about in a given essay becomes—at least implicity, but more often explicitly—the greatest of all. Akhmatova, Tsvetaeva, Mandelstam, Cavafy, and others rotate to the top, previous champions sometimes remembered, sometimes not. To Brodsky, Auden was "the greatest mind of the twentieth century"; the novelist Andrei Platonov (in one of Brodsky's favorite phrases), to say the least, the equal of Joyce, Musil, and Kafka (Proust is always conspicuously absent from these lineups); and as for Derek Walcott, he has given us "an archipelago of poems without which the map of modern literature would effectively match wallpaper." And so on and on.

It is not surprising, then, that Brodsky is at his worst when explicating one of his beloveds' poems. The seventy-two pages on Tsvetaeva's "New Year's Greetings" and the fifty-two on Auden's "September 1, 1939" are the least agreeable parts of this collection, not only because of the hail of superlatives, but also because Brodsky overinterprets wildly, free-associating to the point of making every image, line, word, and sound take on impossible multifariousness. A Strasbourg goose's liver, morbidly hypertrophic as it is, is at least palpably there; the marvels stuffed into a line of Auden's or Tsvetaeva's could not be fitted even into Shakespeare or Dante, and as often as not do not exist. But even when off the mark, Brodsky's enthusiasm is something to marvel at; the ingenuity of his very errors is astonishing.

Finally, this prose has a way of soaring into metaphysical realms where I cannot follow: "Love is essentially an attitude maintained by the infinite toward the finite. The reversal constitutes either faith or poetry." I must not forget, either, the wit that enlivens and endears page after page, or the sure aphoristic touch, as in "By itself, reality isn't worth a damn. It's perception that promotes reality to meaning." Well, Brodsky is a superb promoter of meaning, and the essays on himself when young, on his parents, and on what used to be called St. Petersburg (ironically titled "A Guide to a Renamed City") belong in the anthology any reader carries around in his memory. Let me quote the ending of the last, about those fabled white nights: "On such nights, it's hard to fall asleep, because it's too light and because any dream will be inferior to this reality. Where a man doesn't cast a shadow, like water." I may be infected with Brodsky's disease, but I say only a poet could have written that prose.

[1986]

MEMORABLE LAUGHTER

Milan Kundera, *The Book of Laughter and Forgetting*

MILAN KUNDERA, the Czech novelist and short-story writer, is a grandmaster of irony. His most famous novel, *The Joke* (first published here in a regrettably abridged version but later republished in toto), tells at ample length of the disastrous consequences of a jokey postcard sent by someone who could laugh under—and at—Communism to someone who could not. In one of the finest stories in Kundera's *Laughable Loves,* "Nobody Will Laugh," another casually let-out statement causes a successful *bon vivant*'s downfall. These ironies of fate are handled by Kundera with a condignly ironic style that is calculated to make one undesirable to a totalitarian regime. In 1948, the Communist Party made Kundera a nonmember; when he finally climbed into his rightful place, the fateful events of 1968 turned him into a nonentity, all of whose works were proscribed; in 1979, already domiciled in France, Kundera published *The Book of Laughter and Forgetting,* which finished him off in his country—his citizenship was revoked and he became a nonperson.

But, as the title of another of his novels has it, life is elsewhere, and in twenty languages other than Czech the fifty-one-year-old Kundera is being read and relished for the supreme ironist he is. *The Book of Laughter and Forgetting,* decently translated by Michael Henry Heim, is a construct of curious intricacy that calls itself "a novel in the form of variations." It is in seven sections that could almost pass for unrelated stories, except that there are two pairs with identical titles, and that two sections have the same heroine. The only undeniable link among these seven tales is the author himself, sometimes figuring among the dramatis personae and always providing the ironic commentary of one who perceives life essentially as a series of deprivations and losses, to be combated with laughter or forgetting, two phenomena recurring throughout the book alternately or simultaneously.

There are two kinds of laughter: the diabolic, which is the devil's destructive pointing up of "the meaninglessness of things"; and the angelic, devised by the angels in retaliation, which is the rejoicing in "how rationally organized, well conceived, beautiful, good, and sensible everything on earth" is. Neither laughter is sustaining; man collapses equally under too much disorder and too much order. Only when the two are held in balance is life truly possible, but that seems never to be the case. There are, apparently, also two kinds of forgetting, though here the author is less explicit. There is the kind that enables us to go on living (such as forgetting the death of a loved one), and the kind that robs us of our humanity (such as forgetting our past as individuals, or our history and culture as a people). Unfortunately, it is hard, if not impossible, to reap the benefits of obliviousness without incurring its liabilities.

But there is also another presence—indeed omnipresence—in the book. Sometimes it is grotesque fear, as when the brave young woman editor who helped the proscribed author publish a pseudonymous column on astrology (for Marxists!) is found out and loses control over her bowels. Sometimes it is horror, as when another young woman on a magical island ruled by children realizes that they are lewd, nasty, dangerous. And sometimes it is just a sense of the ludicrousness of things, as when an uneasy orgiast discovers that "Laughter was like an enormous trap waiting patiently in the room with them, but hidden behind a thin wall. There was only a fraction of an inch separating intercourse from laughter," which lurks terrifyingly just "across the border [where] things no longer [have] any meaning." This third presence is the Absurd.

There are ordinary, painlessly perfectible people in this book, as well as a few inspired, painful noncomformists. The former have permanently swallowed the propagandist fantasy of "an idyll, for all . . . a garden where nightingales sing"; the latter are disenchanted revolutionaries who can no longer grasp their youthful actions and who are forever "stalking a lost deed." With awesome gallows humor Kundera depicts the conflict in his country as the clash between believers in the nightingale garden and stalkers of the lost deed. The nightingalists are seduced by those who are "selling people futures for their pasts"; the stalkers reject a world "where every man is a note in a magnificent Bach fugue and anyone who refuses his note is a mere black dot, useless" and to be "squashed between the fingers like an insect."

There is also a super-real realm in the book: angels, devils, and a whole dystopian fantasy island. Yet this is not a fantasy novel but, most nearly, an essay: fictional in form, ironic in tone, wittily and frighteningly alerting us to truths that perhaps only a genius who has been turned too many times into a non-something-or-other can truly apprehend and communicate. Rather than try to explain, let me give you, by way of example, a passage that Jean-Luc Godard, that thieving magpie, incorporates in his latest film without giving Kundera due credit; it concerns the migration of blackbirds from the woods to the city.

> Globally, the blackbirds' invasion of the human world is beyond a doubt more important than the Spaniards' invasion of South America or the resettlement of Palestine by the Jews. A change in the relationship of one species to another . . . is a change of a higher order than a change in the relationship of one or another group within the species. The earth does not particularly care whether Celts or Slavs inhabited Bohemia, whether

Romanians or Russians occupy Bessarabia. If, however, the blackbird goes against nature and follows man to his artificial, anti-natural world, something has changed in the planetary order of things. And yet nobody dares to interpret the last two centuries as the history of the blackbird's invasion of the city of man. We are all prisoners of a rigid conception of what is important and what is not. We anxiously follow what we suppose to be important, while what we suppose to be unimportant wages guerrilla warfare behind our backs, transforming the world without our knowledge. . . .

The Book of Laughter and Forgetting has its eye firmly on the blackbird and so perceives, with the greatest amount of laughter, menacing truths it will not let us forget. It is an unsettling book: magnificent and major.

[1980]

ARDOR OR ARROGANCE

Vladimir Nabokov, *Ada or Ardor:
A Family Chronicle*

ADA or Ardor: A Family Chronicle is Vladimir Nabokov's 600-page novel about an incestuous *coitus interruptus*. Well, not exactly *interruptus*. Van and Ada, ostensible cousins but actual brother and sister, start making love at the age of fourteen and twelve, respectively. They can never have quite enough of each other, yet though circumstances keep separating them, they enjoy brief passionate interludes scattered throughout their lives. Both of them keenly sexual, they indulge in multifarious surrogate sex until, in their fifties, they are permanently united. They spend another half-century as happily senescent lovers: he writing, in the end, this book, *Ada,* and she filling in interstices or commenting in its margins. It is their joint autobiography.

Ada would make a lurid and sentimental tale if Nabokov did not use it chiefly as a receptacle to cram groaningly full of baroque and esoteric devices, stratagems, digressions. The result is one of the most learned, fanatical, pretentious, top-heavy, and mean-spirited books of all time, not so much Nabokov's fictionalized intellectual and artistic autobiography as the record of a prodigiously erudite, insufferably ostentatious, gifted but ungiving mind in an unparalleled display of self-indulgence, self-serving, and hedging self-protection.

The novel takes place on a planet called Antiterra or Demonia, mysteriously related to another planet, Terra, whose very existence, however, is in doubt. Though this setting allows Nabokov to make a few feeble and fatuous gestures in the direction of science fiction, its real purpose is self-gratification. On Antiterra, Nabokov has rearranged our history, geography, and culture in the shape of a giant wish-fulfillment fantasy. North America has become a land jointly settled by Russians, Britons, and Frenchmen, so that its civilization is a blend of the three cultures Nabokov feels most at home with. The languages are, accordingly, Russian, English, and French, spoken parallelly, indeed simultaneously. Hence much of *Ada* is a gallimaufry of Russian and French discourse (the former transliterated and freely translated; the latter arbitrarily sometimes translated, sometimes not) popping up all over amid the English, itself often esoteric enough to have benefited from some sort of translation. The point is to show off Nabokov's dazzling command of the three languages, and although one duly registers dazzlement, one is even more aware of (along with occasional minor lapses in the English) sheer ostentation. Besides, the book might have been a good bit shorter if it didn't, at times, read like its own French and Russian translations. Nabokov uses his three languages (to which he occasionally adds German) for trilingual wordplay, with which this book is hung as with triple tinsel—a tri-denominational Christmas tree, Catholic, Anglican, and Russian Orthodox.

There is also a mixture of times. Antiterra is, in many ways, some fifty or more years behind Terra, and in other ways not. Thus life in the book is a conflation of nineteenth- and twentieth-century existential features Nabokov likes best into a kind of ideal or Nabokovian antitime in which horse-drawn carriages, automobiles, and flying carpets coexist in a fond dream. And there is also a fusion of ages in the characters of

Ada and Van: in their early teens, they expatiate like distinguished scientists and literati; in their declining years, they are still capable of deliciously childish excesses. The attempt is to abolish time and place—which, to be sure, is to some extent the concern of all major fiction; here, however, it is done in a peculiarly narcissistic, self-coddling, and ultimately solipsistic manner.

The style is pure self-indulgence. Not only the polyglot puns, which usually prove wholly unworthy of the elaborate maneuvering required to set them up, but also all kinds of jingling alliterations, assonances, rhymes and near-rhymes proliferate on every page. Add to this recondite allusions to literature and the fine arts, abstruse scientific references (including minidisquisitions on entomology, ornithology, and botany), as well as sesquipedalian and obscure words, including archaisms, neologisms, barbarisms (particularly gallicisms) that Nabokov spawns in unseemly profusion. On top of that, there are anagrams, rebuses, ciphers, sportive references to imaginary works and passages in invented dialects, the whole forming something that frequently resembles a three-or-four-dimensional crossword puzzle.

The very choice of incest as his theme attests to Nabokov's self-love and exacerbated competitiveness. When the children in the novel play at anagrams, the group "scient—insect—nicest—incest" comes up. It suggests a Nabokov who is scient in insects (he is especially known as a lepidopterist), and also one who finds incest, the love of a self-reflecting sister-self, nicest of all. Indeed, Van and Ada are in some senses the same person: Ada, pronounced the Russian way, becomes "ardor," and also "Ah, *da!*"—passionate affirmation; yet it is also the genitive of *ad*, the Russian for Hades, appearing in constructions like "a howl from hell"; in other words, the opposing positive and negative moods of the author. Ada's monogram is an upside-down A, subsuming her two initials, A and V, for Ada Veen. But the V stands also for her "cousin," Van Veen; the Van, short for Ivan, also a phonetic reproduction of Juan (as in the famous Don), and the Veen, I would guess, the Russian pronunciation of "ween"—to think, surmise, conceive—the prime function of the creative intellect. But V. V. are also the initials of Nabokov himself, Vladimir Vladimirovich, referred to in *Ada* as "this brilliant or obscure V. V. (depending on the eyesight of readers . . .)." Van and Ada, in Russian, spell Van *i* Ada, or *Vaniada,* which is the Russian for Vaniad, or the Epic of Van. And so, in incestuous circles, it goes.

There are games of this sort running through *Ada* and, finally, running it through—the poor little butterfly of a tale, impaled on the author's witty erudition, ends up as a mounted specimen in an ultra-chic display case. Take, for example, the elaborate and continuous allusions to Chateaubriand, who had a somewhat more than brotherly affection for his sister Lucile (Lucile-Lucette here becomes Ada's younger sister; Ada's name may derive from Augusta Ada, the illegitimate daughter Byron had by his half sister). Ada and Van are frequently reading novels by Chateaubriand, particularly *René,* which deals with such a guilty passion, and Chateaubriand's name keeps cropping up in various contexts. Most important, Chateaubriand's poem "Le Montagnard exilé" runs, in diverse adaptations, translations, and parodies, like a refrain through the novel. Indeed, the Dore river, *la* Dore, mentioned in the poem, becomes the Ladore of *Ada,* giving rise to puns on "adore," "ardor," and "Ada." Finally, Ada's screen name is Theresa Zegris, the Zegris after one of the Montague-and-Capuletish families in Chateaubriand's *The Last Abencérage.* But all this, like so much more in the book, is mere gamesmanship, and nowise adds depth or significance to the whole.

Even less attractive a trait is the self-aggrandizement, accomplished not only by frequent veiled or unveiled references to Nabokov's own books and other forms of self-praise, but also by the systematic mocking or patronizing of almost every major (and many a minor) writer who might be competition for the Master of Montreux. From Shakespeare and Racine through Eliot and Auden (Nabokov fancies himself a poet as well) to Malraux and Borges, everyone gets the business, Proust and Pasternak most of all. Even writers whom Nabokov favors—Tolstoy, Pushkin, Chekhov—are often treated with condescending banter; and masters in other fields, such as Bergson and Henry Moore, get worked over, too. Indeed, even Albert Schweitzer is ridiculed as "Dr. Swissair of Lumbago," which is the written equivalent of kicking a faithful old dog.

Beyond that, *Ada* was doubtless conceived as a piece of literary one-upmanship. Thus the theme of incest may well have been suggested by an essay of Denis de Rougemont, published in 1959, the year Nabokov began making notes for *Ada*. In this essay, Rougemont argued that truly passionate love could operate only against some terrible barrier, and in our era most barriers are down. There remain political obstacles, as in *Doctor Zhivago*; obstacles of age, as in *Lolita*; and the obstacle of incest, as in Musil's *The Man Without Qualities*. Well, Nabokov makes repeated fun of *Zhivago,* thus disposing of one rival; and writes his, presumably better, novel of incest, thus disposing of the other. Furthermore, the puns and general wordplay are supposed to beat Joyce at *his* game; the large social and high-society canvas, with the narrator's memory triumphing over time and change, is, of course, meant to out-Proust Proust. Borges is minimized not only by jocular digs at an anagrammatic Osberg, but also by a long excerpt from Van's treatise *The Texture of Time,* which in some ways imitates Borges's "A New Refutation of Time," and in others is meant to surpass it.

Finally, there is that most reprehensible device of hedging your bets, of built-in stratagems to disarm all hostile criticism. On the simplest level, this means having the aged Ada, or Van himself, make some depreciatory marginal remark after a particularly purple passage; or of undercutting some emotionally risky sequence by calling attention to the nonagenarian Van's writing this memoir—precarious simplicity protected by an ever-present scaffolding of irony. More elaborately, the whole book purports to mimic or parody the development of the novel and other arts: some scenes are mock-Tolstoyan, some mock-Chekhovian; others are in the manner of famous painters, and still others imitate a shooting script; moreover, we are repeatedly told what would or wouldn't have happened at this point in some earlier phase of the novel's development. I suspect, too, that the principal characters are intended as take-offs on various Russian writers: thus Van is, at times, a latter-day Onegin; his father, Demon, comes out of Lermontov; Demon's mad wife, Aqua, out of Gogol; and so on. All this precludes our judging the book on "mere" narrative and human terms.

And this is where the fundamental failure occurs: Nabokov does not really feel much for any of his characters, but likes to slobber over the charms of Ada or Lucette; he thinks Van, his alter ego, devilishly clever, and Demon wickedly worldly and debonair; on occasion, he can muster up some ironic pity for Marina, the children's absurd mother. But he does not love any of them. As long as thirty years ago, Jean-Paul Sartre rightly wondered, "If Mr. Nabokov is so superior to the novels he writes, why does he write them?" To which the chorus of raves *Ada* has received is the loud but insufficient answer.

[1969]

THE NOVELIST AT THE
BLACKBOARD

Vladimir Nabokov, *Lectures on Literature*

VLADIMIR NABOKOV, who appreciated artfully layered constructions and perceived all art as a fusion of layers in the time-and-space-defying eyes of the great writer and good reader, would have applauded the publishing of his college lectures in *Lectures on Literature*—indeed, he planned to publish them himself. Here, if ever, is a book to be experienced on several levels. To begin with, it is a reading of *Mansfield Park, Bleak House, Madame Bovary, Dr. Jekyll and Mr. Hyde, Swann's Way, Metamorphosis,* and *Ulysses* (the Russian novels that were also part of Nabokov's teaching repertoire will be published in a second volume) by an important novelist who was also an ingenious, albeit highly idiosyncratic critic. It is, next, an evaluation of great—and, in one case, decently minor—novelists by one who was easily the equal of Stevenson, and believed himself the equal of all.

This is, furthermore, a teaching book, and shows us Nabokov the pedagogue, scholar, and annotator, not unlike (in fact, very much like) such characters of his own devising as Pnin, Charles Kinbote, John Ray, Jr., Ph.D., and the compiler of that vast set of notes to the translation of *Eugene Onegin*. Finally, there is a good deal of self-revelation here: *Lectures on*

Literature tells us about as much of Nabokov's likes and dislikes in the art of writing as *Speak, Memory* tells us of his predilections and antipathies in the business of living. There may be even a further level, almost coincidental but not negligible: a refresher course in some magisterial fiction.

To start with the most obvious aspect of the book: Nabokov was a learned, meticulous, fascinating, erratic, and frustrating teacher. A great actor, he would read out—indeed, perform—large chunks of the novels under discussion, thus also saving on the number of original pearls he had to cast before the students. In between the readings came critical evaluations that were often based on chalked-up chronological charts, maps, diagrams, illustrations of how Gregor Samsa looked as a beetle or what sort of orchids Swann's Odette wore—anything that would amuse the literary detective, entomologist, collector of ephemera and curiosities, and creator of worlds elsewhere that was the lecturer.

Nabokov recommends here, "not as a writer's prison but merely as a fixed address, the much abused ivory tower"; in the *Paris Review* interview, however, asked to evaluate his teaching experience at Cornell, he answered: "A first-rate college library with a comfortable campus around it is a fine milieu for a writer. There is, of course, the problem of educating the young." Nabokov wrote out his lectures, as his former student Ross Wetzsteon tells us, "word for word, down to the wryest asides," and, except for minor improvements here and there, never changed them. I suspect that his merry suggestion to have them delivered via tape recorder was not meant to be taken altogether as a joke. As it is, his wife, Vera, who for seventeen years at Wells, Wellesley, and Cornell sat in the front row of all of his classes, typed up his lecture notes, graded his students' papers, and chauffeured him around. So teaching for Nabokov was mostly educating himself. Studying up on *Ulysses,* he told his obsequious Boswell, Alfred Appel, Jr., was the best part of the education he received at Cornell.

Of the one lecture by Nabokov I caught, when he was guest

lecturer at Harvard, I remember only two things: that *Anna Karenina* should really be *Anna Karenin* in English, and that although the lecturer was not against English translations of Russian novels, he preferred them to be diamond rather than Garnett. Still, he must have been a fascinating teacher, what with his dapper appearance, cosmopolitan accent, sophisticated histrionics, and his jokes and word games plying their propaedeutic magic. Coming upon the word "embargo," Nabokov tells his admiring class that, read backward, it spells "O grab me!" In *Bleak House,* "the Dedlocks, I am sorry to say, are as dead as doornails or door locks (the Dead locks are dead)"—though perhaps they are not quite so inert as this elaborately set up dud of a pun. After the phrase "portable hell," comes the jovial reminder that "this is Mr. Nabokov, not Mr. Dickens." Flaubert would write about "eighty to ninety pages in one year—that is a fellow after my heart!" Scott Moncrieff "died while translating [Proust's] work, which is no wonder." "The typesetter of the great Joyce is the godfather of the tiny Mr. [E. E.] Cummings." Kindly Leopold Bloom "even feeds seagulls, which I personally consider to be nasty birds with drunkard's eyes." And so on.

Some of the heartiest jokes are at the expense of despised writers or respected competitors. "The sociological side [of Dickens], brilliantly stressed for example by Edmund Wilson . . . is neither interesting nor important"; "Lady Dedlock is redeemed by suffering, and Dostoevski is wildly gesticulating in the background"; compared to Kafka, Rilke and Thomas Mann are "dwarfs or plaster saints"; Swinburne is identified as "an English post-romantic minor poet"; Freud, the blackest of *bêtes noires,* is a "medieval witch doctor"; and there is a passing reference to "one bore, a man called Stuart Gilbert."

Along with this studied denigration comes also ingenuous self-praise. "Every artist is a manner of saint (I feel that very clearly myself). . . ." "I cannot imagine (and that is saying a good deal). . . ." "Gregor [Samsa] never found out he had wings," Nabokov informs his class—which, though perhaps an entomological truth, is a critical irrelevance—and continues, "This is a very nice observation on my part to be treasured all your lives. Some Gregors, some Joes and Janes, do not know that they have wings." There is no question that Saint Vladimir had little doubt about his own strong opinions and pinions. But what did his winged words do to his students? In the introduction, John Updike tells us about his wife, who took Nabokov's Literature 311-312 (known on campus as "Dirty Lit."), that "she cannot to this day take Thomas Mann seriously."

And how does Nabokov perform here as an interpreter and evaluator of his chosen writers? Not very well on Jane Austen, whom he picked at Edmund Wilson's insistence. He enjoys some of her ironies, pays a wan compliment to her feel for the *mot juste,* makes up some curious critical terminology ("knight's move," "dimpled prose") for her "collection of eggshells in cotton wool," and finally dismisses her in a palinode at the start of his Dickens lectures: "I dislike porcelain and the minor arts. . . ." But at least *Mansfield Park,* as he said elsewhere, was an excuse to read or reread, and to inflict on the students, works mentioned by the characters in the novel, with the result that "I think I had more fun than my class."

Partly, I suppose, because Vladimir Senior used to read Dickens in English out loud to his family, Vladimir Junior is much more at home in *Bleak House* than he was in *Mansfield Park.* He is especially good on the way local color—nature, cityscapes, weather—is tied in with individual personalities, and on the theme of abused but heroically coping children. Rightly, I think, he expostulates: "I should not like to hear the charge of sentimentality made against this strain that runs through *Bleak House.* I want to submit that people who denounce the sentimental are generally unaware of what sentiment is." And he insists that the death of little Jo "is a lesson in style, not in participative emotion."

But it is with Flaubert that Nabokov comes into his own, and here he makes some quite surprising points, such as the demonstration that *Madame Bovary* is in many respects neither realistic nor naturalistic, that "in point of fact, all fiction is fiction. All art is deception." What Flaubert has created is a (very Nabokovian) "world of fancy with its own logic," and *Madame Bovary* is not "a landmark of so-called realism, whatever that is." Nabokov is at great pains to show that the "romantic" world of Emma and her lovers is just as bourgeois and nearly as crass as that of the more obviously middle-class and materialistic characters, and that the only ones who rise above it are little Justin and, in his final ability to forgive and dumbly love on, poor Charles.

For Nabokov, as for his father before him, Flaubert is the supreme master; without him, there would have been no Proust and Joyce ("despite superficial innovations, Joyce has [not] gone any further than Flaubert"), and even Chekhov "would not have been quite Chekhov." It is quite a comedown to go from *Madame Bovary* to *Dr. Jekyll and Mr. Hyde*. Presumably the Stevenson novella (which Wilson advised him against) appealed to Nabokov—though he doesn't say so—because of the theme of the double, or rather the hero's living antithesis, in this case residing in the same body. It is as if Humbert Humbert and Clare Quilty were the same person, which, in a sense, they are even in Nabokov. Certainly our professor is unable to make a very compelling case for Stevenson's greatness, despite all the street plans and house facades he draws for his students (the bipartite Jekyll-Hyde residence is an architectural analogue for the dual protagonist) and makes them copy. He insists on the artistry with which Stevenson (whose name he sometimes misspells as "Stephenson") creates an atmosphere that makes the implausibilities of this story believable and allows it to have "the impact of satisfactory and artistic reality." This phrase is prototypical of Nabokov's artistic philosophy: a novel is real because it has a satisfactory *semblance* of reality, because that semblance is achieved by artistic (artful) means, and because the whole produces the right impact on the reader. But Nabokov is also aware of Stevenson's weaknesses, and this secton reads at times like an uneasy apologia.

With *A la Recherche du temps perdu*, for which he rightly

rejects Scott Moncrieff's now unfortunately unuprootable English title, Nabokov is in his element again. *In Search of Lost Time* is "the greatest novel of the first half of the twentieth century," which, we should recall, is the half that did not produce *Lolita, Pnin, Pale Fire,* and *Ada.* He expatiates helpfully on the ability of Proust "to fill in and stretch out the sentence to its utmost breadth and length . . . in verbal generosity he is a veritable Santa." And, again, he calls attention to the important fact that "Proust's conversation and his descriptions merge into one another creating a new unity where flower and leaf and insect belong to the same blossoming tree." Though he denies having the slightest interest in biographical criticism, he interprets certain of Proust's fictional strategies in terms of the author's homosexuality. There are many fine insights here, but the section ends lamely, perhaps because Nabokov (with some justification) felt that he could assign only the first volume of the huge novel to his students. Even though he does bring in references to and conclusions from other parts of the work, his analyses are largely limited to the actual assignment.

On Kafka's *Metamorphosis,* Nabokov is less interesting than on the other works, possibly because it is the only book he did not read in the original: despite the many years spent in Berlin, he never learned German thoroughly, as he regretfully admits. Nevertheless, he does make some amusing entomological points: "Neither Gregor nor Kafka saw that beetle any too clearly," and he proceeds to show that the creature is no cockroach; we also get such homely historical sidelights as "in Prague, 1912, it was much more difficult to clean and cook than in Ithaca, 1954"; not to mention such odd Nabokovian idiosyncrasies as the opinion that "music, as perceived by its consumers, belongs to a more primitive, more animal form in the scale of arts than literature or painting."

On *Ulysses,* which gets the longest treatment, Nabokov is good, though he deliberately underplays the importance of symbols, is unduly unreceptive to Joyce's wild humor, and repeatedly complains of the book's scatology and obscenity with a prissiness worthy of Pnin. There is a very fine explication of how the stream of consciousness works, a genuine feeling for the characters, an infectious appreciation of how the topography, the city, colors the action. There is also an interesting, though perhaps not entirely convincing, demonstration that the mysterious man in the brown mackintosh is Joyce himself; a provocative assertion that Molly's and Leopold's interior monologues "exaggerate the verbal side of thought. . . . Man thinks also in images," and a disparagement, correct to my mind, of *Finnegans Wake* as "one of the greatest failures in literature," although the ambiguity of "greatest" in this context, necessary to my mind, was not intended by Nabokov. Here, too, there is the one obvious misreading Nabokov commits when he assumes that Buck Mulligan, on the first page of the novel, "tells God to switch off the current." Mulligan is, of course, talking to Haines.

The concluding lecture, entitled "The Art of Literature and Commonsense," is particularly rich in revelations about Nabokov's attitudes toward literature and the nature and role of the writer. Most interesting is the notion that criminals are people lacking imagination; if they had a creative fantasy, it "would have led them to seek an outlet in fiction and make the characters in their books do more thoroughly what they might themselves have bungled in real life." Even more provocative is a passage asserting that "a creative writer . . . cannot help feeling that in his rejecting the world of the matter-of-fact, in his taking sides with the irrational, the illogical, the inexplicable and the fundamentally good, he is performing something similar in a rudimentary way to what—" Here the sentence breaks off: two manuscript pages are missing. Similar in a rudimentary way to whom, one wonders. God, I suspect, somewhat in the manner of that Flaubertian statement about the writer's godlike, invisible omnipresence in his book—an ideal that, according to Nabokov, Flaubert did not truly achieve in *Madame Bovary*. Now, if I interpret the fragment correctly, and if we assimilate it to Nabokov's preceding statement, we get his vision of the writer as a divine criminal or, better, a criminal god.

One of the earliest pronouncements in *Lectures on Literature* proclaims that "great novels are great fairy tales"; Nabokov's former students, like his present readers, are constantly reminded that the greatest folly is to seek psychological or historical reality in a work of the imagination, to read it for moral, existential, social, political—in short, general—ideas, rather than as a specific aesthetic construct, the work of an enchanter, a maker of riddles equipped with elegant solutions. Only a child, Nabokov insists, asks whether a story is true: "literature is of no practical value whatsoever, except in the very special case of somebody's wishing to become, of all things, a professor of literature." But Nabokov does demand, for all his rejection of crude reality—"those farcical and fraudulent characters called facts"—a powerful semblance of reality, which, as he himself might have put it, is not the same as a resemblance. As he said in an interview, unless you know the streets of Joyce's Dublin and what the semi-sleeping car on the Petersburg-Moscow express looked like in 1870, you cannot make sense of *Ulysses* and *Anna Karenin(a)*. In other words, the writer makes use of some specific realities, but only as bait with which to trap the readers into the greater unreality—or greater reality—of his fiction.

The true work of literature has "The Precision of Poetry and the Excitement of Science [Nabokov's capitalization]," we are told here. His ex-student Ross Wetzsteon remembers the phrase as "the passion of the scientist and the precision of the artist." At other times, Nabokov called it "the passion of science and the patience of poetry" or "the precision of poetry and the excitement of pure science." In any of its forms, this leitmotif of the novelist-lepidopterist insists not only on the interpenetration of these seemingly contrary disciplines, but also on the paradoxical nature of each; on the scientific nature of artistic creation, and on the heatedness rather than coldness of science. Yet when he tries to describe to his students what is art, he can do no better than invoke "the telltale tingle between the shoulder blades. . . . It is no use reading a book at all if you do not read it with your back." This theory of literature is a kissing kin to A. E. Housman's definition of poetry as what, when thought of during shaving, makes the skin bristle and the razor inoperative—a sensation whose seat is in the pit of the stomach. But Housman at least has the excuse of never having impaled a butterfly or claimed to be a scientist.

"*Beauty plus pity*—this is the closest we can get to a definition of art," Nabokov tells his students at the beginning of his lectures on Kafka, and he does track down a good deal of pity in the works he discusses. Thus Leopold Bloom's "keen compassion for man-degraded, man-injured animals" impresses the impaler of butterflies; I cited earlier his defense of little Jo's death scene and of Charles Bovary's dumb-animal-like love for Emma. *Lectures on Literature* shows us a Nabokov more human, if not exactly humane, than we get from the novels, the interviews, and such caustic evaluations as Frank Kermode's ("He can sit . . . like the saints enjoying the torments of the damned") or D. J. Enright's ("This author, rich in what is given to few writers and poor in what is given to most men . . ."); indeed, we come across the statement "I take my hat off to the hero who dashes into a burning house and saves his neighbor's child; but I shake his hand if he has risked squandering a precious five seconds to find and save, together with the child, its favorite toy."

This sounds eminently humane, but is it? I suspect that Nabokov admires the saving of the toy more than the saving of the child, because the toy is an artifact related to "those wonderful toys—literary masterpieces" he refers to in "L'Envoi," his annual peroration to his class, in which he also tells them that "the twinkle in the author's eye" when he catches out the murderer or tyrant in his imbecility or vulgarity "punishes your man more surely than the pistol of a tiptoeing conspirator." This would be a hard idea to sell to the victims entering the Nazi crematoria; it is giving art a presumed moral and social efficacy that the old art-for-artists (Nabokov's word) had the good sense not to impute to it.

Still, as Updike in the introduction quotes an ex-student as saying, "Nabokov was a great teacher not because he taught the subject well but because he exemplified, and stimulated in his students, a profound and loving attitude toward it." Yes, and with his customary zeal for artistic perfection, Nabokov tried to make these lectures, too, as artistic as can be. The fine editing of them, despite the incompleteness, repetitiveness, and disorganized state in which they were found, by Fredson Bowers, and the inclusion of Nabokov's drawings, maps, chronological tables, and, above all, photographic reproductions of some of them, along with the marginalia with which Nabokov annotated his teaching copies of the texts, reveal to us the solicitude, the felicitous emendations, as well as the pedantry that went into what he considered the painful, nerve-racking chore of teaching. (In another way, of course, he enjoyed the showmanship of it.)

The pedantry is always there. Nabokov cannot cite a novel mentioned in a book he is teaching without gratuitously giving the date of its composition; he will even draw a supererogatory series of diagrams showing how Jekyll's and Hyde's personalities overlap—something that could be explained in one diagramless sentence; he provides an artful and accomplished drawing of the type of orchid Swann bestowed on Odette. Could that be as important for the understanding of *A la Recherche* as the street plan of Dublin for that of *Ulysses*? Sometimes he writes instructions to himself or his class in Russian, for example the unduly fussy "Open your book!" At other times, he puts accent marks on difficult English words, so that he won't mispronounce them: in "chorister," he puts a *k* over the *ch,* and an accent over the *o*; in "corpuscle," he places parentheses around the second *c.* Despite the now popular belief in his infallible command of English, he makes mistakes: he speaks of killing two birds with a "rock," and perpetrates the sentence "Who else in the book do we have as good people?" And there are puns that the most dedicated paronomasiast would find it hard to love, as when, apropos Freudian interpretations of *Metamorphosis,* he says, "I am interested here in bugs, not in humbugs." But the care with which he corrects the mistakes in the available English translations of *Madame Bovary* and *A la Recherche* is exemplary, and I am delighted to find him worrying about the *mot juste,* as when he says of the latter novel that it "is a treasure hunt where the treasure is time and the archipelago is the past," and then carefully amends "archipelago" to "hiding place."

Yet perhaps the biggest surprise these lectures hold is Nabokov's ability to gush. We catch him referring to "the divine poetry of [Shakespeare's] fantastically great tragedies," or exclaiming about Joyce, "How beautifully the man writes!" or piously pontificating about *Ulysses,* "One thing leads to another in this marvelous book!" One thing leads to another in any book, marvelous or not; but the gush becomes cloyingly sentimental in a statement such as " 'goodness' is something round and creamy, and beautifully flushed, something in a clean apron with warm bare arms that have nursed and comforted us. . . ." Is it possible that Vladimir Nabokov, the archenemy of that middle-class sentiment and middlebrow sensibility that he tirelessly ridiculed under its Russian name, *poshlost,* was capable of a little of it himself? Certainly *Lectures on Literature* affords glimpses of his professorial, avuncular, chattily playful sides, only intermittently crisscrossed by that megalomania that made William H. Gass wonder "why he's never signed his books with a large and simple *N.* It was good enough for Napoleon. . . ."

And then came the success of *Lolita,* affluence, and deliverance from pedagogic drudgery. A dirty little girl put an end to Dirty Lit.

[1981]

SURVIVAL OF THE DIMMEST

Jaroslav Hašek, *The Good Soldier Švejk and His Fortunes in the World War*

JAROSLAV HAŠEK'S *The Good Soldier Švejk and His Fortunes in the World War* has finally appeared in an unexpurgated English version. Few masterpieces have had to wait so long— half a century and another world war had to go by—but slowness and deviousness are characteristic of this Czech novel's antihero. His name, in its German transliteration Schweik, has become identified with a typical mode of contemporary existence—schweikism, a particular blend of stoicism, existentialism, and skulduggery that may be viewed as proof either of modern man's dogged viability or of his insuperable commonness.

Hašek, the creator of Švejk, lived many of his hero's adventures in peace and war. Born in Prague in 1883, the son of a drunken schoolmaster who died when the boy was thirteen, Jaroslav became a near-permanent hookey-player. After a spotty education and a few odd jobs, he settled down to an oddly unsettled life as hobo, hoaxer, boozer, anarchist, and free-lance writer. For one or another of these activities, he had continual brushes with the Austro-Hungarian rulers of the land, and even with his beloved wife, Jarmila, a worthy bourgeoise whom he had obtained with great effort from her conventional parents, and who, after bearing him a son, went back home to them. Hašek consorted with gypsies, had no regular address, perpetrated ever bigger hoaxes, and got to know in passing the insides of several jails and one lunatic asylum, until World War I placed him into that supreme combination prison and madhouse, the Imperial and Royal Austro-Hungarian Army. Prison, because conditions in that vermiculate but megalomaniacal empire's army were viciously inhuman for a common soldier—especially one with an anarchist's police record; madhouse, because it was insane for a Russophile Czech to have to fight his beloved brothers on behalf of hated overlords.

In due time, or even sooner, Hašek managed to defect to the Russians, where he worked himself up from despised prisoner of war to various positions with what was to become the powerful Czech Legion, of which, however, he soon fell afoul. He became a proper Bolshevik and, eventually, a Soviet commissar. In 1920, he returned to the new Czechoslovak Republic as a left-wing journalist, eager to support a wife he brought with him from Russia. But the young republic tended to view him as a dangerous extremist and bigamist; unable to find steady employment, the abstemious ex-commissar relapsed into drunken vagabondage. At his own expense he began to print a projected four-volume war novel about the Good Soldier Švejk, a character whom he had previously used in diverse lesser works. The first installment (1921) proved a success, and a publisher was found for the rest. After the rigors of Russia, Hašek was unable to take his renewed debauches; he died on the threshold of solvency and fame in 1923, at age thirty-nine. His magnum opus, cut off near the beginning of Part Four, was inadequately finished by a friend. But what Hašek did complete proved to be the greatest Czech novel, and the only one with an indisputable place in world literature.

The Good Soldier Švejk chronicles the military misadventures of Josef Švejk, a little fellow who makes a modest living selling mutts as pure breeds, a moderate drinker and immoderate storyteller, dismissed from the peacetime army for idiocy. When World War I breaks out, Švejk is called up again, to be engulfed by the Molochlike machinery of the Imperial Army, as corrupt, stupid, and ruthless an institution as was ever devised for the brutalization, humiliation, and destruction of small but independent-minded chaps from Bohemia. But this shrewd little mongrel-monger will not let himself be devoured. His defenses are imbecility and cunning, the one feigned, the other real.

Up against oafish fellow soldiers, murderous noncoms, and officers who are either demented martinets or silly, self-indulgent loafers, Švejk espouses a five-point program of passive resistance: pretending to be an enthusiastic supporter of Austria, simply dying to die for the Emperor; always going about duties and assignments in the wrong way; being over-ready to admit, indeed proclaim, his idiocy and incompetence; practicing a subtle, intangible irony on his superiors which leaves them disoriented and mildly hysterical; and, now and again, unpredictably deviating into sense and efficiency so as truly to confuse everyone around.

This, of course, cannot be achieved by mere rote determination; it requires a certain innate genius for disorder and guileless sabotage that depends, like the work of any artist, on inspiration as well as on patient persistence. It demands, further, a kind of saintliness: the ability to endure physical deprivations, for the army's chief methods of fighting back are jail and extra duty; and a steady, childlike blue gaze with which to stare down the most menacing NCO, the most furibund officer. Many of these superiors are partly or wholly Czech, but this only makes talking their heads off a little easier; in military zeal manifesting itself almost exclusively in the tormenting of subordinates, they fall scarcely below true-blue Austrians. Still, an occasional decent officer or noncom does crop up, only to be hamstrung in the exercising of humaneness by a system that, sensing its imminent doom, revels in every last shred of tyrannical power.

There is not much plot. Švejk is kicked from unsavory pillar to intolerable post, then reassigned to his peacetime regiment, with which he slowly and circuitously progresses toward the eastern front, managing often to get lost, and almost invariably to trip up his superiors. His repertoire of scrapes and foul-ups, by its variety and preposterousness, preserves a juicy, contraband individuality within the oppressive, dehumanizing routines. Švejk's basic defense mechanism is his garrulity: no matter what anyone says or commands, our good soldier is ready with one or more illustrative anecdotes, ostensibly corroborating the other fellow, but actually under-cutting, derailing, beclouding, or, most frequently, just exhausting him.

Indefatigably and with endless bonhomie, Švejk spins out anecdotes allegedly based on his own past experiences, or those of people he met and talked to. Hilarious, weird, stultifying, absurdist, surreal, or just infuriatingly pointless, the stories of this shaggy-dog-seller-and-teller go on and on, causing despotic superiors and importunate equals either to invoke jail sentences (but to the serene Švejk jail is just another place to gather and disseminate material) or to give up in utter helplessness: bonhomie leads to anomie.

Through medical examinations and courts-martial, as orderly to monstrous, swilling chaplains or pleasantly gallivanting officers, exposed to hanging judges, bestial jailers, or assorted bureaucratic chicaneries, Švejk keeps amiably agreeing, denouncing his ineptitude, and babbling his way to survival. From Prague to Galicia, through Czech, Austrian, Hungarian, and Polish lands, Švejk's disarming chatter and gentle lunacies take the readers on a threefold journey.

We follow, first, the exceedingly droll travels and travails of this picaresque hero who is a new kind of *picaro*: one who does not so much outwit as outnit his adversaries—who fights a stupid power with the power of stupidity, slovenliness, and laziness posturing as serviceability, eagerness, and purely inadvertent lousing up. Such dumbness clearly derives from superior intelligence, and we come to enjoy enormously the small lopsided victories Švejk wrests from the military colossus.

We also journey toward a war. With a prevailing tone of irony or sarcasm, most often good-natured and scabrous, sometimes justly savage (and, on a very few occasions, unjust), *Švejk* lays bare for us the cruelty, idiocy, and sheer waste of war as effectively as any work of art has ever done, and rather better than most. It makes *Catch-22* look like thin gruel, and derivative gruel at that, and compares favorably in all but concision with Voltaire. To be sure, some jokes misfire; the anecdotes will begin to pall. But, in no time, Hašek is back in the realms of crystalline absurdity, quintessential farce, and, behind them, tragic suffering and devastation, neither too obtrusively nor too faintly delineated.

But there is a third, still greater, journey in this novel where so much derives from true experiences, so many characters are based on real people. We are transported to the end of an age, to the crack-up of empires built on aristocratic, capitalistic, and ecclesiastic values. These episodes and anecdotes involving Bohemians, Moravians, Austrians, Hungarians, Germans, Bosnians, Serbs, Poles, Ruthenians, Jews, Tartars—and that would have brought in Russians, too—give us an insidiously growing and at last overmastering feeling of a world in decay, despair, and ferment from below. There is an atmosphere of mistrust and animosity among allies, of increasing resentment among the exploited, and of social, ideational, or simply linguistic barriers to any kind of communication—of which Švejk's unceasing monologues, echoed by the lesser monologizings of many other characters, become the ultimate symbol.

Cecil Parrott's translation and annotations are valiant and sensible, though not unhampered by intractable linguistic and cultural differences. But no matter! The last words of this unfinished novel are "crossing the frontier," and that is exactly what Švejk has done in all directions. Translated into numerous languages, accorded many dramatic, cinematic, and operatic adaptations, projected onto World War II by a play of Bertolt Brecht's, circulated in a cut version among our GIs in that war, Švejk and "schweikian" have become universals like Quixote and quixotic, Rabelais and Rabelaisian, and may turn out to be the emblems of the coming centuries of the common man, unheroic and unepical. Švejk is the first great eponym of the nonepic.

[1974]

ITALIAN
AND HISPANIC
LITERATURE

FLASH DANCER

Umberto Eco, *Travels in Hyperreality: Essays*

THE intellectuals I met on a recent trip to Italy were still wondering why Umberto Eco's novel *The Name of the Rose* was such an enormous hit in the United States, the world, and, more important yet, Italy. Before I had a chance to reply, they were already plying me with their own answers. I heard about how Eco and a bunch of like-minded *littérateurs,* Grupo 63, had put an end to the novel with a plot, and then, when the hunger for a good old-fashioned story became overwhelming, that so-and-so Eco (some said) jumped right in and supplied one. Eco is a great publicist (others said) and knows the right book reviewers, editors, professors all over the world, which paid off. Readers don't want to be entertained any more (one cynic commented); they want to be elevated by boredom.

Needless to say, I wouldn't have got my two centesimi in, even if centesimi still existed (though, I gather, they may be resurrected), but soon I was to be frustrated even more. The editor of this journal [*The American Scholar*] had asked me for a piece explaining the worldwide success of *The Name of the Rose,* but by the time I finally got around to this, it seemed best to do it in the context of a review of Eco's latest American publication, *Travels in Hyperreality.* By the time I got started on that,

363

the *New York Times Book Review* of June 1, 1986, came out with an article by Anthony Burgess on best-sellers in which he explains Eco's triumph as follows:

> Clearly, a mass audience was looking for something other than titillation. The book offered exotic escape, but one could imagine more alluring bolt-holes than an ascetic all-male community. What it offered more abundantly was information. Mr. Eco instructed the reader exhaustively on the life of medieval monks, but he made the way in easy by contriving a cunning anachronism. His William of Baskerville is a Sherlock Holmes transported to the past, and his Conan Doyle provenance was spelled out in his very name.

Burgess's thesis in the article is unimpeachable, albeit fairly obvious. It is that people want to read trash but also want to feel they're being instructed and educated while doing so, which is why they will read a trashy novel by James Michener that they believe (correctly) gives them a lot of Texas history. Or else, as Burgess demonstrates from the example of *Lolita*, they will read high literature as long as they can mistake it for pornography. I myself always thought that for a book to have a great immediate success, it has to be either something low, posing as something high, or something high, passing for low. Thus a Graham Greene or Leonardo Sciascia novel with higher aspirations makes it on looking like a thriller, and a piece of trash by Andrew Greeley or Chaim Potok makes it by passing itself off as a work of religious or theological significance.

But none of this answers why *The Name of the Rose* should make it rather than some other work of a similar sort, and if *Rose*, why so ecumenically as to have made its author a rich man. In his disingenuous little *Postscript to "The Name of the Rose,"* Eco purports to be puzzled by his novelistic success and tries to figure it out. This book, modeled in its specious ex post facto explanations on Poe's "The Philosophy of Composition," is, if anything, even more manipulative than *The Name of the Rose,* but as a piece of highfalutin double-talk it is a

masterpiece of sorts. Take such a statement as the tentative
notion advanced that Adso's, the narrator's, inability to understand anything may have been "one of the features that made
the novel readable for unsophisticated readers. They identified
with the innocence of the narrator, and felt exonerated even
when they did not understand everything."

Adso was, in fact, Eco's excuse for writing a sort of *Bildungsroman,* not so much for Adso (because he, like everyone
else in the novel, remains a cipher, and there is no way for a
cipher to become educated) as for the reader; if, that is, throwing a kind of Baedeker to the Middle Ages pell-mell at the
public can be said to be educational. Eco is, albeit unwittingly,
more honest when he writes of "a huge amount of material . . .
accumulated since 1952, and originally intended for other, still
vague, purposes; a history of monsters, or an analysis of medieval encyclopedias, or a theory of lists. . . . At a certain point I
said to myself that, since the Middle Ages were my day-to-day
fantasy, I might as well write a novel set in that period." I think
that theory of lists is the clue. Eco is a born list maker; nothing
delights him more (you feel it both in his novel and in the
essays of *Travels in Hyperreality*) than making up lists: lists of
architectural details, sculptural elements, bibliographical data,
patristic and other theological lore, aspects of book illumina-
tion, heresies, monsters, holy relics, and on and on. Although
the novel has a plot, the characters disappear behind endless
lists. The book reads like *Middlemarch,* if it had been written
not by George Eliot but by Mr. Casaubon. Was it perhaps
Eco's novel that Dante foresaw in his exclamation in *Paradiso,*
XXX, 116–17: "Quanta è la larghezza/ di questa rosa nell'
estreme foglie"?

Yes, the readers must have felt they were getting an education in a period that had not been extensively dealt with in
fiction. Egypt, the Bible lands, Greece, Rome, the Renaissance—these have been pretty much covered; not so the Middle Ages. Of course, there have been odd novels about a
troubadour or a crusader, about Abélard and Héloïse or the

Albigensians, but they did not catch on; they were either too literary or too specific and did not afford a convenient cross section. It took Eco to figure out that a monastery would make a fine equivalent for a Grand Hotel, and that in trotting out monks with various interests and specialties from all over Europe, and by supplying the monastery with a library to parallel that of Alexandria (and meet with a similar fate), one could write the intellectual, artistic, and craft history of the Middle Ages, and, thanks to a couple of tricky plot devices, the political history as well.

Monks, moreover, excite the imagination, or at least its prurient subdivisions. One envisions homosexual and hetero-sexual orgies, not to mention flagellation, the odd burning at the stake, and other pleasant horrors. That the book delivers relatively little of this doesn't matter; the expectations are sufficiently tickled. Religion, furthermore, is in again, and there is, it seems, renewed interest in Latin in our schools. The Latin passages in *The Name of the Rose,* by the way, are illustra-tive of Eco's shrewdness. They tend to be just easy enough for someone with a modest education to make out the gist; if not, there is usually a translation worked into the text. This raises the question of what language the characters in the novel are speaking anyway. Latin, of course; but then why isn't the entire novel in Italian, which, clearly, stands in for Latin: why are some passages actually in Latin? Worse yet, why are some passages given in both languages? Obviously because Eco wants to impress the reader with his, Eco's, ability to write Latin and also butter him up with his, the reader's, ability to unscramble most of this Latin.

Then, too, Eco has a reputation as a semiologist, and some unfortunate souls doubtless believed that by reading the novel they could get an easy, fictionalized introduction to the arcane but important (so they had been led to suppose) discipline of semiology. Indeed, reviews of the novel made much of the insight that medieval Christian symbolism had a good deal in common with modern semiotics. But as a semiology primer, alas, *The Name of the Rose* is second in uselessness only to books intended as introductions to semiology.

And, further, *Rose* is a genuine cliff-hanger, or page-turner, full of foreshadowing and crosscutting and all the tried and tricky methods of creating suspense. Yet at the same time it exudes learning from every pore and is a kind of cultural *summa* for the Middle Ages. And, surely, credit is due for the amassing of such prodigious information, even if much of it is spewed out in large, unwieldy lumps. It is really essayistic information disguised as fiction, so that it is with relief that one turns to such a volume as the new selection from Eco's short nonfiction of three decades, *Travels in Hyperreality*: the essays here need not pretend to be anything else. They were mostly published as feuilletons in *L'Espresso* and *La Repubblica,* and they are the sort of thing conspicuously lacking from American newspapers.

The pieces in *Travels in Hyperreality* are unequal in value and interest. By far the most rewarding part is the first section, which lends its title to the entire book. (Incidentally, this may be an example of that new type of book whose title is spelled one way by the publisher and another way by the designer. On the jacket—and wherever the jacket's spelling, which is governed by considerations of design, is reproduced—"Hyper Reality" is two words, which is nonsense. Elsewhere, "Hyperreality" is correctly a single word. The day may be at hand when the designer will not content himself with dictating merely the title; give the fellow a finger, and . . .) In this by far the longest of the essays, Eco is traveling through America in search of manifestations of what he takes to be the two dominant American cravings: the need for "the real thing" and the hunger for "more." He concentrates on a variety of museums, millionaires' palaces, fancy hotels, riverboats, theme parks, even cemeteries—Disneylands, Marine Worlds, Forest Lawns, and such—especially in California and Florida, where "the American imagination demands the real thing and, to attain it, must fabricate the absolute fake." The account is primarily of works of art and historical scenes or documents reproduced in various ways so as to make them seem—and in some cases even be—more real than reality. He fans out to cover zoos, television programs with evangelists performing miraculous cures, and life in Los Angeles. Eco's caustic style often scores through poker-faced understatement: "Between San Francisco and Los Angeles I was able to visit seven wax versions of Leonardo's *Last Supper.*" Or: "Los Angeles is . . . a metropolis . . . of seventy-six different cities where alleyways are ten-lane freeways and man considers his right foot a limb designed for pressing the accelerator, and the left an atrophied appendix, because cars no longer have a clutch."

But it isn't all snideness. Eco does recognize that what he calls "the Last Beach ideology"—the American desire to preserve the treasures of European history and art from destruction—has a touching side to it as well as a silly or greedy one, and that, like the American "shrines of the Fake," the European "sanctuaries of the Genuine" with their exclusionism are not above reproach. Eco's targets may be easy, but he dispatches them with admirable brio: "Oral Roberts sees heaven not as the mystic rose but as Marineland. God is a good hippopotamus." Of course, true Dante-saturated Italian that he is, Eco cannot conceive of a Mystic Rose as possibly just as arbitrary and impugnable as a heavenly Marineland. Yet although this liminal section is full of tart descriptions and ironic bull's-eyes, the conclusion is unconvincing—that in this Disneyfied world, "alongside the Good Whale there is the restless, plastic form of the Bad Shark," and that this uncertainty about whether the fake world is heaven or hell keeps the anxious consumer looking for new promises to consume. Would it not seem, though, that on the level of the Absolute Fake, good and evil cease to exist; that it takes a European sensibility trying to outsmart itself to project them onto everything from the San Diego Zoo to the Haunted Mansion, and that continuous consumption stems from a simple voracious appetite rather than from even relatively complex uncertainties?

The next section, "The Return of the Middle Ages," is the only one that remains undated, so that one wonders whether it came out as an advertising adjunct to *The Name of the Rose*. It makes facile parallels between our time and the Middle Ages, and it contains two errors of impressive magnitude. Eco, who fancies himself an expert on America and its popular arts, refers to "Americans [having] succeeded in transforming Rostand's *Chanteclair* [sic] into the *Fantastiks* [sic]." Anyone who knows anything about either *The Fantasticks* or Rostand must know that it is *Les Romanesques* and not *Chantecler* that is the source of that longest-running musical, which has nothing to do with roosters and barnyards. Worse yet, the great expert on the Middle Ages speaks of Gilles de Rais as "having devoured too many children," whereas even such a nonexpert as I knows that Bluebeard subjected those wretched children to sodomy, torture, and murder, but eating them was not one of his practices.

With similar unreliability, Eco writes, in a later section, of "the geisha with the compressed and atrophied foot," although it takes no polymath like him to know that bound feet existed only in China, never in Japan, unless that singular atrophied foot refers to the left one of a geisha who settled in Los Angeles. Now, if you come on strong as a man of encyclopedic knowledge both high and low, as Eco does, you should not commit such whoppers; it makes the rest of us, with our little patches of scattered information, lose confidence in our latter-day Pico della Mirandola and wonder whether his feet, though perhaps not compressed and atrophied, might not be made of clay.

The third section, "The Gods of the Underworld," concerns various cults of unreason throughout the world. In the first essay, Eco begins with the differences between the Superman comic strip and the later movie version, which he finds more mystical. Characteristically, the essay touches promiscuously on such figures as Tolkien, Feuerbach, Fellini, Nietzsche, and Heidegger. There is some diverting juggling with social and cultural phenomena, particularly because of Eco's ability to be both in the stratosphere, with books like *Forme del sacro in un' epoca di crisi* and *Das Heilige,* and in the quotidian mud of movies and comic strips—simultaneously the Superman and the Clark Kent of the history of ideas. But, as always, the fun is marred by two typical disturbing phenomena. One is the grand but unreliable assertion—for example, that speed reading is "already being taught in the universities." I haven't met with it on any American campus and would be very surprised to find it at Eco's own University of Bologna. The other is self-important posturing, as when Eco considers that "as antidote or antistrophe" to these weird cults (and note, by the way, that "antistrophe" where "antidote" would be quite enough), "the arts of the Trivium, logic, dialectic, rhetoric" might serve, save that "anyone who goes on stubbornly practicing them will be accused of impiety."

That last bit is worth pondering. Are there really practitioners of the Trivium who have been accused of impiety? Is this a hard fact or merely a flourish of rhetoric, without logic or dialectic? Consider the essay in praise of Thomas Aquinas from a later section bearing the Boethian title "De Consolatione Philosophiae"; rather arrogantly it ends by listing the probable opinions and positions of Saint Thomas were he alive today. Eco knows "for sure" that he would urge us "to learn from him how you can think cleanly, like a man of your own time. After which I wouldn't want to be in his shoes." This sounds like the same dark threat about the Trivium. Does it mean that, because Eco would not want to be in Thomas's shoes, our semiologist prefers *not* to think cleanly? Or is this just another piece of rhetorical jactitation? Rhetoric without logic, however, leads not to the Trivium but to triviality.

There is something unacceptable about Eco's stance, which tries to be populist and elitist at the same time, and, at all times, paradoxical, challenging, too clever by half. "Terrorism," we read, is a much lesser concern than the coming to power of Communists "because it's a biological consequence of the multinationals, just as a day of fever is a reasonable price of an effective vaccine. . . . [The Red Brigades] must recognize that they are acting out a script already written by their presumed enemies"—that is, the capitalists. This piece of piquant sophistry is in dubious taste in an essay about the Moro assassination, but what can we expect from a social philosopher who in an essay "On the Crisis of the Crisis of Reason" wonders, "Is stylistic evidence valid in establishing what is the 'right' meaning of the *Iliad,* or whether Bo Derek is more desirable than Sigourney Weaver?" The point here is not how Eco answers his own question, but how he formulates it: Homer and Hollywood in felicitous juxtaposition. Again, in an essay on the Falkland war, "Chile refuses to fall in line with Argentina. . . . Castro agrees at once. Castro must be more familiar with Errol Flynn than with Marx."

This kind of grandstanding is typical of someone who tries to be a populist and an elitist at the same time. In "The Multiplication of the Media," from the section "Reports on the Global Village," Eco has a paragraph that begins by asserting that Caravaggio is still recognized as better than his imitators, Balzac still acknowledged as superior to *Dallas.* To prove that this is not just a matter of technique, he continues: "For example, Wenders's film *Hammett* is technically much more sophisticated than Huston's classic *The Maltese Falcon,* and yet we follow the former only with interest and the latter with religious devotion." Who is this "we"? I enjoy *The Maltese Falcon,* but certainly don't follow it with religious devotion. But then, in a long essay, "Casablanca: Cult Movies and Intellectual Collage," Eco informs us that "*Casablanca* is not a work of art, if such an expression still has a meaning." Here the elitist shades into the populist: what is art, after all? A little later in the essay, however, Eco writes, "The boastful *Rio Bravo* is a cult movie and the great *Stagecoach* is not." Could that mean that "the great *Stagecoach*" is, after all, a work of art? Is our populist shading back into an elitist?

But let us return to that *Maltese Falcon* paragraph, where Eco notes that today's "kids pack into a Palasport, but on the first

night it's the Bee Gees and the next it's John Cage or a performer of Satie. . . ." And so on, praising the kids' catholic
omnivorousness, to conclude that, without growing better or
worse, "things have simply changed, and even value judgments must be formed according to different parameters."
There, parameters and all, is the populist speaking. Yet in a
feuilleton on the pop song "Lady Barbara," Eco's conclusion is
"Only when the song has become entirely unpleasant will the
audience feel happy at last." In this contempt it is, of course,
the elitist who gets the upper hand.

There are pieces in *Travels in Hyperreality* on everything from
wearing blue jeans (if Barthes wrote on fashion, can Eco be far
behind?) to sports, from the analysis of a news photograph to
Marshall McLuhan, on whom Eco isn't keen. Throughout,
there are references to the Middle Ages—heralds of, or paralipomena to, *The Name of the Rose.* Always, Eco is best when he
is closest to being a reporter, a travel writer, or a teller of
anecdotes. So "Whose Side Are the Orixà On?"—conversations in situ with practitioners of Afro-Brazilian rites—and
parts of "A Theory of Expositions," on the relative propaganda
merit of various exhibits at Montreal's Expo '67, are much
more enjoyable than the windy speculations in "Language,
Power, Force," a piece dealing with Barthes, Foucault, and the
historians Georges Duby and Michael Howard, where you can
read such things as "It isn't clear if Foucault's view of power
(which Barthes, with genius, exemplifies in the given language) is a neorevolutionary view or a neoreformist one.
Except that Foucault's merit would lie in having abolished the
difference between the two concepts. . . ." Ah, well, an abolished difference need not be clear.

These essays, predominantly, oscillate between opaque hair-
splitting and flashy vulgarization. Thus in the already mentioned essay on Aquinas: "The universe of the early Middle
Ages was a universe of hallucination, the world was a symbolic forest peopled with mysterious presences, things were
seen as if in the continuous story of a divinity who spent his

time reading and devising the *Weekly Puzzle Magazine.*" Then "along comes the mystic, with his nervous, stripped-down intuition, who penetrates with an almost drugged eye into the *garçonnière* of the One, where the sole and true party is going on." This jocular leveling strikes me as no better than the devious overcomplications. And always there is sloppiness, as when, in the same essay, we read about an "Académie de France." There is, however, only an Académie française, which Eco momentarily confuses, I would guess, with the Collège de France. Of course, he knows better, but slovenliness even in small matters is, speaking nonsemiologically, not a good sign.

What I find most objectionable in Eco is what I would call, in his own phrase, "the bricolage of the pop artist [or pop philosopher] who juxtaposes things out of context." Thus in a not uninteresting or imperceptive essay on the ruckus over Antonioni's documentary *China,* in which Eco justly notes the cultural differences between Western socialism and Eastern Communism, he ends by describing a discussion in a restaurant between Antonioni and a young Chinese critic, while "in the corner, ignored by everyone, a young woman with soft, sensual eyes was following the discussion. . . . This was the film actress Maria Schneider, but few would have recognized her."

What a trivial (not Trivial) ending to a respectable essay. Although Eco tries to justify this as a demonstration "that the protagonist of the evening was the Chinese," I think the real motive is showing off: I, Umberto Eco, with my usual savvy, spotted Maria Schneider, whom none of the other journalists and TV crews recognized. What does it matter that Miss Schneider, a usually unkempt, unwashed-looking creature, was not much of an actress, as she demonstrated in Antonioni's *The Passenger* and Bertolucci's *Last Tango in Paris,* the only movies in which she was noticeable? What does matter is that our master *bricoleur* can work her into his essay as a tribute to his perspicacity, his knowledgeableness, his being equally at home in high and low culture—if, as he might say, such categories still have meaning.

The first section of *Travels in Hyperreality* can be recommended to all readers, certainly to all American readers. But to decide whether one wants to read on, one should skip ahead to "The Comic and the Rule," where, along with some pertinent insights, misstatements abound. We read in a single paragraph that "anyone is distressed in seeing *Apocalypse Now*," by which, I'm afraid, Eco means not the wretchedness of the film but the supposed universality of tragedy as opposed to the alleged time-bound nature of comedy; whereas "for Woody Allen you have to be fairly cultivated." But Allen is a success almost everywhere, alas, and degree of cultivation is not the same ball game as time-boundness. The paragraph ends with the assertion that "Alberto Sordi and Totò cannot be exported to a number of countries," though Sordi, at least, has done very well in America and most parts of Europe. As for the allegation that Sid Caesar and Lenny Bruce are unknown in Italy—well, yes; except that, not having made movies, how would they be known abroad?

I suspect that Eco's international success depends not so much on his being tragic rather than comic as on the fact that he writes with such seeming authority on so many subjects that the average reader is awed and taken in. It would indeed require a fairly large panel of diverse experts to show up all of Eco's bluff. It might almost be worth convening it.

[1987]

INCONTINENT IMAGINATION

Gabriel García Márquez, *Collected Stories*

FREQUENTLY the history of literature (or the history of human gullibility) spews up a novel that becomes an "intellectual best-seller"—a book that all persons with literary or intellectual pretensions feel obliged to acquire, and some even to read. It may be the worst work by an established artist whose "best-seller time" has come. This was the case with Nabokov's *Ada,* even though the book was—is—unreadable. Or it may be the tome of a clever counterfeiter, a prestidigitator or *fumiste*—of skill but no substance—as in the case of Umberto Eco's *The Name of the Rose.* Or it may simply be the book of a mediocre but newly emerged writer of strange origin or bent that strikes even some usually judicious people as unusual, original, unique (never mind that it is factitious, trivial, and, to be honest about it, boring). Such a book is—was—Gabriel García Márquez's *One Hundred Years of Solitude,* which earned its author the Nobel Prize, won by such other prodigious Latin American writers as Miguel Angel Asturias (at least unpretentious) and the unspeakable Gabriela Mistral, but never by Jorge Luis Borges, the one who most deserved it.

To read *One Hundred Years of Solitude* is to dive into a mountain of cotton candy head first and brain last, and endlessly, suffocatingly, sickeningly try to eat one's way out of it. This

375

book that, without false modesty, could call itself *One Thou-sand Years of Solitude* is repetitious beyond anything but an old-time movie serial, with characters that even a genealogical chart cannot individuate (why should it? since when is the writer's job done by a chart?); the same sticky-sweet mixture of fantasy and social satire stretches on and on. Its mischie-vousness loses whatever edge it might have through iteration, lip-smacking enjoyment of its own cleverness, and flights into a fancy that seems to me the evasion rather than the extension of truth.

I had no better luck with two short novels by this writer, *The Autumn of the Patriarch* and *Chronicle of a Death Foretold*. Still, it seemed possible that he could achieve more with less—in the short story, which might curb his passion for prolixity. And indeed there are in the *Collected Stories* a few relatively unassuming, predominantly realistic tales that qualify García Márquez as a potential Hispanic Somerset Maugham. There is even one concluding novella in the author's dubious surrealist manner that works well enough, aside from some straining for effect and misfired jokes. For the rest, despite the odd power-ful image and some passages of acerb mockery, these stories are mostly exercises in epigonous surrealism, with fantasy squeezed as desperately and self-destructively as when a nov-ice milkmaid mistakes a bull's scrotum for a cow's udder.

The earliest stories, from the collection *Eyes of a Blue Dog,* are the poorest, though here the author has the excuse of his early twenties. In several of them, the protagonist is either a corpse somehow still alive or a living person relentlessly ver-bose in death. Death-in-life, life-in-death—these parvenu archetypes are pounded in with elaborately contrived, care-fully self-contradictory detail. "Madam," says the doctor in "The Third Resignation," the opening story,

> your child has a grave illness: he is dead. Nevertheless . . . we
> will succeed in making his organic functions continue through
> a complex system of autonutrition. Only the motor functions
> will be different. . . . We shall watch his life through growth,

which, too, shall continue on [sic] in a normal fashion. It is simply "a living death." A real and true death. . . .

Here the preposterous conceit—it has no satirical thrust—has at least a kind of fairy-tale diaphaneity. Presently, pseudo-psychological obfuscation sets in. The living corpse hears terrible noises inside his head: "The noise had slippery fur, almost untouchable," yet our cadaver-hero will "catch it" and "not permit it to enter through his ear again, to come out through his mouth, through each of his pores . . ." etc. But forthwith this "furry" noise "[breaks] its cutglass crystals, its ice stars, against the interior walls of his cranium." Nevertheless, our hero proposes to "Grab it. Squeeze it. . . . Throw it onto the pavement and step on it [until it is] stretched out on the ground like any ordinary thing, transformed into an integral death." Notice that the noise goes from soft and furry to hard and crystalline and back again to something squeezable, thence to something animate that can be stomped on and stamped out with an "integral death." A pious hope, that; in García Márquez no death is integral enough.

Surrealism is all very well if it has some fidelity to its own bizarre self. A Max Ernst must remain an Ernst; it cannot, must not, transform itself into a Tanguy, a Matta, a Wilfredo Lam, at the whim of its undisciplined creator. Let the image be as crazy and hellish as it wants to be, but let it stay in focus. Out of focus, hell itself is not hell any more. It is only an amorphous blur. Yet from García Márquez's paragraphs of chaos a fine image, at times, surfaces—such as that "silence, as if all the lungs of the earth had ceased breathing so as not to break the soft silence of the air."

In the second story, "The Other Side of Death," a similarly living corpse is haunted by a smell instead of a sound. If, in the previous story, the author played around with tenses, here he fools with pronouns:

They were traveling in a train—I remember it now [this "I" comes out of nowhere]—through a country-side—I've had this dream frequently—like a still life, sown with false, artificial trees bearing fruit of razors, scissors, and other diverse items— I remember now that I have to get my hair cut—barbershop instruments. He'd had that dream a lot of times but it had never produced this scare in him. There behind a tree was his brother, the other one, his twin, signaling—this happened to me somewhere in real life—for him to stop the train.

Note the confusion of "they," "I, " and "he" in what is mostly a third-person-singular story. Note also the sloppiness of "other diverse items." And note the theme of the brother, the twin, the alter ego, that crops up with tiresome frequency in these stories—once it is even a mirror image that bleeds when the shaver does not—and later in the same paragraph another García Márquez favorite, the tumor. Here the character notices one on his middle toe, calmly takes a screwdriver out of his pocket "and extracts the head of the tumor with it." And, sure enough, this character, too, "gently wrapped in the warm climate of a covered serenity . . . felt the lightness of his artificial and daily death."

"Bitterness for Three Sleepwalkers" is even less scrutable. It may—just may—be about the death of a mother as perceived by her three sons. In any case, "she," whoever she is, seems to "become dissolved in her solitude" and to have "lost her natural faculty of being present." In "Dialogue with the Mirror," a man "who had had the room before" meditates about the death of a brother. Again the story keeps shifting between a "he" and an "I" and ends with the man shaving before a mirror, which gives the author a chance to have lots of fun with "right" and "left" and "forward" and "backward." In the end the mirror image bleeds, while the man, unbloodied, smells kidneys in gravy and feels "satisfaction—positive satisfaction—that a large dog had begun to wag its tail inside his soul." In the title story, "Eyes of a Blue Dog," a man and a woman inhabit each other's dreams but cannot find each other when awake, because the sleeper, upon waking, forgets the watchword "Eyes of a blue dog" with which to recognize the other. Kipling did this sort of thing better in "The Brushwood Boy."

There follows a straightforward story about a whore who has killed one of her johns and elicits a fake alibi from an ugly restaurateur who adores her and feeds her free of charge. Entitled "The Woman Who Came at Six O'Clock," it is a neatly managed mood piece, situated in the bar-eatery before the evening's clients arrive, and containing such nice turns of phrase as "the man looked at her with a thick, sad tenderness, like a maternal ox." But in "Nabo: The Black Man Who Made the Angels Wait," we are back in the thick of the old farrago with yet another figure hovering in a state that is neither life nor death, and a plot, if that is the word for it, obscurer than any. We get several more such stories, some with ghosts in them, and one, "The Night of the Curlews," that is totally impenetrable. But it is the first to offer a favorite García Márquezian theme: the curious behavior of certain animals. In this instance it is curlews, which blind three men for no apparent reason.

In the stories from the next collection, *Big Mama's Funeral*, Macondo, the mythical locale of most of García Márquez's fiction, becomes more important yet. This Macondo can be anything from a pathetic hamlet to a good-sized town running to seed, and is peopled with the author's stock company of characters who pop up throughout his fiction, short or long. Here the writing is more assured, and some of the besetting mannerisms are kept relatively at bay. They are replaced, however, by new tricks no less annoying. Thus "Tuesday Siesta" is a potentially interesting story about a poor woman who travels wretchedly, with her small daughter, to a distant town where her son, caught in the act of robbery, was killed and buried. She carries a cheap bouquet to lay on his grave, and rouses the indolent priest, during the hot hour of the siesta, for the key to the cemetery. But the townsfolk, aroused by her presence, gather ominously around the priest's house as the story abruptly ends. In Luis Harss and Barbara Dohmann's *Into the Mainstream: Conversations with Latin-American Writers,* we read:

> What he first imagined in the story, says García Márquez, was the part he left out. Though not entirely. Somehow what has been omitted is implicit, therefore all the more vivid and powerful.

Would it were so. We know something about the mother, very little about the daughter, and nothing at all about the townspeople except that they love their siesta. There is not enough to make up for the missing confrontation. There is not even a dénouement, only an anticlimax of the thudding rather than the teasing variety. García Márquez has said that he considers revelations "a bad literary device" and consequently avoids them. The avoidance, I think, is mutual.

Finally, the stories from the *Eréndira* volume, written between 1968 and 1972, are in the author's maturest style and perfectly display its generous flaws and niggardly virtues. Here the surrealism has become formulaic: in "A Very Old Man with Enormous Wings," a senile, moth-eaten angel falls out of the sky and confounds Macondo, which, however, loses interest when the sideshows of an itinerant carnival become more popular. Eventually, the angel just flies away. Conversely, in "The Handsomest Drowned Man in the World," the sea washes up a gorgeous, oversized male corpse, impeccably preserved; as the townswomen all fall in love with him while dressing him in whatever large enough finery they can muster, he has to be tossed back into the waves.

The long and fairly controlled title novella, "The Incredible and Sad Tale of Innocent Eréndira and Her Heartless Grandmother," is probably all the García Márquez one needs to read for a full sampling of his ideas, strategies, and techniques. A mélange of the surreal, scurrilous, and occasionally poetic, it tells of a monstrous, larger-than-life grandmother who, having always exploited her lovely granddaughter, Eréndira, now travels all over with her and prostitutes her to all comers until her alleged debt for supposedly causing their house to burn down is paid back by Eréndira, on her back. The debt is self-perpetuating, and it is only after many years of weird and grueling adventures that the girl, with the help of a lover, manages to do in the grandmother, who takes more killing than Rasputin. Gathering up her ill-gained fortune, Eréndira abandons the lovesick youth and vanishes. Along its way, the novella takes satirical potshots at government, religion, capitalism, family relations, passion, and whatnot, and generally maintains its narrative propulsion despite its curlicues and discontinuities. Though there is wit, horror, and even wistfulness aplenty, the supernatural elements contribute little beyond a superficial exoticism, and one must finally wonder whether the story's eccentricities do not cancel one another out.

Translated conscientiously, though sometimes ungrammatically, by Gregory Rabassa and (the *Big Mama* volume) S. J. Bernstein, these stories sorely lack a philosophical or emotional center. "In García Márquez's world, love is the primordial power that reigns as an obscure, impersonal, and all-powerful presence," wrote Octavio Paz in *Alternating Current*. Obscurity and impersonality, to be sure, abound in these *Collected Stories,* but they contain more obfuscatory deliquescence than concentrated power. And they seem to have precious little to do with love, unless you call love a minor writer's obsession with telling tall tales such as his beloved grandmother told him, a boy of eight, to make him sleep. "Nothing interesting has happened to me since," García Márquez has said, and we are compelled to believe him. But he has certainly learned his grandmother's lessons well: with his fabulating, he can put even grown-ups to sleep.

[1985]

THE MAGICIAN

Jorge Luis Borges, *A Personal Anthology*

WHAT is illusion, what reality? The Romantics were the first to address themselves to this question in Western literature, and it might be presumed that with Pirandello the last juice was squeezed out of it. But no, it is still very much with us— just look at the recent films of Bergman, Fellini, Antonioni, and Resnais. Yet while these filmmakers are mostly transferring battles fought in books and on the stage to celluloid, there is a brilliant writer in Argentina who still has an original way of approaching the problem, and even a new solution to it. For Jorge Luis Borges, reality *is* illusion and illusion *is* reality; being one and the same, both are equally real or unreal. Borges reduces them to an absurd, garishly gesticulating nothingness. But this nothingness is frighteningly real; it is the sum total of multifarious existents that clash and cancel one another out. And so the process continues—the splinters sprouting into new combatants—on and on.

Borges's erudition, choice of forms, and style are all efficient vehicles for his worldview. His learning seems to know no boundaries: a boyhood spent in Switzerland appears to have, in Borges, translated that country's socioeconomic internationalism into intellectual world citizenship. From Old Norse to Anglo-Saxon, from Mid to Far Eastern lore, from the cabala to contemporary philosophy, from the songs of the gauchos to the prose and poetry of the symbolists and even to the "influence of Cecil B. De Mille," everything is grist for his thorough, unostentatious, precise imagination. But this imagination is more than a mill, it is also a volcano, albeit an exquisite one: Borges dreams up new histories and new civilizations (or old ones that never existed), invents heroes and geniuses that never were, but who, mixed in with real ones, become just as convincing as reality, and just as preposterous.

As for the choice of forms, Borges has written poems, essays, short stories, and even, in collaboration, detective fiction. But his most characteristic mode is a kind of tale that partakes of the myth, the parable, the essay, and the prose poem, and whose forebears are Kafka and Mallarmé. To make matters more complicated, the myth, though perhaps based on existing mythologies, departs from them; the parable, though clearly such, leaves us in doubt about its moral; the prose poetry conflicts disturbingly with the cerebral, metaphysical themes; and the essayistic element undercuts the narrative and stresses its fictitiousness, its nonexistence.

But the most magnificent thing about Borges is his style, which deserves that phrase much tossed about in art criticism, magic realism. It is difficult to say whether what he writes is the sheer matter-of-fact description of the ineffable, or the most lyrical hyperbole for something utterly mundane. Thus we read in a poem about a fugitive, "My feet are treading the shadows of pikes/ Pointed at me"—could the literal and the figurative be more inextricably merged? In a tale, we read that "the sky turned the rosy color of a leopard's gums." Fine, we say at first; but, then, anybody's gums are rosy—are a leopard's more so? Or do we merely imagine them more so? Do we even know the exact shade of a leopard's gums? Or, if we don't, is what we imagine perhaps more real than what is?

Within a single tale, as in "The Aleph," the style can shift from a weary skepticism in the very sentence structure and paragraphing to a long, rhythmically rapturous flow as the narration moves from the humdrum to the magical—but is it magical? It is made as believable as the rest, yet in the postscript to the story it is retracted just as naturally. Or is it? The retraction itself is partly undercut. Stylistically, Borges's tales tend to be palinodes within palinodes.

Two recurrent images are prototypical of Borges's art, being, as it were, its cornerstones, its master metaphors. There is, first, the labyrinth. We read, in various pieces, of the world as a labyrinth from which it is impossible to escape; of Ariosto's dreams weaving the skein of that illuminated labyrinth, his work; of a fugitive on horseback creating a labyrinth with his tortuous flight; of the sound of an invisible guitar in the next room creating for an invalid a "meager labyrinth infinitely winding and unwinding." Our dreams are labyrinths that reveal things we forget upon waking; a man, about to be executed, weaves within the last minute of his life a "lofty invisible labyrinth in time"; conversely, Borges's entire life is "the manifold labyrinth my steps/ Wove through all those years since childhood." There is even a mysterious labyrinth in one of the tales "which is a single straight line."

What does this dominant image stand for? The maze is unreality in search of the real. The labyrinth is the frantic attempt to make sense of the jumble that surrounds us— whether it be the journey through life, sounds and sights and movements that crowd us, or dreams and visions that, in the archaic word, "maze" (i.e., bewilder) us. We try to run the maze from this beleaguering confusion toward the clear-cut, the unalterable, the real.

The second master image, fictions, is the other half of our story. In a poem, Borges writes that he "creates a fiction, not a living creature"; not, as he says elsewhere, "a mirror of the world, but simply one more thing added to the universe." All he can create as an artist is "my feeble translation/ Time-bound, of what was a single limitless Word." For, as he again writes, the true work of art that summed up the world may have "consisted of a line of verse . . . of a single word." But this is lost; the legends that are handed down to us are "no more than literary fictions." There is a particular bitterness in that tautology "literary fictions." "Why," asks the rabbi who created the Golem, "did I decide to add to the infinite/ Series one more symbol?" And one of the best-known collections of Borges's works is entitled, redundantly, *Ficciones.*

Fictions are the unreality of what we think most real: art. The author believes he has found his way out of the labyrinth into enduring, immutable reality, the work of art. And, behold, it is only a simulacrum, a verbose translation, one more knickknack added to the clutter of an overcrowded universe—a fiction rather than the Word that captures and mirrors all. At the end of the maze there is a fiction that makes the world even more labyrinthine, and merely extends our predicament.

Is there, then, no continuity, permanence, hope? Well, there is one notion that fascinates Borges and may hold solace. As Marianne Kesting put it, "For Borges the world is a chaotic labyrinth of mirror images, which gains a kind of order only through the recurrence of identities, through repetition." The concept of recurrence itself recurs throughout Borges's work. Thus "the profile of a Jew in the subway may be that of Christ; the hands which give us some coins at a change-window may recall those which some soldiers once nailed to the Cross." Two stories told by Borges are "perhaps . . . a single story. To God, the obverse and reverse of this coin are the same." (But—irony!—Borges is a nonbeliever.) A streetcorner scene "is not merely identical to what was once represented at that corner so many years before, it is . . . the very same." In one of the tales, a character "argues that the number of experiences possible to a man is not infinite, and that a single 'repetition' suffices to demonstrate that time is a fallacy." But comes the typical Borgesian reversal: "Unfortunately, the arguments that demonstrate this fallacy are no less fallacious."

Borges has made a selection from his writings that now appears in English as *A Personal Anthology,* and all the above quotations are taken from it. I cannot always agree with Borges's choices: some of the inclusions are merely pleasant trivia, whereas the omissions comprise such favorites of mine as "The Immortal" and "The Library at Babel." But it is always interesting to see what a master prefers among his works; Borges has moreover arranged these poems, parables, and tales in thematically related clusters, so that the line of force of his thought becomes clear. And some of the most breathtaking stories are here, like the one of the criminal who traps a learned detective by planting esoterically pseudocabalistic clues; or the one about Averroës writing his famous Aristotelian commentaries and coming upon the inscrutable concepts "tragedy" and "comedy," meaningless to the medieval Moorish civilization that lacked a theater. There is the fine story about the "Aleph," a place in which the entire world—past, present, and to come—can be seen, but which turns out to be, possibly, a mere pseudo-Aleph. There is the story of the Druid (if that is what he is) who dreams his own alter ego, only to find that he is himself that alter ego's dream. And several others, in prose and verse, no less remarkable.

But there is also, alas, the translation. The prose fell mostly to Anthony Kerrigan, the editor, and it could hardly have fallen much lower. I am not primarily concerned with gross carelessnesses, as when belly (*vientre*) becomes "chest," or a café with class (*encompetudo*) becomes "renowned." Kerrigan repeatedly misses shades of meaning: a horse cannot, in English, be drinking "crapulous water"—water can hardly be inebriated! But in Spanish *crapuloso* can mean dissolute or debauched; the water could, perhaps, be called "denatured." Kerrigan generally settles for the easy cognate: people are never accustomed to something, always "habituated"; objects are not recovered, they are "recuperated," and so on. This leads to ludicrousness, as when pistons (*embolos*) become "emboli"; and to sheer incomprehensibility, as when the Porte (whose meaning Kerrigan doesn't know) becomes the "Portico." Even Kerrigan's English is defective: frequently ungrammatical ("there are nothing but forms"), it goes through bad usage ("overly," "transpire" for happen) to illiteracy ("thusly" and "imposter"). The meaning is sometimes missed: "He became the other: he had no goal on earth and he had killed a man" is rendered as "He became the stranger: he had no further mission on earth, but he had killed a man." That "but" is particularly misleading.

Alastair Reid, who translated most of the verse, does somewhat better, though the rhythms of the original tend to get woefully disfigured. And where Borges writes a plain "Who will tell us to whom in this house/ Without knowing it, we have said goodbye?" Reid inflates, fudges, and obfuscates: "Who will point out which person, in this house/ To whom we have said, without knowing it, farewell?" That is not even a sentence. Worst of all, instead of a helpful afterword, Kerrigan reprints some letters between Reid and himself that are the height of sophomoric self-display and totally irrelevant.

The translations, then, are, on the whole, regrettable. But it is good to have an addition of any kind to our short supply of Borges in English. Some of the pieces now first available to us serve, in fact, as modest settings for extraordinary gems. "Glory," we devastatingly learn from one of them, "is one of the forms of oblivion." Unfortunately, the reverse is not true: the oblivion we have meted out to Borges will not yield any kind of glory. It merely impoverishes us.

[1967]

TRADUTTORE, TRADITORE— OR THE TRADITION OF TRADUCING

Three Mistranslated Poets: Aleixandre, Montale, Vallejo

VICENTE ALEIXANDRE, the 1977 Nobel laureate, is both amply represented and amply misrepresented by *A Longing for the Light,* a goodly selection from his work, early to recent, made by Lewis Hyde. Roughly half of it is translated by the editor, the other half by W. S. Merwin (unfortunately, one early poem only), Robert Bly, Willis Barnstone, and eleven others. The political credentials of Aleixandre (born 1898 in Seville) are as good as his poetic ones; poor health and isolation removed him from Franco's world; he began publishing in 1926 in Ortega's *Revista de Occidente,* was influenced by Darío, Machado, and Jiménez, and was friends with Lorca, Cernuda, Guillén, and especially Dámaso Alonso. A certain vagueness of poetic profile has nevertheless kept him, perhaps not quite undeservedly, less esteemed than some of his famous contemporaries. Significantly, Neruda refers to him somewhat ironically as the "poet of limitless dimension"; Jorge Guillén numbers him, less than enthusiastically, among the "poets of delirium and free form."

Actually, Aleixandre's work falls, almost too conveniently, into those three phases schoolboys love: early, middle, and late. The early, emerging from a brief dalliance with traditional formalism and *poésie pure,* soon takes the shape of free verse and prose poems redolent of surrealism, the lava of the unconscious gushing forth partly also under the influence of Freud, whom the poet was reading at the time. Aleixandre called this "poetry as it is born, with a minimum of elaboration," admitting the prose poems to be, of all his works, the hardest to read. I find both the prose poems and the *vers libre* of this period unimpressive—too private, nightmare-ridden, undisciplined—which goes, I am afraid, also for three later volumes, up to and including *Mundo a solas* (1936). From this, I quote one quatrain of "El árbol" ("The Tree"), in Lewis Hyde's translation:

Immense knee where kisses will never try to act like false
  ants.
Where the moon won't pretend to be a piece of fine lace.
Because the white foam that might even dare graze it one
  night
is stone in the morning, hard stone without moss.

This excerpt exemplifies Aleixandre's early strategy of evasion, of describing things that are not rather than things that are. "Now the sun isn't horrendous like a cheek that's ready:/ it isn't a piece of clothing or a speechless flashlight./ Nor is it the answer heard by our knees,/ nor the task of touching the frontiers with the whitest part of our eyes," we read in "With All Due Respect," and I respectfully submit: "Don't tell me what it isn't—tell me what it is!" (Stephen Kessler translates *esa dificultad* [this difficulty] as "the task," and *linterna* [lantern] as "flashlight," out of that kind of perverse, translatorish self-importance that runs through this volume.) The sun, we learn forthwith, "has already become truth, lucidity, stability," which isn't much help either in fixing it in our consciousness.

When it is not outright negation, the game is the tenuous equivocation of either-or. A poem in *The World by Itself* is entitled "Guitar or Moon," and an entire collection of 1935 is named *Destruction or Love*. *Or,* even more than *not* and *nor,* is Aleixandre's poetic prop. "In front of me, the dolphins or the sword . . ." "Like that final longing to kiss the shore good-bye,/ or the painful footprint of a hermit or a footstep gone astray . . ." "Bull made of moon or honey . . ." "A horn or a sumptuous sky . . ." "An upward impulse wants to be moon,/ or calm, or warmth, or that poison of a pillow in the muffled mouth. . . ." These fragments represent only the most flagrant *or*'s in four poems from *Swords Like Lips* printed consecutively in *A Longing for the Light*. It is, throughout the earlier works, a pitiless proliferation that contributes to their haziness.

With the collections *Shadow of Paradise* (1939–43) and, especially, *Heart's Story* (*Historia del corazón*) of 1945–53, the middle period gets under way and things look up. These are mostly reminiscences of the poet's childhood in Málaga and love poems; in them, Aleixandre achieves a blend of verdant innocence and lush description of nature, as well as perceptions of love expressed with a very personal *conceptismo*—perhaps a synthesis of Rubén Darío's wildness and Machado's restraint. The rhythms are meticulously balanced, and the long-breathed verses often lengthen out still further at the end of the free-flowing strophes.

A fine example from the earlier tome is "Ciudad del paraíso" ("City of Paradise"), dedicated "To Málaga, my city," yet to which Hyde's translation does signal injustice. "Angélica ciudad que, más alta que el mar, presides sus espumas" becomes "town that stands like an angel over the sea and rules its waves." Even granted that the central panel of this verbal triptych, *más alta que el mar,* with its marmoreal assonance given final chiseling by the framing parallelism of *más* and *mar,* cannot be reproduced in English, something like "exalted above the sea" might come nearer the mark, and "angelic city" is better than "town . . . like an angel." And, "rules the waves" having been preempted by Britannia, I would opt for "rules over its foam," especially since that is what the poet says.

Consider Aleixandre's "Acaso de una reja florida una guitarra triste/ cantaba la súbita canción suspendida en el tiempo;/ quieta la noche, más quieto el amante,/ bajo la luna eterna que instantánea transcurre." "Suspended in time, a sad guitar seemed to sing/ the unexpected song of a flower-filled lattice./ The night was quiet and the suitor even quieter/ under the momentary moon that flows by forever." Thus Hyde; a more Jekyllish translation might run: "Perhaps from a flowery shelf a sad guitar/ sang the sudden tune suspended in time;/ quiet the night and quieter the lover/ under the eternal moon rushing by in a trice." What is particularly inept about Hyde's version is the inversion; the progression from flowery shelf to suspension in time follows the order in which the senses apprehended the phenomena in question; moreover, the song belongs to the lover, not to the lattice. Again, the movement from *momentary* to *forever* is incorrect, and *flows* is too slow; this suggests duration, whereas impermanence is intended: though the moon is eternal, for the lover and for us it rushes by in an instant. And look now at the final couplet: "Allí el cielo eras tú, ciudad que en él morabas./ Ciudad que en él volabas con tus alas abiertas." Hyde translates: "You were the sky and the sky was your home,/ city that used to fly with your wings spread wide." Not so. Málaga, on a cliff overlooking the sea, becomes the sky for someone gazing at it from below; so we must get something like "There you were the sky, city that dwelled in it"—*there* is important, for it means that elsewhere, where the poet now lives, no such guardian city in the sky exists. Again, it is not that the city "used to fly" through the heavens; it still does, only no longer for the absent and sadly older poet. Hence we need a continuous action: "City that flew in it [the sky] with your wings outspread."

The poems in *Historia del corazón* are mostly successful, the vestiges of surrealism discreetly heightening the intensely individual, sensuous perceptions. Especially notable are "The

Old Man and the Sun," "Her Hand Given Over," and "We Feed on Shadow." I quote from the second: "Once more I touch your hand/ . . . to touch/ . . . the skin with its wings and beneath that/ the stony bone that can't be bribed, the sad bone that never gets any/ love . . ." (Hyde). This should read: ". . . feeling under the winged skin the hard, unsubornable/ bone, the sad bone that is beyond the reach of/ love. . . ." (Literally: "as far as which love never extends.")

But in Aleixandre's last phase, things go wrong again. In poems like "If Someone Could Have Told Me" (from *Poemas de la consumación,* 1965–66), surrealism returns with a ravening vengeance; moreover, a fuzzy mysticism and populism set in. There are still fine passages, as in poems like "Whom I Write for" (or "Who I Write for," as Hyde, who, like his associates, is often ungrammatical, would have it) and "To My Dog," containing such a lovely line as "Residido en tu luz, immóvil en tu seguridad, no podiste más que entenderme," which in the original has that pithy lyricism, that one talent of Aleixandre's which it is death to Hyde. This should become something like "Dwelling in your light, motionless in your assurance, you could do no more than hear me." Yet Hyde renders it as "You live in your light, your security does not change, the best/ you could do for me was understand."

One of the few effective late poems, "Llueve" ("It's Raining"), is no less tidily sabotaged by Robert Bly's translation. Take the beginning: "En esta tarde llueve, y llueve pura/ tu imagen. . . ." This becomes in Bly: "This evening it's raining, and my picture of you is raining." Lost are the compression and the word order with its near-chiasmus, so important because it acts as a linking device between perceptions; we need something like "Tonight it rains, as rains your pure image." But, on the whole, the late work is uninspired, and suffers from a facile anti-intellectualism, as in this dictum from "Sound of the War," the last poem in the book: "Whoever touches lives. Whoever knows has died." Aleixandre is worth reading, but in a more fastidious selection and more responsible translation than proffered here.

Another Nobel laureate, Eugenio Montale, receives similarly ambiguous treatment in *The Storm & Other Poems,* now appearing in a complete translation by Charles Wright—complete, alas, only in its inclusiveness. By its inconclusiveness or inexactitude, however, this translation of *La bufera e altro* forfeits any serious claim to completeness. Not much needs to be said about Montale, whose reputation is secure, though, I must confess, he is not a poet to whom I warm easily. Neither his "essentialism" nor his "hermetism" sits well with me, and there are poems in *La bufera* of which I can make very little sense. In the main, I prefer Montale's two previous collections, *Ossi di seppia* and *Le occasioni,* although *The Storm* does contain such justly famous poems as "The Eel" and "Hitler Spring," as well as several wildly imaged but delicately worded lyrics in which, between rampaging skies and uncaring seas, the poet must eke out an ambiguous relationship with nature and a mysterious, many-named beloved, both of whom seem to give with one hand only to take away with the other.

The Ligurian littoral is obsessively present ("each of us has a country like this one, even if altogether different, which must always remain *his* landscape, unchanging"), as is the elusive woman with the clouds of hair and rainbow eyes, and, however muted, the viciousness of war. But much, much is lost in Wright's translation, which sometimes misunderstands, at other times overelaborates and waters down the original. Very seldom does it have anything like Montale's verbal music, granted that our language does not sing as spontaneously as the Italian. But must the English of this poet and professor of English from the University of California at Irvine be quite so slapdash? "You are him," we read; and "you, leapt down from some height, alter its color." There is a ghastly "and, too," *reveille* as a verb, and "different than." We get the overaccusative "that satisfied whomever would face the narrow gate," and the nonobjective "meeting Diotima, she who resembled you"; and there are many missing subjunctives, as in "as though it feeds." Wright is thrown by proper names: *Ariete* (Aries, the ram) is left untranslated; so, too, is *Pafnuzio,* in whom Wright evidently fails to recognize Paphnutius, the hero of Anatole France's *Thaïs*. Again, in English, it must be the "hills of Monferrat," not the "hills of Monferrini," which is the Italian adjective for Monferratian.

Nevertheless, *The Storm & Other Poems* won the PEN translation prize, and was considered for a National Book Award until too many mistakes surfaced, notably *truffatissimi agi* (ill-gotten gains, or comforts) rendered as "wily needles," based on a confusion between *agi* and *aghi*. But consider how Wright wrongs a poem like "The Shadow of the Magnolia," which begins: "L'ombra della magnolia giapponese/ si sfoltisce or che i bocci paonazzi/ sono caduti," literally: "The shadow of the Japanese magnolia is thinned out now that the purplish buds have fallen." But Wright gives us: "The shadow of the Japanese magnolia/ drapes thinner, bonier fingers over the ground now/ that its purple blooms are gone. . . ." This is sticking a cuckoo's egg into Montale's verse, and a cuckoo metaphor it is, those finger shadows draped on the ground. When Montale writes *la via più dura,* Wright carelessly turns the harder way (*via*) into a harder life (*vita*); *le fredde banchine del tuo fiume* ("the cold wharves of your river") becomes "the hoarfrost of your river banks"; constellations that remain "indistinct" in Montale are "unfocused" in Wright; "the shiver of frost does not bend you" becomes "you are not jarred by the stutter and shiver of sleet," with the prolixity weakening the image. Similarly, "the file that cuts finely" turns into "the carver's file, once subtle and true," which is both inaccurate and verbose. "The empty crust of the singer" (presumably the bark of the tree formerly inhabited by songbirds) becomes "the hollow hull," introducing an irrelevant boat image. Montale: ". . . l'oltrocielo/ che ti conduce e in cui mi getto, cefalo/ saltato in secco al novilunio.// Addio." ("The beyond/ that leads you and into which I hurl myself, mullet/ that has jumped onto land at the new moon.// Goodbye.") Wright: ". . . the other side of the sky/ that leads you on. There I swim, break water,/ a fish in the high dry air under the new moon.// Addio." "The other side of the sky" is overliteral and cumbersome, "leads you on" has negative overtones, "I swim, break water" merely breaks wind, and "a fish in the high dry air" is plain nonsense. Moreover, leaving the *addio* untranslated is an affectation—as if, somehow, the Italian word contained profundities the English equivalent could not render.

But it is not only Montale's meanings and images that suffer; his very rhythm and melody are undermined. In the text, the syllabic count does not greatly vary from line to line: "non e più/ il tempo dell'unisono vocale,/ Clizia, il tempo del nume illimitato/ che divora e reinsangua i suoi fedeli./ Spendersi era più facile, morire. . . ." And Wright? "It is no longer,/ Clizia, a season of singing in unison, a time/ when the limitless god devours his faithful, then gives them back their blood./ Giving up was easier, dying. . . ." Note the disparity between the last two quoted verses (the second of which is two verses in Montale), and observe, incidentally, that *spendersi* is to consume or spend oneself, not "giving up." If this is not evidence enough, the reader is invited to examine what Wright does to "The Eel," particularly to its ending, where, for example, *immersi nel tuo fango* ("submerged in your mud") becomes "up to our hairlines in your breathing mud." And such stuff wins translation prizes!

We come now to the winner of the last National Book Award in translation that, in all likelihood, will ever be given: César Vallejo's *The Complete Posthumous Poetry*, translated by Clayton Eshleman and José Rubia Barcia, and published by the University of California Press (1978). Eshleman, the principal translator, writes in his introduction that his goal was a rendering "in which the meaning of every bit of the original is preserved as literally as possible" while also yielding "an engaging poem in English . . . done with grace," which, he finds, is "nearly impossible." In his case, alas, entirely.

Clayton Eshleman devoted years of his life to translating Vallejo without much recognition and remuneration. One must admire his zeal; yet the most stubborn dedication without the needed sensitivity and talent is not worth much. The present version is the second Eshleman published and, in many instances, his nineteenth draft; still, it may be less a service than a disservice to Vallejo if it discourages other publishers and better translators from undertaking this huge task in the near future. The introduction alone contains in its nineteen pages grammatical errors such as "who he began to live with," "identifies with," "intrigued with," "a translation viewpoint," "retraced my direction [i.e., steps]," "neither Neruda or Vallejo," "to even further add," "culminates the relationship," "there are less of [deliberate misspellings]"—to name only the most obvious; and, apropos misspellings, we get "facsimilies" and "expatriots" (for expatriates).

By way of style, Eshleman provides such gems as Vallejo's having "forced the teeth of revolution into the gums of his personal life"; "It was as if a hand of wet sand came out of [Vallejo's] original and 'quicked' me in"; "I now realized that there was a whole wailing cathedral of desires, half-desires, mad-desires, anti-desires, all of which, in the Vallejo poem, seemed to be caught on the edge of no-desire. . . . What made him reach desiring desire? . . . I was in the presence of a mile-thick spirit."

The next problem is that Eshleman uses Vallejo to peddle his own poetry. The introduction is full of such painful irrelevancies (and dangling constructions) as "In giving birth to myself, William Blake's poetry also became very important. I wanted to converse with Blake and knew I could not do this in the sense of Clayton talking with William. . . ." And more, much more, about Eshleman's poetry, complete with bio-bibliographical references, not to mention such lapses in logic as when we read about "dreams in which Vallejo's corpse, fully dressed, with muddy shoes, was laid in bed between Barbara and myself," well before we learn that Barbara was the wife Clayton had prior to his "present wife Caryl." About a bad edition of Vallejo we are told that "in one case one poem [was] made of two, and in another, two poems [were] made into one," which a less than mile-thick mind would perceive as identical statements.

After several variations, the grand theme receives its finest formulation: "We have tried very hard not to make [Vallejo] any more clear in English than he is in Spanish. . . . We do not see ourselves recreating a text in English; rather, we hope to make one in Spanish visible to an English reader." Very well; in that case you print the Spanish text along with a literal translation, possibly at the bottom of the page in smaller print, as in *The Penguin Book of Spanish Verse*. But Eshleman (I tend to exculpate Barcia, who seems to have functioned mainly as an interpreter of meanings and refrained from actual Englishing) will have it both ways; he proudly prints his English facing the originals and goes on to say: "Our goal has been to achieve a translation that reads as great poetry in English while at the same moment it is exactly what Vallejo is saying in Spanish." Even with the modest disclaimer "Obviously, this is not purely possible," this is hopelessly naive or arrogant—especially coming from the coiner of such phrases as "purely possible."

The translator, like it or not, must have an interpretation of what he is translating. If he translates something that, to him, is nonsense, or a set of Chinese boxes with endless meanings within meanings—something so unstable and shifting in value that he cannot get a bead on it—his translation must lack the requisite passion, commitment, shapeliness, and impact. And when poems are as obscure, elusive, remote from reality as Vallejo's (to their detriment, I fear) often are, some kind of meaning must be settled on, lest the reader of the translation be utterly lost. How—to give a hypothetical example—is he to interpret, in a totally unhelpful context, the word *bear*? As giving birth, carrying a burden, or a furry beast? Eshleman admits that some choices had to be made; but when they are not avoided in some way, they tend to be extremely quirky. Frequently there is no way of recreating multiplicity of meaning in another language: puns, overtones, associations, connotations, allusions seldom translate; the best thing is to convey as firmly as can be the chief meaning, explaining the others, if necessary, in a footnote. And one had better make use of whatever beauty, elegance, riches the translator's language possesses, and hope that something emotionally, intellectually, aesthetically equivalent will emerge. As for "great poetry in

English," except on the off chance that the translator himself is a very considerable poet and miraculously in tune with the original, one had better forget about it altogether.

Herewith a small selection from Eshleman's malpractices. I open the book at random at page 11, and find, among other things, "A half of drachm" for half a dram; "The family surrounds the night table [of a dying man] during a high dividend," where *por espacio* means for the space of—i.e., long enough to inherit—a high dividend; "I do not know what this woman is to the sick man, who kisses him and cannot heal him" for "I do not know what this woman who kisses him is to this sick man"; and, just overleaf (page 12), the illiterate spelling "ecstacy." I flip over to page 33, where I find Vallejo's *hun* (for *un*) rendered as "aa": "Time has aa centipedal fear of clocks." Vallejo's frequent capricious misspellings and neologisms present a serious problem for the translator. Except perhaps in a footnote, it is best to ignore them, as David Smith has done in his translation of Vallejo's *Trilce*. In any case, "aa" is impossible; it is the kind of eye- and earsore that *hun,* with its mute *h,* would not be in Spanish.

Take now the moving poem "Altura y pelos" ("Height and Hair"), whose three stanzas all end with a lament in the form of incremental repetition: first, "¡Yo que tan sólo he nacido!"; then, "¡Yo que solamente he nacido!"; and finally, "¡Ay! yo que sólo he nacido solamente!" Eshleman translates: "I who was born so alone"—correct; "I who solely was born"—barbarous; and "Aie! I who alone was solely born"—unconscionable and unspeakable, what with that "Aie! I . . ." only needing one more *ay* to become "The Donkey Serenade." Clearly, we need something like "I who was born so alone"; "I who was only born!"; and "I, alas, who was only born—so alone!" But at least we are spared the utter abomination of "I who so alone've been born!" with which Eshleman came up in an earlier volume of Vallejo translations, *Poemas Humanos* (1968).

Consider a few additional, scattered howlers. "Masterfully" for "magisterially"; "French Comedy" for "the Comédie-

Française"; "smiling at my lips" for "with a smile on my lips"; repeated instances of "aches me" for "hurts me"; the jargon of "intuit" and "incredible amount"; walking "leaned on our misfortune" for "leaning" etc.; frequent occurrences of "who" for "whom"; nonsense words, e.g., "impunibly" and "earth-lyly," where Vallejo uses good Spanish words; "I suffer, like I say" (a very frequent error); misspellings such as "knowledg-able," "stupified," "annoint" (more than once); un-English constructions, e.g., "prying on me," "as it is said" (for "as they say"), "refrain yourself" (for "restrain yourself"), "meaning-possibility"; total illiteracy as in "the corpse might lay down" or "without father nor mother"; an impossible ablative abso-lute: "at the end of the battle, and the combatant dead"; the absurd fondness for omitting the article, as in "where scarlet index, and where bronze cot" or "war gives tomb"; crazy apostrophes, e.g., "t' hell with 'm"; and all those ghastly attempts to reproduce Vallejo's weird spellings with "whasp," "skabbard," "navell," "magesty," etc. etc. And then the tin ear, as in "sick sickle," "wind paper . . . flesh pen" (for "paper of wind . . . pen of flesh"), "wood hearts" (for wooden hearts"), and so on and on.

Eshleman is also careless enough, for all his alleged scruples, to turn "the world looks Spanish until death" into "Spanish unto death"; "judging from the comb" into the nonsensical "off the comb"; "my unconscious" into the literal but un-English "profound I"; "falls to the bottom" into "falls thoroughly." A poem entitled "epistle to the transients" in the text becomes "epistle to those passing through" in the notes.

I wish I could quote entire devastated poems instead of merely this third strophe from "The hungry man's wheel," which concerns stones:

At least the one they could have found lying across and
  alone in an insult,
that one give it to me now!

At least the twisted and crowned, on which echoes
only once the walk of moral rectitude,
or, at least, that other one, that flung in dignified curve
will drop by itself,
acting as a true core,
that one give it to me now!

Even without referring to the original, one can tell that this is not English, and, therefore, worthless. Or take these four verses:

I drink your blood in regard to Christ the hard,
I eat your bone in regard to Christ the soft,
because I love you, two to two, Alfonso,
and I could almost say so, eternally.

This grates as excruciatingly on the ear as on the mind, what with "in regard to," "Christ the soft" (*dulce,* i.e., sweet), "two to two," and that supererogatory *so.*

But let me conclude with a couple of horrible examples from "Los mendigos pelean por España" ("The beggars fight for Spain"), where *encarnizanse en llorar* becomes "they [the beggars] mercilessly cry" rather than "incarnate themselves in weeping," and *arrastrando sus títulos de fuerza* becomes "dragging their titles of strength" rather than "seizing their titles by force." And then we get the unforgettable line "that combat in which no longer is anyone defeated." If at least the judges of the National Book Awards had made clear that this was the best translation into pidgin English!

Vallejo may have been, in Neruda's words, "a poet whose poetry had a rough surface, as rugged to the touch as a wild animal's skin," but that did not prevent Eshleman from making it considerably rougher.

[1980–1981]

SPLIT THREE WAYS

P. N. Furbank, *Italo Svevo: The Man
and the Writer*
Italo Svevo, *Short Sentimental Journey
and Other Stories*

A CRITICAL biography is rarely a complete success: the
author is usually either more of a biographer or more of a
critic, and leans more heavily to one or the other side of the
fence. P. N. Furbank's *Italo Svevo: The Man and the Writer* is,
however, very nearly perfect; its only failing, if failing it be, is
that it strives so resolutely for brevity as to leave us, especially
on the critical side, hungry for more.

And it is a great additional pleasure that such an intelligent,
tasteful, and thorough book should deal with a writer who not
only deserves it because of his excellence, but also needs it
because of his comparative unknownness in this country. Furbank's book is like a large, unexpected inheritance for a noble
pauper—the sense of cosmic justice that emanates from it
makes us all feel a little richer.

If writing is an attempt to settle one's conflict with the
world, an argument with life, no one ever had better credentials for writing than Italo Svevo. Born Ettore Schmitz into
the Trieste of 1861, he was a man split vertically, horizontally,

and diagonally. He was of German-Austrian Jewish parentage, yet his sympathies were with the Italian irredentists. He wanted to be an Italian writer, yet his early education in Germany and his youthful saturation with the Triestine dialect kept him from ever fully mastering literary Italian. Although he was a writer of rare talent and originality—or, rather, because he was—his genius went unappreciated and he was sucked into business, for which he had neither the gift nor the appetite; in order to support his family, he almost completely gave up writing for many years. His very pen name, Italo Svevo (Italus the Swabian, i.e., the German), testifies to his divided self.

Yet if life was unfair to him—he was discriminated against as an Austrian by the Italians, as an Italian partisan by the Austro-Hungarians, and as a Jew by both—life also revealed to him one of its great secrets: its irony. Svevo, the writer of genius, was recognized as such only tardily, fleetingly, and abroad; Schmitz, the distrait and erratic man of affairs, had a very considerable business success and became almost rich. If life was unjust, it was also a huge joke.

With great tact and deft organization, Furbank traces for us this life poor in large events but rich in quaint, footling incidents. Pre–World War I Trieste was a city of Austrians, Italians, and Slavs at loggerheads; an important international port that was utterly provincial and prosaic; a commercial center wholly given over to money-madness. Its life is evoked as skillfully as are the struggles of the writer, the outrageous good fortune of the businessman, the precarious yet genuine happiness of the husband and father.

The liberating impact of the war and union of Trieste with Italy; the renewed urge to write given the stalled novelist by James Joyce (who helped Svevo as much as he was helped by him) and a few French literati; the grudging recognition in Italy, spurred by the poet Eugenio Montale, and the last years of modest, elusive fame, as gratifying as it was frustrating; and the death at sixty-seven from the consequences of an auto accident—all these are beautifully integrated and evaluated in Furbank's book. (What errors there are in it are few and trivial: Goethe wrote "Roman Elegies," not "Italian" ones; the Byzantine emperors were called Comnenus, not Commenus.) There is judicious discussion of Svevo's writings up to, and including, his masterpiece, that great European—that world—novel *The Confessions of Zeno*.

The four best pieces in Svevo's *Short Sentimental Journey and Other Stories* are those that come from the ambience, in time and sensibility, of that late masterwork, *Zeno*. Its protagonist is the hero as neurotic, as compulsive smoker, hypochondriac, sufferer from a premature sense of senility; but Zeno is also the man who becomes so happily absorbed with himself that his failures turn into successes, neurosis becomes livable-with, sickness becomes health. Zeno, moreover, like every other Svevian protagonist, is brazenly and brilliantly Svevo himself, or a large chunk of him. And, most important, Zeno and his book are all wit, all irony, as was Svevo himself.

In the title story, "Short Sentimental Journey," a gentle, ineffectual, uxorious man in his sixties (all of Svevo's heroes are literally or spiritually in their sixties, and they are all aging babies) takes a brief trip without his wife and finds that his longed-for emancipation boomerangs on him. In "The Hoax," an unsuccessful novelist is gulled into believing that an imaginary Austrian publishing house is about to make his literary fortune, but the cruel practical joker accidentally brings about his victim's financial security. In "Death," a loving, elderly husband wishes to set an example of resigned dying to his fond wife, and succeeds only in undermining her simple faith. (This story, like the title one, suffers somewhat from having been left unfinished.) In "Argo and His Master," a dog proves too simpleminded to understand the deviousness of human beings whose very crassness he goes on idolizing.

V. S. Pritchett once described Svevo's hero Zeno as "the clown of the inspiration and the heart," and D. J. Enright has remarked on "the quiet clarity and decency" of Svevo's novelistic style. It is that kind of hero and that kind of writing that breathe in these stories. They are both realistic and poetic, pursuing as they do minuscule occurrences to their ironic roots and their absurd projections on the infinitely wide screen of the universe. It is this analytical intimacy combined with universal debunking that undercut the d'Annunzianism, the grandioseness and "fine writing," of Svevo's contemporaries, and kept him from receiving his artistic due.

In a charming note to his wife, Svevo requested that his funeral be conducted "without ostentation of any kind, even of simplicity." How exquisite and deep, witty and serious that remark is! All of Svevo is: in the house of modern fiction, he is the atrium. The complex elegance of the Proust Salon, the hauntedness of the Kafka Chamber, and the many-layered dreams of the Joyce Bedroom are beyond this delightful central hall, but it opens on all of them: they can all best be reached through it.

In *The Confessions of Zeno* we read, "Life is a little like a disease, with its crises and periods of quiescence, its daily improvements and setbacks. But unlike other diseases life is always mortal. It admits of no cure. It would be like trying to stop up the holes of our body, thinking them to be wounds. We should die of suffocation almost before we were cured." Here, as elsewhere, Svevo saw life as a joke Mother Nature plays on us, and his fiction laughs at it and helps all of us fellow victims to laugh. It is not the least profound view of life. Nor the least tragic.

[1967]

RETURN TO THE SCENES OF CHILDHOOD
The Selected Works of Cesare Pavese

WHEN a writer in the prime of life and at the apparent height of his creative powers commits suicide—Cesare Pavese was not quite forty-two in August 1950 and had just won Italy's most important literary prize—the event is bound to have a deeply disquieting effect. Such an act becomes more than the self-immolation of a private citizen; it is also the silencing of an artist whose continuing awareness the world needs. Worse yet, a brilliant writer is believed to be, rightly or wrongly (or, as I think, both rightly and wrongly), wiser than the rest of us; his rejection of life becomes a slap in the face of all the living.

The usual explanations were offered. After a long, desperate romance with Communism, that god had failed Pavese; after a will-o'-the-wisp love affair with an American movie actress, that goddess also ditched him. These may well enough have been the straws that broke the camel's back, but as Pavese's works, and more particularly his diaries, show, the camel had all along been hanging on by a straw. A sense of his own impotence, both literal and figurative, exaggerated but also real enough, runs through his writing; almost all the works consist, as the present translator and editor, R. W. Flint, justly remarks, of "an elaborate series of leave-takings and strategic withdrawals." Pavese wrote out of a triple deprivation; before life, he remained a child; before the world, an outsider; before love, a failure. But in his writing he was, by an ironic justice, trebly rewarded—in his aliveness to man, to nature, and to those infinitely delicate capillaries of verbiage, of style, that connect the reader with reality.

The facts of Pavese's life, though it stretches through the terrible upheavals of Fascism and war, are relatively simple. Born in 1908 on a hillside estate near Turin, he lost his father, a judge, six years later. When he was ten, the estate had to be sold. The loss of his hill must have been peculiarly traumatic for a boy who was already making up stories about it. In his later fiction, a hill—the Hill—was to become a supreme symbol. Cesare went to school and university in Turin, wrote a dissertation on Whitman, became a teacher and translator of English and American literature. He also edited a magazine, and both because of his articles and for his association with anti-Fascist activists, he was condemned in 1935 to ten months' exile in Calabria.

Back in Turin, he worked as a tutor and on the staff of the leftist publisher Einaudi. More translations followed, as well as his own first stories and novels. (Previously he had published only one volume of verse.) After a brief editorial stint for Einaudi in Rome and rejection by the army, Pavese withdrew, during the last and bloodiest year of the war in Italy, to his mother and sister's farm. Upon the cessation of hostilities, he became editorial director for Einaudi in Turin and joined the Communist Party. More novels and miscellaneous writings followed. In 1950, he was awarded the Strega Prize for *Among Women Only*; that same August, he killed himself.

But let me not add to the Pavese myth, which already overshadows the writings; let me rather hasten to the works, and particularly to those R. W. Flint has translated for us here. For a fuller explanation of Pavese's mainsprings, the reader is referred to Flint's adroit and lively introduction, with which my only cavils are the misquoting of a remark by Antonioni, and the undervaluing of what I consider Pavese's masterpiece, *The Moon and the Bonfire*, the author's last work and true testament. As an addendum, and slight corrective, to Flint's introduction, I recommend Leslie Fiedler's essay on Pavese, reprinted in *No! in Thunder.*

Of Flint's choices, three are beyond questioning. The three novellas, *The House on the Hill, Among Women Only*, and *The Devil in the Hills*, are first-rate works within their somewhat limited scope. The story "The Beach," dating from some years earlier, may deserve the disfavor with which Pavese came to view it. Yet Pavese's main themes and motifs are present even in this lighthearted, immature work, thus making it a useful gauge of the author's growth as an artist. *The Moon and the Bonfire* should also have been included, as Pavese's most rounded statement, technically, poetically, ideologically.

The central theme in all these works is the return to the scenes of childhood, the revisiting of an early environment in and against which the future adult took shape. Characters become aware of choices made in childhood and not then understood, and through this the author illuminates human existence. The principal conflict through which this is dramatized is the juxtaposition and rivalry of countryside and cityscape, of Hill, Seaside, and Town. The Piedmontese author's loyalties are divided, if we look at his situation horizontally, between city and looming hillside; if vertically, between town and alluring beach. These dichotomies take on sociopolitical significance. In the hills are, chiefly, the peasants whom Pavese admires, envies, and, for their brutality, fears; in the city are the workers and proletarian intellectuals, among whom Pavese would number himself, but whose competitive contact repels him; by the seashore are the capitalists, rich idlers of whom he disapproves, yet whose comfortable leisure attracts him.

Plot is the least important element in Pavese's fictions. It usually concerns the ardent yet prickly and fragile friendships among young people, and how these friendships get overturned when sex appears on the horizon. The problem may be the painful attraction to a friend's wife, or some emotional commitment that is never made. Pavese's characters impress us as tiny, unhappy particles, yearning for impossible contacts or dissatisfied with existing conjunctions. In "The Beach," a semifrantic, semi-idyllic summer ends with a sudden pregnancy, removing a young wife from her sundry admirers, of whose number her husband no longer seems to be. In *The House on the Hill,* a rather useless young man (Pavese's alter ego), alone of a group, survives the war, and cannot comprehend why he should have been spared—he who was unable to marry the right woman and be a father to his illegitimate son.

In *Among Women Only* a successful young businesswoman returns to Turin, where she spent her plebeian childhood. She is sucked into a frivolous upper-class circle and observes, while precariously maintaining her own psychosexual equilibrium, how two other young women sink into sardonic ennui and suicide, respectively. In *The Devil in the Hills,* a group of three very young men share a curious holiday with a rich young man and his wife on the slightly older chap's sumptuous hillside estate now running to seed. The fellow is a philosophical drug addict, his wife a charming flirt. One youth has a strange, impassioned relationship with the wild hill, another falls in love with the wife. Tuberculosis suddenly manifests itself in the husband, and the holiday ends abruptly, marking all of them.

It is not in these plots that Pavese's virtues lie. Rather, his strength is in a dual vision that all perceptive critics have remarked on. Italo Calvino, the gifted novelist who was Pavese's friend and protégé, calls this a "lyrical moralist's vision of the world." W. H. Auden speaks of "a mind . . . both highly sensitive and exceptionally intelligent." Leslie Fiedler notes "a control of prose rhythms that makes [Pavese's] language at once absolutely lucid and completely incantatory." What is meant is the perfect coexistence of the felicities of prose and verse.

Consider this sentence: "I see that I have lived a long isolation, a useless holiday, like a boy who creeps into a bush to hide, likes it there, looks at the sky from under the leaves and forgets to come out, ever." There is something so straightforward about this, so brisk and limpid, that we do not notice that the piece of prose is all simile, metaphor, hyperbole. But there is also in Pavese something of that master novelist Proust: the re-creation by the exercise of a hyperpenetrant mind of an age and society in turmoil. Past and present, life and death are held in the balance, creating an endless, mythic Now.

All this is accomplished in intense compression. There is a superb decorum here: the complexity of characters is rendered without psychologizing, without indiscreet prying into private worlds. Instead, there is a tactful—or shy—progression by glints of dialogue and flashes of poetic description, both restrained almost to the point of overscrupulousness. And where Pavese's genius is clearest is in his silences. A boy who met a kept woman reports, "She has a little pocketbook with the mirror all broken. I understand her." The wave of compassion hits between the two sentences, in that discreet but highly charged hiatus. But the pregnant silence may occur even within a sentence. A woman watches her young escort swagger in a roadside café: "It was astounding the way Febo, blond and hairy, took chances in that country place where he didn't know the dialect." There is a gap between Febo's showing off and his hirsute blondness—and it is in this gap that his companion really notices him, becomes concerned and involved.

R. W. Flint's translations seem to me as good as we can expect from an original whose savor is untranslatable, and, despite a few quirks such as the insistence on the subjunctive in indirect question, superior to previous Englishings. Pavese's favorite English word, which recurs throughout his diaries, was "all-pervading." Though Pavese may not be a writer of the first order, there is something about him—and the translation does not lose it—that is insinuating, haunting, and lyrically pervasive.

[1968]

GENERAL
ESSAYS

SPEAKING AROUND
LITERATURE

EXPATIATING on a letter of Herman Melville's, Leslie Fiedler observed that it is the duty of the writer to bite the hand that feeds him, that he must seriously question and criticize the values of the society he lives in. The critic is in the even more awkward situation of having additionally to bite the hands of other writers who supply him with the subject matter of his writing.

When I first heard about a book by the great Carlo Emilio Gadda entitled *La cognizione del dolore*—the cognition, the awareness, the experience of pain—I immediately suspected that it dealt with literary conferences. When I learned that Gadda was unable to conclude his book, that it remained unfinished business, I became sure it must deal with literary conferences. But when I finally started reading it and discovered that it was an eminently sad and serious book rather than a painfully funny one, I immediately realized it could have nothing whatsoever to do with literary conferences.

Literary conferences, I submit, ought to be witty and amusing, lest they become farcical to the point of pain, or excruciating to the point of uncontrollable giggles. This one[1] had a good chance of being genuinely entertaining. It was, after all,

[1] A 1986 literary conference with participants from the United States, Russia, and Italy, held in Sicily. This talk was given on the last day.

co-organized by a magazine that does not really exist. I refer to the *Saturday Review,* once a vaguely respectable weekly that afforded businessmen and housewives, schoolteachers and their students the opportunity to learn from Norman Cousins and an array of middling academics about what was going on in culture. (I know because I occasionally wrote for it.) But quite a number of years ago Cousins sold it to a couple of young hotshot businessmen who turned it into four magazines—the *Saturday Review of Art, Education, Science,* and *Society*—any one of which you could subscribe to, and all of which had one thing in common: a column by the former publisher, Norman Cousins. This version (or versions) promptly failed, and the magazine began to go from hand to hand—it was even bought for a rich kid in his early twenties by his doting family—becoming, by turns, a biweekly, a monthly, a bimonthly, but always maintaining a column by Norman Cousins. Today, save for the title, it has nothing to do with any of its previous selves, though somewhere in limbo Norman Cousins's column doubtless continues to appear.

Yet if one of the organizing magazines of this conference is a myth, and the second one, *Inostranaya Literatura,* is a state organ, the third seems to be alive enough for three. Wherever we have gone in Palermo, copies of *Acquario* have cropped up in stunning profusion. Our hotel rooms were infiltrated by them, eighteenth-century villas seem to be carpeted with them, and had some of the speeches at the conference been shorter, we might have found the time to verify that the lesser streets of Palermo are paved with *Acquario.* Certainly it has followed us to Acireale, and may in due time crawl into our graves with us.

Equally entertaining, and rather more instructive, is the lineup of participants. The American delegation, in particular, shows yet again how amusingly naive the United States is in foreign politics—in this case, literary politics. The American team, if I may use a sporting term, contains novelists, short-story writers, essayists, critics—but not a single poet. Now, as every shrewd and sophisticated country in the world knows, the thing to send to conferences is poets. Why? Because poets are big slingers of words, veritable Davids ready to take on any Goliath, and Davids, moreover, who cannot fail. Should they happen to have an off day, they have two sure excuses: one, that they are used to flying in the empyrean of verse, but that their large, radiant wings prove encumbrances to them in the earthy medium of prose; and two, that though their prose may be mediocre, their poetry is great, something we foreign delegates cannot dispute because we can read it only in translation, and, as everybody knows, the greatness is thus totally lost.

So what do the Italians do? They give us a delegation whose almost every member is at least a part-time poet, and if by some chance he isn't, he is an academic, which is almost as good. For, as Professor Aldo Gargani, for instance, has so brilliantly demonstrated, it is possible for an Italian academic to deliver a paper of a mere twenty pages of prose and make it sound like 10,000 verses of the purest concettistic Gongorism by Giambattista Marino.

The Russians are no less ingenious; they, too, have loaded their delegation with poets of every stripe and from every part of their vast realm: Russia, Georgia, Kazakhstan, even Bulgaria. And if one or another of their delegates is not a poet, he is, like Comrade Felix Kuznetsov, a dazzling actor, able to impersonate a poet flawlessly. He possesses the gift of being able to deliver some thirty pages of prose—and very prosaic prose at that—with the flourishes and bravura, indeed with a whole arsenal of histrionic splendors, to match a Voznesensky or a Yevtushenko declaiming one of his powerful poetic effusions.

On the other hand, here are we, the Americans, vulnerable to the point of nakedness, without so much as one after-hours poet in our ranks. Further, unlike the poets or quasi-poets of the Italian and Russian delegations, we are not even politicians. As a result, we do not speak the lingua franca of literary conferences, which, as becomes progressively apparent, is not

the language of literature but that of politics, or literary politics—as remote from ours as ours is from Italian or Russian, so
that not even the ministrations of the excellent translators can
bridge the gap.

I cannot speak for my American colleagues, but, as for
myself, I have always been in profound sympathy with that
wonderful writer whose time will surely come again, Anatole
France. In his novel set in a lovingly evoked Tuscany, *Le Lys
rouge* ("The Red Lily")—translated into English as *The Scarlet
Lily,* possibly to avoid political misunderstandings—the hero,
who is none other than the author himself, declares: "Je ne suis
pas aussi dépourvu de tout talent pour m'occuper de politique"
(I am not so devoid of all talent as to concern myself with
politics).

But perhaps that is an exaggeration: politics is a necessary
evil and becomes an unnecessary one only when it is practiced
by literary men and women who have no power whatsoever;
or, worse yet, when it degenerates into the kind of literary
politics that nowadays passes for literary criticism in the guise
of one ism or another. The day a melancholy Hungarian
aesthete who was born Lukács György emerged as Georg
Lukács, a German Marxist literary historian and critic driven
by *furor Teutonicus,* was a black one for literature. After that the
isms took over literary discussion, beginning with Marxism
and extending to the recent structuralism and two other isms
that cunningly avoid the suffix by calling themselves semiotics
and deconstruction.

I suggest that all of these are forms of pseudocriticism. It is
the sacred duty of literary criticism to elucidate and explicate,
to make literature more comprehensible and exciting, more
accessible and sustaining to laymen and experts alike. Any
discourse that is more obscure and less penetrable than the text
it purports to illuminate is not criticism; it is aborted poetry,
perverted politics, or pure self-promotion. In my view, the
task of the critic today is to stand on top of a large mound not
unlike the one Heinrich Schliemann stood on in Asia Minor,

and start digging past those layers of useless incrustation, of Troys upon false Troys, until he reaches the true Homeric Troy: literature as it was before the critical isms took over, literature (if I may change my metaphor) as a great feast where you need only the fork of aesthetics and the knife of ethics to dig in. And, of course, a mind—for which Marxism, structuralilsm, semiotics, deconstruction, and the rest have tended to be only crutches, if not actually substitutes.

To put the matter more bluntly: when we have not exhausted the older modes of inquiry, why seek new ones? How do you think Bernard Shaw and Edmund Wilson managed to deal with literature without the benefits of structuralism? What do you think Albert Thibaudet or Benedetto Croce, Erich Auerbach or Kornei Chukovsky would have made of semiotics? And just how far, we might well ask, would Francesco De Sanctis or Fernand Baldensperger or Ernst Robert Curtius have thrown deconstruction?

Do not tell me, please, that the traditional language of criticism is used up, that one can no longer write or speak criticism the way one used to in the not so very old days. If any language were used up, one might assume it to be that of music, or at least of the music made with traditional instruments and traditional notes. Nevertheless, there are or have been in our midst such variously worthy composers as the Englishmen Benjamin Britten, William Walton, and Lennox Berkeley, the Frenchmen Francis Poulenc, Jean Françaix, Henri Sauguet, and Henri Dutilleux, the Swiss Frank Martin and Othmar Schoeck, the German Karl Amadeus Hartmann, the Italian Luigi Dallapiccola, the Pole Witold Lutoslawski, the Finn Aulis Sallinen, and the Americans Samuel Barber and Ellen Taaffe Zwilich, among others. There is no reason to assume that, any more than music, traditional literary criticism is exhausted and can be saved only by new cacophonies.

If I may return to Troy once more, I perceive the Trojans as the true critics, who loved beauty so much that they would not give her up even if she was another man's wife and had been stolen from him. I ask you now: do you want to be of the party of Hector and Helen or do you want to be of the party of the wooden horse, in whose head are hiding Barthes, Foucault, and Saussure, and in whose other end are lurking Jacques Derrida, Harold Bloom, and Geoffrey Hartman?

If you are willing to be true *littérateurs,* you will avoid not only false rhetoric but also facile hope. I am enthralled to learn that the Soviet Union is publishing a new complete edition of one of the world's great poets and prose writers, Aleksandr Pushkin, and that this edition will be printed, as Comrade Nikolai Fedorenko informs us, in thirteen million copies. Of course, even if the great-hearted and poetry-loving Russian people can afford to buy this set of many volumes, that does not necessarily mean that they will read it all, or that, in any event, they will understand it. But let me hope that they will— and that these 13 million sets will miraculously multiply, like the fish and loaves of the Gospel, until every Russian, from the lowest to the highest—especially the highest—has read and fully understood Pushkin's message.

If that happens, there will come a time when a Mandelstam will no longer die in a camp, when a Pasternak will be able to go to Stockholm to collect his Nobel Prize, when a filmmaker such as Sergei Paradzhanov will not be sentenced to five years of jail (although let off sooner) for homosexuality, and when, merely for marching in the wrong peace march and publishing in a trade-union publication, the poetess Irina Ratushinskaya will not be condemned to five years of prison to be followed by seven years of internal exile.

SCHOLARLY WRITING: AN APPRAISAL

I SUPPOSE that the title "Scholarly Writing: An Appraisal" implies in the present context[1] an evaluation of the language or style of American academics who put pen or typewriter keys to paper. It could, therefore, be rephrased as "The English of American Literary Scholarship," except that there is precious little of that around; what there is is mostly the French of American Literary Scholarship, or the Franglish or Amerench of it. This is a language that, even if it is written in English—as it sometimes is—is thought in French; more precisely (or, perhaps, more vaguely) in the French of Saussure and Lévi-Strauss, Barthes and Foucault, and those Frères Jacques of obfuscation Lacan and Derrida, and their various satellites, parasites, and fratricides.

As you can gather, I am especially concerned with that branch of scholarly writing that calls itself literary criticism or metacriticism, and that goes forth under such seemingly diverse banners as those of Structuralism, Semiology, Deconstruction, and What-Have-You, but is really part of the same game—the only game in gown. For whether one sides with Tsvetan Todorov's concept (since partly repudiated by him) of the commentary putting an end to the text by murdering it, or whether one espouses Edward Said's notion that criticism must perceive itself as a beginning and so revitalize itself (a

[1] A symposium of the Modern Language Association in Houston, 1980.

view that, needless to say, has its French antecedents), the learned armies clashing in the night of obfuscation are really of the same devil's party fighting a great fratricidal, as well as soporifically parochial, war.

The crisis in academic criticism—or, if you will, scholarly writing—is, though minuscule *sub specie aeternitatis,* not unlike that greater schism which was defined by one young student as the time when the pope had his head in Rome and his seat in Avignon. Today we must substitute Paris for Rome, and Yale for Avignon, although I do not wish to suggest that critical obscurantism in America did not have autochthonous sources, such as can be found in the works of R. P. Blackmur and Kenneth Burke. I shall never forget the late Sir Maurice Bowra asking me upon his return from a literary conference in Chicago (most likely a meeting of the MLA) whether I could explain to him what language one of the speakers, named Kenneth Burke, had used. I wonder what Bowra would have made of the four horsemen of our critical apocalypse—Harold Bloom, Paul de Man, Geoffrey Hartman, and J. Hillis Miller—who, much more than those Yale Drama School graduates who have lately swamped the New York theatrical scene, deserve the name of Yale Mafia. This fearsome foursome is a true brotherhood, as can be seen not only from their dependably dedicating their books to one another, but also from what, in the manner of their Gallicizing wordplay, I would call the reverence of reference—as when Harold Bloom casually lists the supreme theorists of deconstruction as Nietzsche, Freud, and Paul de Man, as well as himself. This kind of gilding through association runs through the self-congratulatory strummings of the Yale quartet.

Professor Leo Bersani has described in *A Future for Astyanax* Derrida's seminal *Glas* as "a fascinating attempt to move toward authentically new shapes of 'critical' discourse," though he did see fit to enclose the word *critical* in quotation marks—I am not sure whether for his or its protection. New shapes of critical discourse indeed, consisting of a style frenetically abstract, abstruse, and self-referential, and deriving its terminology mostly from science and linguistics, but also from philosophy, sociology, and psychiatry, as well as from foreign languages ancient and modern, and, in the case of Harold Bloom, the Lurian Kabbalah. The result is a kind of linguistic scientism or sciolism—if not, in fact, Scientology—which presupposes the reader's familiarity not only with the writings of the Gang of Four, but also with those of the sages condoned by it. Thus Paul de Man will write matter-of-factly: "This understanding becomes at once the representation of an extra-textual meaning; in Austin's terms, the illocutionary speech act becomes a perlocutionary actual act—in Frege's terms, *Bedeutung* becomes *Sinn.*" And, in my terms, criticism becomes sin.

Bloom, with a naiveté that would be endearing if it were not steeped in self-serving pomposity, gives the show away. In *A Map of Misreading,* he writes: "I remember as a young man setting out to be a university teacher, how afflicted I was by my sense of uselessness, my not exactly vitalizing fear that my chosen profession reduced to an incoherent blend of antiquarianism and culture-mongering." So Bloom proceeded, instead of reducing criticism to an incoherent blend, to elevate it to an even more incoherent mishmash, to use a critical term not unlike such others as *Zimzum, Shevirath hakelim,* and *Tikhun,* favored by him. It seems that now, willy-nilly, "our theoretical critics have become negative theologians," while "our practical critics are close to being Aggadic commentators." Obviously, men like Bloom are not satisfied with being links in a chain, but must perforce be founders of a new critical discipline, if not indeed of True Criticism itself. Thus Bloom invents such concepts as "the strong poet," represented in modern times by "the very old Hardy" and "the very old Stevens," compared to whom Yeats, Lawrence, and Frost are lesser figures with only intermittent strength, whereas Pound and Williams, to say nothing of Eliot, though major innovators, are merely ninety-pound weaklings.

From the notion of "the strong poet," Bloom derives that of

"the strong reader," of whom he offers himself as a prime example, and whom he defines as one "whose readings will matter to others as well as himself," which is at least a certifiable half-truth. The word *strong,* incidentally, seems to derive from the colloquial French *fort,* as when a French schoolboy says to another, "Godard est plus fort que Truffaut," or "Starobinski est plus fort que Poulet." As you know, literary history for Bloom is the misreading or misprision of one poet by another, even as criticism is a similar act of misreading performed by a strong reader on a text, and "does not differ in kind" from what the poet does. At the root of this Yale megalomania, or hysteria, is the need to make criticism (i.e., the middle-aged Bloom) as important as poetry or literature (i.e., the very old Hardy and Stevens). We find this arrogance equally manifest in Paul de Man, when he tosses out in a casual parenthesis that the difference between literature and criticism is delusive. It comes out again, despite a somewhat less apodictic tone, in Geoffrey Hartman's "it could be argued . . . that what a literary critic does is literature." This is not a scandalous remark, but another from the same paragraph in *Criticism in the Wilderness* is: criticism, it is asserted, "can be pedagogic, of course, but it is free *not* to be so."

What I find least tolerable about these Yalies, and others like them, is their belief in their Avignonish infallibility, or in the Gallicizing mode they have adopted. Thus de Man tells us: "The results, in the practice of French criticism, have been as fruitful as they are irreversible." And, of course, the French irreversibility begets an American one; what is sauce for the Strasbourg goose is a bone for the Yale bulldog. Hence the language of our criticism. We find, for example, Hartman writing that "our ideational response to the work of art tends to analyze itself in terms that favor the 'image.'" ("Image," again, is in quotation marks.) Which, if we construe, or deconstruct, it, means that we perceive works of art as images. This, like the Hartmanian reference to an "image/phantasm indeterminacy" and the explanation of phantasm as what "cannot be explained or grounded by the coordinates of ordinary perception, by stable space-time categories," will have to suffice by way of scientism and obfuscation; the arrogance, in turn, comes out even more clearly, albeit obliquely, in the same passage (a discussion of Yeats's "Leda and the Swan") where we read: "Though we grant him [Yeats], provisionally, the authority of his poem . . ." Over and above the poet's provisional reading of his poem comes, of course, Hartman's definitive one.

The new Alexandrinism from New Haven could be summed up as the substitution of hermetics for hermeneutics, as a criticism that is not only free to be unpedagogic—for which read uninterpretive, unexplanatory, unhelpful, and even illogical—but also eager and proud to be so. And, as Bloom has posited in his aforementioned Bloomsday book, it brooks no gainsaying: "As literary history lengthens, all poetry necessarily becomes verse-criticism, just as all criticism becomes prose-poetry." Allow me to give you an example of this prose-poetry—two sentences from de Man's *Allegories of Reading* picked almost at random: "The passage [a couple of paragraphs from *Swann's Way*] is *about* the aesthetic superiority of metaphor over metonymy, but this aesthetic claim is made by means of categories that are the ontological ground of the metaphysical system that allows for the aesthetic to become a category." Whereupon our author notes that the text does not practice what it preaches: "A rhetorical reading of the passage reveals that the figural praxis and the metafigural theory do not converge and that the assertion of the mastery of metaphor over metonymy owes its persuasive power to the use of metonymic structures." Clearly, with writing such as this, especially when it covers hundreds of pages, it no longer matters whether its statements are verifiable or not, for the readers must be either mesmerized into assent or hypnotized into sleep.

How are we to deal with such criticism? Neither the earnest attempt to reason with it in Gerald Graff's *Literature Against*

Itself nor Wayne Booth's efforts in *Critical Understanding* to assimilate it into some sort of critical pluralism will work for me. As Professor Booth himself has noted concerning M. H. Abrams's demonstration of the illogic of deconstruction-isms, "the 'enemy' is somehow untouched by such attacks." ("Enemy" again in those ubiquitous quotation marks.) As I see it, we have two possible choices: either to ignore the Yale tetragrammaton (and others of that stripe) altogether or to laugh it out of—not existence, but importance. What is needed here is a bit of *explication de texte* of this criticism, performed with the skill and wit of a Leo Spitzer explicating an advertise-ment for Sunkist oranges, but with added parodistic or satir-ical laughter. Then perhaps it will no longer be necessary for all good American critics to go to Paris to die, and it will be possible to continue in the tradition of, say, Wilson, Trilling, Jarrell, and Stanley Edgar Hyman—and of my own teachers, Harry Levin, Renato Poggioli, Jean Seznec, and Karl Viëtor.

As for me, I am prepared to be dismissed by my betters from Yale as a middlebrow media critic from Broadway and Hollywood venturing beyond his intellectual means, with, of course, quotation marks around "critic." I am ready for such a *continguity*—the word is, I assume, a typo from page 14 of *Allegories of Reading,* but a great critic's very misprints are misprisions of genius. *Continguity* is, obviously, a nonreduc-tive or metaleptic merging of continuity, contiguity, and con-tingency. Anyway, I respond with Bloom's sublime reply to his critics in *A Map of Misreading*: "I take the resistance shown to [my] theory . . . to be likely evidence for its validity."

SHAKESPEARE AND
THE CRITIC

SHAKESPEARE is the measure of many things, among them
the critic. Just as actors and directors must cut their teeth on
Shakespeare, so the dramatic critic must sharpen his discrimination on him. That is to say, there is no way of being a serious
theater critic without having evolved a set of criteria based on
what one thinks can or cannot be done to Shakespeare. This is
particularly true today when what is known as director's theater is having its anarchic heyday and when every stage director
who wishes to be a playwright, or who wants to make a name
for himself by rewriting a few masterpieces, must improve on
Shakespeare by distorting him into whatever shape the director sees fit to create a sensation with. It would seem that no
sooner had the hack dramatists of the Nahum Tate sort
stopped disfiguring Shakespeare than the actor managers and
star actors fell to it. And when *they* were finally brought to
their senses—or, failing those, to their knees—up rose the
directors to do him in.

It is fortunate that critics and professors don't matter enough
to men and women of the theater, and that some of the weirder
notions about Shakespeare as promulgated by the press and the
academy have left relatively little mark on Shakespearian production. There have, no doubt, been mountings suggested by
the ideas of scholars and critics, but, to my knowledge, only

This essay first appeared in John F. Andrews, editor, *William Shakespeare: His World,
His Work, His Influence*. New York, Scribners, 1985.

the Jan Kott–Peter Brook axis has produced anything like notable damage to Shakespeare in the English-speaking world. Directors such as Laurence Olivier, Peter Hall, and Trevor Nunn have avowed their debt to F. R. Leavis, but this seems to have done no harm to their work. It remains to be seen whether such a potentially deleterious figure as A. L. Rowse with his modernizations of Shakespeare's texts will gain a foothold in the theater.

This is where the critic can be of use. Even if he does not influence what is actually done—and why should he?—he can and ought to have some useful advice about what must not be done. As I see it, the prime function of the modern drama critic in the Shakespearian area is to protect Shakespeare against the directors who want to make director's theater or, to call it by its rightful name, mincemeat out of him. A strong stand against uncalled-for experimentation is greatly needed, as is encouragement of directorial insights that do not obscure but illuminate. There are such ideas, but they are much harder to come by than the other kind, and they are likely to be less splashy—indeed bring no sensational publicity to the director who provides them or the critic who promotes them.

If I have had any governing principle in my reviews of Shakespearian productions, it has been the now highly unpopular one that, by and large, Shakespeare should not be tailored to the audience, but that the audience should accommodate itself to Shakespeare. By this I mean that the theatergoers ought not to be courted by making Shakespeare in various (usually objectionable) ways more appealing to them, but by allowing them to appreciate him in his excellence, which needs very little if any tampering with. I am not saying that a slight cut here or there cannot be countenanced, or that the transposition of some scene (e.g., the killing of the boy in *Henry V*) cannot be defended. But major liberties—and a good many minor ones—should not be taken, especially if their avowed purpose is to make the play more "comprehensible" or "accessible" to contemporary audiences. That kind of education is the job of the schools, newspaper and magazine articles, and program notes. It behooves us to modernize or simplify Shakespeare as much as it does to dilute a vintage wine in order to make it suitable for children, or to convert the outside staircase of a majestic Renaissance palazzo into a slanted platform for the benefit of paraplegics, warm-hearted as such aims may be.

Yet everywhere today critics are hailing this or that hotshot director for having staged a Shakespearian play with the kind of "present-day relevance" that would make students, Broadway audiences, television addicts, and other illiterates become interested in Shakespeare. If Ben Jonson could content himself with few company but fit, Shakespeare, *a fortiori,* can do without those patrons who require Rowse and his likes to reduce him to their level. (Or an Andrei Serban or Peter Sellars [the wunderkind, not the comedian] to reduce him to their *visual* level.) The democratic—or populist—notion that the masses *must* have Shakespeare can only harm Shakespeare and not satisfy the hunger of those who have been bred on television and circused on rock concerts.

In his 1910 lecture "Shakespeare and the Grand Style," George Saintsbury said something of paramount importance about Shakespeare: "It seems as if he had deliberately determined that no special mould, no *recipe* of mixture and arrangement, should be capable of being pointed out as his secret, or even as one of his secrets, of attaining grandeur." If this is so, and I believe that it is, one may want to stress one or another aspect of a Shakespearian play, but not so much as to sacrifice the rest entirely. One should rigorously attempt to offer as faithfully as is humanly possible (and, humanly, a good deal is, but humanity is so easily abrogated in favor of gimmickry) *all* that one can of what is there. And what is there first of all is the language: Shakespeare's poetry aflame even in the prose passages; but that poetry, alas, is often the first to go in contemporary productions. Yet even more fundamental than what directors do with Shakespeare's language is the question of what language the actors speak. If they speak American English, they cannot, in my considered opinion, do full justice to Shakespeare's musical peaks.

I know that faster than you can say Helge Kökeritz, people will point out that Shakespeare's English was different from, say, John Gielgud's or Laurence Olivier's, and more like today's Virginia Tidewater speech. But that is not the point. I recall the late Geoffrey Tillotson's remarking ironically about a production of Shakespeare at Harvard, where he was then guest lecturer—a production wherein the young actors made concerted efforts to sound high Oxonian—"How touching of them to have gone out of their way to study up on Shakespeare's pronunciation." One man's Oxford is another's Ozark.

My point is that no matter how Shakespeare or Burbage or any Elizabethan pronounced those words, the English language has developed a great musicality, a range of pitch and cadence—indeed, a melody—that the American language, a much flatter and unmelodious thing, lacks. And there is no appealing to the past in these matters. It is of small import that Beethoven composed for the fortepiano or that a horn of Mozart's era produced a much more modest sound than today's horns. We have to use the best instruments we have evolved to do justice to the music; in harps, for example, regardless of the "state of the art," the ears of geniuses, we may safely assume, always heard the heavenly variety. To put it another way, we do not stage a Shakespearian play today as it was done at the Globe; or, if we do, it has only curiosity value. Bluntly stated, Shakespeare deserves the best linguistic instruments we have, and the best speech melody, the best music, is to be had in high British speech—even if British actors, as often as not, try to get away from it or cannot manage it any more. American actors trying to reproduce British English run the risk of sounding ridiculous. Still, if, unlike those Harvardians, they can carry it off, by all means let them. If not, let them resort to the best kind of American stage English they can produce—some sort of compromise, or mid-Atlantic, accent. But let the audience realize then that it is getting a second-best bed.

A somewhat similar, though more ticklish, problem in Shakespeare productions in the United States is the casting of black actors. There is no difficulty if the performer can, visually and aurally, pass for white; but I firmly believe, and have often put this belief in writing, that one cannot cast a black-looking or -sounding actor as, say, Mark Antony or Prince Hal. History, even in a work of fiction, has certain prior claims. And, beyond history, plausibility has its unalienable rights: to see a black Benedick or Beatrice does not work because it contradicts too many aspects of the internal logic of the play as well as of the social conditions of the period and place. I think, however, that the world of fantasy escapes such strictures, and that, for instance, the fairies in *A Midsummer Night's Dream* can be played by blacks, provided they are all of them black. What, however, could have been more wrong-headed than David Jones's *Dream* at the Brooklyn Academy of Music, in which one of the four Athenian lovers, and that precisely Lysander, was black? It had to set up the wrong associations in an audience: Egeus simply didn't want his daughter to marry a black.

That is, of course, a matter of the black actor not looking right; as often, though, it is a matter of his not sounding right. The argument presented for so-called nontraditional casting is that in the interest of democracy, fair employment, and social justice, we must be color-blind and tone-deaf. The answer to this is that in art there is no such thing as democracy: you hire someone because he is the best person for the job. And plausibility, homogeneity, seamlessness are part of a good production. There is no way in which either our sense of history or our sense of logic can accept a black Cordelia alongside a white Regan and Goneril. As soon have a white Porgy or Bess. No matter how unnaturalistic a Shakespearian play may be, it needs its foothold in reality from which it can transport us to realms of poetry, symbolism, eschatology. You flout credibility of the humblest sort at the peril of depriving the imag-

ination of a firm launching pad. Start with manifest incon-
sistencies, and disbelief becomes unwilling to let itself be
suspended.

But such considerations are politically odious in this society,
and in vain do I look for critics who will address this issue. It
may be that they don't see it that way, or it may be that they or
their editors or publishers are cowards. Certainly, I have been
accused by entire organizations (such as Actors' Equity) as
well as by individuals of racism for holding such views. And
though some of my colleagues have agreed with me privately, I
have yet to see or hear them make their agreement public.
Need I add that my position does not mean that I am *against*
black actors, only that I am even more *for* Shakespeare, and
opposed to whatever sidetracks his meaning and lessens his
impact.

For related reasons I could not accept the much-lauded and
influential Peter Brook production of the *Dream* for the Royal
Shakespeare Company. It was of no consolation to me that
Brook did not tamper with the text (as he did in his *Lear*);
tampering with the looks of the play can be equally damaging.
Turn the forest outside Athens into a gym, hospital room,
lunatic asylum—or whatever the gleaming white box inside
which Brook staged his circusy nightmare was supposed to
represent—and you start up the wrong reverberations. At the
very least, you make the audience admire the cleverness with
which *you* have transposed the forest, the dexterity with which
you juggle your transposition, and thus deflect the attention
from the essentials to something irrelevant. When Giorgio
Strehler did *The Tempest* at the Piccolo Teatro—another Kott-
inspired production—he unveiled, at the end, his theatrical
mechanism—seemed, in fact, to dismantle the entire orchestra
pit and part of the stage. But this matched Prospero's breaking
his staff, and was an ingenious addition consonant with the
meaning of the play: the director, like the playwright, was
casting off his magic. Meaning was perhaps not deepened,
merely broadened, but it certainly was not altered.

"There is a filiation without the heart," John Donne admonishes in his Third Prebend Sermon. It is up to the contemporary critic to recognize and evaluate to what extent a production of Shakespeare pays him more than lip service. It is therefore encouraging to read the following in the June 6, 1978, entry of *Peter Hall's Diaries*: "I am now militantly classic, which is not popular at the moment when everybody expects to see Shakespeare directed from one single interpretative viewpoint. I don't believe in that any more, so there can be accusations of ordinariness or blankness." Yet the way around ordinariness and blankness is suggested by Hall himself in an earlier entry (September 26, 1977): "The main problem we moderns have with Shakespeare [is] rhetoric." Now, I think that by rhetoric Sir Peter means poetic diction, or, more simply, the problem modern actors have with speaking verse, and modern audiences with listening to it. I can't be entirely sure, but I would like to believe that any good poetry, Shakespeare's or another's, will receive sufficient hearing if properly delivered. (Once again, I am no more concerned with the tone-deaf than with the color-blind.) But how are we to get actors— American ones in particular—to speak poetry well?

The first requirement is for the schools, even on the lowest level, to teach good poetry, to make students memorize it, and to elicit from these students at least the rudiments of the art of declamation. (Shakespeare's songs, by the way, would go over nicely even with young pupils.) The second requirement is for actors, having learned something in school, to develop this skill further, and be able, as their European counterparts are, to give an occasional poetry recital and hold their audience spellbound. In this way rhetoric ceases to be anathema. The trick in the delivery of dramatic poetry is the balancing of two modes. There is the musical mode, which comprises metrics and various aspects of sonority; and there is the intellectual-psychological mode, which comprises the conveying of meaning and the evocation of the feelings accompanying that meaning. Unfortunately, what in the United States passes for truthful,

Stanislavskian acting is in fact Lee Strasberg's bastardization of it (itself a stylization, albeit a grubby one), so that in the postwar years the American stage was swamped with a "Method" that had mostly madness in it, and one that is still surviving directly or indirectly to the detriment of other acting styles, notably the poetic, unnaturalistic, stylized one. In Method acting, getting at some sort of psychoanalytical truth is all, and scansion has never been thought of, much less heard; but never mind metrics, the mere notion of several consecutive words spoken trippingly on the tongue is highly suspect: emotional truth comes not in flowing cadences, only in fractured prose.

Under such conditions, Shakespeare cannot thrive. And, indeed, poetic drama was never undertaken by the Actors Studio; accordingly, acting teachers, actors, and acting students joined in ignoring verse. The upshot is that finding actors who can speak Shakespeare is, in America, even harder than finding directors who can honestly, selflessly stage him. But the delivery of Shakespearian verse—or, for that matter, prose—suffers nowadays from yet another malady: the need to deliver famous lines "originally," i.e., differently at all cost, even if it kills the meaning. Thus odd emphases are thrown onto unlikely words, pauses are introduced where they are uncalled for and withheld where they are needed, and tempo, volume, even minimal audibility are fiddled with in nonsensical ways. Well, not entirely nonsensical; the aim is always to make the actor appear interesting, and interesting he may well be, but not good.

The contemporary critic must defend Shakespeare assiduously against such abuse, because the nobler the monument, the greater the urge of fools to deface it: if there were no guards around at the Louvre, it is on the Venus de Milo that imbeciles would prefer to scrawl their names. Similarly, it is off Shakespeare, by scratching their signatures all over his work, that boneheads and charlatans figure they can thrive best—and often do. And it is not only actors and directors, but also textual editors—especially when directors set themselves up in that capacity—who must be guarded against. I am not even thinking of wholesale philistinism à la Rowse here, but of that odd bit of seemingly harmless updating, as when a director decides that nothing is lost by modernizing Hamlet's "And each particular hair to stand an end,/ Like quills upon the fretful porpentine" into "fretful porcupine." The rationale would be that the meter is not interfered with, the cadence barely, and the meaning made clearer to contemporary audiences. But no: the assonance in *"end," "fretful"* and *"porpentine"* is part of the Shakespearian music, and the internal alliteration in *"fretful"* and *porpentine"* conveys a bristling set of parallelly perpendicular quills or hairs that the *p-c* sequence in "porcupine" undercuts. Besides, it is nice to be reminded of old terms, or of older forms of current words. "Shakespeare works through the living word," observed Goethe, and, true enough, in many cases the fact that a word is still living or partly living is due to Shakespeare. Such conservationism should not be sabotaged.

All this is not to be understood as an attempt to hamstring either the actor or the director. There is such dizzying richness in Shakespeare—such a wealth of legitimate meanings within individual verses, speeches, scenes, characters, not to mention entire plays—that there is room for individual interpretation without having to overstep the boundaries of what is stated or implied—without having to reach for what demonstrably could not have been intended even unconsciously. Only lack of imagination and sensitivity—as well as, of course, excess ego—would impel a lesser man or woman (and who, up against Shakespeare, is not lesser?) to substitute his or her feeble fancies for the supreme dramatist's mighty inventions.

The trouble, to be sure, is that we tend not to have the actors and actresses to embody the easeful masculinity and generous femininity of Shakespeare's heroes and heroines. (It is irrelevant that he himself had to content himself grudgingly with fat Burbages and boy Cleopatras.) Thus an *Othello* directed by Peter Coe for Stratford, Connecticut, and later seen at the

Kennedy Center and on Broadway, used up three Desdemonas without finding a satisfactory one; and a Circle in the Square *Macbeth,* directed by and starring Nicol Williamson (himself rather gross), went through three actresses without hitting upon a suitable Lady Macbeth. (Backstage, they were answering the phone with "Queen for a Day.") Today's unisex young men and women, living in an age of militant feminism and complementary male overcompensation or abjection, are psychologically and physiologically unfit for Shakespearian lovers, quite aside from insufficient or incorrect training.

What devolves on the critic in such an age? The need to develop his standards through voracious seeing, reading, and rereading of Shakespeare, as well as intensive study of historical and critical works. This means perfecting of one's critical taste not only in Shakespearian matters, but also in theater in general, for, to a much greater extent than the uninitiated might think, the two overlap. And it means not calling for notions such as this one from Jonathan Miller, one of Shakespeare's most determined misdirectors: "The bottom line in Shakespearian production is anything goes. If I smear tar over Picasso's 'Guernica,' I've destroyed a masterpiece. If I muck up Shakespeare, I, not he, look like an ass. The text remains, and Shakespeare will survive." That is the Bottom line indeed, and spoken like an ass. For one ass begets other asses, and if they are not stopped, they will be numerous enough to overwhelm and ravish even a clear-eyed Titania.

The question these days is, who will declare mucked-up Shakespeare a scandal? Not the untutored audiences, who don't know any better; not the media, hot for a new work of genius every hour on the hour; not the foundations, itching to make the boondocks awash with classics; not the knee-jerk liberals, feminists, ethnic pride-mongers, and other democratic levelers; and not the critics, vying among one another to be the first to hail the latest reinterpretation and transmogrification of a masterpiece. And that is how the isle gets peopled with Calibans.

INDEX

ABOUT THE AUTHOR

JOHN SIMON was born in Yugoslavia and studied there, in England, and at Harvard, where he got his B.A., M.A., and Ph.D. in comparative literature. He has taught at a number of schools, from M.I.T. to the University of Washington, and has been film critic and language columnist for *Esquire*. He is a frequent book reviewer for *The New York Times Book Review, The Washington Post, The Hudson Review*, the *Partisan Review,* and *The New Republic,* among other publications. His books include *Ingmar Bergman Directs, Paradigms Lost, Uneasy Stages, Singularities, Reverse Angle,* and *Something to Declare*. The recipient of three awards in criticism—the George Jean Nathan award for drama, the George Polk award for film, and the American Academy of Arts and Letters award for literature—he is currently the drama critic for *New York* magazine, film critic for the *National Review,* and culture critic for *The New Leader.*